THE FARMERS' FRONTIER

HISTORIES OF THE AMERICAN FRONTIER

Edited by

RAY ALLEN BILLINGTON

Each volume in *Histories of the American Frontier* offers a lively but authentic account of one period in the occupation of the North American continent. Prepared by recognized authorities, they are designed to be read separately, for each tells the complete story of one phase of westward expansion. Together they will form the first integrated, multivolume history of the American frontier.

America's Frontier Heritage

The Spanish Borderlands, 1492–1846

The French-Canadian Borderlands, 1604–1763

The Southern Colonial Frontier, 1607–1763

The Northern Colonial Frontier, 1607–1763

The Revolutionary Frontier, 1763–1783

The Trans-Appalachian Frontier, 1783–1815

The Frontier of the Old Northwest, 1815–1860

The Frontier of the Old Southwest, 1815–1860

Traders of the Far Western Frontier, 1803–1840

The Overland Migrations, 1840–1860

Mining Frontiers of the Far West, 1848–1880

The Frontier of the Far Southwest, 1850–1890

The Expulsion of the Red Men, 1865–1890

The Transportation Frontier: Trans-Mississippi West, 1865–1890

The Frontier of the Cattlemen, 1865–1890

The Farmers' Frontier, 1865–1900

The Closing of the Frontier, 1890–1960

THE FARMERS' FRONTIER
1865-1900

△

GILBERT C. FITE
University of Oklahoma

HOLT, RINEHART AND WINSTON

New York · Chicago · San Francisco · Toronto · London

*To my teacher and friend
Herbert S. Schell, who first
interested me in agricultural history*

Copyright © 1966 by Holt, Rinehart and Winston, Inc.
All Rights Reserved
Library of Congress Catalog Card Number: 66-15477
2798700

Printed in the United States of America

89012 45 987654321

FOREWORD

THE FARMER is the forgotten man in the folklore of the American frontier. The legendary heroes who have captivated the public since the days of James Fenimore Cooper have been the hunters and fur trappers—the Daniel Boones, Davy Crocketts, Jim Bridgers, Buffalo Bill Codys—whose fantastic exploits provided dime-novel readers with vicarious excitement in the nineteenth century. They have been the cowboys and outlaws who glue modern Americans to their television sets and send hordes of Americans and Europeans alike to cinema palaces throughout the world in quest of a thrill-packed evening. If you mention the word *frontier* to any person, anywhere, you conjure up in his vision the image of a leather-clad mountain man or a gun-slinging cowhand, not an overalled farmer.

This is a major distortion, for if the trappers and the drovers had had their way, there would have been no frontier. Their purpose was to use, not to conquer, the wilderness of western America; they were the friends, not the enemies, of raw nature. Their urge was to hold civilization back, to protect the beaver streams from intruders, to guard the grasslands from the plow, for only so long as there was a wild West would their occupations be secure. Their principal foes were the farmers, for the farmers were the true harbingers of advancing civilization. Not until the forests fell before their axes, their plows broke the prairie sod, and their barbed-wire fences crisscrossed the plains would the West be won.

The farmers carried civilization with them in their wagons and prairie schooners. To later generations they might appear unromantic because they went about the sober business of clearing the land and turning the prairie sod, yet they were the true heroes of the westward march. Their purpose was not to preserve but to subdue nature; to build in the West a patent-office model of the society they had known in the East. And so, as they moved they left in their wake not only abundant farms but burgeoning villages, roads, canals, and railroads; schools, libraries, and theaters; and all other symbols of the maturing social order that was their goal.

This book is about the farmers who won America's last frontier and by so doing wrote a saga of epic proportions. They began their assault during the Civil War, using as a staging area the frontier of farms and villages that had then reached the first tier of states beyond the Mississippi. When they started their march, the Far West was virtually unsettled; a few thousand Americans called California their home, but between the Pacific Coast and the Missouri River only isolated pockets of settlement in Nevada, Utah, Colorado, and at other distant spots challenged nature's monopoly. When the farmers' march slowed at the end of the century, the entire West was occupied, except for the mountain and desert country that still repulsed mankind's advances.

One simple statistic will illustrate the magnitude of this movement: in the 3 decades after 1870 more land was settled and placed under cultivation by farmers than in all the prior history of the continent. During the earlier years—between 1607 and 1870—about 407 million acres were occupied and 189 million were improved; between 1870 and 1900 another 430 million acres were peopled and 225 million of these were brought into production. This was the greatest movement of peoples that the world had known to that day. Surely the story of the conquest of the last American frontier is an epic worthy of greater attention than it has received.

Fortunately that story has found a teller in Gilbert C. Fite, Research Professor of American History at the University of Oklahoma. Born in the Midwest, educated in South Dakota and Missouri, he has lived all of his adult life in the West that he describes in these pages and has dedicated most of his scholarly career to its history. His many books on western farming and western farm leaders have won him recognition as the foremost interpreter of the American frontier during its climactic years. Few students are as capable of describing and understanding the events that he has chosen for his theme.

The results of his dedication and training can be found on the informative pages that follow. They tell the settlement story not only of the Great Plains but of the Pacific Northwest, California during the post-Gold Rush era, and the Rocky Mountain country. Fite has leaned heavily on census statistics to illustrate the movement that he describes; from those same sources and countless others he has mined information that illuminates the economic problems faced by pioneers in adjusting to the unfamiliar environment of a semiarid land. This data allows him to shed light on the adaptibility of frontiersmen and to suggest that those who persisted in growing corn in western Kansas were not as ready to innovate as frontier historians have believed.

However, this book is above all a warmly human document, mirroring the tragedies and triumphs of men and women who braved an unknown land in order to win affluence and a higher place in society. Fite has dug deeply into published and unpublished diaries, letters, and reminiscences. Unlike any other historian he has also used the manuscript agricultural census reports in a number of states. This information on individual pioneers allows him to paint a gripping picture of the life of the ordinary farmer undergoing the hazards of the frontier. The result is often stark tragedy, as winter blizzards, summer droughts, spring grasshopper plagues, and autumn grass fires buffet those hardy enough to brave nature on the Great Plains. Many failed; one of Fite's most interesting contributions is the story of the manner in which bankrupt farmers foresook rugged individualism to plead for public relief. Others succeeded; 2 or 3 years of proper luck and proper climate allowed a newcomer to master his environment and launch himself on the path to success. Thus, the West was settled and the frontier era was brought to a close.

This volume is one of 18 in the Holt, Rinehart and Winston, Inc., Histories of the American Frontier. Like other books in this series, it tells a complete story; it may also be read as part of the broader history of westward expansion told in connected form in these volumes. Each is being written by a leading authority who brings to his task an intimate knowledge of the period that he covers and a demonstrated skill in narration and interpretation. Each will provide the general reader with a sound but readable account of one phase of the nation's frontiering past and the specialized student with a documented narrative that is integrated into the general story of the nation's growth. It is the hope of the authors and editor that this full history of the most American phase of the country's past will help its people to understand themselves and thus be better equipped to face the global problems of the twentieth-century world.

Ray Allen Billington

The Huntington Library
March 1966

PREFACE

FOR MANY YEARS I have had both a personal and academic interest in the agricultural history of the American West. My first boyhood years were spent on a homestead in northwestern South Dakota, which my mother filed on during February 1917. Some of my earliest memories go back to the very end of the farmers' frontier in the United States. My interest in the role of western pioneer farmers, however, has not been determined by nostalgia for a nearly forgotten time and place, although admittedly I hold certain Jeffersonian prejudices about rural America. The main reason for writing a history of the settlement and occupation of the agricultural frontier in the period between the Civil War and the turn of the twentieth century is that there is no book that covers the subject. Agriculture has been sadly neglected by writers and scholars who have devoted their efforts to more exciting but often less important aspects of western history. When we examine all the factors, it becomes clear that the history of agricultural settlement is highly important because farmers, more than any other group, were mainly responsible for finally bringing the frontier to an end.

The West as used in this study covers all the area west of a rough line between Saint Paul and Fort Worth, southwestward to the Rio Grande. The great majority of this vast region was unoccupied when Fort Sumter fell. Although much of Iowa was settled after 1860, I have arbitrarily excluded it from more than incidental consideration because the state as a whole was much less of a pioneer area than Minnesota or the states and territories farther west. The period covered includes the years between the 1860s and the 1890s. In some cases, however, it has been necessary to expand the discussion before 1860 and after the 1890s in order to clarify important developments. In any event, precise dates are not meaningful when dealing with the frontier experience. Within this time and space framework I have tried to present a fairly comprehensive survey of agricultural settlement. My main attention has been devoted to the so-called dirt farmers, and I have dealt with livestock

ix

only as it was a part of general farm operations. The ranching frontier will be the subject of another volume in the Histories of the American Frontier Series.

Throughout the book I have tried to stress the factors that contributed to rapid farm settlement, the methods and scope of operation among pioneer settlers, and especially how farmers adjusted their farm patterns to meet the new physical conditions they encountered on the Great Plains and farther west. The emphasis then is primarily upon settlement and the problems and adjustments that developed within frontier agriculture itself. Space has not permitted a discussion of the broad economic problems that affected agriculture adversely and stimulated the political uprisings among farmers after 1870. Only after we view the over-all picture of western agricultural settlement and understand the difficulties of farming in that region is there a proper basis for comprehending the broader economic problems and issues of public policy, which gave rise to the agrarian revolt. Hopefully, these basic economic problems will be discussed and analyzed in a subsequent volume. This book is more a history of agriculture than of farmers or farm life; a study of settlement and the subsequent working out of agricultural production patterns rather than an analysis of rural social or political problems. Yet, I have included some human interest material, which reveals the great gulf between the hope of farmers, often built on blind faith, and the realities of settlement, which resulted in hardships, sacrifice, and sometimes complete failure. Where possible, I have sought to let farmers present this in their own words.

Many people and organizations have generously assisted me during the period when this book was in preparation. I am especially indebted for a grant from the Social Science Research Council in the summer of 1960, which permitted me to make a special study of hardships among frontier settlers and the response of state governments to the problems faced by pioneer farmers in the late nineteenth century. The University of Oklahoma, especially the Faculty Research Committee, provided me with funds for travel, research assistants, and secretarial help. Most of the writing was done during 1964 under a Guggenheim Fellowship. Without this timely and generous help, completion of the manuscript would have been delayed many months.

I am deeply grateful to an unusually large number of librarians and archivists, but space forbids mentioning more than a few. These include Robert W. Richmond, State Archivist, Kansas State Historical Society; Donald F. Danker, Historian, Nebraska State Historical Society; Robert M. Brown, State Archivist, and Fred Thibodeau, Assistant State Archivist, Minnesota State Archives; Lucille M. Kane, Curator of Manuscripts, Minnesota State Historical Society; and Mrs. Hazel E. Mills,

Librarian, Washington Room, Washington State Library, Olympia. Personnel at the North Dakota Institute of Regional Studies, Fargo, the Oregon State Library, the California State Library, and the North and South Dakota State Historical Societies also provided assistance. Most of all I am indebted to Miss Opal Carr, History-Government Librarian, University of Oklahoma Library, whose efficiency and good humor have been a constant help and encouragement; and to Mrs. Alice Timmons, Library Assistant in the Phillips Collection, and Jack D. Haley, Assistant Archivist, University of Oklahoma Library, for their many kindnesses.

A number of individuals have read and made helpful comments on parts of the manuscript. They include Donald F. Danker, Hiram M. Drache, Herbert S. Schell, Homer E. Socolofsky, Clifford E. Roloff, James H. Shideler, Robert G. Dunbar, Thomas Le Duc, and Edward Everett Dale. My colleague Donald J. Berthrong has generously shared his wide knowledge of the West with me during the writing of this book, and his insights and suggestions have been uniformly useful. While the criticisms of these readers have been invaluable, I am responsible for the final product and they are in no way to blame for any shortcomings.

My typists have made the writing of this book immeasurably easier, and I want to express my keen appreciation to Josephine Soukup and Mary Jo Sletten for their patience and efficiency. Finally, I express fond appreciation to my wife, June, whose complete indifference to this project left me free and undisturbed for research and writing.

Gilbert C. Fite

Norman, Oklahoma
March 1966

CONTENTS

	Foreword	v
	Preface	ix
	List of Maps	xiv
1.	The Unknown Land	1
2.	Land and Immigration Policies in Minnesota, Dakota, Nebraska, and Kansas	15
3.	The Upper Midwest and Central Prairie Frontier, 1865–1875	34
4.	Destitution on the Frontier in the 1870s	55
5.	Bonanza Farming in the Red River Valley of the North	75
6.	The Great Dakota Boom, 1878–1887	94
7.	The Central Plains Frontier, 1878–1896	113
8.	Agricultural Settlement in Oregon and Washington	137
9.	The Farmers' Frontier in California, 1850–1900	156
10.	The Rocky Mountain Farming Frontier	175
11.	Pioneering in West Texas, Indian Territory, and Oklahoma, 1860–1900	193
12.	The End of the Farmers' Frontier	215
	Notes	225
	An Essay on Bibliography	247
	Index	263

LIST OF MAPS

The Farmers' Frontier, 1865–1900	END PAPERS
Physical Features of the Western States and Territories	5
States and Territories West of the Mississippi, 1870	38
Westward Settlement between 1860 and 1890	127
Oklahoma Indian Lands, 1889	204

◁ **1** ▷

The Unknown Land

As the green grass of spring began to cover some of the scars of Civil War in 1865, many Americans turned their faces toward the West. In this respect the men and women who had been engaged in that bloody conflict were no different than their ancestors. Americans were a pioneering and an agricultural people who had experienced a constant love affair with the land. They had steadily edged their way westward from the Atlantic Seaboard and gradually pushed back the frontier in search of fertile acres, as well as other resources, until by 1860 they had reached the Missouri River and a few miles beyond. Many Americans had moved across the great interior section of the United States and settled in California and Oregon where farming had become well established by the 1850s. But the only major settlement of Americans before the Civil War between Kansas City and Sacramento was the Mormons around Salt Lake City. Yet, despite the constant move westward, more than half the continent was still unoccupied when the guns grew silent at Appomattox. Millions of acres of land, enough for hundreds of thousands of farms and ranches, were pasture for roaming buffalo and the home of wandering

2 - The Unknown Land

Indian tribes. The Great West was there for the taking, and men and women from the East, the Midwest, the South, Europe, and even the Orient conquered it, or were conquered by it, during the next generation.

In 1860 the edge of settlement ran along a jagged, irregular line running southwestward from west of Saint Paul to the Rio Grande somewhere near Del Rio, Texas. In Minnesota settlement was confined largely to the southeastern part of the state, along the Mississippi northwest of Saint Paul, and southwest as far as New Ulm. Despite the fact that Minnesota had been in the Union for 11 years, the northern and western half of the state was an unsettled frontier still awaiting the forester's ax or the farmer's plow. Farther west, people had just begun to trickle into the extreme southeast corner of Dakota along the Missouri and Big Sioux rivers above Sioux City, Iowa. From there the rough line of pioneer settlement followed southward along the western edge of the first tier of counties in Nebraska and through the third layer of counties west of Missouri in Kansas to the northern boundary of Indian Territory, or what later became Oklahoma. Most of the population in Kansas was located east of a north-south line running through Topeka.

Farther south, Indian Territory was closed to whites except as they might lease land from the Indians, but in Texas farmers and ranchers had pushed into unoccupied areas of the west-central part of the state. By 1860 the edge of population in north Texas was west of Gainesville, just about at the 98th meridian. The settlement line then shifted southwestward to around present Breckinridge about 75 miles west of Fort Worth, then south to Mason and Llano counties, and finally on southward to the Rio Grande.[1]

In some places, tongues of settlement, the cutting edge of the frontier, extended still farther west. The frontier line was really never a line at all, and the term can only be used to give a general measure of the course of settlement. A few people had gone far beyond the more settled communities. Most of northwest Iowa remained unoccupied in 1860, and many central Texas counties had room for thousands of additional farmers, although the edge of settlement had passed those areas.

Almost all of the Great West between the Pacific and a line drawn roughly from Saint Paul to Fort Worth awaited exploitation in 1860. This vast region contained about 1,200,000,000 acres of land but only 1,542,580 people. There were abundant resources of minerals, timber, and, most important for this study, farmlands within this great undeveloped area. Only in the states of Minnesota, Kansas, Texas, and California had any substantial number of farms been established when Lincoln entered the White House. These states had 18,181; 10,400; 42,891; and 18,716 farms respectively. But in all the remaining portions of the West, there were only 19,098 farms, containing a mere 7,437,819 improved acres out of a total of more than 1 billion acres.[2]

Although the Great West, as it was often called by contemporaries, was potentially rich agriculturally, it differed from the humid East and South where Americans had been establishing farms for generations. The land beyond the 98th meridian consisted of the outer edge of the prairies, the Great Plains, the Rocky Mountains, the intermountain dry desert country, and the Pacific Slope. By 1860 settlers were approaching the western edge of the humid and subhumid prairies of the Midwest where ordinarily there was enough rainfall for crop production, and in Kansas and Nebraska a few farmers were within 100 miles or so of the Great Plains.

Labeled for years on school maps as the Great American Desert, the Great Plains extended about 1300 miles from Canada to Texas, varying in width from 200 to 700 miles. This vast region was bounded on the west by the Rocky Mountains and on the east by a transition zone in the vicinity of the 100th meridian. It included the eastern parts of Montana, Wyoming, Colorado, and New Mexico and the western parts of Texas, Oklahoma, Kansas, Nebraska, and the Dakotas.[3] Perhaps no region of the United States came to excite more optimism or was filled with more grim human tragedy than this great stretch of country.

Indeed, from the time when explorers such as Zebulon Montgomery Pike and Major Stephen H. Long had traversed the region in the early nineteenth century, it had been widely held that the Plains was unsuitable for human habitation. Long wrote that the region was "almost wholly unfit for cultivation, and of course uninhabitable by a people depending upon agriculture for their subsistence."[4] Thomas J. Farnham, a Vermont lawyer who traveled throughout the West in 1839, described the region east of the Rockies as a "burnt and arid desert, whose solemn silence is seldom broken by the tread of any other animal than the wolf or the starved and thirsty horse which bears the traveler across its wastes."[5] This was, of course, an exaggeration, but certainly the Plains differed greatly from the region farther east. The terrain varied from extremely flat, as found in parts of the Texas Panhandle, to gently rolling, and even rough country as seen in the Nebraska sandhills. In its virgin state, vegetation on the Great Plains consisted mostly of short buffalo and grama grasses. Except along the streams and rivers, trees were almost nonexistent. The region was drained by the Missouri, Platte, Arkansas, and Red (of the South), which rose in the Rocky Mountains and flowed eastward to the Mississippi Valley. The Missouri River carried a substantial body of water the year-round, but the Platte, Arkansas, and Red, along with smaller rivers like the Canadian, Cimarron, Republican, Solomon, and Cheyenne, had most of their runoff during the spring. Throughout much of the year these riverbeds looked like crooked and barren wastes, and were completely dry or contained a small stream of water meandering along trying to escape absorption by the sand.

4 - The Unknown Land

Going westward from Kansas City, one soon recognized that he was approaching a markedly different geographic area. The altitude gradually rose to 4135 feet at the western boundary of Kansas and to 5280 feet at Denver. Most of the Great Plains region had an elevation of more than 2500 feet. From the viewpoint of agriculture, the most important feature of the Great Plains was its semiaridity. However, the amount of rainfall varied greatly. In certain parts, the Plains during some years might be completely arid while in others it was almost humid with two to three times the ordinary rainfall. On the average, annual precipitation was between 15 and 20 inches a year or only about half as much as in the central part of the Mississippi Valley. At Lubbock on the Staked Plains of West Texas annual rainfall was about 18 inches; at Denver it was 14 inches; at Scottsbluff in western Nebraska, 16 inches and at Bismarck, North Dakota, 15 to 16 inches. There are other places where the yearly rainfall did not exceed 12 inches. Summers on the Plains were dry and hot, and the high winds caused rapid evaporation of the limited moisture.

Beyond the Great Plains were the Rocky Mountains, a region that by the time of the Civil War had been thoroughly explored and publicized by fur traders, army officers, miners, and travelers. Although the Rockies were high and rugged, they were not continuous all the way from Mexico to Canada. Throughout the mountains there were many valleys, or "parks," and plains, often above 7500 feet, suitable for grazing and farming without irrigation. Between the main Rocky Mountain system and the Sierra Nevada-Cascade chain was a broad region some 600 miles wide and about 1100 miles long, which consisted of mountains, valleys, high plateaus, and deserts. This intermountain region was the driest section of the United States. The part of the area centering in Nevada and western Utah was known as the Great Basin. Precipitation was as little as 4 or 5 inches annually. The Columbia Plateau farther north consisted of eastern Washington and Oregon, and parts of western and southern Idaho. Part of this region received sufficient moisture to raise grain crops and became an important area of farm production. For example, the average annual rainfall at Moscow, Idaho, was about 22 inches. The Colorado Plateau covered southwestern Colorado, southeastern Utah, northeastern New Mexico, and northern Arizona. This was a high, dry region suitable mainly for grazing livestock.

Much of the southern part of the intermountain area, made up of southern New Mexico and Arizona, and the southeast part of California, was a true desert. In the mountains of northern New Mexico and Arizona yearly precipitation reached as much as 30 inches, but in the desert valleys rainfall was almost totally lacking. The average annual rainfall at Yuma and Phoenix, Arizona, was $3\frac{1}{2}$ and $7\frac{3}{5}$ inches, respectively, and

The Unknown Land - 5

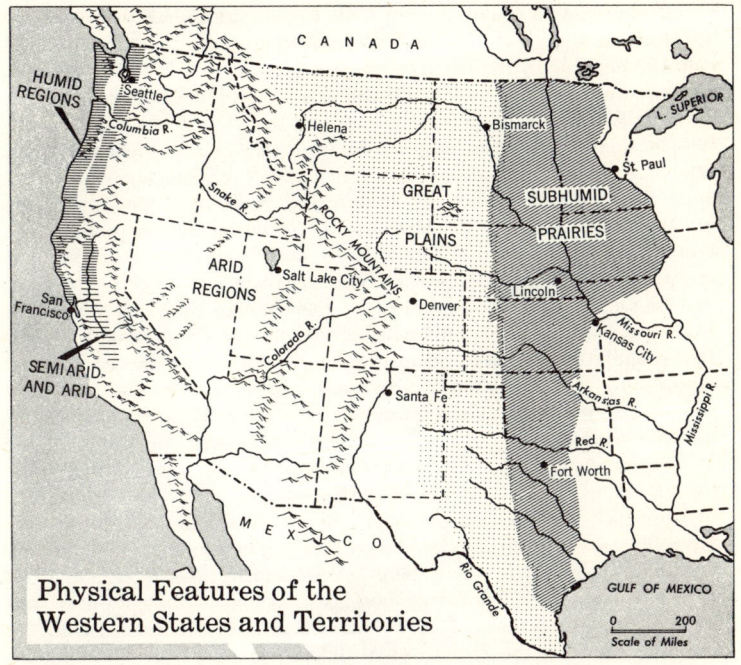

Physical Features of the Western States and Territories

at Blythe in southeast California, only $4\frac{1}{10}$ inches. The biggest problem facing farmers in the Intermountain region, both in the days of original settlement and later, was that of obtaining sufficient water for irrigating crops. The major rivers in that region included the Columbia and the Snake in the North and the Rio Grande and Colorado in the South. The soils in the mountain valleys, plateaus, and desert areas were generally productive if sufficient moisture was available.

Between the Sierra Nevada-Cascade ranges and the Pacific Ocean was another distinct geographic area, which by 1860 was the most extensively settled part of the American West. Thousands of settlers had gone to the Willamette and Columbia River valleys in Oregon and Washington, and to California, especially around San Francisco and Sacramento, during the 1840s and 1850s. From northern California to the Canadian border was a well-watered area, which received plenty of rain for successful agriculture. The annual rainfall at Eugene, Oregon, in the Willamette Valley, was about 38 inches while as much as 83 inches fell at Aberdeen, Washington, on the coast. Much of this area, however, was mountainous, and a heavy cover of timber made it unsuitable for farming. In California the great Central Valley stretched from Bakersfield in the south to Redding in the north. This area contained rich and productive soil but was short on rainfall. Precipitation varied from about 6 inches a year at Bakersfield to around 23 inches at Red Bluff.[6]

Considering the West as a whole, it was an area of great variations in terrain, climate, and soils. One problem, however, was common to the entire Great Plains, Rocky Mountains, and parts of the coastal states region—that was water. Much of the area could be farmed productively without artificial watering, but a large portion of the West required irrigation for successful farm production. Other parts were only good for grazing. To complicate matters, at the close of the Civil War there was a great lack of knowledge and understanding about rainfall, irrigation, suitable crops, soils, and other matters relating to successful agriculture; nearly all the 109,048 farms in the western states and territories were scattered along the eastern edge of the unsettled West where rainfall was generally adequate.[7] The over-all prospects and potential for farming in most of the vast region west of Omaha were virtually unknown.

Probably less was known about the conditions of agriculture than any other aspect of the region's economic resources. The numerous explorations sponsored by the federal government to learn more about the West had been accompanied by botanists, zoologists, topographers, and other scientists, but these observers had been mostly concerned with the flora and fauna of the region. They did not provide much information about the prospects for agriculture. Only in a few instances had serious efforts been made to evaluate the agricultural potential of various parts of the West.

In 1859 and 1860 Colonel W. F. Raynolds led an exploring party up the Missouri to Fort Pierre, then headed southwest to Fort Laramie by way of the Black Hills, and northward to the Yellowstone River. The expedition returned by Fort Union and the Missouri River to Omaha, having followed a long circular route over the northern Great Plains. Raynolds reported that "probably over three-fourths of the country over which the explorations of my party extended possesses a soil that, other conditions being favorable, would render a generous return for the labors of the husbandman." He thought that the grass on the Plains would furnish excellent pasturage and with enough rain "would yield abundantly such crops as are suited to the latitude." But he added that "the dryness of the climate must . . . constitute a very serious obstacle to successful agriculture. . . ."

Raynolds, moreover, made some unusually sensible observations about the Northern Rockies and Great Plains. He did not automatically discount their worth for agriculture providing the right crops and sufficient moisture could be obtained. But in 1859 it was not known what crops might be best suited to that northern latitude and neither did anyone really know much about the rainfall pattern. Raynolds regretted that the "question of the amount of rain-fall in the country was not fully impressed upon my mind at the commencement of the expedition" so he could have made more careful observations and calculations. He declared that "careful and reliable data on the amount of rain-fall will alone determine the productiveness of the vast region between the Missouri and the Rocky Mountains."[8]

Most of the army officers who traveled throughout the West, and the scientists who accompanied them, did not believe that the Great Plains and Rocky Mountains held any future for agricultural production. Commenting on the country between Omaha and Utah in 1866, General W. B. Hazen wrote that west of Fort Kearney the Plains and Rocky Mountains were worthless for farming. Half the region had no value at al, he declared, and the other half was fit only for pasture. Hazen believed that of the land suitable for grazing only about one acre in a thousand could be made productive "by irrigation and in no other way." He predicted that the Great Plains and the Rocky Mountain region would in "time be settled by a scanty pastoral population," but that was all. "No amount of railroads, schemes of colonization, or government encouragement," he said, "can ever make more of it."[9] General John Pope was even more pessimistic. In 1866 he wrote that the Great Plains "is beyond the reach of agriculture, and must always remain a great uninhabited desert. . . ." The Rocky Mountain region, he said, was no better adapted to farming except "the streams being more numerous, and the timber more abundant, it is more practicable to form settlements and to cultivate the valleys of the streams by irrigation." But Pope believed that only a small amount of land could be brought into production by this means and that output would never exceed local consumption.[10]

General W. T. Sherman's evaluation was equally gloomy. Writing from Fort Sedgwick in northeastern Colorado in August 1866, Sherman said that it was "impossible to conceive of a more dreary waste. . . ." He added later that the Platte Valley had good grass and "looks as though by irrigation it would produce wheat, barley, etc.; but the government will have to pay a bounty for people to live up here till necessity forces them." Sherman, however, was enthusiastic about the agricultural progress along the eastern base of the Rockies north of Denver where settlers had been irrigating for about 6 years. He urged that irrigation be encouraged "to its very utmost limit."[11]

Additional information and evaluations were obtained by geological expeditions into the western states and territories. On March 2, 1867,

Congress authorized geological explorations in Nebraska and the next year the commissioner of the General Land Office was permitted to extend the survey to other parts of the West. F. V. Hayden, who had made several scientific trips throughout the West, was placed in charge.[12] Subsequently, he and others made extensive geological and geographical surveys of the western territories. Most of the comments on agricultural prospects in the region were incidental to other investigations and shed little light on the prospects of farming west of the Missouri River. The scientists did, however, try to make one thing clear as early as the 1860s —most of the land yet remaining to be occupied between the Missouri River and the Pacific Ocean lacked the necessary rainfall for dependable crop production.

In a section entitled, barrens, or "plain" lands, the commissioner of the General Land Office wrote in 1868 that the Great Plains was an impediment to western settlement, that it cut the nation off from the mining settlements in the Rocky Mountains, and that the question must be answered as to how to "relieve this belt from natural inarability, and make it fit for the habitation of man." Anticipating that an answer must be found for the problem of aridity, the commissioner had asked the surveyors general in different areas to state their opinions. On the basis of these reports, he concluded that "any considerable portion of this territory" could be made productive only through irrigation.[13]

In the annual reports of the United States Geological Survey on the territories after 1868 there were many miscellaneous comments on the problems and prospects of agriculture in different parts of the West. For example, in one section of the report dealing with explorations through Minnesota, Dakota, and Nebraska in 1872, Cyrus Thomas reported that his chief objective had been to "examine into and report upon the agricultural resources of Dakota Territory" and the surrounding area. He actually included very little material on this subject, but Thomas did emphasize that there was a zone somewhere between the western edge of Iowa and Missouri and the Rocky Mountains where rainfall was too skimpy for assured crop production. While recognizing that there was no exact line of demarcation between the humid and semiarid areas, he insisted that it was necessary to determine the aproximate belt in order to protect unsuspecting settlers. "The individual who has gone beyond this line and opened a farm upon the broad prairie, depending upon the rain-fall alone to supply his crops," Thomas continued, "has learned by sad experience that knowledge which ought to be supplied to the public." He then accused land speculators and other promoters of presenting a false picture of agricultural prospects on the Great Plains. "I dislike to make such statements," Thomas wrote, "but I deem it my duty to speak plainly on this point."[14]

Despite numerous explorations and surveys, the agricultural qualities of the West remained largely unknown as late as 1870. Moreover, the meager information available was buried in dusty government reports not easily accessible to the public. What General Hazen said about the Great Plains in 1875 applied equally well to other parts of the West. "The government had," he wrote, "year after year, at great expense, sent parties of scientific men to traverse these countries; to gather up, describe, and publish all that could be found out relative to beasts, birds, insects, fishes, and every conceivable creeping, crawling, or flying creature; also correct reports of its geology. But I have never known any one charged to learn and report that most important of all items, 'whether it is good for agriculture.' "[15] The plant and animal life did not seem to suggest to many contemporary observers how the western plains, mountains, valleys, and deserts might be adapted to the agricultural needs of man, except as an area for grazing. Perhaps this is not surprising, considering the current scientific knowledge of climate, soils, rainfall, and irrigation.

By the late 1850s and 1860s other observers were presenting an entirely different view of agricultural possibilities in the Great West. Sharply attacking the idea that the Great Plains was a desert in any ordinary meaning of the word, western boosters presented flattering accounts of the region between the Missouri River and the Rockies. Their ideas were in direct conflict with the pessimistic statements of Army generals and other observers. In 1857 William Gilpin of Independence, Missouri, wrote that the popular misapprehension about the Plains was as great as the general view of the Atlantic Ocean at the time of Columbus. Admitting that the climate was greatly different from that of the humid East and that there was a scarcity of timber, he argued that substitute resources were available. He said that bituminous coal and dried buffalo dung were abundant and would serve for fuel. Buildings, he explained, could be constructed out of adobe brick and even fences could be made from this sun dried material. Gilpin believed that enough water could be found in the creek and river valleys to provide irrigation water for all kinds of crops, making "this country a permanent home for man." Moreover, he predicted that pastoral husbandry would succeed and develop rapidly. Then, he said, there would come a systematic order of farming, "the culture of cereals, hemp, tobacco, fruits—and the production of meats, leather, and wool."[16]

Crossing western Kansas the same year, Albert D. Richardson noted that it would be better for a farmer to drive 25 miles or so to a creek or river bottom for wood than to settle in an area where forests had to be cleared before crops could be planted.[17] John K. Wood, an army man who traveled west of the Red River of the North into Dakota in 1863, said that the beautiful prairie of that area was the finest land he had ever seen.[18] In 1867 General William J. Palmer reported that the Arkansas Valley was exceedingly rich and that 50 bushels of corn to the acre could be raised above Fort Lyon in southeastern Colorado. He mentioned other small and large valleys that were also favorable to farming. Palmer declared that the western half of the continent was not "an agricultural paradise," yet it was continually inhabitable and contained "frequent and extensive districts of great attraction to the farmer." Furthermore, he emphasized that it was a wonderful area for the grazier. Even though irrigation was necessary in much of the West, Palmer thought this might be a blessing by freeing farmers from the vagaries of the seasons.[19]

Samuel Bowles, editor of the Springfield (Massachusetts) *Republican*, crossed the Plains in May 1865. While he referred to "the great central desert of the continent," Bowles hastened to explain that the Plains was not really a desert and certainly not worthless. He believed that the Plains had a tremendous potential for ranching and, once the railroads arrived, "it will feed us with beef and mutton, and give wool and leather immeasurable."[20] In his book on *The Mines of Colorado*, published in 1867, Ovando J. Hollister included a chapter on agriculture in which he emphasized that bountiful crops could be grown on the plains along the eastern side of the Rocky Mountains. When it was discovered that the uplands would produce as well as the river bottoms, he said, "the 'desert' theory was finally dismissed in Colorado, and farming took its rightful place, as the second if not the first great industry of the new State."[21]

Describing his trip between Omaha and Denver, William Prescott Smith, an eastern businessman, said that he kept asking himself as he rode along in his pullman car, where is that great American desert that he had learned about in school? "Here is a vast and beautiful expanse," he wrote, "teeming with milk and honey, and literally blooming with flowers. Here are pleasant grazes and fertile plains." This easterner declared that "here the forests, too will come, and here even at man's bidding, every product of the earth that ministers to human contentment . . . will come."[22]

By the late 1860s the old desert concept of the region west of Kansas City, the idea that farming could never succeed there, was in retreat before the optimistic pen pictures painted by enthusiastic travelers, editors, and businessmen. But more important for the agricultural settlement of all the west were the activities of independent pioneer farmers who did not wait for outside advice or direction. No amount of uncertainty or lack of knowledge regarding the true agricultural nature of the West stopped farmers from growing crops wherever they found it possible and profitable to do so. By 1860 agriculture was well developed in parts of California's Central Valley, in the Willamette Valley of Oregon, and by the Mormons around Salt Lake City. By the time of the Civil War the farmers' frontier had become comingled with the mining, transportation, and military frontiers all over the Far West. High prices of provisions at the mines provided incentives for agricultural production, and the demands of trading posts, military forts, and other isolated settlements encouraged farmers to grow crops locally.

Farming quickly developed to meet the needs of miners in 1858 and 1859 around Denver, Golden, Colorado Springs, and other towns in Colorado. D. K. Wall had a commercial garden at Golden in 1859, and in December of that year William Kroenig, who irrigated from the Huerfano River about 135 miles south of Denver, supplied the Denver market with corn, corn meal, potatoes, and other vegetables. In the census of 1860 for Colorado, 195 persons gave their occupation as farming. This was dwarfed by the 22,086 miners, and nearly equaled by the 175 saloon keepers, but it indicates that a good many settlers on this frontier turned to agriculture.[23] Moreover, Coloradans were impressed with the possibilities of agriculture in the arid West when large quantities of commodities were hauled to Denver from the Mormon settlements. The *Rocky Mountain News* reported on October 5, 1860, that "there arrived yesterday a vast quantity of fresh eggs, butter, a large quantity of onions, barley, oats, etc., only fifteen days from the City of the Saints. . . ." The writer added that 12,000 sacks of flour and 5000 bushels of corn were on the way from Utah. "Nobody here dreamed of any supply of provisions coming from the West," he concluded.[24]

Colorado's agricultural production expanded rapidly after 1860. Writing in the Central City (Colorado) *Miner's Register* in August, 1862, one observer declared that the valley ranches [farms] would produce abundant supplies of vegetables, that grain crops were practical, and that "all kinds of farming can be as profitably carried on in this country as in any other on God's green earth."[25] Indeed, this seemed to be the case. A correspondent for the *Rocky Mountain News* reported in October 1861 that he had ridden down the Platte Valley and observed many fine farms.[26] One farmer declared that by 1863 about 33,000 bushels of wheat were produced in the Platte Valley alone. At times there were even temporary surpluses. The *Miner's Register* announced in May 1863 that thousands of bushels of potatoes were "rotting for the lack of purchasers and consumers."[27]

The development of agriculture around the Colorado mining camps was duplicated, if on a somewhat lesser scale, at many other places throughout the West. Near Fort Benton on the upper Missouri River in Montana there was a thriving little settlement by the early 1860s. Fort Benton served as a transportation and forwarding center to the Montana goldfields, and settlers there grew farm products for the local trade.[28] As miners rushed to Bannock and Helena farmers were not far behind and they began raising cattle, wheat, and potatoes in the Bitterroot, Beaverhead, and Prickley Pear valleys.[29] Farmers also settled at Bozeman near Fort Ellis. Walla Walla in southeastern Washington became an outfitting point for the Idaho and Montana goldfields and this business activity gave a sharp impetus to agriculture. In 1859 Walla Walla County produced 22,305 bushels of oats and 4749 bushels of wheat, plus other crops.[30] General J. A. Rawlins wrote in 1866 that the road from Boise, Idaho, to Walla Walla covered a rich and beautiful country and that, "no place along the route do you pass many miles without passing houses and well cultivated fields."[31]

Thus the activities of miners, of the army, and of transportation companies drew pioneer farmers into isolated areas of the West, where they sought to grow some of the scarce and expensive provisions needed during initial settlement. Military posts were often moved or abandoned, placer mining played out, and way stations were forsaken when no longer needed, but the farmers usually stayed on, at least some of them, and established permanent communities. By the end of the Civil War these agricultural pioneers were spotted widely over the Far West. They were in the Bitterroot and Gallatin valleys of Montana, along the Snake River in Idaho, around the gold diggings in Colorado, along the Rio Grande in New Mexico, and in the Salt Lake Basin.

The vanguard of this last agricultural frontier was beginning to form a big vise around the vast region yet unsettled, and in many areas it had penetrated to its heartland. Farmers were not only moving from east to west, from Illinois or Iowa to Colorado, but from west to east, from California and Washington to Montana, Idaho, and Utah. Agriculture would have spread throughout the Far West in time without any special impetus, but without the markets provided by miners, freighters, and the army, the penetration of pioneer farmers surely would have been much slower. This blending of many frontiers was responsible for bringing such a rapid close to the American frontier experience, and caused the director of the census to write in 1890: "Up to and including 1880 the country had a frontier of settlement, but at the present the unsettled area has been so broken into by isolated bodies of settlement that there can hardly be said to be a frontier line. . . ."

The output of these widely scattered frontier farmers in the early 1860s is unknown because they did not keep reliable records. But certainly the aggregate must have been substantial. In any event, by 1865 patterns of production had been established throughout the Rocky Mountain region all the way from the Rio Grande to the Snake. One fact became absolutely clear at the outset; irrigation was necessary to produce crops in most of the mountain and intermountain region. It was not yet known, however, to what extent irrigation might be applied, just what crops were most suitable for the different areas, or where markets could be found to absorb greater production. Vast quantities of land were available for agriculture if the proper crops were grown and water was available.

Although the beginnings of agriculture were being made in scattered parts of the Far West during the early 1860s, and in some limited areas even earlier, the main interest of pioneer farmers was then in the prairie region of northwestern Iowa, southern and western Minnesota, southeastern Dakota, and the eastern portions of Nebraska and Kansas. Except for the lack of trees, this upper midwest prairie frontier with its level and slightly rolling terrain, rich brown soil, and fairly dependable rainfall was not very different from the areas farther east. Here emigrants from Ohio, Indiana, or Illinois felt at home. They could use about the same agricultural techniques and grow the same crops of corn and small grains, and do so on much cheaper land than was available in the old Northwest. Certainly, under the agricultural technology of that day, the region west and southwest of Saint Paul to eastern Kansas was the most promising farming area in the United States not then under the plow.

Glowing reports on the area's agricultural prospects came from all along the edge of the prairies. A Dakotan writing from Union County in January 1868, said he could hardly forbear the "most extravagant language when I attempt a description of this beautiful country. . . ." Boasting of this situation, a Dakota territorial legislative committee declared at Yankton in 1869: "Here is a place for a man to rebuild his fortune again; here there need be no destitute, for all that will work there is abundance; here is a land yielding bountifully, open to all nations, where all may enjoy the blessings of a home." The committee further exclaimed that "the capacity of our territory for raising immense herds of cattle, and for the production of large crops of corn, wheat, oats, rye, barley, buckwheat, potatoes, sorghum, melons, fruits and vegetables, demonstrate the ability of our country to sustain a dense population."[32] Following a trip to the Red River Valley of the North in 1869, Paul Hjelm-Hansen wrote that it had many advantages for farmers. "The soil," he said, "is of the richest sort and easily cultivated, for there is neither stone nor stump to bother the plow." Hjelm-Hansen believed this region would be ideal for Scandinavian immigrants.[33]

The rich acres on the edge of the prairies, and even farther west, caused many land-loving Americans to wax eloquent in their praise of the region. In July 1867 the editor of the *Kansas Farmer* traveled to Fort Harker, the current terminus of the Union Pacific Railroad, Eastern Division, about 200 miles west of Lawrence. "But what struck with peculiar force was the vast areas of unimproved land, rich as that on the banks of the far famed Nile," he wrote. "Land before us, land behind us, land at the right hand, land at the left hand—acres, miles, leagues, townships, counties,—oceans of land, all ready for the plough, good as the best in America, and yet lying without occupants."[34]

Indeed, by the late 1860s a new agricultural image of the western edge of the prairies and even of the Great Plains had emerged. The westward push of pioneer settlers, extension of the railroads, land and townsite promoters, immigration agencies of the western states and territories and local newspapers all had a part in this image building. Before long, people would be foolishly saying that rainfall followed the plow and that there was no real geographic or climatic barrier to the westward advance of the agricultural frontier. Scientists in the United States Geological Survey continued to warn settlers throughout the 1870s about the true climatic nature of the Great Plains, but dry government reports could not compete successfully with the glowing promotional literature written by enthusiastic local editors, or published by railroads, states, territories, and other interested groups.[35] Restless pioneers were in no mood to be denied a part of what they considered their national heritage. They were determined to push west despite warnings that it was hazardous to go beyond the 98th or, at most, the 100th meridian. However, when young men mustered out of Grant's and Lee's armies in 1865, it was not necessary to test the agricultural possibilities west of the 98th meridian. There were still millions of fertile acres within the zone of reliable rainfall. The westward rush was on.

◁ **2** ▷

Land and Immigration Policies in Minnesota, Dakota, Nebraska, and Kansas

*I*n June 1873 Jane M. Grout was with a train of emigrants heading westward from Winnebago in southern Minnesota. West of Jackson she observed three other wagon trains of settlers plodding toward the setting sun. On June 17 the group with which Jane Grout was traveling camped near Worthington and, after a short stay, moved on farther west to Luverne in the extreme southwestern corner of the state. This young lady was fascinated by the rich, treeless prairie land of southwestern Minnesota and confided to her diary that the "farther we got the better I like it."

These fertile prairies on the unsettled frontier held a compulsive appeal for many restless and seeking Americans. Writing from Beatrice, Nebraska, in November 1872, Uriah W. Oblinger, a young Indianan who was homesteading in Fillmore County, declared: "Ma you can see just as far as you please here and almost every foot in sight can be plowed." He added that a "man can come here with $500 and manage properly and in a few years he can have a good comfortable home in a beautiful looking country. . . ." James M. Ross who had been in Nebraska 4 years wrote to his father in Illinois that "the longer I stay in this country the better

15

I like it. I like its pure dry atmosphere and its deep loose soil and the dry rolling prairie...."[1]

Jane Grout, Oblinger, and Ross were representative of the thousands of emigrants from the Midwest and East who swarmed over the inviting prairie lands of southwestern Minnesota, northwestern Iowa, southeastern Dakota, and eastern Nebraska and Kansas in the late 1860s and early 1870s. And they were being joined by thousands of land-hungry immigrants from northern and western Europe. On June 3, 1869, the Sioux City *Times* reported that "eight hundred Norwegians are enroute between Chicago and Sioux City bound for Dakota...."[2] Among the settlers were young men who left their families and struck west to make their fortunes. Oblinger said that in his vicinity about one-third of the claims were being taken up by single men like himself. There were also young families like that of James Ross who told his father that "I am well satisfied that I can do better here [Nebraska] than I can in Illinois."[3] Some were old men who had failed and who were looking for another chance in a new country. Others joined together in colonies, thinking perhaps it would be easier to conquer this farming frontier in groups rather than alone.

Land was the greatest undeveloped resource on the upper midwest prairie frontier. It was land, which most pioneers hoped to exploit, either by actual farming or by holding it for speculative gain. The three main ways of acquiring land were by purchase, preemption, or under the Homestead Act of 1862. Known as "an act to secure homesteads to actual settlers on the public domain," the homestead law was cast in a democratic mold and was a victory for those who believed that it was socially and economically important to people the land with small proprietors. President Andrew Johnson said in 1865 that, "the lands in the hands of industrious settlers, whose labor creates wealth and contributes to the public resources, are worth more to the United States than if they had been reserved as a solitude for future purchasers."[4] Alvin Saunders, territorial Governor of Nebraska, declared: "What a blessing this wise and humane legislation will bring to many a poor, but honest and industrious family. Its benefits can never be estimated in dollars and cents."[5] Although this early exuberance over the Homestead Act later proved to be somewhat unjustified, it did represent a great democratic principle of trying to give more people a propertied stake in society.

Under the Homestead Law, a male or female citizen over 21 years old, the head of a family, or a person who had declared his intention to become a citizen, was permitted to file on 160 acres of the public domain. The only cost was a filing fee of $10, plus some other small miscellaneous charges. After making improvements and residing on the tract for 5 years, the applicant could apply for the final patent, or title. If a homesteader did not want to fulfill the 5-year residence requirement, he could, after

6 months, gain title to his land by paying the government $1.25 an acre in cash ($2.50 in designated railroad land grant areas). This was known as commutation of a homestead. Although the commutation provision opened up a way to violate the democratic intent of the Homestead Act and made it possible to monopolize land, the law specifically sought to promote actual farm settlement. Section 2 provided that every person applying for a homestead had to swear that it was "for his or her exclusive use and benefit, and that said entry is made for the purpose of actual settlement and cultivation, and not, either directly or indirectly, for the use or benefit of any other person or persons whomsoever. . . ."[6]

Settlers could also obtain land under the preemption law of 1841. This measure permitted a qualified person to acquire 160 acres of government land for the minimum price of $1.25 an acre. The preemptor also had to make some improvements and live on the land about 14 months before he could gain final title. As was true under the Homestead Act, the preemptor had to swear that the land was for his own exclusive use and that it was not being acquired for sale or speculation. The laws permitted a settler to file for both a homestead and preemption claim, making it possible to acquire a total of 320 acres directly from the federal government.

The third principal method of getting land was by purchase. This had always been the main way of acquiring land on the American frontier and it continued to be the most usual means to obtain a farm after 1865. Despite what appeared to be liberal land laws, which were aimed at helping actual settlers acquire a farm for little or no cash, there was much less land open to public entry than was generally assumed. This was because the federal government gave away millions of acres to the states for educational and other purposes, and to the railroads in order to stimulate the rapid building of transportation facilities in the West. Moreover, additional millions of acres acquired when Indian titles were extinguished were put up for sale and specifically barred from homestead and preemption entries.[7]

For example, when Kansas entered the Union, the state was given 3,495,494 acres for education and internal improvements, and additional land was turned over to the state later.[8] Land grants and land controlled by railroads in Kansas amounted to 10,340,512 acres, or about one fifth of the entire state. In Nebraska the Union Pacific was granted 4,846,108 acres and the Burlington approximately 2,400,000. Thus while 1,471,761 acres were acquired in Nebraska between 1863 and 1872 under the Homestead and Preemption acts, land granted to railroads, and that bought with agricultural college scrip and with soldiers' bounty land warrants amounted to 9,435,796 acres. About 40 percent of the land in Kansas was withdrawn from the public domain, removing it from homestead or preemption entry.[9] These millions of acres owned by the railroads, the states, and those held for sale by the federal government were sold at the most favorable figure obtainable. Moreover, those who had land for sale often owned the most desirable tracts. In Nebraska, for example, much of the best land in the Platte River Valley was owned by the Union Pacific.[10]

Consequently, when the settler arrived in southwestern Minnesota, southeastern Dakota, northwestern Iowa, or eastern Nebraska and Kansas in the late 1860s and early 1870s, he frequently found that much of the best land was already owned by the state, corporations, or land speculators and was unavailable for homesteading or preemption. Therefore, he had to buy land. Much of the advertising to attract settlers to the Western states and territories in this period emphasized that good lands were for *sale*.[11] Even where land was available for homesteading, many farmers continued to purchase their farms from the federal government, state, railroads, or large holders because much of the land subject to homestead entry was likely to be far from transportation facilities and distant from markets. It was thought good business to pay $2.50 to $10 an acre for choice land near the railroad, rather than obtain free land or pay the government price of $1.25 an acre and be forced to locate 20 to 50 miles from transportation.[12]

There were harsh complaints against those who moved in ahead of the actual settlers and through grants or purchases acquired and held large quantities of the best land for speculative gain. The Saint Paul *Weekly Pioneer* bitterly declared on January 4, 1867, that "almost two whole counties have been entered with college scrip and land warrants by speculators. . . . These two counties had far better have been visited by the locusts of Egypt or the grasshoppers of the Red River than by these speculators." Because of the practice of holding land for speculation, the editor continued: "Whole townships have been *doomed* as the homes of whippoorwills and owls—and 'No Admittance' written over them with 'agricultural college scrip,' to the hardy pioneers in search of homes."[13] Evidences of extensive land holdings were reported by other frontier newspapers. The Nebraska City *News* for example, declared in September 1867 that "seven thousand acres of land lying west of Lincoln [Nebraska] were entered by a gentleman from Pennsylvania last week."[14] The editor of the *Kansas Farmer* complained that "the settlement of the state is retarded by land monopolists, corporate and individual." The worst offenders, he said, were the owners of college scrip. He argued that Kansas would have been much better off if the state contained "but two classes of land owners—the government and the actual settler. The public lands should have been kept for homesteads and pre-emption." This Kansan believed that the government should have given money or credit to the railroads and agricultural colleges, rather than land.[15]

By the late 1860s and early 1870s, criticisms of land monopoly, along with a growing concern about the disappearance of good public lands upon which settlers could establish a farm under the homestead or preemption laws, prompted congress to review its land policies. In March 1870, William S. Holman of Indiana offered a resolution in the House of Representatives stating that "the policy of granting subsidies in public lands to railroads and other corporations ought to be discontinued...," and that public lands should be held for "the exclusive purpose of securing homesteads to actual settlers under the homestead and preemption laws...."[16] The next year Congress discontinued granting land to railroads. Moreover, both major political parties became concerned with the land question by 1872. The Liberal Republicans, with Democratic support, and Republicans stated in their respective platforms that the national domain should be "held sacred to actual settlers," and "for free homes for the people."

Part of the resentment against those who held large acreages for speculation was due to the fact that farmers themselves were a breed of land speculator who objected to seeing their opportunity for speculative profits reduced. Many pioneer farmers had no intention of developing their homestead or preemption claim. Like the big speculator, thousands of small farmers were convinced that they could make more money by getting land cheap, or for nothing, and holding it for increased prices, than by the slow, hard work of farming.[17]

Commenting on small-scale speculation in 1879, the editor of the *Kansas Farmer* complained that a large number of settlers "have no other purpose than to go on the outskirts of the settlements, pre-empt the best lands," build a cabin, and stay only long enough to secure a patent so the land could be mortgaged or sold. "This is averse to the intention and spirit of the law," the editor continued, "and no such scheme of small speculation should be permitted. The restless spirit which consumes his day in squatting, does not add to the wealth of the nation or contribute to the welfare of society...." This writer suggested that the time of residence should be extended to 10 or even 15 years. Thus, he said, "the mania for frontier wandering would be sensibly checked," and "the frontiers would be much better improved if they were not advanced so rapidly...."[18]

Despite the fact that millions of acres fell into the hands of corporations and speculators who held them for profitable prices, there was no real lack of good land on the Minnesota, Dakota, Nebraska, and Kansas frontier in the late 1860s and early 1870s that could be obtained free or at very cheap prices. Between the western edge of settlement in 1865 and a line roughly from Valley City, North Dakota, to Hutchinson, Kansas, there were millions of unoccupied acres of productive land that farmers could obtain by homesteading or preemption. There would have been millions of additional acres if the federal government had not given land to railroads and if former Indian lands had been opened for public entry rather than placed on the market for sale. But until at least the middle of the 1870s there was enough good land for homesteading and preemption within areas of fairly dependable rainfall for about all of the farmers who actually wanted to farm. It was not until the late 1870s when settlers had to push farther west into areas where the soil was poorer and rainfall scarcer that the problem of getting a good quarter section became acute and the question of reserving land for actual settlers became a national issue. By that time, however, it was too late to do much about reserving land for farmers because most of the area susceptible to farming under conditions of natural rainfall and the then known agricultural technology was already in private hands. It should be emphasized again, too, that many of the "actual settlers" about whom so much was said in and out of Congress never intended to farm their homesteads. They were nothing but small-time speculators.

After 1873 land could also be obtained from the federal government under the Timber Culture Act. The purpose of this law was to promote the planting and growth of timber on the western prairies. It was argued that groves of trees would reduce the winds, attract increased rainfall, and provide lumber for building and fuel. Under this measure, a person could obtain 160 acres of government land in return for planting and cultivating 40 acres of trees. At the end of 10 years, later reduced to 8, final title would be granted if the settler could prove that the specified number of trees per acre were healthy and growing. Since it was not feasible for most farmers to plant and care for 40 acres of trees, an amendment in 1878 reduced the acres to 10. Between 1873 and 1880 some 64,535 original entries were made for 9,346,660 acres, mostly in Kansas, Nebraska, and Dakota. Even though a farmer might have already filed on a homestead and preempted land, he could also enter what was known as a tree claim. Consequently, many of the entries under this law were by farmers who wanted to get more land and expand their operations. A relatively small amount of land was obtained under the Timber Culture Act, and up to 1904, final patents had been issued on some 9,745,000 acres.[19]

Although the westward movement of settlers continued during the Civil War, not many homesteads were filed in the states and territories of this north central frontier until the late 1860s. The first homestead was filed by Daniel Freeman a few miles west of Beatrice, Nebraska, on January 1, 1863.[20] Up to 1868 more homesteads were entered in Minnesota than in any other state. During the 6 years from 1863 to 1868, inclusive, 19,251 persons filed on approximately 2,500,000 acres there. This was more than the combined total of Dakota, Kansas, and Nebraska, which had 1205, 6244, and 7858 entries, respectively, during that period. In 1869 Nebraska drew the most homesteaders, and the next year Kansas took the lead with 5024, or 2000 more than Minnesota.

The first real boom in homesteading on the Minnesota-Dakota-Nebraska-Kansas frontier, however, took place in the early 1870s. In 1871 entries in these states and territories totaled 20,237 and covered 2,571,209 acres. When a new land office was opened at Concordia, Kansas, on January 16, 1871, there was a mad scramble to file claims. A receiver at the office recalled: "The door was opened—a shout—a rush—a scramble over each other—a confused shouting of the number of the range and township, as a half-dozen or more simultaneously presented their papers to the officers. . . ."[21] Kansas alone had more than 9000 entries in both 1871 and 1872. Not until the hard times of the middle 1870s was there a marked decline in filings, and this was only temporary. Thousands of homesteaders on this frontier received final patent through the regular homestead procedure before 1880 after living on their land for 5 years. Others took advantage of the commutation feature so they could gain full title more quickly.[22]

Despite this record of homestead settlement in the 1860s and 1870s, the Homestead Act has been severely criticized on the basis that it really did not help a great many farmers get established on the land. It has been charged that the law was superimposed on a land system that continued extensive sales of public lands, that the commutation privilege permitted the act to be abused, that it encouraged monopoly and speculation, and that it perverted the law's democratic aims. Moreover, critics have held that 160 acres was not enough land on which to make a living in much of the West still available for settlement after 1862. To put it another way, the law was not suited to the geography of the Great West.[23]

Although the Homestead Act had many weaknesses in both form and administration, most of the critics have misjudged its value as a farm-making measure, at least on the upper midwest prairie frontier. Moreover, much of the complaint completely ignores the time and circumstances under which the law was passed and placed in operation. While it is true that the Homestead Act was not suitable for much of the area west of the 100th meridian, no one in 1862 was thinking of applying the law to the arid and semiarid portions of the West. Indeed, most Americans who thought anything about it were convinced that much of the Far West could never be settled by crop farmers under any circumstances. When the measure was enacted, settlement was still well within the humid region of the Mississippi Valley, where 160 acres was sufficient for the average family.

Furthermore, the establishment of a family on a quarter section of land was deeply ingrained in American thinking by 1860, and it was too much to expect that Congress should have passed a different type of law that would have been more appropriate to the Great Plains, Rocky Mountains, and intermountain plateaus. Lawmakers in Washington were not prophets, and they had no way of knowing how rapidly the rest of the prairie lands would be settled and how soon farmers would be pushing out onto the barren plains. The state of agricultural technology in the 1860s actually held the size of operational farms down to 160 acres, or smaller, for most families. As will be shown subsequently, as late as the 1880s, except in the areas of bonanza farming, it was not practical for an ordinary farm family to try to cultivate more than 160 acres.

Some critics have suggested that if a person tried to sell his homestead, it should have reverted to the public domain, thereby keeping more land for actual settlers and reducing speculation. The main weakness of this argument is that to deny a person who acquired a homestead the right to dispose of it to his best advantage ran counter to the basic concept of private property, which was so strong in nineteenth-century America. To make a man farm his homestead or require that it revert to the public domain was contrary to every idea regarding the sanctity of property ownership. Owning land in fee simple had been a basic American tenet since colonial times and this meant that, once acquired, a man could do as he pleased with his land. In a nineteenth-century context the idea that a homesteader should not have been able to sell his land comes close to being "un-American."

Others have argued that the federal government should have provided transportation and at least part of the initial capital to help poor workers get from their eastern homes to homesteads in the West. While there is much to be said for this position when considered from an economic and social point of view, it again totally ignores the prevalent attitudes and beliefs in the nineteenth century regarding the place of the federal government in society. Practically no one except the socialists believed that the federal government should assume this kind of responsibility in the role of economic development.[24]

An even more important criticism is that, after all, not many settlers actually obtained free land under the homestead law. The truth of this charge depends on the time and place under consideration. It is definitely not true if applied to the Minnesota-Dakota-Nebraska-Kansas frontier in the late 1860s and 1870s when thousands of farmers acquired 160 acres free, except for the filing fees. Between 1860 and 1880 some 251,984 new farms were created in that area. It is impossible to calculate just how many of these were opened up in 1861 and 1862 before the Homestead Act became effective. During the entire 20-year period there was an average of 12,595 new farms established annually in those states and territories. Expansion was less rapid in the early 1860s than later, but it can be safely assumed that at least 10,000 of the 251,984 farms were started in 1861 and 1862. This leaves the creation of approximately 242,000 new farms between 1863, when the homestead law went into operation, and 1880. During that time 86,169 farmers in Minnesota, Dakota, Nebraska, and Kansas obtained patents to their homesteads through the regular residence requirement. Another 50,673 who had filed entries before June 30, 1880, gained their title in the same manner during the next 5 years. Thus, between 1863 and 1880, 136,842 of the 242,000 new farms were settled as homesteads and title was acquired through cultivation and residence. This was about 56.5 percent of the total farms created on that frontier, during that period. About two thirds of the farms in Minnesota were originally established by homesteaders.[25]

All things considered then, it appears that the Homestead Act has been unduly criticized, at least as it operated down to about 1880. During the first 2 decades after the law was passed, it was especially important in helping to people the upper midwest and central prairie frontier with operating farmers. On that frontier the democratic objective of giving more people an economic stake in society was, to a considerable degree, achieved. However, serious abuses did multiply when settlers reached the Great Plains, where a 160-acre farm was not likely to become a successful economic unit without at least partial irrigation. Congress did not make a mistake in passing the Homestead Law, but it did fail miserably in not enacting new legislation about 1880 that more accurately fitted the remaining public domain, including the Great Plains, and forest and desert lands. The Desert Land Act of 1877, for example, did not fulfill the needs of western farm settlers.[26]

This measure provided for selling 640 acres of land at $1.25 an acre to a settler who promised to irrigate it. Twenty-five cents an acre had to be paid at the time of filing and the other dollar within 3 years. When this law was passed, Congress may have had the best intention of trying to promote the establishment of individual farms in the semiarid and arid West, where the environment ruled out the traditional homestead of 160 acres. However, enactment of the Desert Land Act showed how little legislators knew about the cost and problems of farm-making in much of the Far West. The average settler with limited capital was in no financial position to undertake the heavy expense of irrigation to bring arid land into production. Consequently, this law was of little or no value to actual farm settlers in the 11 western states and territories where it applied. Fraud and corruption were rampant as ranchers and speculators perjured themselves after pouring a bucket of water on a section and swearing that the land was being irrigated.

When the Homestead Act was passed, little was known about the agricultural possibilities of the semiarid and arid regions, but this was not true by the late 1870s. The annual reports of the United States Geological Survey of the territories covering the years 1868 to 1883, John Wesley Powell's *Report on the Lands of the Arid Region of the United States,* published in 1878, reports from the commissioner of the General Land Office, and other studies and observations had provided fairly accurate information on the land and water resources of the West. Therefore, there was no excuse for Congress to continue laws such as the Homestead Act or to write new measures that did not correspond to the needs of actual settlers; unless, that is, the lawmakers purposely planned to help timber, mining, and ranching corporations rather than the small farmer. The point is that Congress had reliable information in 1880 that it did not have in 1862.

The most serious abuses under the land laws occurred after about 1880, when relatively little good land suitable for nonirrigated agriculture remained open for homesteading. In the better farming areas, which were homesteaded in Kansas, Nebraska, Dakota, and Minnesota, commutation was never a serious problem and did not promote land monopoly. The reason for this was simple: farmers wanted to farm. When commutation did occur and the title changed hands, the land was usually acquired by another farmer. The degree of land monopoly in those relatively good farming areas was fostered mainly by railroad grants and college scrip purchases and not by the commutation privilege of the Homestead Act. However, after 1880 timber and mining companies, as well as ranchers, took advantage of the commutation provision and acquired thousands of acres for the minimum price of $1.25 an acre, or a little more. At the end of the century after the good farm lands in Minnesota were gone, it was found that of 1865 commutations between 1899 and 1903, 1659 were in the timber or mineral belts of the state. And about 89 percent of those commuted in the timber belt were transferred to other parties, mainly to lumber companies.[27] In short, the great fault of Congress in developing land policy was the failure to make basic changes when the good agricultural land was occupied and in failing to adjust public policy to the geography of settlement.

But in the first decade following the Civil War these questions were neither of practical or academic interest. Free or cheap land was available and it drew a torrent of people into the West until pioneer emigration was slowed temporarily by the hard times, droughts, and grasshopper plagues of the middle 1870s. Even though the population of Minnesota, Dakota, Nebraska, and Kansas increased from 312,907 to 941,279 between 1860 and 1870, this flow of settlement was not considered fast enough. Every western state and territory wanted more people. After all, population was the greatest resource for economic growth. Without people the natural resources could not be developed. Not only did the state and territorial governments have a stake in obtaining more settlers, but the railroads could not sell their lands or build up their carrying business unless there was a steady increase in population. Every serious observer recognized the need for both more producers and consumers.

In his inaugural address in January 1860 Governor Alexander Ramsey of Minnesota declared: "Give us the capital of more men and we will vivify [and] infuse the breath of life into the dead capital of millions of acres now growing only prairie flowers. . . . Immigration will multiply capital, diffuse wealth, sell our town lots [and] increase activity in every pursuit and business. . . ."[28] The state immigration commissioner in Nebraska wrote early in 1872 that, "Nebraska needs thrifty and industrious settlers to develop the resources of her great landed estate," and another Nebraskan declared: "landless men want lands, and menless lands want men—to unite men and lands in a sacred loyalty to each other's service of the state, is the worthy mission of our great and successful immigration scheme."[29] James S. Foster, the first commissioner of immigration for Dakota Territory, expressed the situation well when he said: "Immigration is the life of business in a new country. It gives patronage to the railroads; it encourages manufacturers. . . . It builds up cities and towns, and makes a market for the products of the farmer. All classes and every branch of business feel its favorable effects."[30]

Recognizing this situation, the state and territorial governments, the railroads, and other agencies became active farm-makers. All kinds of advertising and promotional campaigns were undertaken to lure people from the older Midwest, the East, and Europe to lands on this upper midwestern prairie frontier. In fact, this was considered not only a proper role of government, but an indispensable function.

Minnesota was extremely active in trying to attract immigrants. A Board of Immigration was established as early as 1855 and, even before that, strong individual efforts were made by officials like Henry H. Sibley and Governor Alexander Ramsey. In 1864 the legislature authorized the secretary of state to carry on promotional activities, and, while administrative procedures underwent many changes in succeeding years, the purpose was always the same—"to do everything which may enhance and encourage immigration to our state."[31] Agents were appointed, and thousands of reports, pamphlets, and other pieces of literature were published and distributed to prospective settlers in the United States and abroad. Besides being written in English, many of the promotional pamphlets were made available in Swedish, Norwegian, German, and Dutch translations. The virtues of Minnesota were also advertised in newspapers throughout the eastern United States and in northern Europe.

Official efforts were also made to promote emigration into Dakota Territory as early as 1862, but it was not until 1869 that an official commission was approved. No special funds were provided by the territory for this purpose until 1871. However, once organized, Commissioner of Immigration James S. Foster distributed thousands of copies of his *History and Emigrants Guide*, his annual report, and special pamphlets published in English, Swedish, and other languages. As the contest for settlers increased, territorial legislators appropriated $3000 annually for 1875 and 1876 to expand the activities of a new bureau of immigration created in 1875. Superintendent Fred J. Cross advertised the territory by distributing thousands of copies of a pamphlet, *The Free Lands of Dakota*, plus other promotional literature, and he exhibited Dakota agricultural products at several midwestern fairs.[32]

At the same time Kansas was attempting to lure emigrants to the Jawhawk State. Agents were sent out as early as 1864, and when the Kansas Board of Agriculture was formed in 1872, its main task was to promote settlement in Kansas. The board's Annual Report and special publications contained a great deal of material on the opportunities for farmers in Kansas.

Nebraskans did somewhat less with official promotion than did surrounding states, but as early as 1864 the Nebraska Immigration Association, a private promotional agency, was chartered by the territorial legislature to publicize the territory and "induce" immigration. An official immigration organization was set up in 1870, and money was appropriated to distribute pamphlets and later to pay traveling agents.[33] In one publication the Board of Immigration welcomed "every robust immigrant, however unblessed with the goods of fortune," and said that the state's "broad productive acres need thousands of workmen." "Land for the Landless! Homes for the Homeless!" was one popular and appealing slogan. The land commissioner praised the soil, climate, productions, and opportunities for farmers in Nebraska, and added that "epidemic diseases are unknown."[34]

There were a number of non-official agencies and many individuals who were also active in promoting emigration into the unsettled West. These included steamship companies, who were interested in selling transatlantic tickets, land companies, religious and philanthropic groups, newspaper editors, immigrants who wrote letters to relatives and friends back home, and ethnic groups, who formed special societies to encourage immigration to their state. The Scandinavian Immigration Society, for example, was formed in Minneapolis in 1869 and for the next few years employed agents and distributed favorable publicity about Minnesota. Agents for land companies fanned out across northern and western Europe urging prospective immigrants to settle in specific areas where their employers had land for sale.

Everywhere on the upper midwest prairie frontier local businessmen and newspaper editors boosted their communities in the most glowing terms. One Minnesota editor, for example, dedicated a pamphlet entitled, *Waseca County in Minnesota as a Home for Immigrants* to "laboring men who earn a livelihood by honest toil, to *landless men* who aspire to the dignity and independence which comes from a free home on God's green earth; To all men who wish for homes in a beautiful, fertile, productive country."[35] Thousands of foreign immigrants were attracted to this last prairie frontier by letters from relatives and friends who had already preceded them to America. Not all of these personal reports were favorable, but the general tone was that the United States held wonderful opportunities for farmers as well as those interested in other occupations.

People were so important to the economic development of new areas that active competition to attract immigrants developed among the states and territories. The standard argument in favor of setting up some kind of official immigration agency was that settlers would be drawn off to other states unless something were done. In supporting a more vigorous official policy to promote immigration, one Saint Paul editor wrote: "Will the citizens of Minnesota look calmly upon the vast army, which is about to make its exodus from the East . . . to seek homes in the West, and allow them to make choice of Missouri, Kansas, Iowa or Nebraska, without even stretching out the hand of friendship, or lifting a voice of welcome."[36] In its report for 1867 the Minnesota Immigration Board asserted that its promotional activities must be continued because of competition from surrounding states and territories. Governor Marshall told the legislature in 1868 that he did not really favor supporting the work of an immigration board, but that Minnesota must continue its efforts because "other new states are putting forth efforts to control and direct immigration to their territory." Minnesota, he continued, must have its "just share" of immigrants.[37] Uneasy because settlers were crossing open lands in western Iowa and going beyond the Missouri River, the editor of the *Iowa State Register* at Des Moines declared in 1870 that "great blanks on our prairies are marked by blank leaves in the ledger of our Commerce, and keep our State back from its predestined wealth and greatness."[38]

Sometimes editors and immigrant agents pictured a neighboring state or territory in the most unfavorable light. In the middle 1860s Dakota was presented by some writers in neighboring states as a barren, grasshopper-ridden, Indian-infested desert where no farmer was likely to succeed. Moses K. Armstrong, a land speculator and ardent defender of Dakota, wrote in March 1864 that "all the little hungry newspapers along the line of the Fort Dodge and Marshalltown road are continually howling in the ears of immigrants the most pitiful lies" about Dakota. After raking Iowa with his searing satire and criticism, he concluded that the area around Fort Dodge and Webster City was "a prairie, where the cows give blue milk, and the wind whips the long-tailed pigs to death."[39]

Railroads were among the most active agencies seeking emigrants.

28 - Land Policies in Minnesota, Dakota, Nebraska, Kansas

An advertising pamphlet for the Missouri-Pacific Railroad and the Kansas Real Estate Association, 1888. (The Kansas State Historical Society, Topeka)

The Illinois Central had set the pattern for other lines that acquired millions of acres of land from the government farther west.[40] The Union Pacific, Northern Pacific, Burlington, Santa Fe, and other lines all organized elaborate promotional campaigns to lure people to their lands in Minnesota, Dakota, Nebraska, Kansas, and areas beyond. Usually administered through the land department or a company immigration bureau, the railroads distributed millions of pamphlets, maps, circulars, handbills, and other kinds of advertising tracts. These were published in many languages. In 1882 alone the Northern Pacific distributed 632,590 copies of its promotional publications written in English, Swedish, Dutch, Danish, and Norwegian.[41]

The railroads also advertised extensively in newspapers in the East and in northern Europe. The advertising usually contained a description of the country where lands were available, the price and terms for purchasing farms, and instructions on how to reach the "promised land." For example, in 1874 the land department of the Santa Fe published a pamphlet entitled, *Five Hundred Thousand Acres of the Best Farming and Fruit Lands Located in the Limestone and Blue Grass Region of Kansas.* . . . Besides describing the country and telling how land could be obtained, beautiful farms were pictured, which must have excited any lover of the soil who had the slightest yearning to own a farm. Many of the booklets included exaggerated statistics on farm production. The tendency was to present the unsettled country in the most favorable light. Promoters boasted about cheap lands, abundant crops, and financial independence for the hard-working pioneer. Even the climate was praised; doctors, it was said, were hardly ever needed in the West. While railroad and other promotional literature often misrepresented true conditions on the upper midwest prairie frontier, settlers were also given accurate information. A Santa Fe pamphlet of 1879 told easterners: "We cannot advise any married man to come here [Kansas] with less than $800 or $1000, to make a start on a farm . . . and then it will take plenty of grit, hard work and rigid economy to get through the first year or two. . . ."[42]

At least through the 1870s there was often a close relation between the state and territorial governments and the railroads in their promotional efforts. In 1871 when Hans Mattson agreed to go to Europe for the Northern Pacific in search of immigrants, he said that as an agent "for a great railroad company," he could be of more service in the economic development of Minnesota than he could as Secretary of State, a position from which he resigned.[43] The railroads also contributed to the state immigration agencies and in some cases without such financial support the state organizations could have done very little because of insufficient appropriations.

Some of the most effective advertising of the frontier, however, was provided at almost no cost to the railroads or the official promotional agencies. This was the writings and published interviews of newsmen who accepted the railway-sponsored excursions into the areas open for settlement. In June 1875 Colonel A. S. Johnson, land commissioner for the Santa Fe, arranged a trip for about 225 editors, many of them from the Ohio and Mississippi valleys, into western Kansas. Crops were good, the grass was lush, and the entire country looked like the Garden of the West, a name some writers gave the area, and abundant food and drink were provided at the Santa Fe's expense.

The stories and editorials that followed this trip must have warmed the heart of Colonel Johnson as they were better than any kind of paid

An advertisement for the Atchison, Topeka and Santa Fe Railroad, 1881. (The Kansas State Historical Society, Topeka)

advertising. The editors later passed a resolution thanking the Santa Fe for sponsoring the excursion, and declared: "we have been profoundly impressed with the immense agricultural resources of the country traversed by the Atchison, Topeka & Santa Fe road, the evidences of which we have witnessed; that we are convinced that its capabilities for raising cattle, corn, and all the products necessary to the sustenance and comfort of human life, can hardly be realized and appreciated until they have been seen." They were compelled to repeat in all seriousness what some had taken lightly, "Go West, young man, go West."[44] One editor from Indiana wrote: "I never saw finer country in the world than that part of Kansas passed over by the Atchison, Topeka & Santa Fe road. Corn waist high, wheat in the shock, oats in fine condition, and vegetables in abundance." Another editor who had been born on an Illinois farm where corn had been a major crop reported that "yet I must confess to the superior excellence of these valleys over anything I have ever seen elsewhere."[45]

But the railroads did much more than advertise the West. They developed a wide variety of practical programs to locate farmers directly on railroad-owned land and also furnished transportation to those who settled on other lands as well. The companies sold land exploring tickets to farm seekers, and if a buyer took 160 acres or more the cost of the ticket would be credited to the purchase price. Some railroads gave settlers additional credit if they broke and planted a certain amount of land the first year. Moreover, the companies shipped personal belongings of the emigrants at low rates, or sometimes free of charge, and established emigrant houses where families could stay without cost while they searched for a suitable farm. The Burlington set up an emigrant home at Lincoln, Nebraska, and other roads provided or helped to support similar homes elsewhere. Indeed, the railroads played a major role in the rapid agricultural settlement of the upper midwest prairie frontier. They were highly important as farm-makers. Unlike the situation east of the Mississippi River where the railroads did not move very far into unoccupied areas, in some of the western states and territories the lines were built far ahead of settlement. This was especially true of the Union Pacific, Northern Pacific, and Santa Fe. The purpose of railroad interest in settlement was, of course, to sell company land. Most of the railroad land on the upper midwest prairie frontier was sold at between $2.50 and $10 an acre. In the period from 1872 to 1873, the Northern Pacific priced its lands in western Minnesota from $2.50 to $8, depending on its distance from the railroad, while the cost of Union Pacific lands in Nebraska varied from $2.50 to $10 an acre. The majority of Santa Fe land in Kansas brought $5 to $6 an acre in the early 1870s and the Burlington realized an average of $6.07 per acre for its Nebraska lands between 1870 and 1880.[46] In some special cases the prices were above $10, but ordinarily farmers found good land up to the middle 1870s all along this frontier at less than this figure. Railroad lands could be purchased for both cash and on time payments. Credit policies varied, but usually a farmer could take from 4 to 10 years to pay for his land.

In 1870, for instance, the Union Pacific offered good Nebraska land at $5 an acre with one fourth in cash and the remainder in three annual installments. A farmer was generally granted a 10 percent discount for paying cash. The Burlington offered cash sales and both short- and long-term credit extending to as much as 10 years. The directors explained in 1873 that settlement was not stimulated so much by low prices "as by easy payments, enabling settlers with very small means to meet their engagements out of the products of their land."[47] By charging higher than government prices for land and offering long-term credit, speculation was reduced and the railroads got what they really wanted, namely, agricultural settlement.

In order to dispose of large blocks of land and build up business along their lines, the railroads were especially active in getting colonies of people to settle on their tracts. In 1870 the Union Pacific advertised that railroad and homestead land could be obtained in large blocks "enabling communities to lay out town sites, erect mills, build churches and school houses, and make other improvements in the most eligible locations."[48] Jay Cooke, financier of the Northern Pacific, wrote in the same year that one of the main objectives of the Northern Pacic was "to promote, so far as possible, immigration by colonies, so that neighbors in Fatherland may be neighbors in the new West."[49] Here were appeals to group settlement, which would obviate the lonesome, isolated pioneer existence.

Most settlers on this upper midwest prairie frontier seemed to believe that railroads were the key to economic development. The demand for transportation to open up new areas was very strong and writers became almost lyrical when they set out to explain the value of railroads. Although Grangers began attacking railroad abuses in the early 1870s, grass roots support for more railroad mileage continued strong in almost every community as the settlers pushed farther west. Land grants to railroads found many more criticis in the settled Midwest than in the developing areas of Minnesota, Dakota, Nebraska, and Kansas.

The editor of the Saint Paul *Daily Press* wrote in 1872 that "the policy of adequate land grants in aid of railroads through the underdeveloped regions of the West has proved incalculably the most beneficent use of the public domain, which has ever been instituted." Railroads, he continued, were the "primary and indispensible agencies" on which a developing country had to depend. He criticized those who talked about denying grants to railroads so that land could be reserved for actual settlers. This was "absolute nonsense," he wrote, because to offer a man a homestead with no means to market his produce is "to set before him a Barmecide feast of empty dishes." Praising the railroads as colonizing agents, the writer concluded that they were "an absolute necessity as the primary condition of western settlement."[50] During the spring of 1871 when the tide of emigration rushed westward along the Northern Pacific track in western Minnesota, the same writer declared that this "illustrates in a marked manner the mighty power of this railroad as a colonizing agency."[51] A year later the same paper stressed how the railroads served as town builders as well as farm-makers. Breckinridge, the temporary terminus of the St. Paul and Pacific Railroad, had 30 buildings, the editor exclaimed, when only "a month or two ago the prairie thereabouts was innocent of an inhabitants." Towns like Moorhead, Fargo, and Grand Forks would all develop rapidly and the entire Red River Valley would "soon be a hive of industry, thanks to the great civilizer—railroads."[52]

A writer for the *Minneapolis Tribune* said that the territory between Saint Paul and Fargo was "utterly unfit for the residence of man" before the Northern Pacific was built. "But no sooner does this iron artery of trade and commerce penetrate its borders than the 'wilderness blossoms like a rose.'" The writer added: "There is nothing which so rapidly pushes forward the car of progress and civilization as the railroad locomotive."[53]

Another Minnesota editor declared that farmers above all others needed railroads. Once built, continued the editor, railways provide "a home market for surplus and brings in capital and opens up greater competition in mercantile channels and in innumerable ways enures to the farmer's interest." On another occasion this writer said: "It certainly cannot require a great amount of argument to prove that it requires a railroad to properly develop a new country."[54]

In Nebraska *The Daily State Journal* at Lincoln took the same attitude. The editor argued that the Northwest would have been a howling wilderness "had not a portion of the vast lonely and worthless prairie been given to build through it these great highways of commerce, over which the immigrant hastened to make his home on the frontiers." Then emphasizing the role of railroads in economic development, the editor exclaimed: "when the government gives a land grant on the frontier to a railroad, it gives something absolutely worthless, until the road is built, and which confers for nothing, a vast boon upon the people of this and future generations."[55] Other writers emphasized the value of railroads by pointing out how they helped to increase land values.[56] These attitudes continued for a number of years especially in the more remote communities still seeking transportation. When the Missouri Pacific reached Stockton in northwestern Kansas, in November 1885, a local farmer recorded in his diary that it was certainly "a grand achievement for the people of this part of Kansas...," and ended with, "Whoop La Hurrah."[57]

When the long established habit of pioneering was coupled with the enticements offered by government land policies, attractions by railroads, and community and state promotional activities, the upper midwest prairie frontier succumbed to settlement in a few short years after the Civil War. By 1875 farmers were beginning to move out onto the Great Plains in Nebraska and Kansas. Areas around Lincoln and Topeka, which had been largely unoccupied in 1865, had become well settled communities a decade later.

◁ **3** ▷

The Upper Midwest and Central Prairie Frontier, 1865-1875

*A*lthough the upper midwest and central prairie frontier (Minnesota, Northwest Iowa, Dakota, Nebraska, and Kansas) filled up rapidly during the Civil War and in the decade that followed, settlement was by no means steady or uninterrupted. After the Sioux Indian uprising of 1862, for example, there was a sharp but temporary break in the movement of people to south-central Minnesota and Dakota. Scores of pioneers southwest of the Minnesota River abandoned their farms for the safety of more settled communities, while probably half the hardy farmers who had moved into Dakota left the territory in the fall of 1862.[1] Many people also abandoned their new homes in Dakota during 1863 because of severe drought and ravaging grasshoppers. In 1864 another grasshopper plague caused additional settlers to forsake the valleys of the Missouri and Big Sioux and move back to Iowa or some other more favorable location. Only 64 homesteads were filed in Dakota in 1864 following 2 very bad crop years. As Moses K. Armstrong wrote: "Unremitting drouth and clouds of grasshoppers swept the bloom from the fields and the verdure from the plains. . . ."[2]

Frontier farmers in Minnesota were hard hit during 1866 when their late-planted crops were ruined by an early frost. The following winter found so many pioneers suffering want and privation that Governor William R. Marshall paid out $6946 in emergency relief to buy food as well as seed for spring planting in 1867.[3] Following this bad year, homestead entries in Minnesota dropped from 3789 in 1866 to 2985 in 1867. Entries declined even further in 1868 before rising again.[4] Settlers farther south were also confronted with difficult conditions. In 1866 grasshoppers ravaged parts of Kansas and caused heavy losses to farmers. One editor wrote on September 4 that within a few minutes after their appearance everything green was covered and "in less than two hours the leaves were stripped from trees, bushes, corn, and etc."[5]

But Civil War, Indians, grasshoppers, severe winters, and other hazards did not stem the pioneer tide. Between 1860 and 1865 the population of Minnesota rose from 172,022 to 250,099 an increase of 45 percent. By 1870 the state had 780,773 persons. The number of farms advanced from 18,181 to 92,386 in the decade of the 1860s, which demonstrated how rapidly the virgin prairies were being carved into homes. But even with this rush of settlers, native and immigrant alike, most of western Minnesota still awaited the plow in 1870. Such potentially rich counties as Nobles, Rock, Murray, and Pipestone in the southwest, and the counties bordering the Red River farther north, were practically uninhabited.

Farmers were also pushing rapidly into the rich prairie lands of northwestern Iowa. The *Iowa State Register* reported in December 1865 that "a tide of immigration has been constantly pouring into the Northwestern portion of this State. . . ." In 1871 the secretary of the Iowa Agricultural Society predicted that before the end of another year "the free lands of Iowa will be a thing of the past." Several colonies settled in northwestern Iowa during the 1870s adding to the heavy flow of individual migration.[6] The speed of settlement can be seen by looking at Clay County. Between 1860 and 1880 the number of farms rose from only five to 697.

In Dakota conditions began to improve in 1866. Governor A. J. Faulk told the legislative assembly that it would not be long before the natural advantages of the territory would draw men of capital "or until our Territory is dotted over with farms, groaning with their abundant crops—a garden of fruitfulness, and the abode of a large and growing population."[7] And Faulk was a good prophet. During the next 3 years crops were good and a boom psychology pervaded the southeast section of the territory. The Sioux City and Pacific Railroad reached Sioux City, Iowa, in 1868, providing prospective emigrants with transportation right to Dakota's door. At Vermillion, the only land office in the territory, 186

36 - Upper Midwest and Central Prairie Frontier, 1865-1875

A street in Moorhead, Minnesota, 1872. (Minnesota Historical Society)

land claims were registered in May 1869 and 300 in June.[8] The three southeast counties were fairly well occupied by 1870, and settlers were going farther up the Big Sioux and James River valleys and scattering out over the tablelands in between. In 1868 and 1869 a total of 1137 homestead entries were filed and by 1870 the number of farms in Dakota had risen to 1720, compared to only 123 a decade earlier.

Westward expansion was especially rapid in Kansas and Nebraska. In 1865 there were only 140,179 people in Kansas, and the outer fringe of settlement was at Salina. By the end of the 1860s, however, farmers were taking up land in Russell, McPherson, Rice, Sedgwick, and other counties in the central part of the state. After 1870 there was a veritable flood of land seekers to that region. In 15 months during 1871 and 1872 the Concordia land office alone received 7000 homestead and 4000 preemption entries.[9] The great majority of settlers on this central Kansas frontier were native Americans from the older Middle West. Illinois, Iowa, Indiana, Missouri, and Ohio furnished by far the greatest number of pioneers in the area from Wichita north to Concordia. For example, Rice County, which was organized in 1871, had only five people in 1870 but this number increased to 2453 by 1875. All but 225 were native Americans and more than one-fourth came from Illinois.[10] There was a marked increase in homesteading as pioneers moved farther west in Kansas where more public land was available. Between 1868 and 1870 homestead entries increased from 1496 covering 166,214 acres of land, to 5024 filings on 646,609 acres. In 1871, 9456 settlers in Kansas filed on 1,261,622 acres, and the amount was nearly as great in 1872. The number of farms in Kansas rose from 10,400 in 1860 to 38,202 in 1870 and to 138,561 by 1880.[11]

In Nebraska farmers were rapidly taking up land in the east central part of the state during the late 1860s. Between 1860 and 1870 the number of farms increased from 2789 to 12,301. Not many settlers had gone beyond York County, which contained 604 persons and 232 farms in 1870. Homestead entries and railroad land sales reflected the demand for new farm homes. The number of homesteads filed in Nebraska increased from 2844 in 1868 to 6021 in 1871. Moreover, from 1871 to 1873 the Burlington Railroad sold 247,315 acres to 2058 purchasers in Nebraska and hundreds of farmers also bought land from the Union Pacific.[12]

A statement of a traveler along the old National Road in 1817 seemed applicable to the last farmers' frontier of the early 1870s. "Old America seems to be breaking up and moving westward," he wrote. If this observer a half century earlier was hardly ever out of sight of people going to Ohio, it was difficult in the late 1860s and early 1870s to travel about the upper midwest prairie frontier without seeing wagon trains, individual families, and railroads loaded with emigrants and their goods moving relentlessly toward the open lands. Ferries across the Mississippi River below Saint Paul were often jammed with people, wagons, livestock, and other belongings as westbound settlers looked toward western Minnesota, Dakota, or Nebraska. The newspapers gave almost constant attention to this tide of emigration. A La Crosse, Wisconsin, editor observed that "all the ferries between St. Paul and Prairie du Chien" were "crowded daily in the transportation of emigrants from Wisconsin and Illinois."[13]

In spring of 1867 a writer for the Saint Paul *Pioneer* reported that "settlers continue to pour in like a flood" and that Saint Paul was full of enterprising strangers.[14] By July so many Swedes and Norwegians were going to Minnesota that the editor said: "It seems as if the Scandinavian Kingdoms were being emptied into this State."[15] Horace Greeley, who visited Kansas in October 1870, wrote that settlers were "pouring into Eastern Kansas by car-loads, wagon-loads, horse-loads, daily. . . ."[16] In May 1871 a Nebraska traveler said he counted more than 200 emigrant teams between Lincoln and the Big Blue River to the west. In some areas the government surveyors could not keep up with the rush of settlement and they pleaded for larger appropriations and more help. W. H. H. Beadle, Surveyor General of Dakota Territory, wrote in August 1870 that settlers were already beyond the lines of survey. Emigrants who had come across Iowa and Minnesota by wagon, he said, had taken up 70,000 acres in June alone.[17]

While most settlers had traveled westward by wagon before 1870, expansion of railroad mileage contributed greatly to the speed and ease with which farmers could reach unoccupied lands after that date. The

Northern Pacific was completed to Moorhead, Minnesota, on the Red River in 1871; the Burlington reached Kearney, Nebraska, where it made connections with the Union Pacific in September 1872; the Santa Fe arrived at Emporia, Kansas, in 1870 and built westward to the Colorado line 2 years later. The Missouri, Kansas, and Texas arrived at the northern boundary of Indian Territory in March 1871. Moreover, many shorter railroads and branch lines spread out from the main rail centers. As was true in many parts of the West, the transportation and agricultural frontiers joined together to conquer vast unsettled regions. Hundreds of emigrants, however, continued to make their way west in wagons just as their forebears had done. Crossing southwestern Minnesota in June 1873, one traveler mentioned seeing three wagon trains besides her own, one of which had 11 teams.[18] By the early 1870s much of the available land was a considerable distance from track, and even if a family traveled from Illinois to Topeka or Lincoln by rail, it was likely that the rest of the way had to be reached by wagon.

Regardless of how a pioneer traveled to an unsettled area, his first

A claim shanty built in Clay County, Minnesota, 1870. (Clay County Historical Society)

tasks were to select land for homestead or purchase, build some kind of shelter, and to get a crop planted. If the settler planned to homestead or preempt land, he first found a desirable tract and then went to the nearest land office to file his entry. When he bought land from a railroad or other private party, an agent usually assisted him in getting located. In many instances a man would leave his family behind, go west and select his farm, and then return home to get his wife and children. Single men often migrated to the frontier, obtained land, and later married a girl from back home or found a companion in the new country. Western promoters urged eastern girls to go west because

> *There is no goose so gray, but, soon or late*
> *Will find some honest grander for a mate*[19]

The first settlers in a new community usually chose land immediately adjacent to the rivers and streams or on what were known as the second or third bottoms.[20] There they found a little timber for fuel and housing, and, besides, water was likely to be nearer the surface than on higher ground. Discussing the availability of land west of Concordia, Kansas, Amos Cutter of the land office wrote in April 1872 that very little land remained for homesteading along the rivers and creeks but that upland farms could be found in all the counties west of the Republican River.

The first home built by emigrants on the upper midwest prairie frontier of western Minnesota and southeastern Dakota was usually a crude dugout or sod house. There were a few log houses and occasionally someone had enough money to build a frame structure. However, it generally took a few years for the ordinary pioneer to earn enough money to build with lumber. Jane Grout recorded in her diary that, as her party traveled west of Winnebago City, Minnesota, in 1873, earlier settlers were planting trees around their sod houses. In one community she saw a single frame house in an area completely surrounded "by little sod ones," a sight, she said, which looked odd to someone from Wisconsin. Most newcomers in eastern Nebraska and Kansas built log houses but, after about 1870 when settlement extended farther west, sod houses and dugouts were the most common type of pioneer home. One observer declared that there were no frame houses among rural settlers in Barton County, Kansas, in 1871.[21]

If a farmer were fortunate enough to get settled on his land, break 10 or 15 acres, and then raise a crop of sod corn or wheat, and perhaps some potatoes, he at least had food for the coming winter. However, many emigrants moved to their new homes in the late summer or early fall, which was too late to plant and harvest any crops. These people often suffered severely because they did not have sufficient cash to meet their immediate needs for food and clothing to say nothing of capital to develop their farms. Most pioneers had very little money or property. Their belongings often consisted of nothing more than a few household goods, a wagon, plow, a team of oxen, one or two milk cows, and perhaps a horse or two. With very limited resources, a settler's success in establishing a farm often depended on when and where he located as much as it did upon his ambition or managerial abilities.

If a farmer happened to settle on his land during a period of rising prices and was then fortunate enough to have a good crop the first year, he could make enough money to support his family and add a little to his meager capital. Two or 3 such years in a row might put him well on the way to becoming a successful farmer. On the other hand, if a poor pioneer settled too late to plant a crop, if drought, frost, hail, or grasshoppers destroyed it, or if prices were low, a major crisis developed because of lack of money to see the family through until another harvest. Under these conditions, the settler immediately became mired in debt if, indeed, he could hang on at all, and 2 or 3 such years together usually brought him to the verge of bankruptcy. Finding themselves in this condition, thousands of settlers on the agricultural frontier packed up their few belongings and returned to the East. A bankrupt homesteader might

Upper Midwest and Central Prairie Frontier, 1865-1875 - **41**

A frontier woman gathering cow chips for fuel on the western plains. (The Kansas State Historical Society, Topeka)

sell a relinquishment on his homestead to a new settler or to a more successful neighbor. In hard times a relinquishment on 160 acres could be bought for as little as $50, and sometimes less. Many settlers met some of their expenses by finding off-farm work, especially on the railroads. At times these pioneers traveled many miles in search of employment, which would provide a few dollars in cash.

Good crop years during initial settlement were crucial to most settlers. When Governor Marshall of Minnesota asked the legislature in 1868 to provide relief for suffering frontiersmen, he explained this situation clearly. The chief causes of distress, the Governor said, "appear to have been the advance beyond the older and productive settlements in the year 1866, of a class of settlers who were wholly dependent on the crop they should raise the first year—the year of their settling. Many of them arrived so late that the earlier frost of that year cut off their crops. The long winter of '66–'67 exhausted the resources of these people —compelled them to use their seed grain for subsistence and left them helpless for the future."[22] When grasshoppers ravaged parts of Kansas in 1874, Governor Osborn, in asking the legislature for help, explained that "the new settlers in the western counties who had not yet got the soil ready for wheat were relying upon the usual crop of corn for their winter's subsistence, but this has been swept away and many of them are left without the means of support."[23] Similar conditions were common on the outer edge of settlement at other times and on other frontiers.

During the hard times in western Kansas following 1879 the state provided help for destitute settlers. Of the 84 settlers who applied for relief from Gove County in 1881, 50 had been there only 2 years, 25 had lived there 1 year, and only nine had been in Gove County as long as 3 years. The relief applications show that most of those who applied had been in western Kansas only since 1879. A dry and difficult year followed in 1880 when the crops failed and most settlers found themselves destitute by the spring of 1881.[24]

Despite intermittent hard years, settlers on the Minnesota-Dakota-Nebraska-Kansas prairie frontier were much more likely to succeed as farm-makers than those who pushed farther west onto the Great Plains a short while later. The natural conditions of soil and rainfall were much more favorable on the prairies, and crop failures were rather exceptional in northwest Iowa, southwest and western Minnesota, southeast Dakota, and eastern Nebraska and Kansas. But when farmers reached the 98th or 99th meridian and continued even farther west in search of land, they entered a region where drought was common and crop failures frequent under the then-known systems of farming. Indeed, during the late nineteenth century a series of good years was the exception rather than the rule. Because reserves were absolutely necessary to carry a farmer over frequent bad times when he settled on the Great Plains, sufficient capital became more important than it was on the prairie frontier farther east. And when a settler moved even farther West to areas where irrigation was essential for crop production, capital assumed greater significance because of the expense of developing water systems.

Shortage of capital was one of the greatest obstacles to successful farm-making after 1865. Even though a settler might homestead his land or buy it cheap on long-term credit, he still needed money to develop his farm and get him through periods of crop failure. Ideally, a settler required funds for a house, well, fencing, machinery, and livestock. Assuming that a farmer homesteaded his land, it was often stated in the 1870s and 1880s, and by historians later, that a settler should have at least $1000 in order to get properly established and equipped. As mentioned earlier, the Santa Fe Railroad warned eastern families in 1879 not to move to southwestern Kansas unless they had $800 to $1000 to start a farm. But, as a matter of fact, thousands of farms were established and developed into reasonably good homes with a much smaller initial investment. There were also many failures, but through luck, grit, sacrifice, and careful management, many succeeded.

Success was possible because there was very little initial cash outlay for some of the essentials necessary for home- and farm-making. A dugout, which was dug into the side of a hill and built up in front with sod or lumber could be made at practically no expense other than a door and window, and even these were not absolute requirements. A Nebraskan quoted the cost of items to finish a dugout in 1872 at only $2.78. A sod house could be completed by purchasing a door and windows, and a few rafters to hold up the roof in case logs or poles were not available. Plaster for the inside was made by mixing clay and ashes. One pioneer said that a sod house was "made without mortar, square, plumb, or greenbacks."[25] In any event, it cost very little. Not much cash was needed for fuel because where wood was unavailable pioneers burned twisted hay or dried animal dung, commonly called cow chips. In some areas coal was mined locally at very small expense.

Moreover, most farmers on the prairie frontier could dig their own wells, and if at first there was not enough money for a pump or windmill, the water could be drawn in a bucket. There were many places even on the Great Plains where water could be obtained at less than 50 feet below the surface. In Solomon township of Norton County in northwest Kansas, most of the wells were less than 100 feet deep, and quite a number of them were not more than 30 feet.[26]

Fencing, on the other hand, was expensive, but not many settlers built costly fence at the outset. The average farmer fenced his land gradually, obtaining the money from the sale of crops and livestock over a period of years. Meanwhile, children herded the livestock to keep it out of growing crops. The idea that a farmer made, or even needed to make, an immediate outlay for fencing is erroneous. Kansas, Nebraska, Dakota and some other western states and territories enacted herd laws, which required that owners of cattle that ran at large were responsible for keeping them out of farmers' fields. When fences were an absolute necessity, farmers built a small amount of wire fencing or used cheap local material where possible. Hedge and stone were used in parts of Kansas.[27]

The matter of fencing can best be seen by looking at some local situations on the Kansas frontier in the 1870s. The state census of agriculture for 1875 shows that in Center township, Norton County, which was organized in 1872, not a single one of the 78 newly arrived emigrants had any land under fence. In Solomon township in the same county only three out of 59 farmers reported any fence. Charles Thresher, who

The interior of Elam Bartholomew's sod house in Rooks County, Kansas, about 1900. (The Kansas State Historical Society, Topeka)

settled near Topeka in 1872, did not fence his "south 80" until 1880 by which time he had acquired enough money to make this investment.[28] The expense of fencing was not necessarily a part of initial capital requirements.

At the outset most settlers had very little investment in machinery. A wagon was necessary, but many pioneers had this before migrating west. If one had to be purchased, the price in the 1870s was between $75 and $125. A team cost around $150. A plow could be purchased for $15 to $30, and a harrow for even less. With this much equipment an emigrant could put in his first crop. In 1870 farmers in Chippewa Falls township of Pope County, Minnesota, reported the value of their machinery at from a low of $10 to a high of $200. Most farmers had less than $100 worth of machinery. Assuming an undervaluation, this was still a very small investment.[29] Many farmers did much of their work by hand during the first years of settlement. Elam Bartholomew, who settled in Rooks County in northwestern Kansas in 1875, recorded in his diary on June 27, 1877, that he and four neighbors planned to work together through harvest "running three cradles and sufficient additional force to rake, bind and shock the grain." Bartholomew cut hay with a scythe and planted corn with a hand planter.[30] If a farmer did not have a team and plow, he could hire breaking done at from $2.50 to $4 an acre, and the wheat, corn, or potatoes could be planted by hand. Although chances of success were much better if a settler had more capital, thousands of farms were established with less than $500.[31]

The experience of Fred A. Fleischman, who filed on a quarter section in Wood County, Dakota, on June 4, 1879, illustrates how a poor man could make a successful start if he settled in the right place and happened to begin at the right time. Fleischman first arranged to have 20 acres plowed at a cost of $60. Then in the spring of 1880 he borrowed $200 from his brother in New York and with $225 he had saved, he moved to his place and began farming. With this amount of money he was even able to build a frame house. That fall prices were reasonably good and he sold $170.55 worth of wheat and oats. The next year 213 bushels of wheat brought him $223.71, or better than a dollar a bushel. He also sold $128 worth of oats and other items, which gave him a total income of $371.89 for 1881. Meanwhile, he plowed more land, and in 1882 he sold $1241 worth of produce, about half of which was wheat. After beginning farm operations with less than $500, about half of which was borrowed, within 3 years Fleischman found himself in a good home and with a fairly well developed farm. It is important to note that during the years when Fleischman was getting established, the weather was favorable and prices were quite good. These circumstances were very important in helping him get properly situated, and he was still farming after 1900.[32]

Even though many farms were successfully established on the prairie frontier, and even on the Great Plains, with limited capital, the margin between success and failure was often very narrow. It might be drought or rain, hail or sunshine, grasshoppers or absence of insects, and health or disease among livestock that made the difference between bankruptcy and survival. Soil varieties were also important. While low prices, high transportation costs, and other economic problems made it difficult to succeed at farming, thousands of farmers actually made fairly comfortable homes for themselves and families after 1865 even when confronted with these difficulties. Very few farmers, however, could stay solvent in the face of the twin handicaps of low prices and crop failures. Low prices were bad, but not necessarily fatal. Low prices and crop failure together most generally assured ruin for the frontier settler, and for many others as well.

Bad conditions had the first and greatest impact on the farmer of limited capital. Gradually, however, more land was brought into production, livestock multiplied, and if crops and prices were not too bad, the farmer gradually accumulated more property and improved his situation. But when farmers tried to establish a successful commercial operation with such slender resources—one or two cows, 8 or 10 acres of wheat or corn, and a few potatoes—almost any natural calamity such as the death of a cow, crop failure, or family illness could mean quick and irreparable ruin. The surprising thing is not that many pioneers failed to establish going commercial farms in the 1870s and 1880s, or fell heavily into debt, but the remarkable thing is that so many of them succeeded.

Some of the foreign immigrant groups arrived in the West with more money than most native settlers. In April 1878 Mrs. Mattie Oblinger of near Sutton, Nebraska, wrote to her parents in Indiana that some Dutch families were moving into the neighborhood. They had more money, she said, and had bought three quarters of land and were building frame houses and even frame barns. That, she added, was "stylish for Fillmore [County]." Some of the Mennonites who arrived in Kansas in the 1870s carried substantial sums of money, and one group reached Topeka in 1874 with $2 million.[33]

Most settlers who went to the frontier and began to farm planned to build up their capital out of production from their land and livestock. They also hoped to benefit from increased land values. The manuscript census and diaries of individual farmers indicate, however, that capital formation was a long, slow process on most western farms. Charles Thresher near Topeka owned 158 acres. In 1872 he listed his net worth, including land and buildings, at $4126. By 1880 he was worth $5033, and by 1885 $6097. While this increase amounted to $2781 in 13 years, $2000 of this came from the rising value of his farm.[34] Thresher had made a living for himself and his family during that time, but he had added very little to his capital for operations. In other words, income from his production was little above his current consumption. This was the situation for thousands of farmers on the Western Prairie and Great Plains frontiers.

Most farmers reinvested into the farm practically everything they made. Although this seemed necessary in order to establish a profitable operation, it meant that families postponed or gave up convenieces and pleasures that might have taken money away from needed farm improvements. After paying for machinery, barns, fencing, and operating costs, there was not much left over for furniture, books, travel, and other things, which might have made life more enjoyable. This is no doubt one of the main reasons why so many farm women came to dislike the farm. When the question arose as to whether to spend the limited money on new curtains for the house or repairs for the reaper, the decision was usually to buy the repairs. The repairs were absolutely necessary if harvesting was to continue, while the old curtains could be made to last a little longer. Farm women resented always having to postpone conveniences and pleasures, and to be told that they would have to wait for next year.

At the outset most frontier farmers operated on a very small scale. Although they raised crops and livestock for the commercial market, most pioneer families produced much of their own living and in the first years had little to sell. The scale of operations and the economic position of western farmers after the Civil War can best be seen in the manuscript census and in diaries kept by individual farmers. Pope County in western Minnesota received its first emigrants in the late 1860s. In 1868 only 2721 acres were under cultivation. The census of 1870 shows that farmers generally had 125 to 160 acres of land, but in 1869 most settlers cultivated less than 25 acres. In Anderson township no farmer had more than 20 acres improved, and of the 32 farmers in Chippewa Falls township the improved acreage varied from a low of 4 to a high of 40. Wheat was the main crop, but most farmers reported raising less than 100 bushels. Practically every settler raised from 10 to 50 bushels of potatoes. The majority of farmers reported owning one or two milk cows, and a few had as many as three or four. In addition, most pioneer families in Pope County had a team of oxen and one to eight head of "other cattle." In Chippewa Falls township there was only one horse listed in 1870. Butter was a main cash product, and farmers reported producing anywhere from 75 to as much as 300 pounds annually.[35]

Much the same picture emerges wherever one looks at other sections of the frontier in the 1870s. Russell County, Kansas, was organized in 1872 and by 1875 had a population of 1052. In Center township there were 84 farmers in 1875, of whom 60 had the traditional quarter section of land. Sixteen settlers had only 80 acres, one had none, and seven owned more than 160 acres. The two largest landholders each reported 480 acres. Seventy-one of the 84 farmers reported having grown corn in 1874, mostly less than 15 acres each. Over half of them had less than 10 acres. Sixty-two of the settlers in this township also grew wheat, but they usually had less than 10 acres, with 4 to 8 being common. Some farmers also grew a small amount of barley, rye, or oats. Potatoes were raised by almost every farmer. Of the 84 farmers in the township, 55 reported owning milk cows. Of these, 25 had only one cow, and 16 possessed only two. Forty-three settlers had "other cattle," but usually less than 10 head. Twenty-four farmers owned neither stock cattle nor milk cows. Fifty-two of the farmers owned one or more horses; 11 had only one, while 25 owned two head, or a team. Only one-third of the settlers reported having one or two swine.[36]

It is clear from the census data that most frontier farmers began in a very small way. They had very little machinery or livestock, and they farmed only a few acres. They produced part of their own living by growing potatoes and other vegetables, wheat for flour, and by raising livestock for meat. But they were by no means totally self-sufficient and some food items like sugar and coffee had to be purchased, along with clothing, utensils, and farming equipment. These other supplies were obtained with money obtained from selling butter, a few bushels of grain, or an occasional hog or calf. Butter was an especially important income producer for frontier farmers. In the 1870s it usually brought between 10 and 15 cents a pound. Some households were actually kept solvent through the sale of butter. The census records reveal that during a year many settlers produced more than 100 pounds, much of which was marketed. In August 1876 Mrs. Mattie Oblinger wrote her parents in Indiana that "we have been very busy and most of the time without stamps and money. We have managed to keep ourselves in groceries such as we were compelled to have by selling butter and a few vegetables. . . . Uriah [her husband] is going to town tomorrow afternoon and I want to send a little butter and potatoes and corn and pickles and get some groceries. . . ."[37] In the first year or two of settlement the average frontier family might handle less than $50 in cash and even after several years income and expenditures many times did not exceed $300. In 1873 Charles Thresher near Topeka took in $259.39 and spent $379.10; in 1876 his receipts were $316.12, and his expenditures $337.90.[38]

Spring wheat was the main crop grown by farmers on the Minnesota and Dakota frontier in the late 1860s and 1870s. Most settlers considered wheat the ideal crop. It was easily grown, it could be eaten, stored, or transported, and it could always find a market. Although it might be risky, many pioneers considered wheat growing to be the best and fastest way to increase their incomes. Although in 1872 the commissioner of statistics recommended more diversified agriculture, he concluded that "at least while emigration lasts, and the necessity of the settlers demand quick returns for labor and money expended, wheat culture will undoubtedly remain the principal business of a majority of Minnesota farmers."[39] Reports of successful operators undoubtedly encouraged greater concentration on this crop. In 1872 a writer for the *Farmers Union* commented on the good crops and prices that prevailed. Then he told about a farmer near Shell Rock who had moved to his place only 3 years before $1200 in debt. With the current wheat crop this farmer would pay off his debt, and besides, during the 3 years he had added an equal amount to his farm property and equipment.[40] In 1877 the commissioner of statistics wrote that "the profits of our wheat farming are so alluring, that the small farmer, struggling with poverty, and a large family, often becomes a gambler with wheat and risks his all on the hazard of a crop." He emphasized that wheat farming "requires adequate capital as much as any other business," and again urged farmers to diversify their operations.[41]

By 1872 some 61 percent of the cultivated acreage in Minnesota was in wheat, and more than 22,000,000 bushels were produced. The westward advance of wheat growing was evident by 1870 when Minnesota moved into sixth place among the wheat-producing states. Iowa also grew a great deal of wheat, although corn was the main crop there. But by 1870 Iowa ranked second only to Illinois in wheat production. In

Harvesting with a team of four oxen. (Minnesota Historical Society)

Dakota farmers also emphasized wheat, and the territory's 1720 farmers produced more than 170,622 bushels in 1870.

In Minnesota both pioneer and better established farmers had a mania for wheat-growing in the late 1860s and throughout the 1870s. In Chippewa Falls township of Pope County not a single farmer reported growing any corn in 1869. In 1871 Jackson County farmers in the southwest part of the state planted only 382 acres of corn compared to 2437 acres of wheat. A minister at Cottage Grove, Minnesota, said in 1866 that "nothing interests the people of this community more than the price of wheat." On another occasion he declared that around Cottage Grove "men work in wheat all day when it does not rain, lounge around talking about wheat when it is wet, dream about wheat at night and I fear go to meeting Sabbath Day to think about wheat."[42] In 1870 Governor Austin said that "in the wheat record of Minnesota may be read the history of her marvelous advancement." But he warned that overproduction had caused low prices and said that the "remedy is to be found mainly in a more diversified agriculture." Others also preached diversification. Comparing wheat growing to a lottery, the editor of the *Farmers Union* called it "a risky business." The farmer, he said, took a chance on the weather, insects, prices, and other unpredictable factors. "Don't risk your *all* on wheat," he argued, "raise corn and hogs, oats, barley, hay, flax, potatoes, sheep, cattle, poultry, bees—anything that is profitable so that if anyone of these calamities befall you as they have thousands of wheat growers in the west this year, you may have some other reliance to depend upon."[43] But Minnesota farmers continued to rely heavily on wheat. Seventy percent of the state's improved acreage was in wheat by the late 1870s; and by 1880 production had nearly doubled that of a decade earlier, reaching 34,601,030 bushels.

Some large-scale wheat operations developed in Minnesota. Oliver Dalrymple, who later made history in the Red River Valley of North Dakota, was one of the state's largest wheat growers. By 1872 he had 2300 acres in cultivation near Hastings. His land was divided into three farms, Grant, Sherman, and Sheridan. Considering the price of his land, fencing, and costs of operation, Dalrymple figured that he had made 20 to 25 percent average profit on his investment during the previous 6 years. Moreover, his land had risen in value from $10 an acre to $40 an acre. In 1872 he raised 50,600 bushels of wheat and sold it for $53,130. Dalrymple told a reporter for the *Farmers Union* that this kind of farming paid him larger returns than any other enterprise he could have entered. The writer added that "Minnesota has room for twenty thousand just such farms requiring only intelligent management to give equally good returns.[44]

While wheat was the main cash crop produced in Minnesota and Dakota by pioneer farmers as well as those who had been established longer, not many settlers placed their full dependence upon wheat. Frontiersmen usually raised varying amounts of oats, barley, corn, flax, potatoes, and other vegetables. Most settlers also cut and stacked a considerable amount of hay, which was usually abundant. This was fed to cattle and horses. Pioneer families seldom had more than five or 10 head of cattle, but income from the sale of livestock products was important in helping to meet living expenses. The vast majority of settlers sought a degree of diversification in their production. At least they tried to produce a good share of their own food. But even diversification did not assure success on the farm. A drought or grasshopper plague that ruined the wheat also destroyed other crops as well as the hay for livestock. However, it seems true that the more diversified farmer usually did better at least during the initial years of settlement and with limited capital.

The first crop planted by settlers on the Nebraska and Kansas frontiers was usually corn rather than wheat. Many farmers who had come from Ohio, Illinois, Indiana, Missouri, and other parts of the older Middle West considered Kansas and Nebraska potentially rich corn country. Indeed, the eastern parts of these states were well suited to corn culture, but even after pioneers pushed 100 to 200 miles west of the Missouri River where the climate was too dry for assured corn production, they still clung to planting corn. Settlers on the Kansas frontier had come from corn growing areas and as one authority observed, they "tended to follow the natural course—that of planting the accustomed staples until local conditions of climate, soil and marketing directed otherwise."[45] In 1870 corn production in Kansas reached 17 million bushels compared to only 2,391,000 bushels of wheat; in Nebraska the ratio was about two to one in favor of corn. The pioneer counties in Kansas placed an especially heavy emphasis upon corn. In McPherson County, which later became a great wheat producer, only 5138 bushels of wheat were reported in 1870 compared to 40,540 bushels of corn. In York County, Nebraska, settlers grew 10,700 bushels of corn and 8876 bushels of spring wheat.[46]

Corn had a number of advantages for pioneer settlers in certain areas. It could be planted by chopping a hole in the sod with an ax or with a simple hand planter after the land had been broken. It could be ground into meal for food and could also be fed to livestock. Wheat was not considered a good feed for animals, except poultry. Moreover, the acre production of corn was usually much higher than that of wheat, although the price was often less than half as much. But price was not so important to the pioneer farmer who consumed much of his own production and who lacked adequate transportation facilities to get a crop such as wheat to market.

Pioneers on the Nebraska and Kansas frontier clung to corn as their principal crop even as they pushed westward to the 100th meridian and beyond. As late as 1880 Kansas counties like McPherson, Reno, and Sedgwick, which later became leading centers of winter wheat production, still grew much more corn than wheat. Sedgwick County produced more than four times as much corn as wheat in 1880. The state census of 1875 shows that pioneer farmers in Solomon township of Norton County, which was on the 100th meridian, were trying to grow corn in that semiarid region. Of the 59 farmers in the township, 52 reported corn. However, wheat was gaining in popularity and 39 farmers had either spring or winter wheat, or both.[47] As farmers moved up the Republican and Platte rivers in Nebraska they also relied heavily on corn. By the late 1870s western settlement had reached Dawson, Gosper, and Phelps counties just about at the 100th meridian. In 1879 the farmers there produced two to four times as much corn as wheat.

The experience of Kansas farmers with wheat was not especially encouraging up to 1870, or even for several years afterward. Intermittent drought, grasshoppers, chinch bugs, and other problems caused more discussion that actual production of wheat. The editor of the *Kansas Farmer* wrote in September 1867 that "no crop, in our country, has met with so many discouraging failures and disastrous defeats as wheat." Yet, he said, it was an extremely important product, and "no other state in the union is urged by so many considerations of pride and interest to try wheat raising in Kansas." Then the editor appealed "to every Kansas farmer in the name of duty and interest, to test the wheat producing quality of his land at once. Let every man put in at least one acre of wheat this fall, and another in the spring.[48] But, production rose slowly and it was not much greater in 1872 than in 1868. By 1874, however, production had climbed to 9,881,000 bushels or about six times the crop of 1868. The increase in wheat production was not considered rapid enough by some Kansas leaders. In 1875 the President of Kansas State Agricultural College declared that: "As in most Western States, corn has been the leading crop; the statistics show that it is far from being either the most certain or the most profitable." Then he added: "Don't put all your eggs in the corn basket; put most in the wheat basket, it is safer."[49] But by 1880 only four counties in the state produced more wheat than corn. It is significant that these counties were on the extreme western frontier, indicating that farmers were beginning to realize that western Kansas was definitely not a corn country.[50]

Both spring and winter wheat were raised in Kansas during the early years. In 1870 about 55 percent of the wheat acreage was in spring wheat, but there was a strong trend in the 1870s toward the winter variety. By 1875 winter wheat comprised some 76 percent of the crop. Farmers discovered through practical experience that the soil and climate of Kansas were more suitable to winter wheat than to spring wheat. One of the main considerations was to have a crop that matured early, before the summer droughts occurred. Moreover, settlers gradually adopted improved practices, such as drilling the seed into the ground, which helped to assure a better winter wheat crop. New varieties of wheat introduced during the 1870s improved both quality and production.

The wheat boom in Kansas during the 1870s was based on soft winter varieties, including Michigan White, White Bluestem, Early May, Red Amber, and Mediterranean Red. There were numerous other varieties, and farmers in different sections of the state favored the kind that seemed to do best in their particular locality. Among the hard winter wheats brought to Kansas was Turkey Red, introduced by the Mennonites, probably in 1874.[51] Within another decade hard winter wheat was rapidly becoming the great cash crop of central Kansas.

Other crops raised by Nebraska and Kansas farmers were about the same as those grown by settlers in Minnesota and Dakota. These included oats, which usually ranked second or third among the grain crops because of its feed value, along with barley, rye, and a small amount of buckwheat. Some farmers also raised broomcorn and sorghum. Kansas farmers produced 2,500,000 gallons of sorghum in 1874. Vegetables, especially potatoes, were a staple product on practically every frontier farm.

Farmers on the edge of settlement depended heavily upon livestock for their subsistence. However, as pointed out above, the average pioneer on the Kansas-Nebraska-Dakota-Minnesota prairie frontier in the late 1860s and early 1870s had only a few head of cattle, hogs, or horses. Yet, the one or two cows were extremely important in helping to make a living by providing milk, cream, and butter. Moreover, these cows were often the foundation for a larger herd. Since pasture and hay were cheap and plentiful, many farmers considered it good business to increase their cattle numbers. The number of milk cows in Kansas, for example, rose from 123,440 in 1870 to 418,333 a decade later; the increase in Minnesota was from 121,467 to 275,545; in Nebraska 28,940 to 161,187; and in Dakota from 4151 to 40,572. Nebraska farmers increased their nonmilk cattle some 12 times in the 1870s, while in Dakota and Kansas the number rose by about five times. In Minnesota the increase was a little more than double.[52] Not many settlers on the frontier kept sheep. Although the number of sheep rose sharply in Minnesota, Dakota, Nebraska, and Kansas after 1870, the increase occurred as much among the established farmers as in the new settlements. Sheep required considerable care, were subject to disease, and losses were heavy because of dogs and coyotes.[53]

Most frontier farmers, as well as those who had been settled for a number of years, maintained a combination grain-livestock enterprise. The relation of crops to livestock varied with individual producers, but relatively few farmers concentrated on a single aspect of farming. Even in areas where wheat was the main cash crop, farmers raised some other commodities, as well as livestock. There was a great deal of talk about diversification in the 1870s, but actually most farmers normally diversified their efforts and investment without advice from the farm journals or the colleges of agriculture. Yet greater diversification was continually presented as the means to solve some of the farmer's problems. So long as the mania for wheat growing continued in Minnesota, farmers lagged behind those in southeast Dakota, Nebraska, and Kansas in diversifying their operations, but there, too, specialization gave way to varied farm enterprises throughout most of the state by the early 1880s.

Rapid westward migration to the upper midwest prairie frontier is reflected by the striking increases in population, in the number of farms, and in the acreage under cultivation. The number of people in Minnesota, Dakota, Nebraska, and Kansas grew from 1,001,279 in 1870 to 2,364,448 in 1880, while the number of farms increased from 98,809 to

301,769 and the improved acreage rose from 4,982,781 to 24,641,374. In other words, population increased about two and one-third times, the number of farms rose threefold, and the improved land in farms jumped approximately five times.[54] Although this was a remarkable record of expansion, the conquering of this agricultural frontier did not come without great hardships to many settlers.

◁ **4** ▷

Destitution on the Frontier in the 1870s

*F*arming always has been a risky, uncertain, and sometimes heartbreaking business, but pioneer settlers in the 1870s on the upper midwest and central prairie frontier were confronted with an unusual series of hardships. Prairie fires, hail, drought, and, worst of all, grasshoppers plagued farmers in many parts of this area well into the middle years of the decade. These and other natural hazards were spotty and unpredictable, but thousands of farmers both on the frontier and in the older settled regions suffered heavy losses. Because of their limited resources, pioneer farmers were less able to stand a loss of crops than their better established neighbors. However, there were few farmers in this region who were financially able to weather a grasshopper invasion or drought without having to make genuine sacrifices. As if the physical problems were not enough, farmers were adversely affected by periodic low prices. Indeed, these were times of trouble on western farms.

There were periodic droughts that damaged crops in the late 1860s and 1870s, but it was not often that a farmer lost everything because of dry weather. Rather, a drought usually meant only partial loss of crops.

In Nebraska and Kansas, for example, corn might not mature, but could at least be cut for fodder. However, hail, fire, or grasshoppers could bring total destruction to crops, and in the case of fire and hail, buildings and personal property might be lost as well.

In 1871 hail and prairie fires in southern and southwestern Minnesota caused heavy losses to farmers and left scores of pioneer settlers nearly destitute. In July hail wiped out crops over a large area of Blue Earth County and families who had been merely poor before the storm were now in dire want. One observer wrote that the Butternut Valley had been "sorely afflicted" with hailstorms and smallpox, and that most of the people were new settlers "and poor at the beginning." Moreover, by December 1871 the weather was extremely cold and many pioneers could not keep warm on their straw-filled mattresses with scanty coverings. One farmer wrote a representative of the governor: "I have been trying to live on my place and with sickness and bad luck in crops have well nigh run out of everything—I have been sick for months and my wife is not well from exposure and hunger and I thought that there was no other way than to ask you to help me—If you can let me have $25 and some close [sic] for my wife and daughter and myself as we have not close to cover our backs or heads—And if I can't get the money I shall lose my place after livin' from hand to mouth for three years on the frontier."[1]

So many letters and reports describing destitution on the Minnesota frontier reached Governor Horace Austin in the fall and early winter of 1871 that he appointed special investigators to look into the situation. In October Mark D. Flower traveled through Jackson, Cottonwood, Martin, and other counties in that area to obtain firsthand information on conditions. Flower's letters to Governor Austin reveal tragedy and discouragement, which were even too much for hardy pioneers. He told of a young man and his wife who had just settled on a homestead near Windom and who had "expended all of his means in building a house and in laying in a winter's supply of provisions. His house and furniture burned, together with all of his supplies." In another case, a family had lost a barn and granary that held 43 bushels of wheat, 15 bushels of oats, two pigs, tools, and 25 tons of hay. All that remained was a cow and calf, one yoke of oxen, and a yearling. The family of five, Flower said, was "extremely destitute, nearly naked and too poor to clothe themselves." From the appearance of the country around Saint James the "fires were awful," he added.

As Flower traveled over the southwestern frontier counties of Minnesota he came upon case after case of people left destitute by prairie fires. Many of these pioneers had settled only the year before and had absolutely no reserves to meet such difficult and unexpected circumstances.

A Norwegian farmer near Mountain Lake had lost his stable, 150 bushels of wheat, 30 bushels of corn, and 26 tons of hay. He only had 20 bushels of potatoes left. Unless outside aid came, Flower wrote, this settler would starve or have to desert his homestead. From Blue Earth City, Flower wrote that one farmer had nothing remaining after the fire except "a good-looking wife," which was perhaps better than another farmer who needed help. His "old lady" was "husky," Flower reported, and "will weigh 180 lbs." A man with an invalid wife and two children had lost his hay, corn, and stable. He had planned to sell the corn to clothe his family, "but all is gone." Indeed, scores of farmers were in a grim struggle with solvency by the winter of 1871–1872 in parts of Minnesota.[2]

In order to help the suffering pioneers in the winter of 1871–1872, Governor Austin appealed to the public for contributions of cash and commodities. Within a short time clothing, flour and other food, as well as cash, were pouring into the Governor's office. The money received was turned over to the county treasurers who distributed small amounts to the most needy. Records in the Governor's relief file show that many destitute families were given from $5 to $25, depending upon their circumstances. While this was a small amount, it made the difference between stark poverty and outright starvation. In some instances, relief commissioners working out of the Governor's office distributed money directly to needy families as they went through the countryside surveying conditions. For example, C. H. Johnson who was in charge of state relief in Meeker, McLeod, Wright, Sibley, and Carver counties distributed $370 in aid to 24 farmers.[3] Between October 14, 1871, and February 14, 1872, a state relief fund of $19,508.73 was distributed. While much of this was raised in Minnesota, several thousand dollars came from sympathetic people in the East.[4]

Relief supplies raised from private sources and distributed by state and county officials was good, but it was not enough. It kept people from starving, but did not provide financing to help plant another crop. Hundreds of settlers needed seed. In this situation needy farmers turned almost automatically to county and state governments. Frontier life may have encouraged independence and self-reliance as men struggled to establish homes against heavy odds, but it is abundantly clear that pioneer settlers did not hesitate to seek government aid in times of economic crisis. Doctrinaire beliefs about the role of government in economic affairs had no place in the thinking of western farmers during periods of want and distress. They relied on government because it was the only practical agency capable of helping them.

Although Governor Austin praised the voluntary system of relief, he told the legislature in January 1872 that more must be done. Additional requests for aid were coming in, he said, and quite a few farmers would require assistance until the next harvest. Under growing pressure for state assistance, the legislature passed a law on February 29, 1872, "to aid citizens of Minnesota who have suffered loss or damage by fire or storm during the summer and fall of 1871." The original House bill asked for an appropriation of $20,000, but the amount was finally cut to only $2000 for the purpose of buying seed wheat and other grain.[5] Farmers were to make applications to their county commissioners and, if a request for aid were approved at that level, it was then sent to the State Auditor and Treasurer for final approval and payment. No claim could exceed $50. The legislature had not done much, but it had at least recognized the problem and taken some action.

Minnesota farmers somehow survived the disasters of 1871, but worse conditions were ahead. In 1872 the pioneers in Becker and Clay counties in the Northwest had their crops eaten by grasshoppers. Then on January 7, 8, and 9, 1873, a tremendous blizzard swept over much of Minnesota, freezing unsheltered livestock and causing several deaths. A resident at Worthington wrote on January 21 that the widow and five children of one victim could not attend the funeral because they did not have sufficient clothing. The remains of this poor settler, he said, were interred by the Grand Army of the Republic. Another family west of Marshall was overtaken by the storm, and all were frozen to death except the wife. An investigator for the Governor found that 18 people had died of exposure, others had their legs frozen and amputated, while many lost cattle, horses, and other livestock.[6]

Minnesota lawmakers again moved quickly to meet this crisis. On January 22, 1873, the legislature appropriated $5000 to provide medical care and "other relief."[7] The Governor was to spend this money at his discretion and a year later he reported that the full amount had been disbursed. People in 34 counties had received an average of $36 per family. Part of the funds had been used to pay doctor and hospital expenses, but there was not enough money to pay all of the doctors who "attended upon the partially frozen."[8]

No doubt many settlers were beginning to wonder if some irate Moses was calling on an angry God to punish the people, because like Pharaoh of old, more plagues were to come. In 1873 the first of a series of grasshopper infestations destroyed the crops of hundreds of farmers in southwestern Minnesota, Dakota, and northwest Iowa. Although grasshoppers periodically ravaged crops all along the upper midwest prairie frontier from Wichita to Saint Paul during the middle 1870s, they struck with unusual fury and frequency in Minnesota. Wherever grasshoppers invaded an area, damage was usually spotty and uneven. While some local communities might be completely devastated, farmers only a few miles away might be spared. But in 1873 hundreds of Minnesota farmers lost all or a large part of their crops, and, in some cases, these were the same families who had recently met the unkindly fate of snow storms, prairie fires, and hail. The persistence of these natural disasters was a heartbreaking and bankrupting experience.

When it became evident that hundreds of farmers in southwestern Minnesota, northwestern Iowa, and southeastern Dakota could not support themselves during the coming winter, local and state relief committees were set up to solicit and distribute food and money to the destitute settlers. Coal, grain, food, clothing, and other supplies were given to many needy families. Some of the cash had to be used to pay transportation on the goods, but the railroads made their contribution by lowering freight rates on relief commodities or by hauling them free of charge. One official estimated that two railroads in Minnesota contributed transportation worth at least $5000 if regular rates had been levied.[9] The main relief committee in Minnesota was set up by the Saint Paul Chamber of Commerce and was headed by General H. H. Sibley. This group solicited some $6506 in cash, plus clothing, bedding, coal, and food. In Iowa the money and goods solicited by General N. B. Baker's state relief committee provided food and clothing for hundreds of settlers.[10]

With the approach of winter, however, it became evident that voluntary efforts would not be sufficient. Relief committees as well as state officials were flooded with letters and petitions describing the pitiful conditions among farmers. Many of the needy called for state aid. General Sibley explained to the new governor, C. K. Davis, in January 1874 that he had just received word of many families who were still in extreme need. He thought there were at least 600 families in southwestern Minnesota who "must be supported during the winter and spring." Moreover, they needed seed grain. Private relief had been helpful, Sibley explained, but it was then about exhausted and was "not commensurate with the wants of the stricken settlers." In his last message to the legislature, Austin, the outgoing Governor, explained the plight of new settlers who had lost their crops, and declared that there would be terrible suffering "if not relieved by the hand of charity." Like Sibley, he believed that the means must be found to help farmers get seed grain.[11]

There were similar demands for state aid by citizens of northwestern Iowa. The Board of Supervisors of Palo Alto County passed a resolution asking the state legislature to appropriate $5000 to help the needy of that county. The petitioners said that "unless aid is procured in some manner, the prosperity and well being of this portion of the state will be materially affected and its development greatly retarded. . . ."[12]

On January 31, 1874, the Minnesota legislature passed a law appropriating $5000 for "the relief of the destitute inhabitants and settlers upon the frontier." This was a straight relief measure and the funds were to be distributed under the governor's supervision. Although the value of goods given to any family was usually less than $10, many people were kept from starving and freezing with these funds. For example, one family got 50 pounds of pork, 100 pounds of flour, and 50 pounds of corn meal for a total value of $8.95. This figure shows that the difference between existence and starvation was a thin line for some pioneer families. But the vital matter of getting seed to plant in the spring of 1874 still remained. To meet this problem, the legislature appropriated an additional $25,000 on March 2 for the purchase of seed grain. This program was also to be administered by the Governor, but no family could receive more than $35.[13]

The Iowa legislature was even more generous. After defeating a bill designed to loan $100,000 to poverty-stricken farmers, another measure was approved on February 26, which provided $50,000 as an outright donation to supply destitute settlers with "such seed, grain and vegetables as may be deemed necessary." During the next few months the Iowa Commissioners who were in charge of the program distributed wheat, corn, oats, potatoes, and garden seeds to 1750 families, expending $36,369 of the appropriation.[14]

Congress also took notice of the grasshopper plagues on the frontier. On June 18, 1874, an act was passed permitting farmers in specified areas of Iowa and Minnesota to be absent from their homestead or preemption lands until May 1, 1875, without losing their rights under the residence requirements of the law. A settler could now seek work elsewhere and not have to worry about someone contesting his claim or losing time required for final proof.[15]

Despite the voluntary and state efforts to relieve distress on the frontier, reports of destitution continued to reach officials. On February 6, 1874, a single girl, Jennie Flint, of Murray Centre, Minnesota, wrote to Governor Davis that she must apply for assistance for herself and her 71-year-old father "as we are here in this far western country and very poor withall." Then she continued:[16]

> We have no money nor nothing to sell to get any more clothes with as the grasshoppers destroyed all of our crops what few we had for we have not much land broke yet as we have no team of our own we have to hire one in order to get it worked what little we have to sow so you see it is rather hard on us to hire so much and get along. We managed to raise a few potatoes and some corn and a little buckwheat and that is all we have to depend upon. We are very bad off for bedding not having but two quilts and two sheets in the house and have to make them serve for two beds. We have to use our clothing that we wear on the beds to keep us from suffering with the cold and then it [is] most impossible to keep warm for our house is so open. . . . we have not got

our house plastered as yet only on the outside with mud could not get any lime to do it with for we had no money nor could not get any. We almost perish here sometimes with the cold. . . . Now if you will be so kind as to send us some bedding and clothes and yarn to knit us some stockings with we have no wool nor yarn. Or send us some money so we can get them ourselves we would be thankful. . . .

The spring of 1874 brought new hope to the frontier communities of Iowa and Minnesota. Most settlers had made it through the winter with the help of private and public aid, and had planted a few acres with seed obtained through the state governments. Hope sprang eternal in the breasts of most farmers who always looked ahead to "next year." But before the crops matured in the summer of 1874 an even more extensive grasshopper plague struck western farm communities. Unlike 1873 when most of the damage was confined to Minnesota and Iowa, the next year there was widespread devastation from Texas to the Canadian border. Now Dakota, Nebraska, and Kansas farmers also had their crops devoured. Before the grasshoppers arrived in Kansas, severe drought scorched many areas of the state. On July 25 the mercury shot up to 110 degrees at Junction City, and a few days later the grasshoppers descended on the Kaw Valley and ate up what little crop the drought had left.[17]

One correspondent wrote that the grasshoppers came like a mighty cloud, blotting out the sun. Then they settled everywhere "devouring everything green, stripping the foliage, and off the bark, from the tender twigs of the fruit trees, destroying every plant that is good for food or pleasant to the eyes, that man has planted. . . ." Describing the situation further, this writer said that a person must keep his mouth closed to "eschew an involuntary morsel."[18] The editor of the Wichita City *Eagle* described the devastation in that area as follows: "they came upon us in great numbers, in untold millions, in clouds upon clouds, until their fluttering wings looked like a sweeping snowstorm in the heavens, until their dark bodies covered everything green upon the earth. In a few hours many fields that had hung thick with long ears of golden maize were stripped of their value and left only a forest of bare yellow stalks that in their nakedness mocked the tiller of the soil. . . ."[19]

As was often the case, drought and grasshoppers came the same year, but as was also generally true, some areas were damaged worse than others. This was the situation in 1874. In Kansas, for example, a partial wheat crop was harvested before the grasshoppers arrived, but the corn crop on which so many farmers depended was nearly a total failure. A Council Grove farmer wrote on August 10 that "there has been no rain here of consequence for a couple of months, and between the drouth, the chinch bugs, and the grasshoppers, we will be forced to go to Egypt or somewhere else for our corn."[20]

Nebraska settlers, especially in the central and western counties, also

62 - Destitution on the Frontier in the 1870s

Grasshoppers stopping a western-bound train on the Union Pacific Railroad in Nebraska. (Nebraska State Historical Society)

suffered heavily from the twin plagues of drought and grassshoppers. Corn and potatoes, the staple crops of most pioneers, were consumed, leaving the fields barren. Governor Robert W. Furnas told the Nebraska legislators that western pioneers had lost their corn, which meant an "entire year's labor," and that they "had no means to support themselves and families during the winter, or to provide for next year's crops."[21] According to one report, in Hamilton County only hay and squash remained. Where women had previously said, "Come to dinner" they were now saying "Come to squash."[22] In southeastern Dakota garden crops, potatoes, corn, and some small grains were lost. From Sioux City to Yankton, a distance of about 60 miles, nearly all the corn was destroyed.[23]

The situation was even worse in Minnesota, where farmers had suffered so much the year before. In most of the southwestern counties, as well as in northwestern Iowa, the vegetable crops were almost entirely ruined in June and grainfields were consumed as if by fire. Traveling from Mankato to Le Mars, Iowa, one observer said that fearful destruction had been accomplished. A minister-farmer from Redwood Falls, Minnesota, returned home on June 12 from a trip to Saint Paul. "But what a destruction had the 'army of God' wrought" during his absence, he wrote. His 40-acre field of wheat had been demolished, and the grasshoppers were ravenously eating the oats, potatoes, and corn. This minister had hoped that some in his congregation would escape, but, he said, the Lord made no exception. "Joyful and hopeful that they would pass us and pitying at the same time the country where they were going to, we at once saw our hopes destroyed, for the Lord ordered them to swallow up also the few fields in our neighborhood, which had been spared up to this time. In what masses and with what fury they fell over the wheat, then already in ears, I cannot describe."[24]

Under these conditions suffering was widespread, but as usual it was far worse among the newly settled farmers on the frontier. Without cash reserves or credit, hundreds of settlers suffered extreme want. In some cases this was the second or third successive year of disaster. Letters appealing for some kind of help bombarded state and territorial officials during the summer, autumn, and winter of 1874–1875. An elderly farmer from Watonwan County, Minnesota, wrote Governor Davis that his crops had been destroyed 2 years in a row "and we can see nothing but starvation in the future if relief does not come. . . . Oh, most honorable governor, I hope you will help us poor old mortals. . . ."[25] A fearful wife described her's and the children's plight to an absent husband who was away looking for work. They were short of food and clothing, she said, the wind whistled through the wretched old house, and something must be done quickly "or we may suffer greatly and may die. I am actually scared," she concluded.[26]

A visitor to Harlan County, Nebraska, in late October reported that in two townships more than 40 families would need aid within 2 weeks. Major N. A. M. Dudley declared that of the 800 people in Red Willow County in western Nebraska, 544 of them would require help during the coming winter. "Of these 544 needy people," he wrote, "it was found that 100 had either no food or less than a five day supply."[27] Appeals from Kansas settlers to state officials were equally numerous and pathetic.

People tended to turn to the state government for help because county governments, the usual source of local relief, were financially unable in the frontier regions to meet such major crises. The tax base in western pioneer counties was severely limited. Most money was raised by taxing land and real property, but in the frontier counties settlers had very few personal belongings, and if they lived on a homestead the land was not taxable until after final entry had been made. Moreover, during years of drought and grasshoppers, farmers could not even pay the taxes they did owe. This meant that counties had to sell bonds to raise additional funds, but these counties had a poor credit rating and their bonds were usually heavily discounted. Local resources were simply not adequate on the frontier to meet the relief needs, so people looked to the next nearest source of help—the state.

64 - *Destitution on the Frontier in the 1870s*

An illustration from *Harpers Weekly*, July 3, 1875, showing settlers clearing the field of grasshoppers. (The Kansas State Historical Society, Topeka)

The editor of the Saint Paul *Daily Press* wrote on May 23, 1874, that the "friendly offices of the state" were necessary to prevent suffering and starvation among Minnesota's pioneers. A citizen of Saint Peter urged Governor Davis "to put the case before the next legislature . . . and recommend . . . that we might get some assistance in our great misfortune." Another correspondent from Lyon County said that if the federal government did not provide help "it will be the duty of the state to make such appropriations." A group of citizens from several of the surrounding counties met at Windom on May 26, asked for a federal appropriation for relief, and pleaded with Governor Davis to lay their needs before Congress.[28]

Nebraska and Kansas citizens also called for state help. The editor of the *Daily State Journal* at Lincoln wrote that voluntary contributions were nearly exhausted, and the only power left "to feed the hungry, to clothe the naked, and to furnish seed in the spring to those who have nothing to plant, will be the legislature of our state." The Grand Island *Times* asked: "Can't the legislature make appropriations so that any deficiency may be supplied in the case voluntary contributions . . . are not sufficient to furnish seed to our farmers for next year's crops?"[29] In Kansas the Ellsworth *Reporter* said that "there will have to be an appropriation" to help farmers buy seed for 1875 and he thought $200,000 was not excessive. In any event, "aid should be given with no niggard hand."[30] Recommending a direct appropriation of $50,000, the editor of the *Kansas Farmer* urged the legislature to make this the first order of business in January 1875.[31]

While discussion continued as to how, and to what extent, state government might help destitute farmers, private relief organizations were formed to raise money and supplies for the needy settlers. In Minnesota General Sibley again headed a statewide relief committee. Several Minnesota counties contributed to the relief fund, which along with private contributions, gave the Sibley committee $18,959 to distribute. By January 1, 1875, $15,551 of this amount had been expended.[32] A Territorial relief committee in Dakota solicited some $4000, mostly in eastern states.[33] These funds were used to buy food, clothing, fuel, and seed wheat for suffering farmers. On September 18, 1874, the Nebraska Relief and Aid Society was organized at Lincoln for the purpose of collecting money and supplies to distribute among the poverty-ridden settlers of that state. Between September 28, 1874, and May 1, 1875, this organization raised $74,035 in cash and thousands of additional dollars' worth of commodities.[34] The Kansas Central Relief Committee was set up in October 1874 and, like the committees in Dakota, Minnesota, and Nebraska, made a nationwide appeal for assistance. These calls for aid were resented by speculators and land boomers, who feared the affect of adverse publicity, and they hurt the pride of many people, but conditions were too serious to let pride or prejudice interfere with assistance from any available source. The Kansas Committee received and disbursed $73,863.47 in cash during the period from 1874 to 1875. Besides this, it collected 265 carloads and 11,049 packages of goods valued at $161,245.[35] Railroads in the devastated states again hauled many of the supplies free or at reduced rates.

Money and provisions for settlers on the frontier came from a wide variety of sources. Relief committees in the larger western cities, such as Kansas City, Omaha, and Saint Paul raised thousands of dollars, mostly among businessmen. People in smaller towns and farmers outside of the afflicted areas also responded to pleas for help. Much of the money, clothing, and food, however, was contributed by easterners whose compassion was stirred by the heart-rending stories of suffering on the frontier.

Although voluntary contributions helped thousands of frontier settlers to keep alive during the winter of 1874–1875, the amounts raised and distributed were clearly inadequate. Continued pleas for assistance indicated that there was not enough to meet the demands for immediate relief to say nothing of the critical need for seed grain. Governor Thomas A. Osborn of Kansas was the first to recognize the problem as a matter with which state government should deal. On August 28, 1874, he called a special session of the legislature to deal with privation on the frontier. He announced that he regarded "the first duty of the state of fostering care and protection for all her citizens." When the lawmakers met on September 15, the Governor estimated that some 15,000 people, mainly in western Kansas, needed assistance.[36]

Although there was considerable demand from the stricken sections of the state for direct appropriations for relief, the legislature refused to take this course. Rather, a law was passed authorizing the counties to issue relief bonds and use the proceeds to buy clothing, feed, and fuel for the destitute residents. However, bonds could be sold only after a favorable vote of the people in each county. Since county bonds would be heavily discounted in the regular money markets, legislators authorized issuance of up to $73,000 in state bonds to raise money to buy the county securities. The function of the state then was to act mainly as a banker or bond buyer for any county that voted to issue relief bonds. The law did provide some small direct appropriations to specified counties out of money raised by selling state bonds. For instance, Rush and Decatur counties were each to receive $1000.[37]

Very little money was raised for relief purposes in Kansas under the county bond law. People in most areas of privation had not wanted this kind of relief in the first place. A reporter for the Wichita City *Eagle*, who covered the special legislative session, declared on September 17, 1874, that members from the older settled portions of the state only wanted state backing for county bonds. But the new counties, he said, were not asking to borrow. "We are in favor of a direct appropriation of money to the poor fund of each county desiring aid. . . ." The editor later attacked representatives from eastern Kansas for raising constitutional objections to direct appropriations. "Constitutions and official oaths," he declared, "were made for the people and by the people, and not the people for the constitutions." He admitted that from a financial and constitutional viewpoint the legislature might have acted wisely, but "from a moral, compassionate, or charitable point their action was cold, selfish, heathenish."[38]

When the regular legislative session met in Topeka in January 1875, a further effort was made to get a direct appropriation for relief and seed grain. By that time Governor Osborn estimated that more than 32,000 people needed rations.[39] The proposal that received most serious consideration would have permitted the state to sell bonds up to a maximum of $95,000 for relief purposes. However, the measure was defeated because of a conflict over whether it should be a loan or a gift to the counties. Governor Osborn sent another special message to the legislature on March 2, recommending that $50,000 be appropriated to buy seed for

A painting of Kansas by Henry Worrall designed to contradict the charges that Kansas was dry and barren. (The Kansas State Historical Society, Topeka)

needy settlers. "I know of no channel through which the public money could flow with a probability of more beneficial results," he said, but the lawmakers failed to take any action.[40] While representatives of the State Central Relief Committee were traveling near and far soliciting money and goods for starving citizens, all that the legislature did in 1875 was to appropriate $6000 to pay freight on commodities gathered by the relief committee, and another $5000, which was given to the executive committee of the grange for the same purpose.[41]

Meanwhile, legislatures in Nebraska, Minnesota, and Dakota were also wrestling with the problem of how to provide supplies and seed for poverty-stricken frontiersmen. Governor Furnas of Nebraska said in August 1874 that local aid would be provided where possible but "in cases where this cannot be done, the state ought, and will render needed relief."[42] When the legislature met several months later, it passed a bill permitting the state to sell $50,000 worth of bonds to raise funds for seed grain.[43] A board of relief was established to handle the money, but the actual distribution of seed was to be made by the Nebraska Relief and Aid Society and the grange relief committee, which had firsthand knowledge of settlers' needs. However, nothing was appropriated to buy food and clothing and those in want had to continue relying on voluntary contributions.

Governor John L. Pennington of Dakota Territory initially tried to play down the damage there,[44] but by December 1874 the needs of destitute settlers were too evident to deny. Consequently, he asked the territorial legislature to take whatever action "enlightened statesmanship may suggest. . . ." He emphasized that agriculture was the basis of all other profitable enterprises, and concluded: "I earnestly invoke the fostering care of the law-making power for the aid and protection of the tillers of the soil."[45] In January 1875 the legislature passed a measure that authorized the sale of $25,000 worth of territorial bonds as a means of raising money for relief and seed. Upon advice from Washington, Pennington vetoed this law, but the legislature promptly passed it over his objections. However, it was never implemented, and people suffering as a result of drought and grasshoppers in Dakota had to rely entirely on private charity.[46] Farmers who lost crops in northwest Iowa in 1874 also had to depend upon voluntary contributions.

It was in Minnesota that the legislature came to grips most realistically with the problem of grasshopper devastation. Governor Davis refused to call a special session in 1874, preferring to rely upon county and private help until the regular session met in January 1875. Meanwhile, strong popular pressure developed to help the suffering settlers, some of whom had lost their crops for 3 successive years. General Sibley told Governor Davis that it would "result in injury to the state" to appeal for money and commodities outside of Minnesota, and he urged "speedy action" on an appropriation of $100,000 for relief and $50,000 for seed. On January 28, 1875, the state legislature appropriated $20,000 "for the immediate relief of suffering settlers on the frontier." These funds were to be administered by the Governor who immediately appointed representatives to disburse the funds. A report dated March 2 illustrates the kind and amount of help given to individual farmers. In part of Jackson County 69 settlers were given assistance in amounts usually ranging from $2 to $4 per family. One farmer got 1 pound of coffee, 4 pounds of sugar, ½ pound of tea, some tobacco, ½ gallon of oil, and 5 yards of calico for a total value of $2.30.[47] Others received flour, meat, coal, and other commodities, but almost always in very small amounts.

While most of the direct relief was distributed in February 1875, the legislature was considering what to do about seed grain. On March 5, $75,000 was approved for this purpose. At the same time the lawmakers reimbursed the counties and certain individuals who had advanced money to the relief fund in 1874 to the extent of $17,300. Altogether, the Minnesota legislature appropriated $112,300 for relief and seed grain.[48]

In the minds of many people, local and state aid were considered entirely insufficient to meet the problems of the widespread want and privation in 1874–1875. Although the Kansas legislature failed to provide any funds for relief, the House and Senate passed a concurrent resolution on January 30, 1875, calling on Congress to appropriate $100,000 "to aid the settlers on our western frontier in the purchasing of seed and to aid in their support the coming year."[49] As early as May 1874 a group of citizens meeting at Windom, Minnesota, urged Governor Davis to send a representative to Washington to lay the needs of suffering farmers before Congress. Congressmen and Senators from the states also pleaded for assistance. In January 1875 Representative Stephen A. Cobb of Kansas introduced a bill to appropriate $150,000 for grasshopper sufferers. He advanced a most intriguing argument in favor of his bill. Since the federal government had enticed settlers into the west by offering them free land, he said, it should now come to their aid.[50]

Even before Congress began to discuss special legislation to provide relief to poor frontiersmen, the federal government was actually becoming involved in helping needy westerners through the army. In fact, it was General E. O. C. Ord at Omaha who was among the first to impress the seriousness of the situation upon Washington. As early as October 24, 1874, General Ord described the pitiful conditions found among Nebraska settlers and asked permission to distribute rations of flour and pork among the most destitute.[51] His request, however, was denied. But General Ord kept pressing the matter of relief until on November 11 Secretary of War William W. Belknap recommended to President Grant that he authorize the distribution of surplus army clothing to freezing farmers. Belknap emphasized that no law permitted such action, but he thought that Grant would be justified in ordering the issue of clothing in light of the emergency and then hope for subsequent congressional approval.[52] The next day Grant authorized the army to proceed with its program. On November 23 General Ord and General John Pope at Omaha and Leavenworth, respectively, received orders granting them permission to distribute clothing to the needy in Nebraska and Kansas.

During the next 3 or 4 months, thousands of clothing items were distributed by army personnel. Included were 10,004 heavy infantry coats, 2382 uniform coats, 16,186 pairs of shoes, and 8454 woolen blankets.[53] Lieutenant Theodore E. True found almost unbelievable conditions in parts of Nebraska early in 1875. After calling on several families in Dawson County, he wrote in his diary: "It was pitiable, in most instances, upon entering the poor huts to see women and children crouched shivering around their dull fires in the midst of a cloud of pulverized snow driven in upon them by the storm."[54] In these cases surplus army clothing was a godsend. Conditions of individual settlers were so bad that army officers sometimes gave destitute families supplies without any official authorization. Major N. A. M. Dudley told of a boy arriving at Fort McPherson, Nebraska, with his feet wrapped in cotton bandages. The lad stated that he had left his mother and five brothers and sisters at home without any food. After the soldiers gave him some shoes and enough clothing to keep him from freezing, Major Dudley directed the supply officer to give the boy two sacks of flour and 30 pounds of bacon, and concluded: "if the Commissary General elects to do so, he can deduct its value from my pay."[55]

On February 10, 1875, Congress gave official approval to what the army had already been doing and in addition authorized the distribution of food "to prevent starvation and suffering . . . to any and all destitute and helpless persons living on the western frontier who have been rendered so destitute and helpless by ravages of grasshoppers. . . ." An appropriation of $150,000 was made for this purpose.[56] The Omaha *Daily Republican* credited this measure largely to the work of General Ord. The need aroused "him to efforts which knew no cessation, till the nation and the government had taken measures equal to the necessities of the case," the editor declared.[57] The Commissary-General of Subsistence immediately ordered Generals A. H. Terry, Ord, and Pope who commanded the Military Departments of Dakota, Platte, and Missouri respectively to survey the needs and enroll those who should receive help. Army personnel was to administer the program. It was hoped to provide rations for one month to each needy person over 12 years of age with ¾ pound of pork, 1 pound of corn meal, and beans, coffee or tea, salt and sugar in the same amounts given to enlisted men. Children were to receive a half ration.

During the next few months the army distributed 1,957,108 rations to 107,535 adults and children in Minnesota, Dakota, Nebraska, Kansas, Iowa, and Colorado. Although there was not enough food to provide each needy person with a 30-day supply, in many cases this help seemed to be the difference between life and death.[58] "Sufferers in Kansas and Nebraska received the great bulk of food distributed." A farmer from Reno County wrote Governor Osborn that his family of six had drawn rations for 20 days, including 25 pounds of corn meal, 18¾ pounds of pork, and 3¾ pounds of beans.

Besides direct federal relief of this kind, Congress approved a law on January 25, 1875, permitting the commissioner of agriculture to make a special distribution of seed to those areas devastated by grasshoppers. Lawmakers appropriated $30,000 for this purpose. While this measure had strong support in the afflicted regions, Representative Charles W. Willard of Vermont declared that he could not imagine any justification for such an appropriation. "It certainly is unknown to any provision of the constitution," he said.[59] Necessity clearly overrode any narrow interpretation of the Constitution and the commissioner of agriculture proceeded to distribute 703,989 packages of vegetable seeds, 7544 quarts of oat seed, plus small amounts of other grain.⁶⁰ One Nebraska pioneer put his request to verse:

> *Uncle Sam, it appears, has consented at last*
> *To scatter a few of his coppers*
> *In behalf of those who, in the year that is past*
> *Were cursed and cleaned out by the hoppers*
> *Now I, being one of ten thousand in need,*
> *Would willingly better my status;*
> *So, if you can't give me my quota in seed,*
> *Just send me a peck of potatoes.*

Want and privation were more widespread on the upper Midwest and central prairie frontier during 1874 and 1875 than at any other time during the settlement of that region. Even with the combined efforts of private relief, county and state aid, and federal help, there was untold suffering. Many of the men left home in search of work, leaving their wives and children alone, fearful, and in dire need. Army investigators found home after home where the mother and children were facing cold and hunger, hopefully awaiting word from the absent husband and father, or praying that help would come from some relief agency. The women displayed almost unbelievable courage in face of the most terrible circumstances. Reports of those who handled relief are filled with statements describing how women refused to give up. One little girl told an army officer that her father believed the family would starve when the present supply of flour was exhausted. But she quoted her mother as saying: "God will take care of us."

The support for frontier relief went beyond humanitarian considerations. There was the matter of keeping settlers from deserting their new farms and returning to their former homes. If this should happen, the effort and expense of immigration commissions, railroads, editors, and all kinds of promoters would end in vain. Indeed, fear that people would be forced to leave was a sharp prod behind all of the state and territorial relief efforts. No unsettled community dared run the risk of losing population that was the main factor in economic development.

A resident of Windom, Minnesota, wrote to General Sibley that he feared some of the settlers would "move out in the spring rather than try another year of frontier life," and urged immediate shipments of pork and beans into the area.⁶¹ In pleading for help, the Saint Paul *Daily Pioneer* declared on February 8, 1874, that prompt state action was necessary "or very many of the people will leave the country with their families." To permit this would be shortsighted policy and poor business for the state, the editor declared. When the bill was introduced to appropriate funds for helpless settlers in Iowa in 1874, it was held that such action was "not simply a matter of humanity" but "a matter of justice to men who are engaged in the work of rescuing one of the fairest portions of Iowa from the wilderness—as a matter of profit to the State at large."[62]

Writing about state backing for county relief bonds, a Nebraska editor said that if the state ultimately had to pay the bonds "no injustice will be done, for the general good of the whole state demands that the settlers be retained within her borders."[63] Early in 1875 the Omaha *Daily Republican* declared that the future of Nebraska depended upon the settlers getting seed grain. If nothing were done to help the farmers, it would "exclude from our vast unoccupied domain for years to come the thousands from the Old World who are anxious for a home in this." The editor added that it simply was good business to help settlers obtain seed. In this case, he said, "prodigality becomes true thrift, economy ruin."[64] While a variety of voices called for government relief, local promoters in all the afflicted states and territories insisted that the reports of drought and grasshoppers were greatly exaggerated and that there was not much genuine need among settlers. They resented anything that might retard settlement. These professional boosters were more interested in their own long-range welfare than in the immediate needs of the poor pioneers.

Despite the efforts to tide settlers over rough times, many of them did abandon their new homes in 1874 and 1875. In some localities the frontier receded in face of bitter privation. It is not known just how many people left the newly settled regions, but contemporary accounts indicate that a good many moved to the older Midwest and East. Writing from Fairmont, Minnesota, in June 1874, one observer said "many have already left" and others would have to follow if outside help did not arrive.[65] The Manhattan *Nationalist* reported that "the drought and grasshoppers combined have discouraged a great many people, and teams pass through town every little while on their way east."[66] Even before the grasshoppers arrived in Kansas, some farmers were leaving because they had no water. Ellis County actually had fewer people in 1875 than in 1870.[67] After investigating destitution in north-central Kansas, one official estimated that at least 600 families had forsaken a six-county area between August 1874 and January 1875.[68] Many settlers also left central and western Nebraska, and Dakota. Drought and grasshoppers not only temporarily depopulated some frontier areas, but news about "droughty Kansas" and reports of privation among Western settlers that circulated through Eastern newspapers discouraged emigration into parts of the upper midwest and central prairie frontier from 1873 to 1877. Besides this, these were depression years, which tended to slow up the westward movement.

The slowing down of migration to the frontier was reflected in the decline of homestead entries. In 1874 settlers filed 16,018 claims in Minnesota, Dakota, Nebraska, and Kansas, but the figure decreased to only

8284 in 1875. During the next 2 years homestead entries continued at a slow pace, dropping to 7236 in 1877.[69] However, the remarkable thing is not that natural hazards and hard times discouraged so many emigrants during the middle 1870s, but that the frontier continued to draw so many people despite severe and prolonged hardships.

The recession of the frontier was short-lived, and farmers continued to push westward. Except for a few areas, Kansas, Nebraska, and Dakota settlers harvested good crops in 1875. Comparing the crop years of 1874 and 1875, Governor Osborn of Kansas declared that "rarely has a transformation been more complete and surprising than that which a single year has brought about." Most settlers in Nebraska and Dakota also had abundant crops in 1875, and fairly good conditions continued the following year. Although Minnesota farmers suffered most from grasshopper infestations, damage occurred on a lesser scale in 1875. However, devastations were horrible in 1876. The grasshopper menace seemed so serious and widespread that Governor John S. Pillsbury called a regional conference to consider the matter.

The Governors of Minnesota, Nebraska, Kansas, Iowa, Missouri, and Dakota Territory met at Omaha on October 25, 1876. Insisting that grasshopper devastation was a national problem, the conference called on the federal government to help in the fight against the insects. Apparently doubting the will or ability of Congress to act, the Governors also asked people in the afflicted areas to offer special prayers for deliverance.[70] One young man suggested that if prayer worked, it would be the most economical approach. But neither God nor Congress came to the immediate help of Minnesota farmers who had considerable portions of their crops destroyed again in 1877.[71] The worst, however, was over, and grasshopper damage in 1878 was slight. But between 1873 and 1877 these pests caused millions of dollars in damage and created untold hardships for thousands of frontiersmen as well as the more established farmers.

Farmers on the upper midwest prairie frontier undoubtedly suffered much more during the middle 1870s from natural disasters than they did from the Panic of 1873 and the subsequent hard times. Although the prices of farm commodities declined, this was not a life or death matter to the pioneer who provided much of his own living, including food. So long as he had corn or wheat for meal or flour, some vegetables, and a few head of livestock, he could get by with amazingly little cash. Western farmers hoped to have some surplus for sale, but most frontiersmen were not yet drawn so completely into the commercial complex that farm prices determined their success or failure. This condition, however, did not last long, and as new settlers sought to expand and develop their operations by acquiring more machinery, extending their fence, or improving their buildings, they needed cash, which could be obtained only from selling crops and livestock. Under these conditions prices became of utmost importance.

Poor crops in much of the frontier region during the 1870s contributed to better than normal prices, considering depression conditions. The trouble was that many farmers had nothing to sell because their crops were destroyed by drought or grasshoppers. Wheat brought as much per bushel in Nebraska in 1875 as it did in 1870, and between 1874 and 1878 Minnesota farmers generally received from 80 cents to $1 a bushel. Kansas farmers received 90 cents for wheat in 1874, although 2 years later the price had dropped to as low as 30 cents at some interior markets.[72]

The discouraging circumstances so prevalent over much of the upper midwest and central prairie frontier in the 1870s began to give way to a new wave of optimism by 1877 and 1878. In the spring of 1877 the Omaha *Herald* recorded that the prospects for emigration to Nebraska "were never higher."[73] The *Kansas Farmer* was filled with accounts of pioneer settlers who had carved successful farms from the raw prairie in only a few short years. A correspondent from Reno County, Kansas, declared early in 1877 that "we are having quite a large immigration this spring." Eighty people had arrived the week before and more were coming, he said. "There is still plenty of room, you are welcome," read the enticing invitation.[74] And so after a slackening of the westward push in the middle 1870s, the stage was being set for a new boom period all along the prairie-plains frontier.

◁ **5** ▷

Bonanza Farming in the Red River Valley of the North

*A*lthough quarter-section farmers swarmed over the frontier in the 1870s, they were not alone in forming the cutting edge of agricultural settlement. One of the most interesting and significant phenomena was the establishment of large farms operated on strict business principles. The bonanza farms represented in agriculture many of the same characteristics and patterns found in the business world—large-scale and sometimes corporate organization, absentee ownership, professional management, mechanization, and specialized production—all of which were being applied in the industrial sector of the economy in the late nineteenth century. There were a few large or bonanza farms scattered all over the West in the 1870s and 1880s. But nowhere did bonanza farming reach such extensive proportions and play such a major part in the agricultural settlement of an important region as in the Red River Valley of North Dakota and Minnesota.

The Red River Valley is an unusually flat, fertile plain stretching northward about 300 miles to Lake Winnipeg from the tri-state juncture of the Dakotas and Minnesota. About two thirds of it lies south of the

Canadian boundary. The land is so level that one early observer said he should be "hopelessly homesick for some unevenness for the eye to rest upon." He declared, however, that with transportation this area would become "one of the richest wheat gardens of the West."[1] Indeed, most of the early observers of this vast prairie were lyrical about its agricultural possibilities. One speaker told his Boston audience in 1871 that a fabulous wheat country would be opened when the Northern Pacific reached the Red River. If it were not for the river, he told disbelieving New Englanders, a farmer could plow an uninterrupted furrow that would equal the distance from Boston to Philadelphia. After the Northern Pacific reached Fargo later the same year, a correspondent at Duluth declared that within a short time, long trains would be laden with wheat coming out of the Red River Valley.[2]

Although wheat and other crops were raised at Pembina as early as 1820, farming did not attain any importance in the Red River Valley until after 1870 when permanent settlers began to move into the Fargo-Moorhead area. James Holes settled on the Dakota side in 1871, and by the following year he sold produce as far away as Bismarck and Winnipeg. By 1873 R. M. Probstfield and several other farmers around Moorhead were raising a small amount of oats, wheat, and garden vegetables. The success of these early farmers in the lower valley and the completion of railway connections with Duluth and Saint Paul opened the way for additional settlement. However, the development of large-scale, commercial wheat farming was tied closely to the Panic of 1873, the bankruptcy of Jay Cooke and Company, and the Northern Pacific's policy of exchanging land for its depreciated securities. These events took place just at the time it became evident that the Red River Valley was ideal for wheat. It was in 1874 that a farmer on the Sheyenne River about 6 miles west of Fargo raised 1600 bushels on 40 acres, an event that brought favorable publicity to the region.[3] The limited efforts of the Northern Pacific Railroad to sell its lands in the Red River Valley met with only meager success. Between June 15, 1872, and September 30, 1873, the company sold only 46,119 acres, principally on the Minnesota side of the Valley. Six individuals bought 13,832 acres, or nearly one-third of the total, while the rest was purchased by what James B. Power, land agent for the Northern Pacific, called "actual settlers." The average sale to this latter group was 123 acres. However, after the failure of Jay Cooke and Company and the fall in Northern Pacific bond prices in 1873, holders of these securities moved to exchange their depreciated bonds for company land. Power recalled that by late 1873 he was receiving many inquiries about taking advantage of this privilege.[4]

From September 30, 1873, to September 29, 1875, the railroad sold 483,141 acres for an average price of $5.04 an acre. However, 23 persons purchased 304,965 acres, or some 63 percent of the total, mostly with

Bonanza Farming in the Red River Valley - 77

Amenia, North Dakota, in the 1880s. The small building in the upper right is a claim shanty. Picture shows large-scale wheat raising in the Red River Valley. (North Dakota Institute for Regional Studies)

depreciated bonds. Northern Pacific bonds averaged around 10 to 20 percent of their face value during these years, which meant that the cash cost to these large purchasers was approximately 50 cents to $1 an acre. Among the early buyers were officials of the Northern Pacific as well as other investors. President George W. Cass initially got 4400 acres; Benjamin P. Cheney 3164 acres; Frederick Billings 28,672; and the Amenia and Sharon Land Company composed of New York and Connecticut investors, 28,352 acres. During this period most of the sales were confined to about 30 miles west of Fargo and within 5 or 6 miles of the Northern Pacific track.

Even more railroad land was sold in large tracts during succeeding years. After 1875 first mortgage bonds of the old company could be exchanged for preferred stock of the reorganized Northern Pacific. At times this stock was traded for land when its value was as little as 10 cents on the dollar. From September 30, 1875, to August 31, 1878, about 40 purchasers acquired 587,270 acres or an average of 14,680 acres each. Among the large buyers were the Grandin brothers, John L., and William J., of Pennsylvania, who got 61,104 acres; and the Maine Savings Bank of Portland, which acquired 17,300 acres. Others bought additional large holdings, and during the 8 years and 5 months ending November 30, 1880, the Northern Pacific sold 2,851,314 acres of land for an average price of $4.08 per acre. Power figured that "fully seven-tenths of the entire area was sold to original bond holders." The cash cost to those who exchanged preferred stock for land was about 65 cents an acre.[5]

This then was the basis of land acquisition that made possible the bonanza farms in the Red River Valley of the North after 1875. In order to gain unbroken control over their vast holdings, some purchasers acquired the intervening government tracts with Indian scrip or by other means. Not all of the land taken was in the valley, but most of it was located there. Of course, the Northern Pacific sold some land to small farmers and an increasing number of settlers took up government land by homesteading and preemption. However, it was the large-scale,

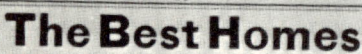

An advertisement for homes in the Northern Pacific Country.

specialized agricultural operations that placed their mark upon the region and that were so unlike farming on most western frontiers.

Bonanza wheat farming in the Red River Valley was begun in the summer of 1875. Upon the recommendation of Power, Cass and Cheney employed Oliver Dalrymple to manage and develop their Dakota wheat lands about 18 miles west of Fargo. As mentioned earlier, Dalrymple was probably the largest and best-known wheat grower then living in the Northwest. The agreement called for making Dalrymple a conditional partner by permitting him to acquire some of the land if the wheat-raising enterprise were successful, and eventually Dalrymple got several thousand acres around Casselton, Dakota. Dalrymple was the manager for absentee owners who hoped to profit from their investments in wheat lands. The other capital and operating expenses for which Cass and Cheney were responsible included machinery, buildings, seed, horses, and labor. There would be none of the long, slow, lonesome struggle to develop farms on the Cass-Cheney lands. Enough money, men, and machinery would be provided to bring large acreages into production quickly.

In June 1875 plowing began under the immediate supervision of Dalrymple's nephew, and before work was halted, 1280 acres had been turned. Evidently five other operators were also preparing wheat lands during that summer, for Dalrymple wrote to the Grandin brothers in March 1876 that six farms would be in crop during the coming season.[6] Dalrymple sowed wheat in April, and a few months later harvested about 13,500 bushels from the two sections of land, or about 11 bushels an acre. With more acres and a better crop Dalrymple raised approximately 75,000 bushels the next year. When word of this success spread eastward, there was a rush to buy depreciated Northern Pacific stock, which could be exchanged for land.

Meanwhile, Dalrymple, who was about penniless because of losses suffered by speculating on the grain market, wrote to his brother William in Pennsylvania asking to borrow $2000 to buy 1280 acres of "the best wheat land situated on the line of a railroad" on his own account. He wanted in addition $3500 to pay for breaking the land, which cost from $2.75 to $3 an acre, and $4500 with which to construct houses and barns on each 160 acres. These buildings would be occupied by families who would work the wheat land. Dalrymple said that he could repay the $10,000 from the receipts of the 1877 crop. By that time, he predicted, the farm would be worth $20,000. He suggested that each brother would share equally in the land as well as in the cost of improvements and cultivation. Dalrymple explained that he had cleared $100,000 in one 4-year period on his Minnesota wheat farms, and that the chance to obtain the best wheat lands at cheap prices close to the railroad would not last long.[7] In response to this plea, William advanced his brother some money.

Those on hand recognized that the best lands were rapidly being acquired and that they must act fast or be left with having to choose from second-rate property. Dalrymple explained to the Grandin brothers in March 1876 that they were really 2 years behind in choosing the best lands, but that it was still possible to acquire suitable acreages. "We must get ahead of the crowd this year," he concluded. In asking his brother for money, this seemed to be just what Dalrymple was trying to do.[8] Power reported to George Stark, vice-president of the Northern Pacific, in September 1876 that, considering the quality of land and its proximity to the railroad, "the *cream* has been taken." Most of the unpurchased railroad lands, he said, were in the timbered or brush areas of Minnesota or the upland prairie of Dakota west of the Red River Valley. Power declared that this upland prairie west toward Bismarck did not interest purchasers because it was not known whether it was good for agriculture. It was Power's opinion, however, that area could be profitably cultivated.[9]

Following 1876 Dalrymple expanded his own Alton farm as well as those of Cass and Cheney. Located about 18 miles west of Fargo near Casselton, the heart of the Cass-Cheney-Dalrymple farms formed a compact body about 6 miles long and 4 miles wide, extending on both sides of the railroad. By 1877 Dalrymple had 4000 acres in wheat, and 2 years later this had grown to more than 10,000 acres. Dalrymple's example set the pattern for others. The Amenia and Sharon Land Company sent two of its major stockholders, E. W. Chaffee and Edward Gridley, to select land in the Red River Valley in 1875. Power helped them locate 42 sections, and they began farming operations in the fall of 1876 by having 640 acres plowed and prepared for seeding the next spring. Chaffee, who became the company's farm manager, spent $23,043 in 1877 for horses, machinery, seed wheat, labor, and improvements.[10] This would have been enough capital to establish 30 or 40 ordinary frontier farmers on homesteads.

At about the same time the Grandin brothers began developing some of their vast holdings located about 30 miles north of Fargo. They employed Dalrymple to manage some of their Dakota agricultural affairs and he eventually acquired one-half interest in the south unit of the Grandin farms.[11] The Antelope farm in Richland County south of Fargo was developed on land purchased by the Maine Savings Bank of Portland. In 1879 Henry S. Back was employed to make improvements and start the farming operations.[12] The Dwight Farm and Land Company selected 16,000 acres in Richland County in 1879 and by 1882 had 8000 ready to sow to wheat.[13] The Donaldson-Ryan farm at Kennedy, Minnesota, contained 33,000 acres and in 1884 reportedly produced 230,000 bushels of wheat.[14] There were many other bonanza farms started between 1876 and 1880 in both North Dakota and Minnesota.

The organizational and managerial practices adopted by Dalrymple were followed by most of the other large investors in wheat lands. Dalrymple originally divided the Cass-Cheney-Dalrymple farm into subdivisions of 1280 acres. Later some of the divisions consisted of as much as 1600, 2000, or even 5000 acres. A house was constructed on each subdivision for the local foreman and quarters were built for the laborers who were employed during spring planting and at harvest and threshing time. Stables, machine sheds, a blacksmith shop, and granaries were also built. Elevators were later constructed so that grain did not all have to be marketed at threshing time when the cost of hiring teams was high. The day-to-day management of each subdivision was in the hands of a foreman.

Although Dalrymple only visited the farms periodically, he maintained over-all supervision and assumed full managerial control. He made the basic decisions on how much to plow and plant, what wages to pay, what machinery to purchase, and whether to store or sell the wheat crop. Unlike other large businesses where a number of the directors might know a good deal about managing the firm, large-scale farming was an enterprise about which eastern businessmen knew nothing. Therefore, they had to rely exclusively on the man chosen to run their agricultural operations. They had to trust him to conserve their capital and to produce a satisfactory return on their investment. Undoubtedly, the reason Dalrymple's services were in such demand was because he was one of the very few men who had had successful experience in large-scale wheat farming. It was assumed that if anyone could make wheat-raising a paying venture, it should be Dalrymple. When urging his brother to invest in wheat lands in 1876, Dalrymple declared that "for ten years I have been the largest wheat grower in the Northwest and ought to know something about wheat lands and wheat growing."[15]

The cultivation of extensive acreages required a degree of mechanization not found anywhere in the United States, except in the Central Valley of California. In his second year, 1877, Dalrymple had 26 breaking plows, 40 plows for backsetting or turning the broken sod, 21 seeders, 60 harrows, 30 self-binding harvesters, and five steam-powered threshers, each of which had a daily capacity of 1000 bushels. There were 80 horses and 30 wagons on the Cass-Cheney-Dalrymple farms. During spring planting, 50 men were employed to operate the necessary machinery, and they sowed 220 acres of wheat a day. At harvest time 80 to 100 men had to be hired.[16] As more acres were planted it was necessary to invest more capital in machinery and to increase operating expenses by hiring additional laborers.

All of Dakota Territory raised only 2,830,289 bushels of wheat in

1879 but more than half of this amount, 1,530,727 bushels, were grown in the three Red River Dakota counties of Richland, Cass, and Traill, where the bonanza farms were developing. Cass County alone, center of Dalrymple's operations, produced more than one third of all the wheat grown in Dakota that year.[17] Reporting on his trip to the Cass-Cheney-Dalrymple farms, a writer for *Harper's Magazine* said that the "railroad train rolls through an ocean of grain."[18]

By 1879 and 1880 newspapers and periodicals all over the United States were beginning to carry accounts of the extensive farming operations and fabulous profits from wheat growing in the Red River Valley. The *Nebraska Farmer* reported the large returns of one Dakotan and concluded that this was "evidence that farming on a big scale pays in the Red River Country." The editor warned small farmers, however, that they might not be able to do so well. In April 1879, Governor William A. Howard of Dakota told a New York *Tribune* reporter that "people of the East are beginning to find out that we have the finest wheat lands that the sun ever shone upon." Then he recounted the experience of George W. Cass. According to Howard, Cass had planted 4000 of his 10,000 acres to wheat and after spending $50,000 for land and equipment, he had sold enough grain in one year to pay all expenses as well as the cost of the land. "A single crop gave him his magnificent domain of 10,000 acres with all the stock and improvements he has upon it," the proud governor announced.[19]

On September 20, 1879, the *Commercial and Financial Chronicle* devoted about half of an article on wheat growing in the United States to large-scale operations in Dakota. Referring to "a new system" of raising wheat, the writer said: "It is no longer left to the small farmer, taking up 160 acres of land, building a log cabin and struggling to secure himself a home. Organized capital is being employed in the work," he wrote, "with all the advantages which organization implies. Companies and partnerships are formed for the cultivation precisely as they are for building railroads, manufactories, etc. . . ." Then the reporter figured a hypothetical case of expenses and profits for an operator cultivating three sections of land. He estimated that it would take $16,055 to buy land and equipment to start farming. At the end of 4 years expenses would total $49,385. The returns based on current experience would amount to $51,440 in that period. In other words, the wheat grower would have about $2000 cash profit, plus a farm worth $40,000 after 4 years. While the writer did not guarantee such favorable results, he said they seemed entirely reasonable. The New York *Tribune* copied part of this article under the subheading, "A striking revolution in this form of agriculture."[20]

An article, "The Bonanza Farms of the West," which appeared in the

Atlantic Monthly in 1880, promoted this same idea. A new agricultural development in the great Northwest, said the writer, "has forced itself upon the public attention, that would seem destined to exercise a most potent influence on the production of all food products, and work a revolution in the great economies of the farm." Along the same line, the *Prairie Farmer* told its readers that Dalrymple's experiences showed how capital could be profitably employed in raising wheat on a large scale. A booklet entitled, *The Land of Golden Grain*, distributed by the Land Department of the St. Paul, Minneapolis and Manitoba Railroad in 1883, completely abandoned reality and linguistically flew to the land of make believe. The author referred to the Red River Valley as "paradise regained—the farmer's Elysium—a realm of peace, plenty and prosperity." "Any land," he continued, "will pay for itself at present prices in one or two crops." He declared that "God's star-gemmed skies never domed a lovelier domain."[21]

By 1880 everything was set for an unprecedented wheat boom in the Red River Valley. The area had become widely publicized, eastern capital was flowing in by the hundreds of thousands of dollars and managerial and farm organization patterns had been experimented with and proven successful. The state of agricultural technology had developed to a point where an almost unlimited amount of plowing, seeding, harvesting, and threshing could be done if enough man power and horse-power were provided. Especially important were the twine self-binder and the steam-powered threshing machine. Some harvesting machines that bound grain with wire were still being used in 1880, but they were being rapidly replaced by models using twine. Crop failure or low prices, possibly both, were the only dangers on the horizon, but these did not seem serious because both crops and prices were good in 1879 and 1880. Wheat in Cass County, Dakota, averaged nearly 20 bushels to the acre in 1879 and brought about 80 cents a bushel.

While a relatively few bonanza operators acquired a disproportionate amount of land in the Red River Valley and stimulated national interest in the region, they made up only a minor part of the population. Small farmers were as anxious for wheat profits as eastern and foreign investors, and after 1875 they rushed into the valley seeking both railroad and government land on which to establish wheat farms. Power reported that between September 1875 and August 1878, about 500 settlers had bought tracts from the Northern Pacific ranging in size from 80 to 320 acres.[22] There was an even stronger demand for homesteads and preemption claims. Power wrote in the spring in 1879 that most of the people arriving in the valley were seeking government land.[23] From July 1, 1878, to June 20, 1879, 295,233 acres were entered at the Fargo land office under the homestead act and 246,722 acres under the timber culture law. In the first 6 months of 1879 only one land office in the United States, Kirwin, Kansas, received more homestead entries than Fargo. This surge to acquire government land continued at even a faster pace in 1880. During the fiscal year ending June 30, about 449,664 acres were filed on under the homestead law at the Fargo office, and the new land office at Grand Forks received entries for 160,746 acres between January 1 and June 30, 1880. By 1880 homestead entries in Dakota considerably exceeded those of any other state or territory. Filings under the timber culture act in Dakota were 868,749 acres, nearly double that of its nearest rival.[24]

By the spring of 1880 farmers were squatting on land yet unsurveyed, land offices were besieged with farmers wanting to register entries, and the hotels in Fargo and Moorhead were crowded with hopeful pioneers. Writing to Frederick Billings in April 1880, Power said he had visited Fargo the week before and the town was "packed with land seekers, the majority looking for government lands, a few with considerable capital for opportunities to speculate, some for nonresident lands and some for improved farms." The greatest demand, however, was for land near the railroad. The wheat boom by both large and small producers in the Red River Valley was well under way and promised to develop far beyond what most people could imagine.

During the next decade the type and extent of agricultural operations in the Red River Valley brought worldwide attention to the region. In 1882, A. R. Dalrymple, superintendent of the Grandin farm, reported raising 142,523 bushels of wheat, 21,453 bushels of oats, and 8577 bushels of barley. Following further expansion, a tremendous crop of 214,234 bushels was grown in 1886 by which time 9650 acres were in wheat. Although 11,222 acres were planted to wheat in 1890, the somewhat smaller yield resulted in a crop of 180,774 bushels.[25] Dalrymple's operations in the middle 1880s were described by the Dickinson *Press*. He had 32,000 acres in wheat and 2000 acres of oats. These 34,000 acres were divided into three farms of about the same size, each of which had its own headquarters, superintendent, bookkeeper, foreman, and other officers. The three main farms were further divided into sections of 2000 acres, which were supervised by a foreman. Each division had a boardinghouse for the workers. In the spring about 500 men were employed on all the farms, and during harvest this number increased to 1000. These men were recruited from the itinerant farm labor force, and they arrived at the time of year when workers were needed. In the fall all the men were dismissed except a few who were retained to feed and care for the 400 to 500 horses and mules. Each of the headquarters had a store from which provisions were requisitioned by the boardinghouse cooks. Dalrymple said that "The whole thing is so systematized that we can tell to a cent the cost of victuals for a man and the cost of seeding, repairing, or plowing an acre of ground." In 1885 the Dalrymple-Cheney farms produced 210,000 bushels of wheat.[26] Dalrymple reported to the *Dakota Farmer* that his total crop for 1890, probably including that from his own lands as well as farms which he supervised, would reach at least 450,000 bushels.[27] However, since wheat was bringing only about 60 cents a bushel in 1890, Dalrymple's net income was probably not as good as in the early 1880s when he raised less but received 80 cents a bushel and more for his crop.

In 1881 the Amenia and Sharon Land Company raised 15,500 bushels of wheat, in 1882 the amount had risen to 25,000 bushels and by 1885, to more than 47,000 bushels. By December 31, 1888, the company valued its lands, machinery, improvements and 100,000 bushels of wheat at $485,051.[28] Some years the company had fabulous business success. In 1883 one section of land produced 11,676 bushels, which sold for 80 cents a bushel and made a clear profit of $2198, or about $3.50 an acre, more than the original price of the land. Other large farms included the Antelope, Dwight, Fairview, Spiritwood, and Cleveland in North Dakota and the Lockhard and Keystone operations in Minnesota. Moderately extensive farms of from 2000 to 3000 acres were opened in all of the Red River Valley counties.

Whether it was during the breaking and plowing season, planting, or harvesting and threshing, the grandeur of the West seemed to be reflected in the massive operations on Red River Valley wheat fields.[29] In the early fall on large wheat farms as many as 40 to 50 plows might be seen moving across the flat landscape like an army in formation, leaving behind an ever widening strip of freshly turned earth. After harrowing the land, a score or more of seeders or grain drills planted the wheat, usually in April, and then in August the self-binders would make a long procession through the fields cutting as much as several hundred acres per day. As many as 100 reapers were sometimes used on the largest enterprises. The wheat was shocked by hired laborers and then a short time later it was hauled to the threshing machines, which by the 1880s were usually powered by monstrous steam engines. In 1889 Governor Arthur Mellette listed the machinery requirements for a 10,000 acre farm. They included 60 gang plows, 60 seeders or drills, 150 wagons, 50 to 60 self-binders, 10 threshing machines, and 10 steam engines. To operate this machinery and do the other necessary work, 250 men and 300 horses were considered necessary.[30]

The establishment of bonanza farms as well as medium-sized and even small pioneer operations, where a settler might not break more than 20 or 30 acres a year, soon made the Red River Valley the nation's leading wheat region. In the decade between 1879 and 1889 wheat acreage in the six Minnesota counties and nine counties in North Dakota, which were all or partially in the valley, rose from 130,877 to 2,450,658 acres. Production climbed from only 2,498,642 bushels to 29,340,512 bushels in the same decade.[31] By 1890 western Minnesota and the Dakotas produced more wheat than any comparable area in the United States. The scope of grain growing is also reflected in the size of farms. In 1889 the average farm in North Dakota included 277 acres, compared to 181 acres in Kansas and 190 acres in Nebraska. In Cass and Traill counties there were 98 and 52 farms, respectively, that contained 1000 acres or more. No county in either Kansas or Nebraska had as many large farms as did Cass County, North Dakota.

Although bonanza farming came to be associated in the public mind primarily with the Red River Valley, such operations were not, of course, confined to that area. In southwestern Minnesota a number of farmers grew between 1000 and 2000 acres of wheat, and some even more.[32] There were also a few extensive farms in Nebraska and Kansas. However, as will be shown later, the other major area of bonanza wheat farming was in the Central Valley of California. Although the regions were 2000 miles apart, bonanza farming in the Central Valley and the Red River Valley developed at about the same time and in much the same manner.

Bonanza farming played an important part in advertising and settling the northwestern Minnesota and eastern Dakota frontier, but by the late 1880s this type of agriculture was on the decline. Resident managers were complaining that it was extremely difficult to make money raising wheat, and many of the large property holders were selling off part of their land to small farmers or renting it to individual operators on a share basis. A Mr. Rogers reported as early as 1886 that his large-scale operations near Bismarck had not been satisfactory and he had then contacted Dalrymple and Cheney for their views. According to Rogers, Dalrymple and Cass expressed the opinion that the days of large profits in wheat growing were at an end and that some bonanza farmers were already dividing their land into small tracts and leasing them.[33] The Amenia and Sharon Land Company had operated its lands as one large unit during most of the 1880s, but by 1889 it was beginning to sell some smaller tracts and rent others. By the early 1890s much of its land had been divided up into small units. What caused the trend away from bonanza farming? Why was it that the large, supposedly efficient operator did not crowd out all or most of the small producers? The answer seems to be fairly simple: bonanza farming was never as profitable over the years as the promoters, speculators, and publicists claimed.

On April 20, 1889, A. R. Dalrymple wrote to his Uncle William in Pennsylvania that "it seems as if the time has come when there is no money in wheat raising." Looking back at the previous year, he explained that he would lose money on his own farm and that the same situation existed on the Grandin farm. It was in a discouraging tone that Dalrymple closed his letter by saying: "Can anyone do anything to make a living besides raise wheat?" The next month Dalrymple reported that Grandin was working from daylight until dark trying to sell land and that he had disposed of one section near Hillsboro for $20,000 or $31.25 an acre. Later in the year following a poor crop Dalrymple sadly explained to William that they must "look for some other business to pay our debts."[34] This was by no means an isolated case. At about the same time officials of the Amenia and Sharon Land Company were worrying about their investments. There was talk about assessing the stockholders for more capital to pull the agricultural operations through another year. Some company properties were actually being sold and the firm's Dakota agent feared that the stockholders would insist on further liquidation. This company was also looking for land buyers.[35]

Even Oliver Dalrymple, the king of bonanza farmers, was being pressed by creditors throughout the 1880s. In December 1885, the McCormick Harvester Company intimated that it would take legal action against Dalrymple to collect a $21,185 bill for wire and twine. This account extended back nearly 6 years. Dalrymple successfully pleaded for more time to meet this obligation, and as late as 1888 the McCormick firm still had not collected the account.[36]

Thus by the late 1880s the bonanza wheat boom was stalling and many of the big operators were going through an agonizing reappraisal of their business activities. Correspondence by agents and investors is filled with complaints of losses, the prospect of additional assessments on the stockholders, pleas for extended credit, and a desire to sell part of their lands. What had happened to the rosy prospects of a few years earlier when it was commonly said that extensive wheat farming would insure good profits and eastern investors furnished a steady flow of capital to the Red River Valley? Was not size and efficiency the answer to the usual low returns from farming?

As mentioned earlier, bonanza farming was characterized by investment of large amounts of capital, a high degree of specialization in production, use of the latest agricultural machinery, and hired management. The combining of these factors was supposed to produce efficiency and profits. However, nonresident capitalists soon found that there were some basic differences between managing a large-scale farm and operating, for example, an iron mine or a manufacturing plant. The main difference was that the bonanza farmer could not regulate his production nor determine the prices of the things he bought or sold. Since he could not determine his output or influence the price of wheat, the manager or agent on a bonanza farm was faced with tough problems of management. Consequently, regardless of his size, the bonanza farmer was in the same unfavorable economic position as his smaller neighbor. The fact that operations were highly capitalized even increased his problems in some respects because it was absolutely necessary to earn a large amount of cash regularly to pay cash operating expenses and returns on investment.

Indeed the employment of large amounts of capital in agriculture presented its problems as well as its advantages. The cost of wheat production could be lowered, but even this did not assure profits, particularly in years of poor crops. It was not uncommon to spend as much as $20,000 to $30,000, besides the investment in land, to open up and begin developing a large wheat farm. B. S. Russell who supervised the Spiritwood farm spent $60,100 during 1878, 1879, and 1880 to bring the farm into production. This included $17,000 for breaking, $9000 for machinery, $6500 for buildings, plus other expenditures.[37] Besides outlays of this type there were costs of management, labor, machine repairs, supplies, lumber, and taxes. In 1883 the operating expenses on the Amenia and Sharon Land Company were $59,242, of which $16,044 was for hired labor. Wheat sales that year brought $35,605, which left a large deficit even after $15,886 worth of land was sold.[38]

Heavy expenditures for capital improvements and operations meant that to operate profitably the individual or company had to be assured a dependable income. The only thing that could provide this was a good wheat crop and favorable prices every year. But these two essential factors were often missing and, in any event, were completely outside the control of even the most skilled agricultural manager. It is easy to see the effect of a complete or partial crop failure, or a sharp drop in prices, on the bonanza farmer who had taxes, interest, labor, and other current operational bills, which had to be paid in cash. The big profits for wheat growers that were projected in 1879 and 1880 were based upon a crop of around 20 bushels to the acre and a price of 80 cents to $1 or more a bushel. This favorable combination of production and price turned out to be quite abnormal. Because of a short United States crop in 1881, local wheat prices rose above $1 a bushel, but they never reached that figure again in the nineteenth century. In 1884 Dakota wheat prices fell to less than 50 cents a bushel under the weight of a large crop. In 1886 and 1887 prices were between 50 and 60 cents. While they increased to around 90 cents in 1888, profits were reduced by a partial crop failure. Even in the so-called good seasons there were likely to be spotty failures that hurt individual producers. Moreover, prices also fluctuated greatly. In 1880 the Amenia and Sharon Land Company sold its wheat for 90 cents a bushel, in 1883 it brought 75 cents, and by 1887 it had declined to 60 cents.

Furthermore, production was not only determined by the acreage planted, but by rust, insects, drought, floods, and other natural phenomena. For instance, A. R. Dalrymple reported that he had finished threshing on the Grandin farm in September 1882, but that those who did not get done suffered heavy losses because of 3 weeks of rain.[39] No doubt in some instances local agents and managers overemphasized the natural difficulties in order to explain their failure to return more money to investors, but there is little doubt but that unfavorable weather and insects cut down on income. The correspondence and reports of local managers are filled with accounts of light crops, insect damage, the effects of drought, and other unfavorable conditions. Thus it was not possible to make future plans and to figure potential income by multiplying bushels times price because even the best manager could not regulate or influence these factors.

There were also difficult problems associated with absentee ownership and local management. It was not easy to get qualified managers who knew about farming and were also skilled enough to direct bookkeeping operations, and to do the buying and selling. At the outset of Dalrymple's operations, for example, Power reported to George W. Cass that it was impossible to present accurate accounts for the years of 1876 and 1877 because Dalrymple had run "his business in the usual western way," meaning that it had been a sort of hip-pocket operation. Power said that there were no vouchers for some purchases, nor a full account of labor charges. Although Dalrymple and other large-scale wheat growers employed bookkeepers, when genuine cost-accounting methods were applied, profits shrank rapidly. The crop on the Cheney farm in 1877 brought $21,345, but his profit was only $940.43 after charging off depreciation for machinery, livestock, and other improvements.[40]

Major managerial decisions on a bonanza farm centered around such questions as whether or not to build an elevator or granary, what supplies and machinery to purchase, and when to sell the crop. For example, should the grain be sold at threshing time or should it be held in hopes of getting a higher price. If the wheat was to be stored, it meant added capital outlay for granaries and elevators. Yet this had to be balanced off against the fact that it was usually cheaper to hire teams to haul the wheat in the off season than it was during threshing. Actually there were many decisions to be made, and a wrong move could easily cost dearly. For example, A. R. Dalrymple declared that in the fall of 1888 he decided to hold some of his own wheat as well as part of that on the Grandin farm because it would only bring 60 cents a bushel. However, by the spring of 1889 he said the price locally had dropped to only 40 cents and that his creditors were pressing him.[41] In 1891 many wheat producers held their wheat because they believed the short crop in Europe would force prices upward to perhaps as much as $2 a bushel.

However, wheat from other parts of the world filled the demands, and when American farmers saw prices were not going to rise, they flooded the markets with wheat. Early in 1892 the price dropped sharply, causing great losses to growers who had stored their 1891 crop.[42]

The uncertainties inherent in agriculture plagued large wheat growers, and year after year insufficient income to cover expenses and dividends caused eastern investors sleepless nights. William Dalrymple, who had backed his brother Oliver, was so pressed by debt that at times he was nearly beside himself with worry. His relatives in Dakota wrote in 1882 and 1883 how hard times were and explained that nothing could be repaid to William. N. M. Dalrymple wrote to his uncle William on August 10, 1883, that expenses on the Alton farm took all the money that he could scrape together. He said that he expected the biggest wheat crop ever harvested in the Red River Valley, but he failed to mention sending any funds to William. So far as the Pennsylvania Dalrymple was concerned, all of the talk of a big crop was nothing but prospect and promise.

Although wheat did make growers large profits during some years this was probably the exception rather than the rule. Power reported that profits on the Cass farm in 1877 were $26,859. In 1886 stockholders in the Amenia and Sharon Land Company received $42,245 in dividends.[43] But large operating profits do not seem to have been the ordinary thing, despite glowing reports in local newspapers and boasting by some of the bonanza farmers themselves. The available records indicate that the large operators made their real money by selling both wild and improved lands to small farmers. By the 1880s much of the unimproved land in the Red River Valley brought from $10 to $15 an acre and improved farms sold from $20 to $40 an acre. Those individuals and companies who bought large tracts for $4 and $5 an acre with depreciated railroad bonds made excellent profits, but they made most of their money as land speculators, not as wheat farmers. In fact, some years land had to be sold in order to raise enough funds to operate the large farms.[44]

The decline of bonanza wheat farming in the Red River Valley was caused more directly by the poor crops of 1888, 1889, and 1890, which greatly intensified the basic economic problems of large wheat growers. Both drought and a frost that struck in August sharply cut wheat production in 1888. Even Oliver Dalrymple said that farmers were trying to grow wheat at below the cost of production, and suggested to Governor L. K. Church that tax payments be postponed until October 1, 1889.[45] But such an extension would have been of little value because 1889 was even a worse year. Much of the wheat was a total failure, and thousands of acres were plowed under because they were not worth harvesting. George Parr, who lived in Walsh County north of Grand

Forks, wrote in the fall of 1889 that "we crowded in every available acre, to try to retrieve our losses of last year . . . but it turned out a very unwise one in many instances." In 1890 Red River Valley farmers experienced another partial failure due to drought. Parr wrote that on land 10 to 15 miles west of the river production was about 8 bushels to the acre. In the western part of Walsh County, he said, hundreds of acres of wheat had been choked out by weeds.[46] Although a bumper crop was raised in 1891, much of the grain was lost because of heavy rains during threshing. Some wheat was still standing in the shock in the spring of 1892.

Conditions became so bad among farmers in Dakota during 1889 and 1890 that statewide relief efforts were undertaken to help the destitute. The publicity that now went out from the Dakotas was in sharp contrast to the optimistic reports of a decade earlier, which had helped to lure eastern capital into bonanza wheat farming. Although most of the destitution was in the newly settled regions of the state far west of the Red River Valley, such publicity was not conducive to continued investment in large-scale wheat operations. Even the vaunted efficiency of large operators could not win the fight against the twin enemies of low production and poor prices. An additional factor in the decline of bonanza farming was a rise in taxes.[47]

Of course, these same conditions also hurt the small farmer. In fact, if the large producer could not make decent returns from wheat farming, how could the small and less efficient farmer hope to establish a profitable enterprise? As bonanza operations were getting well underway in 1879 and 1880, one observer gave the small farmer very little chance to succeed against his big neighbor. Looking at the size, capitalization, organization, and efficiency of the bonanza farm late in 1879, one writer declared: "against the unlimited use of this combination of capital, machinery, and cheap labor the individual farmer, either singly or in communities, cannot successfully contend, and must go under."[48] What had happened to this seemingly logical conclusion?

In the first place, it should be emphasized that the small farmer in the Red River Valley, or elsewhere in the West, probably did not make much money in the 1880s and 1890s. In many cases he was in debt and sometimes on the edge of bankruptcy. Nonetheless, the smaller farmer who diversified his operations probably had as much or more staying power than his large, highly capitalized, and specialized neighbor. This is not to stay that he made as much money, but his situation was such that he could continue to farm with a relatively small amount of cash income.

The small farmer did not have much cash outlay for management or labor because this was supplied by himself and family. Furthermore, it was not necessary to pay any cash return on investment. Properly figured, a farmer should have income to cover his labor and investment costs, but most farmers in the nineteenth century did not do this kind of bookkeeping or quit farming if their income did not cover these items. If they made a living for themselves and their families, paid their minimum operating costs, and had enough to pay interest and taxes, they could keep farming indefinitely. Lower income often resulted in more debt and reduced living standards, but the established farmer could usually get through a crisis if it were not too long. Moreover, a farm was a home and farming a way of life as well as a business for millions of ordinary farmers.

On the other hand, bonanza farming was strictly a business for the Grandins, the Amenia and Sharon Land Company, and other large operators. Their farms had to be run on a business basis with proper returns paid on investments. If they could not pay for management, labor, operating expenses, and other costs and still have money left for dividends and interest on their investment there were no sentimental or practical reasons to continue. When cash returns dried up because of poor yields or low wheat prices as was true in 1889 and 1890, it made good sense for these big operators to sell or rent part or all of their land and invest their money in something that would produce better dividends. The main advantage of holding their land was that it would probably rise in price, but even this prospect was not enough to keep the huge bonanza farms intact.

The unfavorable years of the late 1880s and early 1890s were not, however, without their indirect benefits to agriculture in the Red River Valley. The hard times were at least partially responsible for bringing about some much needed adjustments in the region's farming practices. For example, it was found that summer fallowing would greatly increase grain yields, especially in periods of drought. This was the practice of working the land but only sowing a crop every other year. In this way more moisture was stored for the alternate years when crops were planted. Dalrymple began to summer fallow in 1886, but this practice spread slowly. However, the results of leaving the land lie idle periodically became clearly evident during the dry years of 1888, 1889, and 1890. Even in the extremely dry season of 1889 some wheat on summer fallowed ground made more than 25 bushels to the acre compared to only 3 or 4 bushels on land that had been consistently planted to wheat. Moreover, there was a tendency by farmers to shift away from exclusive reliance upon wheat and to raise other grains and livestock. Some of the bonanza farmers raised livestock and actually contributed to diversification in the area. In one of his open letters to the *Cultivator and Country Gentleman*, George Parr declared that mixed or diversified farming was much safer for any farmer than concentration on wheat growing.[49] Adjustments that resulted in placing somewhat less emphasis upon wheat were healthy for the region's farmers.

Although the strictly bonanza operations declined in importance after 1890, many large farms continued to be operated in the Red River Valley. By 1900 Cass County had 155 farms, which each contained over 1000 acres. But these were mostly locally owned and run as family farms, rather than on the order of Dalrymple's massive operations.

Bonanza farming in the Red River Valley had an important influence upon agriculture throughout the great unsettled West. It advertised the agricultural resources of the region as perhaps nothing else could have done. The reports of quick and large profits, even if exaggerated, excited the imagination of thousands of restless settlers and stimulated the rapid westward movement of the 1880s. Moreover, it is likely that the highly mechanized operations of large-scale farmers encouraged the more widespread use of machinery among smaller farmers who read about or witnessed first hand the new horse- and steam-powered equipment. The business that bonanza farming produced in the Red River Valley was highly important because it helped greatly to place the Northern Pacific Railroad on a sounder financial basis. This, in turn, permitted the company to build into western North Dakota and on to the Pacific Coast, where it played a significant role in the agricultural settlement all the way to Puget Sound. Farm expansion in both Washington and Oregon was closely associated with completion of the Northern Pacific and some of its branch lines. Finally, bonanza farming helped to present the West as a large, rich, expansive region only waiting to be exploited by the settlement of hundreds of thousands of additional farmers. It was both a part of, and a stimulant to, the Great Dakota Boom.

◁ **6** ▷

The Great Dakota Boom, 1878-1887

While bonanza farmers were conquering the Red River Valley frontier, thousands of pioneers rapidly occupied the rest of eastern Dakota. Farmers swarmed over the inviting prairies east of the Missouri River, and between 1878 and 1887 the region experienced an unprecedented boom.

Agricultural settlement in Dakota up to 1878 was confined mainly to the southeast and part of the Red River Valley in the northeast. There were a few farmers in the James River Valley northward from Yankton and between the James River and the eastern border, but the central and northern area all the way to Jamestown was a great uninhabited prairie. But by the middle 1880s farmers had settled much of the high plains between Huron and Pierre in the southern part of the territory and between Jamestown and Bismarck farther north. Between 1880 and 1890 the population of Dakota jumped from 135,177 to 511,527, while the number of farms rose from 17,435 to 95,204. In other words, during a single decade the population increased about 3¾ times and the number of farms, 5½ times.

The beginning of the Great Dakota Boom coincided with the widespread discussion over just how far west farmers could go with reasonable expectation of success. By the late 1870s there were a number of authorities who believed that in many places farmers had reached, or even passed, the place where they could succeed on a quarter section of land using traditional agricultural methods and organization. Among the foremost critics of attempts to establish 160-acre farms on the Great Plains was Major John W. Powell, eminent scientist and explorer who became chief of the United States Geological Survey in 1881. Viewing the rapid westward advance of farmers onto the western prairies and Great Plains, Powell felt that settlers should be warned as to what to expect.

In a speech before the National Academy of Sciences in April 1877 Powell discussed the remaining public domain. With the aid of maps and charts he divided the United States into arid and humid regions. Powell showed all the United States west of a rough line from central Texas and Indian Territory, and central Kansas, northeastward to western Minnesota as being arid except for a small strip along the Pacific Coast. While much of this vast western area was suited for grazing, Powell said, it was unfit for farming. With some exceptions in Texas and Indian Territory, Powell declared that there was not much good land left in all of the West on which a poor homesteader could settle as there was in a single county in Wisconsin. This speech was part of Powell's campaign to get the homestead law modified so that farmers could obtain more acres for grazing, which he believed was the only reliable type of agriculture on the Great Plains and other parts of the unsettled West not subject to irrigation.

Major Powell believed that natural geographic conditions in most of the West required a different type of agricultural organization, and that the policy of giving 160-acre homesteads to farmers in the arid and semiarid regions would only lead to disappointment and bankruptcy. A New York *Tribune* correspondent wrote that Powell had raised a matter of grave and general interest. "If it is true that there is scarcely any good land left fit for a poor man's farm," said the writer, "the sooner the fact is announced the better."[1]

The suggestion that settlement had reached the safe limits for crop production under conditions of natural rainfall by the late 1870s aroused the fighting spirit of westerners. Railroad and land companies, townsite promoters, and all kinds of speculators considered Powell a troublesome ignoramous who had better stick to his books. James B. Power, Northern Pacific land agent, explained to the editor of the *Pioneer Press* in Saint Paul that farmers had already demonstrated that the country as far west as Bismarck was "well adapted to successful agriculture." Power argued that every year the so-called arid region was being settled by "practical men who form their opinion of the fertility of the country and its adaptability for settlement by the practical test of cultivation rather than the statements in essays by a whole school of such scientists as Major Powell." If Powell was as much in error about other parts of the so-called arid region as he was Dakota, Power declared that "no reliance can be placed upon any of his statements as to the agricultural value of any country." Moreover, Power concluded, if Powell hoped to deter emigration into the West he would fail.[2]

Power and Powell represented two extreme points of view; both were partly correct and partly wrong. Powell wisely pointed out the dangers of trying to apply the traditional methods of farming practiced in the humid areas to regions that received less than 15 or 20 inches of annual rainfall. On the other hand, Power was right in saying that the westward movement could not be deterred by Powell-type reports. It is characteristic of people to believe what they want to believe, and in the late 1870s and 1880s they wanted to believe that the West still offered great agricultural opportunities. To some extent they were right.

Besides, was not the climate changing as settlers pushed their farming operations onto the edge of the Great Plains? Within 6 weeks after Powell spoke, the Wichita *Weekly Beacon* editorialized: "Rain, rain, rain, rain, will it never cease."[3] One Nebraska observer wrote that "as the plains are settled up we hear less and less of drouth, hot winds, alkali, and other bugbears that used to hold back the adventurous." He said that the "theoretical farming limit" of the 100th meridian would move westward if, indeed, it did not "cease to exist altogether."[4] After compiling information from numerous sources, the editor of the *Prairie Farmer* wrote in 1880 that "cultivation of the soil increases rainfall on what have been called the arid plains of the West, has been, and is now being demonstrated in those regions."[5]

Most scientists scoffed at this idea, but many laymen argued that plowing and loosening the soil permitted it to absorb more moisture, thereby giving greater evaporation and in turn producing more rain. A series of years between 1878 and 1886 when an unusual amount of moisture fell throughout much of the Great Plains seemed to bear out the position of the laymen against that of the geographers. All the way from the Canadian Border to Indian Territory restless pioneers rushed onto an unusually wet Plains fully convinced that they were helping to change the climate with their plows and tree planting. Two Nebraska professors, Samuel Aughey and C. D. Wilber, wrote a small pamphlet in 1879 entitled *Agriculture Beyond the 100th Meridian* in which they declared: "It is clear that rainfall is and has been increasing from year to year."[6] One emigrant on the Southern Plains was heard to remark: "The Lord just knowed we needed more land, an' He's gone and changed the climate. It's raining more out here than it use to."[7] Warnings like that by J. A.

Bent of Lawrence, Kansas, had no effect in slowing the tide of emigration. Bent wrote that it was especially dangerous for the poor pioneer to venture onto a plains homestead without enough livestock or money to see him through the unfavorable seasons. Another resident of eastern Kansas warned that the region west of the 98th or 99th meridian was different and "to advise the uninformed immigrant to go out there and engage in farming is little short of a crime."[8]

Meanwhile, in 1878 Major Powell completed his *Report on the Lands of the Arid Region of the United States* in which he tried to present an accurate and realistic picture of the American West. Powell defined the arid region as that area west of a meandering line following roughly the 100th meridian, but usually east rather than west of that line. He denied that settlement and cultivation increased the amount of rainfall, and argued that agriculture throughout most of that vast region west of the 100th meridian must center around grazing and irrigated farming. Powell recommended "pasturage farms," a unit of 2560 acres with access to a small amount of irrigable land, and group settlement, which could provide satisfactory local social organizations. Since the cost of developing irrigation from the larger rivers and streams was beyond the means of ordinary settlers, Powell favored the cooperative use of labor and capital to build the necessary waterworks. The present land policies, Powell said, were not suitable to the needs of actual settlers in the arid region, and he prepared legislation to provide for the establishment of irrigation districts and grazing homesteads. But these bills found little support either among the public or in Congress.[9]

But neither science nor common sense were any match for the pulling lure of the land. Settlers rushing to get their 160 acres in Dakota were in no mood to worry about the region's geography in light of the current good crops in that region. They tended to agree with the writer from Nelson County, Dakota, who declared: "a limitless expanse of fertile but idle soil, extorts a cry for the plow. A million plows are wanted in the Territory of Dakota."[10] By the middle 1880s the Dakota Boom was at full tide. At the same time there was another rush to obtain land in western Nebraska and Kansas, and eastern Colorado. Settlers were showing the doubters that the Great Plains could be farmed successfully.

A number of factors contributed to the unprecedented boom in Dakota after 1878. The early success of bonanza farming in the Red River Valley advertised Dakota as a paradise for the wheat grower. Moreover, railroad expansion, which had been held up by the Panic of 1873 and the subsequent depression, was revived after 1878. During the next 10 or 12 years, hundreds of miles of track were laid throughout Dakota. The Commissioner of Immigration wrote in 1887 that, "A Dakota town old enough to be divested of swaddling clothes, and without expectations of additional railway facilities, is yet to be heard of." "Expectations" frequently failed to materialize, but scores of villages and towns were connected by rail as the Northern Pacific, the Chicago, Milwaukee and St. Paul, the Chicago and Northwestern, the St. Paul, Minneapolis and Manitoba, and other roads extended their main and branch lines.[11] By 1887 the Territory had more than 4000 miles of railroad, which linked farmers directly with eastern markets. One resident wrote that the railroads had contributed to the settlement of Dakota's agricultural and grazing lands in 5 years what it would have taken a century to accomplish without "its powerful influences."

As was true on other agricultural frontiers, the railroads provided quick and easy transportation, sold land to settlers, and carried on an intensive promotional campaign. One pamphlet published by the Chicago, Milwaukee and St. Paul in 1882–1883, advised: "Read, Ponder, and—Go West." This publication told of happy farmers who had raised 20 bushels of wheat to the acre and, it was said, paid for their entire farms in one year. The writer declared that the reason so many people were going to Dakota was because "all draw prizes." Hundreds of settlers, the author declared, had emptied their pockets and paid the necessary $14 to file on a homestead, which within 2 or 3 years were worth $2000 to $3000.[12]

The most important influence that drew people to Dakota, however, was that age-old desire for land. With real estate values rising in the East and Midwest, farm-makers and speculators had to look farther west to find free or cheap land ready for the plow. Vacant Dakota lands seemed ideal for settlement. They were fairly level, free from stones and stumps, and highly fertile under favorable moisture conditions. With local exceptions, between 1878 and 1886 Dakota, like other parts of the Western Prairies and Great Plains, received considerably more moisture than usual. In the spring of 1882, for example, low places as far west as the Missouri River stood full of water, giving the impression that Dakota was a land of abundant rainfall. Moreover, Dakota had an unusually large amount of land, which could be entered under the homestead, timber culture and preemption acts. Considering all factors, there seemed to be no more favorable place in the United States for the poor farmer to settle and prosper than in Dakota. The commissioner of the General Land Office wrote of Dakota in October 1879 that "immigration has exceeded the largest estimates, and Dakota is believed to lead all other lands, States, and Territories in the number of acres settled upon during the year."[13] The boom was rapidly gaining momentum.

Thousands of prospective settlers flooded the territory's land offices. Statistics cannot properly convey the feverish rush for Dakota lands, but figures on land disposal are perhaps the best measure of the boom. During the 10 years from 1880 to 1889 a total of 41,321,472 acres, an area larger

Threshing wheat in Dakota in the 1880s. (Jennewein Western Library, Friends of the Middle Border, Mitchell, South Dakota)

than the state of Iowa, were entered under the public land laws. In 1880 and 1881 between 2 and 3 million acres were filed on annually, but in 1882 the figure rose to 4,360,131, in 1883 to 7,317,236, and in 1884 shot up to an almost unbelievable 11,082,818 acres. This was nearly 40 percent of all the land that the federal government disposed of in 1884 and nearly twice as many acres as were entered in a single year in any other state or territory between 1860 and 1900. For the year ending June 30, 1883, near the height of the land boom, there were 22,061 homesteads and 11,199 timber culture entries filed in Dakota. This was 39 percent of all the homesteads entered in the United States that year and 54 percent of the timber culture claims. In the next fiscal year settlers in Dakota filed 14,086 homestead and 11,179 timber culture claims, which was 25 percent of the homesteads and 40 percent of the timber culture filings in the entire United States.

The swift settlement of this agricultural frontier can be seen by looking at the Huron land office. Within a year after its establishment in 1883 the Huron office was doing more business than any other land office in the United States. In fact, the 1,815,460 acres of public lands that the government disposed of through the Huron office surpassed the entries for any entire state or territory, except Nebraska. Most of the land entered at Huron lay between the 98th and 99th meridian in the east central part of what became South Dakota, and during 1884 about 4191 homesteads covering 634,632 acres and 3034 timber culture entries totaling 479,585 acres were filed on. The old phrase "doing a land office business" was certainly applicable to the Huron land office.[14] Farther north the land offices at Aberdeen, Bismarck, Fargo, and even Devils Lake were doing a large business by the middle 1880s.

Thousands of farms and scores of towns and villages were established as people flocked to Dakota. Governor N. G. Ordway did not exaggerate when he reported in 1883 that "the progress and development of Dakota during the past year has been almost phenomenal. The tide of emigration which set in strongly in 1880 has been constantly increasing, . . ."[15] No frontier was ever praised in more glowing terms. "This is the sole remaining section of paradise in the western world," said one observer, "all the wild romances of the gorgeous Orient dwindle into nothing when compared with the every-day realities of Dakota's progress."[16]

Between January 1 and August 1, 1882, some 400 carloads of emigrants' supplies and goods arrived at Watertown, and in April 1883 about 250 carloads reached Huron. Farther south, settlers left the railroad at White Lake or Kimball and "then as fast as teams could be hired, and as fast as teams could take them, they rushed for" Jerauld County and the surrounding area then being opened for settlement.[17] A Saint Paul paper reported April 12, 1883, that the previous week 1000 cars of emigrant goods had left for Dakota and that the night before two passenger trains loaded with settlers departed for that territory. Mitchell, Huron, Aberdeen, Jamestown, and other towns were jammed with emigrants, railroad cars were packed with people and their belongings, and extra cars filled the sidings and served as temporary homes for the eager landseekers. The editor of the *Dakota Farmer* declared in March 1884 that "no country before has been able to draw the stream of emigration so long and without any diminution." "The Almighty," he continued, "seems to have preceded us and prepared a quarter section already to sow. . . ." Settlement was so rapid in Brown County that as early as 1884 one resident declared that the county had no good land left.[18]

Although the rush of people into Dakota after 1878 was essentially an agricultural boom, all phases of the territory's economy were affected. Towns and villages sprang up as if by magic. One contemporary said: "Language cannot exaggerate the rapidity with which these communities are built up. You may stand ankle deep in the short grass of the uninhabited wilderness; next month a mixed train will glide over the waste and stop at some point where the railroad has decided to locate a town. Men, women, and children will jump out of the cars, and their chattels will be tumbled out after them. From that moment the building begins." The Watertown *Times* reported that villages of 500 to 1000 inhabitants have grown up in 12 months. Mitchell was established in May 1879, got railroad connections in September 1880, and by 1882 had 1200 people.

Redfield, farther north, was platted in July 1882 and by November contained a population of 1000. Minot, in the northern part of the territory, boasted of 1000 people after only 5 weeks of settlement.[19] Jealous of this influx of people and accompanying property boom, eastern realtors were said to grumble that in Dakota "every townsite was a city, every creek a river, every crop a bonanza, every breeze a zephyr and every man a damned liar."[20]

As on other frontiers, hundreds of Dakota settlers arrived with very little equipment or capital. They threw up a sod or cheap frame house sometimes covered with tar paper, and with a team of horses or oxen, a wagon, and a plow, they began farming. These pioneers hoped that the first crop would provide enough money for a living and further development of the farm. The territorial manuscript census of agriculture for 1885 reveals that a good many farmers had nothing but a bare quarter section of land during their first year of settlement. In some cases, of course, these propertyless farmers did not intend to farm but homesteaded or filed on land under the timber culture law in hopes of being able to hold it awhile and then sell a relinquishment. But those without equipment who intended to farm usually hired a few acres broken and if the crop of wheat was good, they were gradually able to buy some machinery and livestock. Fortunately for those of such limited capital, the series of good years in Dakota during the decade before 1887 made it possible for thousands of nearly penniless farmers to become established operators. Between 1868 and 1890 final homestead entries in Dakota numbered 39,442. This was more than 41 percent of the total farms reported in the two states by the census of 1890. Dakotans also made final entry on 2409 timber culture claims up to June 30, 1890, and several thousand more later. Most of these homesteads and "tree claim" farms were acquired during the boom period.[21] The public land laws, including the preemption act, were highly important contributors to farm-making in Dakota, especially east of the Missouri River.

Many homesteads and timber culture claims were commuted for cash by smalltime speculators, often single women, who filed on a homestead and then sold a relinquishment for anywhere from $50 to $400. Most relinquishments probably did not command over $100.[22] In the 9 years between June 30, 1880, and July 1, 1889, for example, 26,721 homesteads were commuted in Dakota. This was about 30 percent of the total homestead entries in Dakota during that period. The commutation privilege in the Homestead Act did permit petty speculators to make a few dollars by filing the initial entry and waiting until a person came along who wanted to farm and was willing to purchase the relinquishment, but it did not slow down settlement in eastern Dakota nor lead to land monopoly. Individual farmers got the land, although actual settlers in

Sod buildings on Albert McKinstry's farm in Central Perkins County, northwestern South Dakota, about 1905. The author spent his first years on a homestead only a few miles from the McKinstry place. (Jennewein Western Library, Friends of the Middle Border, Mitchell, South Dakota)

these commutation cases did not get it free. However, it cannot be assumed that all of the commuted homesteads represented this kind of speculation. Many farmers paid for their farms rather than wait 5 years to get title so they could use the land as security for credit. Moreover, some settlers expanded their farms by purchasing a relinquishment on a quarter section nearby. The evils associated with commutation in the Dakotas took place mostly after 1898 as the more arid parts of the area were being settled.[23]

As had been true in the earlier period of settlement, the first crop planted by most Dakota pioneers in the 1880s was wheat, for homesteaders were as much infected with the wheat fever as their bonanza neighbors. Brown County, which lay between the 98th and 99th meridians in the east-central part of the territory, experienced a tremendous wheat boom after 1880. One farmer recalled that he filed on a homestead and adjoining timber culture claim, and immediately set to work to break as many acres as possible. He boarded with a neighbor and lived in a tent on his homestead land. By working hard himself and hiring some breaking done, he broke 90 acres and planted about 50 acres of sod crops. The next year he sowed wheat that made 21 bushels to the acre as well as oats and corn, which also did well. After selling his crops and paying his bills, he had $1295 in cash at the end of his second year. Farmers all over Brown County were reporting wheat yields of 25 to 40 bushels to the acre in 1882. As one writer said, wheat had been "gloriously crowned

The interior of a Dakota home about 1890. (Minnesota Historical Society)

king." Indeed, people were "set crazy" by the tremendous crop of that year. Quick profits could not only be realized from actual wheat growing, but also from the increase in property values associated with the boom. One story told of a man who bought a relinquishment claim for $130, "plowed two acres, built a house, and sold out for $1,500."[24]

A young Minnesotan who settled in Brown County in the fall of 1880 acquired 480 acres under the homestead, tree-claim and preemption laws. Over the next few years he plowed more and more of his land. In the spring of 1885 he sowed 215 acres of wheat and raised 5176 bushels, which sold for 70 cents a bushel. Meanwhile, he had acquired machinery and livestock, and saved some cash. By 1885 his land was worth $20 an acre or $9600, and his other property brought his assets to above $10,000. Beginning with a two-horse team and a wagon in 1880, this pioneer farmer had built himself a $10,000 estate in 5 years. Orange Judd, editor of the *Prairie Farmer*, who reported this experience, declared that "Mr. Greeley's advice is still applicable."[25]

Publicizing experiences of this nature only added to the excitement and expectancy of potential settlers. The Aberdeen land office was opened on October 1, 1882, following the great wheat crop of that year. The first day nearly 1000 homestead entries were filed. The number of farms in Brown County increased from only 28 in 1880 to 2441 in 1885. The wheat yield was not very good in 1883 because of dry weather, but the next year 25-bushel wheat was common and expansion continued. The 1884 crop in Brown County alone was estimated at 1,867,801 bushels.[26] Under the influence of "wheat fever," similar expansion occurred throughout the entire upper James River Valley and westward to the Missouri River. Up to 1885 most of the settlement occurred between the 98th and 99th meridians, but during the next few years farmers pushed to the 100th meridian and a little beyond in the north-central part of the territory. By 1886 and 1887 the counties bordering on the east side of the Missouri River between Pierre and Bismarck were becoming well settled.

During the boom of the 1880s, the vast region west, northwest, and north between Mitchell and Bismarck, a distance of some 400 miles, was rapidly transformed from open prairie to settled farms. Considering 21 pioneer counties in that region, the number of farms increased from only 439 to 19,262 in the decade after 1880.[27] This was entirely apart from the wheat and land boom, which was occurring simultaneously in the Red River Valley farther east.

Although spring wheat was the leading crop of Dakota settlers who occupied the central and northern parts of the territory in the 1880s, additional crops were not ignored. Oats and corn were the other most important cereals, followed by barley, rye, and flax. Although this was not a favorable area for corn, many pioneers planted it as a sod crop the first year, and sometimes continued to grow it thereafter. The publicity connected with wheat growing has led some writers to dismiss corn as totally unimportant among pioneer Dakota farmers, but this was not the case. The territorial manuscript census of agriculture shows, for example, that of 30 farmers in Rosette Township in Edmunds County, 11 grew wheat and 10 produced corn in 1884. There were 38 settlers in Logan Township in newly settled Hand County in 1884 and 30 reported wheat and 10 planted a few acres of corn.[28]

The *Dakota Farmer* reported in 1887 that "each year witnesses the widening of the corn belt in Dakota, and the gradual conversion of the farmers of the most northerly localities to the belief . . . that corn can be grown anywhere in the Territory." A Sully County farmer wrote that he believed corn was the most profitable crop in central Dakota if it were marketed through livestock.[29] But farmers gradually learned that it was foolhardy to depend on a corn crop between the James and Missouri rivers in the north-central part of Dakota. During the dry year of 1889 corn in Faulk County went about 2 bushels to the acre. Wheat did not do much better, but generally wheat was a more reliable and profitable crop than corn. Even in the older settled region of the southeast where a corn-livestock type of farm organization eventually developed, wheat continued to be the leading grain crop even after 1890.

The Dakota agricultural boom continued through 1885 and into 1886 as thousands of additional farmers kept streaming into the territory. They

The Great Dakota Boom, 1878-1887 - **105**

A copy of a large colored poster advertising the McCormick harvester and twine binder. McCormick Collection. State Historical Society of Wisconsin)

plowed up the rich buffalo grass and planted grain in its stead. The 720,000 acres of wheat planted in the banner year of 1882 rose to 1,540,200 in 1884 and to 2,675,350 by 1886. The vast increase in the acreage of wheat and other cereal crops was made possible by mechanizing farm operations. Dakota farmers bought thousands of plows, seeders, drills, harrows, and particularly self-binders. In the summer of 1884 one firm in Huron sold 108 carloads of reapers in Beadle and Hand counties, and the *Dakota Farmer* reported that as many more had been sold by the agents of the same company in Spink and Faulk counties. By 1884 and 1885 an increasing number of Dakota farmers were abandoning the practice of backsetting and were using discs to pulverize the broken sod. Despite warnings that farmers should not go into debt for machinery, hundreds of them bought all kinds of equipment on time believing that good years would continue and that farm machine notes could be paid off easily.[30]

The crops of 1885 seemed to substantiate even the most optimistic view of the territory's agricultural future. Reports of good sod corn, flax that made as much as 25 bushels to the acre, oats that went 50 to 70 bushels, and wheat that made as much as 25 bushels an acre all encouraged additional emigration. The Faulkton *Times* reported on September 24, 1885, that the local fair had been a huge success and redounded to "the glory and credit of the people. . . ." Producers in that area, the editor said, had been blessed with big crops of grain and vegetables. Orange

Judd traveled from Huron to Pierre in the fall of 1885 and reported that people were rejoicing in their abundance. Corn in Hand County, he said, had made 40 bushels to the acre, oats 30 to 50 bushels, and wheat 15 bushels. He declared that most of the good government land in Hand County had been taken up, although the first settlements had occurred only 5 years before. However, if a person wanted to start farming, he could get land from those who wished to leave. "There is a considerable class of inefficients, and of uneasy people, ready to sell out at the first fair offer, often at a good deal less than the real present value of the land," Judd advised.[31]

Settlement was so rapid in Dakota that there was very little of the lonely pioneer life so often associated with the frontier. A correspondent from Faulk County declared that in 3½ years after the beginning of settlement, the county was "thickly dotted with dwellings, and thousands of acres of golden grain are undulating in the breeze." Between 1880 and 1885 the total population of Faulk County jumped from 4 to 3120. In the second year of settlement in Clark County a resident wrote that there was a compact settlement of enterprising and well-to-do farmers in his township. The territorial manuscript census of agriculture in 1885 reveals that after a year or two of settlement many townships had from 25 to 40 farmers. Since there were 36 sections in each township, when a family settled on a quarter of land, it was probably not more than a mile or 2 from the nearest neighbor.

The Dakota frontier was occupied by both native Americans and foreign immigrants. Although most of the foreign born were located in the older, settled, eastern counties, some immigrants pushed westward to the edge of settlement. For example, hundreds of German-Russians settled in McPherson County, most of which lay between the 99th and 100th meridians. Groups and colonies also settled on the Dakota frontier where they could get land under the Homestead Act. The largest number of foreign born Dakotans came from the Scandinavian countries, Germany, Canada, and Russia. By 1890 some 44.5 percent of the population in North Dakota was foreign born. In South Dakota it was 27⅗ percent. The percentage of foreign born in the Dakotas was much higher than in Nebraska and Kansas where the frontier was settled mainly by native born citizens.[32]

The first signs that the Great Dakota Boom had begun to decline came in 1886. Governor Gilbert A. Pierce reported that "the year has not been altogether as prosperous as desired," because of a general business decline and local drought conditions, which had reduced the wheat and oat crops.[33] Actually, the territory's production of wheat averaged only about 1 bushel less per acre, but some localities had very poor crops. Moreover, the price was 11 cents a bushel lower than the year before, and wheat sold at from 48 to 52 cents a bushel. In some parts of the territory drought struck again in 1887 and 1888.

Unfavorable weather conditions and low wheat prices hit the specialized grain grower especially hard, and small farmers, as well as the bonanza operators, began to complain that there was no profit in raising wheat. A Clark County farmer reported that over a 5-year period he had failed to make any money raising wheat and that in 1888 he would not plant a single acre. Another observer wrote early in 1887 that the future of wheat raising did not appear bright and that a crisis had been reached in Dakota farming. Many discouraging experiences with wheat raising were reported to the editor of the *Dakota Farmer* in 1887 and 1888.[34]

The decline and even disappearance of wheat profits stimulated the whole question of diversified farming. Farmers were advised to concentrate less on wheat and to grow other crops, plant a garden, get some poultry, milk a few cows, and raise livestock. The farmer who did this would be much better off, said the editor of the *Dakota Farmer*, than if he made "calculations based on the expectation of a big grain crop and enormous prices."[35] The *Northwestern Farmer and Breeder* published at Fargo urged farmers to engage in dairying so they could sell enough cream to pay their living expenses. Following several years of raising wheat in Hand County, a farmer near Miller cut his acreage sharply and urged other farmers to follow his policy of diversification. The producer who abandoned grandiose plans in regard to wheat and took a basket of eggs and a pail of butter to town would return home light-hearted and out of the clutches of unnecessary debt, he wrote.[36] Creameries were established in several communities after 1886, indicating the growing emphasis upon dairying.

Although wheat acreage continued to rise in the late 1880s, more and more farmers did diversify their operations. They raised a larger amount of feed grains and more and better livestock. In the southeast part of the territory a grain-livestock economy had developed by 1890 and in some counties corn had become the leading crop. But even in the newly settled north-central part of the territory, similar changes were occurring. In 1885 a Dakota Stock Breeders Association was formed at the Territorial Fair in Huron, and within a few years quite a number of farmers were raising purebred livestock. In 1886 J. B. Spaulding of Hamlin County advertised 200 head of purebred, registered shorthorn cattle for sale.[37] The first carload of cattle ever shipped out of LaMoure County in the northern part of the territory were sent to an eastern market in the fall of 1887. According to one observer, this showed that farmers were awakening to the advantages of diversified farming. "Two years ago a cow was a curiosity in these parts. Everybody was here for the sole object of raising wheat—nothing else—but the last two years have opened their eyes, and this country will henceforth be noted for its stock as well as the wonderful number one hard."[38] Moreover, by the middle 1880s farmers on the high plains around Highmore and Blunt were experimenting with alfalfa. Since it would withstand drought and was a good feed for livestock, alfalfa was considered an especially promising crop. "I look to alfalfa as the stepping stone to profitable stock raising, a sure foundation for any country's prosperity," wrote one farmer.[39]

The wheat and land boom in Dakota was really over by 1887, but if any life remained, it was destroyed by the terrible drought of 1889. The first two tiers of counties west of the Minnesota border were not greatly affected, but farther west the damage was devastating. Wheat averaged between 8 and 9 bushels to the acre over the entire territory, but many fields yielded less than 5 bushels per acre and some none at all. In Edmunds County only 207,703 bushels were produced on 60,113 acres, or less than 4 bushels to the acre. In nearby Faulk County the average was even lower.[40] Writing from Faulkton, one farmer said that crops had been poor in 1887, 1888, and now again in 1889, "leaving the farmers as poor as poverty itself." Then he told how his 50 acres of wheat, 30 acres of oats, 25 acres of barley, and 19 acres of flax had been burned by the hot winds until scarcely anything was worth harvesting. His entire wheat crop from 50 acres brought him only $41.48, while the seed and threshing cost $56.04, to say nothing of other expenses.[41]

Conditions became so bad by the winter of 1889-1890 that many people were in dire want. In Miner County where wheat and corn averaged between 2 and 3 bushels to the acre some 2500 individuals were reportedly threatened by death from starvation. Governor Arthur C. Mellette of the new state of South Dakota toured the devastated areas in December 1889 and found that in parts of Clark, Faulk, and Miner counties there were at least "600 families who are almost absolutely destitute, except as they are helped."[42] The situation was fully as bad in North Dakota, especially in the newer settled counties. T. H. Helgesen, state commissioner of agriculture and labor, estimated that there were at least 5000 people in his state who needed assistance. After returning from a trip through several hard hit North Dakota counties, Helgesen wrote to Governor John Miller that "I found the people really more destitute than I had expected. They are in great need of almost everything."[43]

Early in 1890 the North Dakota legislature considered a bill that would have provided loan funds of $100,000 to buy seed wheat for needy settlers. This measure was defeated, however, and another measure was passed appropriating $2500 for direct relief. The South Dakota constitution prohibited state appropriations for relief, and, consequently, the lawmakers did not provide any money for needy citizens. They did, however, authorize boards of county commissioners to lend money to farmers with which they might buy seed wheat. This measure was not implemented to any great extent and was therefore of little help. When the states failed to act decisively in this matter, the needy had to depend primarily on private relief. Committees were set up in both North and South Dakota to solicit outside aid, and by early 1890 carloads of coal, grain, clothing, food, and other supplies were reaching the needy areas. Governor Mellette wrote in February that if it had not been for the charities from adjoining states and from eastern Dakota "many of our people must have perished during the past winter."[44] Contributions, mostly from outside the state, amounted to $39,627.46 in South Dakota.[45] The discussion of state aid, the setting up of solicitation committees, free shipment of donated supplies by the railroads, and distribution to needy settlers were all reminiscent of conditions and procedures in the 1870s when destitution stalked the Minnesota, Nebraska, and Kansas frontiers. And again it was the newly settled pioneer farmer who suffered most.

Boomers and promoters resented the unfavorable publicity associated with the relief efforts. While admitting that there was some hardship, the editor of the *Yankton Press and Dakotan* sharply criticized what he called the "damaging falsehoods" emanating from eastern newspapers. Some of the stories, he wrote, were "sufficient provocation for a declaration of war." After attacking the Chicago press for "systematically libeling the Dakotas," the Yankton editor declared that "this crusade against the Dakotas is one of the meanest on record." Under these conditions, Dakotans were having a struggle to maintain their agricultural prestige.[46] Although at first Governors Mellette and Miller tried to play down bad conditions, they had to recognize reality. Actually, they were in a dilemma. If the states moved to help the destitute, it would prove the widespread need and advertise the Dakotas as a poor place to emigrate. If, on the other hand, they did nothing, people were likely to leave the states and this would deter economic development. A lumber dealer from Aberdeen wrote Governor Mellette: "The greatest crisis in the history of this region is now at hand, and if we want to prevent depopulation, we must do something, . . ."[47] The editor of *Conklin's Dakotian* published at Watertown said that if people left because of crop failure and poverty, Dakota would be set back a decade. "If these people are driven out in large numbers as paupers and mendicants we can never induce others to come in and fill their places," he argued.[48] Thus, regardless of how distasteful it was to solicit outside help, Dakotans buried their pride and made a strong effort to help people so they would not leave. Some, of course, cursed Dakota and departed, but not large numbers.

Despite the hard times, and perhaps because of them there was continued pressure to open more lands for settlement. The Sioux reservation was the center of intense interest by land speculators and farmers after 1887. Stretching from the Missouri River on the east to the Black Hills on the west, and from the Nebraska border almost as far north as Bismarck, this area contained some 22 million acres, or about one fourth of Dakota Territory. In his report to the Secretary of Interior in 1887, Governor Louis K. Church urged that at least half the vast area be thrown open to settlement. Continued agitation bought the desired results early in 1890. Meanwhile, hundreds of boomers had gathered at Pierre and Chamberlain awaiting official word of the opening. When the announcement came at 3:30 P.M. on February 11, a cannon was fired at Pierre, the legislators rose in their seats and cheered, and hundreds of people drove their teams across the river on the ice and rushed to locate land. The army, which had not been officially notified, held back the boomers for 2 days at both Pierre and Chamberlain, but then the settlers hurried over the river bottoms and rolling plains in search of farms and locations for townsites. On February 12 the Yankton *Press and Dakotan* reported that "every incoming train [to Chamberlain] is heavily loaded with settlers bound for the reservation, and the stream of humanity crossing the river is almost continuous. Several thousand have already begun the erection of homes, the new arrivals being forced to go further into the interior."[49] Actually, this description was grossly exaggerated and the small boom of settlement soon dissipated. The area was not fully occupied until after 1900.

Although the number of farms in the Dakotas increased by nearly 20,000 between 1890 and 1900, mostly in North Dakota, the Great Dakota Boom was over. The 7 or 8 years following 1890 were difficult ones for many Dakota farmers, especially those in South Dakota. Periodic crop failures and low prices following the Panic of 1893 left many farmers heavily in debt and barely able to make a living. The crops of 1890 were poor in many communities, and those of 1893 and 1894 were even worse. The drought of 1894 was so severe that scarcely anything was raised in the western counties. The situation was particularly bad in South Dakota, where in 1894 the corn averaged only $4\frac{1}{5}$ bushels per acre and wheat $6\frac{3}{5}$ bushels. The average wheat yield in North Dakota was higher because of better crops in the Red River Valley.[50] Moreover, wheat prices had dropped to about 45 cents by 1894 and fell even lower the next year. Early in 1895 the South Dakota legislature authorized counties and townships to provide seed for drought-stricken farmers and some counties made no effort to collect taxes in 1894.[51] Under these discouraging circumstances some settlers left the Dakotas in search of better opportunities elsewhere.

Sixteen of South Dakota's 53 counties lost population between 1890 and 1900. The heaviest losses occurred in the area between the James and Missouri rivers, which had been settled during the boom of the

1880s. Total population in 12 of these counties dropped from 76,943 in 1890 to 64,491 in 1900, a decline of 16 percent. Besides the drop in rural population, people left the towns and villages as well. Not all of the newly settled counties in South Dakota lost population during the difficult 1890s and no county in North Dakota experienced a decline. However, population did fall in some individual townships in North Dakota.[52]

By the late 1890s better crops and higher prices created a new spirit of optimism. Hope seemed to spring eternal on the frontier. After 1900 a new boom occurred as thousands of settlers pushed onto the unoccupied lands west of the Missouri River, commonly called the West River Country. During the next 15 or 20 years thousands of acres were acquired both for farming and ranching. However, this land was all west of the 100th meridian and the meager and uncertain rainfall made crop farming under the current agricultural practices a highly risky business. As far as grain farming was concerned, the best of Dakota lands had been settled before 1890.

So long as farmers continued to concentrate on grain growing, lack of land was not a problem as they advanced farther west. In other words, the land laws with their emphasis upon 160-acre tracts did not interfere with or retard successful farming west of the 98th and 99th meridians, as has so often been claimed. It should be emphasized in the first place that most farmers who went west of the 98th meridian acquired more than the traditional quarter section. A settler might file a preemption claim, a homestead, and a timber culture entry for a total of 480 acres. This apparently was not common, but many did get an additional 80 acres or another quarter directly from the government through purchase. Thousands of commuted homesteads were acquired by farmers who wanted to expand their operations. In 1890 the average-sized farm in South Dakota was 227 acres and in North Dakota, 277 acres. In the counties between the James and Missouri rivers the averages tended to be higher.

Although farms in Dakota averaged 227 acres in 1890, the average acreage of cereals on each farm was only 73 acres. By 1900 the average production of cereals was 118 acres per farm but by that time the average size of farms had increased to 362 acres. The situation was similar in North Dakota where the average acreage of cereals was 117 and 124 per farm in 1890 and 1900, respectively, while the average size of farms was 277 and 342 acres. It is obvious that farmers did not lack for land.[53] Moreover, in 1900 there were only about 18 head of cattle per farm on those that reported in North Dakota and 32 head on the average South Dakota farm.

Thus farmers up to the 1890s were not fully utilizing all the land they had. Those who failed did not do so because of inadequate land, but from lack of capital, poor management, the wrong combination of production, or factors such as unfavorable weather and low prices, which were completely outside of their control. Despite the hard times of the 1890s, grain farming did not retreat in the Dakotas. Some farmers gave up, but others took over their holdings and worked out a type of farm organization that fit the land and climate. Farmers gradually adjusted to the geographic conditions by resorting to summer fallowing, planting more drought-resistant crops, placing greater reliance on livestock, and resorting to irrigation where water was available. The Plains of Dakota severely tested the ingenuity and persistence of pioneer farmers, but thousands of them succeeded in establishing decent homes in spite of the many problems.

Most of Dakota east of the Missouri River was occupied during the boom years between 1878 and 1887. The frontier of agricultural settlement pushed across the raw prairie and rapidly transformed it into settled farms. Expanded railroad mileage, the availability of large quantities of public land, which could be entered under the federal land laws, a series of good crops, and organized promotional effort all combined to bring this farmers' frontier quickly to an end. Except for the bonanza farmers, the frontier experience in Dakota was similar to that in other areas of the West, which was settled during the late nineteenth century. Most pioneers began in a small way with limited land and capital. They lived simply and frugally and provided much of their own living. But the speed of settlement minimized the isolation and loneliness of pioneer life. Until the late 1880s and early 1890s when farmers were struck by the twin enemies of low prices and crop failures, eastern Dakota was considered one of the most desirable parts of the remaining agricultural frontier.

◁ **7** ▷

The Central Plains Frontier, 1878-1896

A correspondent from western Kansas wrote in the fall of 1878 that Edwards County, which was located beyond the 99th meridian, "is no longer on the verge of civilization. For the past six months," he continued, "the hardy pioneers, strong, daring and confident men from the north and east, have ventured a hundred miles to the westward." There settlers could be seen in sod shanties or in dugouts "as contented and happy as a preacher, as comfortable as a king." Such was the picture presented of western Kansas by an enthusiastic resident at the beginning of a period that experienced rapid settlement and within another decade had brought an end to the agricultural frontier in Kansas.[1]

Although it was questionable whether the new emigrants were "happy" and "comfortable," there was no doubt but that in 1878 and 1879 a rapid influx of farmers poured into western Kansas and Nebraska. The droughts, grasshoppers, and hard times of the middle 1870s were temporarily past and the tide of emigration again picked up momentum. An Ellis County observer wrote in June 1878 that "incessant breaking for wheat can be seen in all directions." From Mitchell County came the report that a large amount of new land had been broken and that the crops were splendid. The Dodge City *Times* was boasting of the agricultural prospects presented by Ford County, which was astride the 100th meridian, and the editor declared: "Eastern readers, you are welcome to share our prosperity and good luck in Kansas."[2] By 1880 several hundred farmers had settled in eastern Ford County, and the cattlemen were in retreat before the onward rush of the sodbusters.[3]

A similar situation was occurring in southwestern Nebraska. In 1878 and 1879 settlers advanced into the new counties along the Republican River and scattered over the area between the Kansas border and the Platte. The land office at Bloomington in south-central Nebraska received homestead entries covering 307,131 acres during the year ending June 30, 1879. During the next year homestead filings at North Platte farther west and north reached 173,857 acres, nearly double the figure for 1879. By 1880 Frontier, Red Willow, and Hitchcock counties had 241, 438, and 199 farms respectively. Much of the newly settled area was west of the 100th meridian.[4]

Attempts by John W. Powell, officials of the General Land Office in Washington, and others to discredit the agricultural possibilities of lands west of the 100th meridian brought stronger and more bitter reactions from residents in Nebraska and Kansas than from Dakotans. This was primarily due to the fact that by 1880 settlers were already at or beyond the 100th meridian on the Central Plains Frontier. In Dakota, on the other hand, there were still millions of acres of unoccupied public lands between the 98th and 100th meridians. Thus when a special commission of which Powell was a member reported on the land laws and their operation in the West early in 1880, Kansans and Nebraskans took sharp issue with recommendations that the plains west of the 100th meridian should be reserved principally for grazing homesteads. Even before this 690 page document was published, the Nebraska Board of Agriculture attempted to refute the implication that western Nebraska was unfit for ordinary farming. In calling on Professors Samuel Aughey and C. D. Wilber at the State University of Nebraska for their opinions, the board wrote: "We note with anxiety movements tending to 'condemn as agricultural,' and 'denominate, *for all time to come*, only as pasturage lands,' that portion of the state situate[d] west of the one-hundredth meridian." The Nebraska scientists replied that the soil was fertile west of the 100th meridian and that moisture was usually sufficient for crop production. Moreover, rainfall was gradually increasing. Those who would deny these lands to farmers and maintain them as pastures, Aughey and Wilber concluded, would be perpetrating a "fearful robbery," and should "receive public execration."[5]

The unusually abundant rainfall and good crops harvested by the pioneers in 1878 stimulated a rush of emigration that seemed to make discussion of the agricultural potentialities of the Central Plains entirely irrelevant. Norton County, located on the high plains of northwestern Kansas, reported 7001 people in 1880, compared to only 899 5 years earlier. Farther west on the 100th meridian Hodgeman and Trego counties, organized in 1879, boasted a population of 1704 and 2535 respectively the following year. More than 1000 farms were reported in those two pioneer counties by the census of 1880. The land office at Wakeeney in Trego County entered 108,542 acres under the Homestead Act for the year ending June 20, 1880. The rapid westward advance in 1879 is reflected by the fact that 11,337 homesteads were entered in Kansas and 4905 in Nebraska, covering 2,288,127 acres of land.[6] By 1880 there was a scattering of agricultural settlement over the vast plains area between Dodge City, Kansas, and North Platte, Nebraska.

The new boom had scarcely begun, however, when it was cut short by a widespread and severe drought that caused tremendous hardships among new settlers. In contrast to the heavy crops in 1878, which had encouraged rapid westward migration the following spring, the crops of 1879 failed in most frontier counties. Wheat averaged about 2½ bushels to the acre in Pawnee County, Kansas, and this was fairly typical of some 12 or 13 counties in western Kansas. Corn made 6 to 8 bushels, and the yield of other grains was equally poor. The situation was nearly as bad in parts of southwestern Nebraska.[7] To make matters worse, conditions were no better in 1880 throughout much of the central plains region. With two crop failures in succession, many of the newly settled emigrants who had expended their slim capital were destitute. By the winter of 1880–1881 a crisis had developed on parts of the frontier. In response to this need, the Kansas legislature on February 15, 1881, appropriated $25,000 for the direct relief of suffering settlers on the western frontier.[8]

The applications for relief tell a great deal about the frontier settlers and their experiences. Many of them had come to the western counties of Kansas in 1879 and had suffered from two crop failures in a row. There were people of all ages, including one old man of 80 who had settled all alone on a homestead in Gove County west of the 100th meridian the previous October. There were big families with six or seven children who were near starvation. A farmer near Dodge City had settled there in April 1879. Although he had 50 acres under cultivation by 1880, he had raised nothing of consequence in either 1879 or 1880 and desperately needed food for his wife and six children as well as seed for the coming spring. So many farmers rushed to file applications for relief in Norton County that the officials ran out of printed forms and the applicants simply wrote out their requests in longhand. Of the 125 who applied for help in Norton County, more than half had lived there only

2 years or less. The newly arrived, undercapitalized settler suffered the most. Largely dependent upon his first and second crop to get a start, the pioneer farmer had nothing to fall back on if these failed. Success or failure was determined for thousands of settlers by the whims of nature, and the time and place of settlement.[9]

While a tremendous land and agricultural boom was occurring on the Dakota frontier in the early 1880s, agriculture on the Central Plains of Kansas and Nebraska was developing much more slowly in the face of unfavorable weather conditions. The population of several frontier counties in Kansas actually declined between 1880 and 1882, and one observer in Pawnee County was right when he said that settlers were cursing droughty Kansas and leaving for other places. Pawnee County lost more than 1000 people in the period from 1880 to 1882. Elam Bartholomew, who lived in Rooks County where conditions were somewhat better, recorded in his diary that "thousands of acres of wheat in western Kansas" had already been killed by the prolonged drought. People were getting "the blues badly" and, on the extreme frontier, settlers "are commencing to turn their faces toward the land of the rising sun."[10] Some counties that had been organized for a decade and settled for 5 or 6 years also experienced an exodus of settlers. The population of Phillips County dropped from 12,014 in 1880 to 8446 2 years later.

Discouraging reports continued to come out of western Kansas. On November 28, 1882, a resident of Graham County wrote: "We are having a bad time generally in our county this fall. Have not had rain enough since the 10th of July to wet the ground two inches deep. Wheat and rye that was sown two months ago are dead." Only in 1 year during the last 5, he said, had there been a decent corn crop in his area. In 1882 the cornstalks were not even big enough to burn and "more than half the people are compelled to use cowchips and sunflower stalks for fuel." Nine out of 10 families, he explained, lived in sod houses or dugouts and were having a hard time. This discouraged farmer declared that "five years experience in this county has convinced me that the farmer must leave here and make room for the stock raiser." During this period he estimated that 1000 families had come to the county to farm and after 1 to 3 years they returned to their "relatives east, poorer, sadder, and much wiser."[11]

Under these conditions it is not surprising that there was a sharp drop in homestead filings in 1881, 1882, and 1883 in both Kansas and Nebraska. In fact, more homesteads were entered in Kansas in 1879 alone than in 1881, 1882, and 1883 combined, although the decline was not so severe in Nebraska. Total crop acreage expanded only modestly. The 2,215,937 acres of wheat in Kansas in 1880 was higher than in most of the subsequent years in that decade, although there was a considerable increase in corn. Unlike Dakota where the pioneer crop was generally wheat, most settlers on the Kansas and Nebraska frontier planted corn as their first crop in the 1880s. But over-all, the early 1880s was a time of slow agricultural development on this Central Frontier.

But pessimism and discouragement were washed away by the increased rainfall and improved crops in 1883 and 1884. It was almost miraculous how a few good rains could change the attitude and outlook of people in an entire region. The Kansas City *Journal* reported in March 1884 that "for more than four weeks almost every train from the east has been loaded with large parties of excursionists . . . seeking homes in various portions of Kansas."[12] A writer for the Chicago *Inter-Ocean* said in the fall of 1884 that many people were leaving Illinois and other midwestern and eastern states for Kansas. "The time has come when Kansas was considered a droughty state, but that day is past, and her reputation for sure crops is becoming widely known."[13] This article assured prospective settlers that southwestern Kansas was the place for persons who were willing to help build up a new country. "Land is cheap and a good home can be made to pay for itself in a few years," wrote this observer. A new boom in western Kansas and Nebraska was in the making. It reached its crest in Nebraska in 1885 and in Kansas the following year.

From 1884 to 1887 settlers, speculators, and town boomers completed the settlement of the western one-fourth of Kansas and Nebraska, which lay between the 100th and 102d meridians. As farmers moved into the last three tiers of counties in Kansas they could see the deserted claim shanties that had been abandoned 3 or 4 years before by drought-stricken pioneers. But the remains of former failure did not deter the new invasion of the high plains. The editor of the Dodge City *Times* wrote on December 18, 1884, that the large cattle ranches in that area would surely have to give way to smaller herds owned by farmers. Speaking at the Nebraska State Fair in September 1885, Orange Judd, editor of the *Prairie Farmer*, spoke of the remarkable agricultural development of western Nebraska and again attacked the "Great American Desert" idea.[14]

By the spring of 1885 a torrent of settlers were flooding onto the last Kansas and Nebraska frontiers. The Larned *Optic* declared that "the largest immigration ever known in the history of the state is now steadily flowing into southwestern Kansas." The farther west one went, the greater the boom, he added. A writer for the Kinsley *Graphic* declared in April that "the immigration boom continues to increase." He said that this time people were coming to stay. "Come on!" he wrote, "there is still plenty of room; land is cheap here yet, and thousands of acres for sale. . . ."[15] Another observer said that the tidal wave of settlement marching westward in Kansas had never been equaled in the state's en-

118 - *The Central Plains Frontier, 1878-1896*

Emigrants entering the Loup Valley, Custer County, Nebraska, 1886. (The Nebraska State Historical Society)

tire history. More rainfall and better crops were not only drawing new emigrants, but those who had settled a few years before were now in a position to build improvements, buy machinery, and expand their operations. One writer said of southwestern Edwards County in Kansas that the area was "literally spotted with new frame and board houses with here and there a sod house."[16]

Again, a favorable combination of circumstances stimulated the rapid advance of pioneer settlement. The revival and expansion of railroad building after about 1878 was an important factor in extending the farmers' frontier in Kansas and Nebraska. Many small companies were organized and laid hundreds of miles of track, while the larger established firms increased their already substantial mileage. The Union Pacific in Nebraska and the Kansas Pacific and Santa Fe in Kansas had provided transportation to the western edge of those states, and beyond, in the late 1860s and early 1870s, but in the 1880s these companies built numerous branch lines that extended railroad service to formerly isolated western communities. The Missouri Pacific put together a large railroad network in Kansas during the 1880s. By 1885 a growing number of communities on the Central Plains Frontier were served by two railroads, and in some cases three. Even such previously isolated Kansas counties as Seward in the southwest and Greeley on the extreme western border had railroad transportation by the late 1880s.

The rapid extension of railways, often financed by local bond issues, provided more efficient transportation and brought markets closer to even the most isolated pioneer farmers. Moreover, railroads helped to influence the pattern of settlement, although they did not by any means determine it. In parts of western Kansas and Nebraska settlers moved many miles from the main railroads and branch lines did not reach some pioneer communities for several years. It was a decade, for example, between original settlement in Rooks County, Kansas, and the arrival of the railroad at Stockton, the county seat. The financial and business activity associated with railroad construction was both a part of and a contribution to the boom on the Central Plains Frontier during the middle 1880s.

Abundant rainfall was an even more important factor in encouraging rapid westward migration because it helped to create the optimistic impression that agriculture could be established on a profitable basis in western Kansas and Nebraska. This in turn would support industries, railroads, and towns. The entire boom psychology that developed in the middle 1880s was closely associated with adequate moisture in an area that had recently suffered from severe drought. Moreover, capital was readily available as eastern investors poured millions of dollars into western Kansas and Nebraska, securing their loans with farm real estate mortgages. The manager of one loan company declared later that "during many months of 1886 and 1887 we were unable to get enough mortgages for people of the East who wished to invest in that kind of security."[17] Although all kinds of townsite boomers, railroad promoters, and business speculators were drawn to the Central Plains Frontier in the middle 1880s, it was the pull of free or cheap land that was mainly responsible for enticing farmers to the area. The urge to own or speculate in land was never more evident than on the Kansas, Nebraska, and Dakota frontiers in the years from 1885–1888.

Western land offices were inundated with applications for pre-emptions, homesteads, and timber culture claims. In Nebraska the number of homestead entries in 1884 nearly doubled the year before, reaching 8887 and covering 1,362,186 acres. The number of homestead entries reached their peak in Nebraska during 1885 when they totaled 11,293, but the demand was still heavy in 1886 when 10,269 entries were filed. In six southwestern Nebraska counties there were 2577 and 2899 homestead filings, respectively, in 1885 and 1886. These farmer-homesteaders west of the 100th meridian applied for 859,609 acres of land.[18] Writing on *Nebraska Her Resources, Advantages, Advancement and Promises*, former Governor Robert W. Furnas declared in 1885 that rainfall was moving west, and the man who put up a sod cabin, planted corn and other cereals, raised livestock, and worked diligently would assure him-

Peter M. Barnes and his family in front of their sod house near Clear Creek at the south edge of Swiss Valley, Custer County, Nebraska, about 1887. (The Nebraska State Historical Society)

self "an early reward." In the spring of 1886 there was a tremendous rush of people into southwestern Nebraska. In one 6-week period it was estimated that 3000 people stopped at Benkelman in Dundy County in the extreme southwest corner of the state, and that 2000 of them had taken up land. By 1887 the land boom in western Nebraska was beginning to decline, but still 7120 homestead entries were filed covering more than 1 million acres.

Homestead entries in Kansas during 1884 totaled only 3547, which was about the same as in each of the 3 previous years. However, in 1885 the number jumped to 9954 and the next year skyrocketed to 20,688. This was second only to the all-time high of 22,061 filed in Dakota in the fiscal year of 1883. Total applications for government lands in Kansas in 1886 amounted to 5,636,824 acres more than one tenth of the entire area of the state. During the 3 peak years of the Kansas land boom, 1885, 1886, and 1887, there were 43,426 homestead entries filed and 24,496 timber culture claims. This was a total of 67,922 entries and covered 10,551,785

The Central Plains Frontier, 1878-1896 - **121**

A farm home in Custer County, Nebraska, about 1888. Corn growing in the background. (The Nebraska State Historical Society)

acres of land. Even though a large number of farmers filed both a homestead and a timber culture entry, the total number of land claims reflected a tremendous rush of new settlers into the western one-third of of the state. As was always the case on the frontier, some of those who filed on public land never intended to live on it or to engage in farming. Speculation was their true purpose. A writer for the *Kansas Farmer* said that one of the worst things about western settlement was the fact that many who took up claims had no intention of making homes, but filed for "the sole purpose of selling out. . . ."[19] However, thousands of pioneers who entered homestead and timber culture claims intended to farm and to establish permanent residences in their communities.

Agricultural pioneering on the Kansas and Nebraska frontier changed very little between the 1870s and the boom of the 1880s. Farmers tried to raise the same crops, lived in the same kind of sod or cheap frame houses, settled on the traditional 160 acres of land with very little capital to develop it, and during the initial years operated on a very small scale. The only difference that could be observed was that settlers were just farther west by the 1880s. The manuscript census of agriculture for 1875 and 1885 at or near the edge of settlement appear remarkably the same.

122 - *The Central Plains Frontier, 1878-1896*

Stacking alfalfa in Buffalo County, Nebraska, 1900. (The Nebraska State Historical Society)

In fact, if the census were not dated it would be hard to tell from internal evidence whether the data were from Cloud County, Kansas, between the 97th and 98th meridians in 1875, or Norton County, on the 100th meridian, more than 100 miles farther west in 1885. The patterns of farming were just the same.

Norton County located on the Nebraska border is fairly typical of the farming frontier on the semi-arid plains of Kansas and Nebraska in the middle 1880s. By looking at one township in some detail it is possible to get a clear picture of the general situation. There were 32 farmers in Solomon township of Norton County in 1885, of whom 30 were owners, one a renter, and one farmer was unlisted. Twenty-six of the 32 settlers had 160 acres, two had 320 acres each, one had 205 acres, and another had only 40. Two farmers had no land. Of the 5045 acres in farms, only 300 were under fence. Twenty-seven of the township's settlers planted corn, and 16 grew winter wheat. The average acreage of corn per farm reporting was 21 and of wheat, 13. A few farmers also grew a little oats, rye, spring wheat, and sorghum, while most of them raised anywhere from ¼ to 1 acre of potatoes. The majority of settlers did not own much livestock. Twenty-five of the 32 farmers had milk cows, but 18 owned three or less. Twenty farmers also reported a few head of other cattle, but this usually consisted of a calf or two and did not represent any kind of a stock herd. Twenty-two of the 25 farmers who had milk cows produced butter, and a majority of the settlers reported making 100 pounds or more. Ten said they sold poultry products in 1885, and 23 had usually only one, two, or three head of swine.[20] An examination of townships in Ford and Rawlins counties of western Kansas does not show any significant variation from the pattern of farm operations described here. The general picture was one where most farmers on the frontier had the traditional 160 acres of land, they raised a few acres of corn or wheat, or both, owned a few head of livestock, and sold meager quantities of dairy and poultry products. Farmers were by no means self-sufficient, but their production of salable crops and livestock was usually so small during the initial years of settlement that they were only in the beginning stage of commercial operation.

The worst speculative features of the boom in western Kansas and Nebraska during the middle 1880s took place in the nonfarm sectors of the economy rather than in agriculture. Bonding for railroad building; speculation in town lots, which saw prices of raw prairie in some places advance to as much as $800 per lot; and construction of public and commercial buildings best reflected the fervor of speculation. These various speculative ventures, as well as the prospect of engaging in agriculture, drew thousands of people into the Central Plains Frontier. The 32 counties covering the western third of Kansas had only 38,271 people in 1885, but this figure had shot up to 139,393, 2 years later, or an increase of some 370 percent. In western Nebraska the picture was much the same.[21] Meanwhile, crop acreage expanded only from 180,107 to 479,379 in the same period, or about 265 percent.

As the boom began to recede in western Kansas and Nebraska in 1887 it gained momentum in eastern Colorado. In the fall of 1886 the editor of the *Colorado Farmer* wrote that for a long time the arid lands of eastern Colorado had been considered unfit to maintain a farming population outside of limited areas of irrigation. However, he said, the production of corn, oats, alfalfa, and potatoes in 1886 had demonstrated that settlers on the high, dry plains could raise sufficient crops to support themselves and their livestock. "We are satisfied," continued the editor, "that nothing now but absolute failure and famine can at present stop the immigration into this country and we will have to await the irrefragable evidences of events and time to finally settle the differences of opinion as upon a similar question it has been settled in western Nebraska."[22]

Whatever doubts existed about the farming prospects of eastern Colorado, they were temporarily removed during the following year when an increasing number of settlers harvested good crops. The rush to get land in eastern Colorado now duplicated the slightly earlier surge of settlement in Dakota and western Kansas and Nebraska. In 1887 the number of homestead entries jumped to 5081 from only 1808 the year before, and in 1888 they climbed to 6411, more than were filed in any other state or territory that year. During 1887 and 1888 a total of 15,225 timber culture claims were also filed in Colorado and many settlers seriously attempted to grow trees. In these two peak years of the boom in Colorado, 4,217,045 acres of land, mostly in the eastern plains section, were entered under the homestead and timber culture laws. Most of the emigrants were native Americans, many of whom had lived on previous frontiers farther east. But they were farmers and they intended to farm. To be sure, they knew little or nothing about the limitations and requirements for dry land farming in a semiarid region, but this did not deter them and they attempted to farm in much the same manner as they had done in more humid country.[23] The extension of railroads into eastern Colorado, especially the Rock Island, which built from the western boundary of Kansas to Colorado Springs in 1888, also contributed to rapid settlement.

By 1887 and early 1888 Colorado writers were exuberant about the so called "rain belt" on the state's eastern plains. In an editorial, "Some thing About the 'Rain Belt,'" the editor of *Field and Farm*, published in Denver, said that during the 28 years he had been in Colorado, he believed "25 would have witnessed good crops in this 'rain belt' had they been planted and had the plow share been sent deep in the virgin earth." In the fall of 1888 this same writer reported that crops in eastern Colorado were excellent. "Corn is king," he said, "and the yield has been a grand one." But farmers were becoming interested in winter wheat production and it seemed to this farm journalist that eastern Colorado was ideally suited for wheat. "With adaptation to the conditions of the country, the proper cultivation of the right kinds of crops and above all diversified methods of farming, will make the rain belt win every time," he enthusiastically concluded.[24]

Like other western communities, eastern Colorado had its full quota of promoters and boomers. On April 15, 1887, for instance, the *Elbert County Democrat*, owned incidentally by the Burlington Townsite Company, said that Burlington and the area around it (later Kit Carson County) was booming. "Elbert County," he said, "is an extension of the beautiful lands of Western Kansas, and is productive beyond computation. . . . The question of moisture is no longer a speculation, but it is an assured fact. . . . All that is needed is to plow, plant and attend to the crops properly; the rains are abundant."[25]

A pamphlet published by the Burlington Railroad in 1887 entitled, *Eastern Colorado*, declared that the "rain belt" had moved westward to within 80 miles of Denver, and that the tablelands of eastern Colorado "are not to be excelled in productiveness by any country upon earth."

A sod schoolhouse in Cherry County, Nebraska, about 1900. (The Nebraska State Historical Society)

Repeating the corn-is-king theme, the writer said that this crop would give "horney-handed sons of toil" a "splendid remuneration for the labor expended in growing it." Such misplaced optimism, of course, had no basis in fact, but many people believed it. "Their belief," said one authority on Colorado agriculture, "was founded on blind faith; their faith on supposition, and supposition arose as ozone from the exquisitely colored prairies on a May morning after a spring rain. . . ."[26]

Like their neighbors in western Kansas and Nebraska, the first settlers planted corn. In 1889 the eight eastern counties of Colorado bordering Kansas had 35,978 acres of corn compared to only 3978 acres of wheat. This pattern of crop production shows to what extent the eastern Colorado frontier was simply an extension of the frontier of western Kansas. Most of the settlers were poor, and poverty, ignorance, and habit combined to cause them to establish the same farm practices to which they were accustomed. Under the circumstances of inadequate capital, lack of knowledge about the region's true geographic characteristics, and failure of all branches of government to provide any kind of advice or leadership, the poor pioneer can hardly be blamed when he

126 - *The Central Plains Frontier, 1878-1896*

A dugout in Custer County, Nebraska, known locally as the Preacher's House, about 1886. (Nebraska State Historical Society)

failed. And hundreds of those who rushed into eastern Colorado in 1887 and 1888 did fail. Nature refused to give them an even start in the race for agricultural success. The crop of 1888 was fair, but in 1889 and 1890 searing drought wiped out the crops, leaving hundreds destitute. The Census of 1890 reported only 3535 farms in 15 counties of eastern Colorado, and some of these were along the Platte and Arkansas rivers where irrigation was possible. This indicates that many people had already left and that thousands more had filed on government land with no intention of living on it.

The land and agricultural boom on the Central Great Plains Frontier of Nebraska, Kansas, and Colorado had collapsed by 1889. Spotted but widespread and damaging drought in that year was a major factor in reversing the economic expansion all along the agricultural frontier. In fact, many local areas had suffered from drought intermittently since 1887. But even before the worst of the drought in 1889 and 1890 the boom was fading. In western Kansas, for example, towns, railroads, and commercial enterprises had developed on a speculative basis and had grown far beyond their need to service the surrounding farm communities. Moreover, outside capital began to dry up, which resulted in a decline in building and the employment and profits connected with construction. The booming towns of 1886 and 1887 now had no function but to supply the commercial needs of farmers and they were greatly overexpanded for that purpose. Consequently, the towns lost population and some of them totally disappeared.

The Central Plains Frontier, 1878-1896 - 127

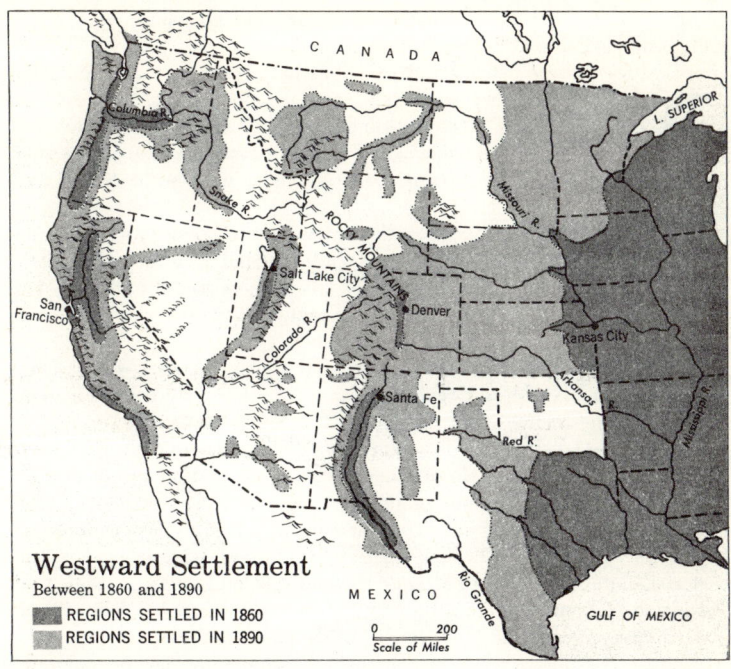

Westward Settlement
Between 1860 and 1890
- REGIONS SETTLED IN 1860
- REGIONS SETTLED IN 1890

The droughts of 1889 and 1890 created a crisis in scores of frontier counties because they climaxed several years of spotty and partial crop production. Hundreds of farmers who had settled in western Kansas, Nebraska, or eastern Colorado during the previous 5 years now found themselves in dire straits. Wheat and corn averaged only a little more than 4 bushels to the acre in Grant County in southwestern Kansas in 1889, and some of the nearby counties produced even less. The situation was extraordinarily critical for hundreds of farmers because the complete failure of crops over a wide area came upon the heels of a boom when many settlers had gone heavily into debt. Loss of crops not only made it impossible for people to pay their debts, but it was a question of just surviving unless outside relief arrived.

The appeals for help began reaching state officials late in 1889. On November 30 the county commissioners of Grant County, Kansas, asked Governor Lyman Humphrey for aid. Writing from the same county, one citizen said that "most all the people here that could leave have done so and what is here are too poor they cannot get away and are in need for they [sic] been here for four years and raised no crops." Another resident wrote the Governor that unless help came from outside the community "we will have to abandon our claims, and go where we can get something to live on."[27] The County Commissioners of Stevens County appealed for private charity and said that help must come immediately or "terrible suffering and starvation must be the result."[28] People in eastern Colorado were also petitioning the Governor for state aid. Farmers in western Nebraska raised better crops in 1889 than their neighbors to the south and west, although there were some local areas of failure.

To meet the condition of settlers in western Kansas, private donations of food and coal were collected and distributed among the needy early in 1890. But despite this relief, it seemed that only state aid and the prospect of a crop grown from state-financed seed would keep many citizens from abandoning their homes.[29]

That eternal hope for a crop the following year, which was so characteristic of farmers on the Great Plains, was shattered by the even more severe drought in 1890 that stretched all the way from the Texas Panhandle to the Canadian border. One farmer in Kansas told the Governor that he did not raise a grain of wheat from 14 acres, that rye seeded on 8 acres had been blown out of the ground, and that "we won't get a bushel of corn." He concluded that "we are in a bad fix now we appeal to you for some help."[30] Calling for relief for drought-stricken settlers in eastern Colorado, the *Rocky Mountain News* said on January 3, 1891, that "hundreds of families are on the verge of starvation and helpless women and children look imploringly to . . . other parts of the state for relief." A reporter for the *News* who had visited families in eastern Colorado wrote that farmers were paying 2 and 3 percent interest a month on chattel mortgages and that one family had nothing in the house to eat except a half sack of flour and a side of bacon. In western Nebraska it was estimated that 2000 families were in dire want. The Omaha *Daily Bee* said that these poor people had been "kept from freezing to death by a providentially mild winter. Thousands of women and children are today subsisting upon Andersonville fare. . . ."[31]

Under these circumstances, farmers on the Central Plains Frontier again turned to their state legislatures for help. Whatever constitutional or philosophical objections may have existed to direct state relief were pushed into the background by the necessities of the moment. Retiring Governor John M. Thayer of Nebraska told the legislature on February 5, 1891, that voluntary contributions of food, clothing, and coal had been gathered and distributed while the people were waiting for the legislature to act. He recommended a state appropriation of $200,000 for relief purposes. Thayer said that 6011 families in western Nebraska required fuel and provisions, and 9938 families would need seed grain in the spring. Responding to this plea and to direct requests from those in need, the legislature provided a total of $200,250 from direct appropriations and the sale of bonds to be distributed by a special relief committee. Most of the money was spent for food and grain. Besides the state appropriation, volunteer relief committees continued to distribute thousands of dollars' worth of supplies.[32]

In Kansas the story was much the same. The need was great, there were demands for state aid, and when private charity fell short, the legislature provided some help. A representative of Governor Humphrey, who toured several western counties in January 1891, reported that there were 50 to 100 families in each county who would be unable to live through the winter without assistance.[33] The Kansas legislature did not appropriate money for direct relief, but in March it did make $60,000 available to needy farmers with which to buy seed grain.

The situation in eastern Colorado where some farmers had raised little or nothing since they first settled in 1887 or 1888 was even worse than in Kansas and Nebraska. By early 1891 hundreds of settlers in the so-called rain belt were existing on private charity raised in Denver and Colorado Springs. Farmers petitioned the legislature for state aid and the newspapers added their voices to the demand. The Denver *Times* declared that public sentiment demanded "relief from the legislature and the response should be prompt."[34] On March 3, 1891, the Colorado legislature appropriated $21,250 to be distributed among eight needy counties to buy seed for spring planting.[35] Although this measure was challenged in the courts, it was upheld.

Fortunately for the settlers on the Central Plains Frontier, rainfall was abundant in 1891 and they raised extraordinarily good crops. Also 1892 was a favorable year. However, drought and crop failure returned to many communities in eastern Colorado and western Kansas and Nebraska in 1893. While conditions were bad in many areas, they were nothing compared to the destitution caused by drought and grasshoppers in 1894. This was one of the driest years on record when no more than 8 to 9 inches of rain fell over much of the Great Plains, and thousands of farmers had a total crop failure. The pitiful condition of some families was almost unbelievable. On June 29, 1894, a housewife who lived near Mendota, Kansas, wrote to Governor Lewelling: "I take my pen in hand to let you know that we are starving to death. It is pretty hard to do without anything to eat here in this God forsaken country. . . . My husband went away to find work and came home last night and told me that he would have to starve. He has been in 10 counties and did not get no work. It is pretty hard for a woman to do without anything to eat when she doesn't know what minute she will be confined to bed. If I was in Iowa I would be all right. I was born there and raised there. I haven't had nothing to eat today and it is 3 o'clock." A resident near Jetmore,

Kansas, wrote that two-thirds of the people in his vicinity had to depend on cow chips for fuel and since people had to sell their cattle some families had to go as far as 13 miles even to get any cow chips. With the temperature 16 degrees below zero and 5 inches of snow on the ground, "what are the people to do," he asked.[36] From Blaine County, Nebraska, a farmer wrote that he had raised nothing but a few early potatoes and that he and his family of seven could not subsist until spring without assistance. An elderly Nebraska woman wrote that she and her grandsons had been living on boiled weeds and bread and butter.[37]

The same methods used to provide relief in earlier crises were again adopted to help needy settlers. In Colorado the Denver *Republican* headed a relief drive to obtain food and clothing for the destitute families in the eastern plains counties. Thousands of pounds of supplies were distributed, as well as a substantial amount of cash.[38] The legislature appropriated $32,250 to help farmers purchase seed grain, but this law was vetoed by the Governor.

Voluntary relief efforts were also carried on in Kansas and Nebraska. Cash donations to the Nebraska State Relief Commission totaled $28,999.38, and the state legislature appropriated $50,000. Most of these funds were expended for flour, coal, and other provisions. Although nearly half the state appropriation went for freight, the railroads hauled goods free of charge or at reduced rates during part of the crisis period.[39] An additional $200,000 was appropriated in Nebraska "for the purpose of procuring seed, and feed for teams, for the destitute farmers. . . ."[40] In Kansas a relief committee and J. K. Hudson of the Topeka *Capital* solicited 99 carloads of provisions, plus $3,154.59 in cash. On February 9, 1895, the Kansas legislature provided $100,000 with which to buy seed grain. This was administered through county officials and was given to farmers as a loan rather than as an outright gift. The legislature also authorized several counties to sell bonds for relief purposes.[41] Early in 1895, Senator Richard Pettigrew of South Dakota introduced a measure to appropriate $300,000 of federal funds to supply seeds to drought-stricken farmers in the West, but his amendment never passed. Arguing in favor of this bill on March 2, 1895, the *Nebraska State Journal* said the federal government really had a responsibility to help suffering pioneers because it had lured them into that unfavorable region. The government had become *"particeps criminis,"* in the whole affair, said the editor.

The crop failures among frontier settlers in the 1890s were accompanied by extremely low prices. Indeed, prices were generally considerably lower than in the years following the Panic of 1873. Wheat dropped to less than 50 cents a bushel, and corn was so cheap it was sometimes burned in place of coal. Livestock prices were also distressingly low. Thus farmers in the west were hit by the twin blows of cheap prices and poor crops. The editor of the Goodland *News* in Kansas summarized this situation when he wrote on January 24, 1895, that settlers had not been driven out of the region so much by "natural repulsion of climate as to an unusual bunching of reverses." This situation had far-reaching implications for the entire Central Plains agricultural frontier.

In the first place there was a sharp decline in both farm and town population. Thousands of people who had settled in western Kansas and Nebraska and in eastern Colorado during the unusually wet 1880s deserted their homes after 1889 and sought a more favorable environment. In Kit Carson County in eastern Colorado some people slipped away in the night to avoid their creditors, and one man "left his cattle and farm machinery that were mortgaged on the prairie."[42] This county lost 36 percent of its population in the 10 years after 1890. The population of nearby Kiowa County declined from 1243 to 701. In 24 counties of western Kansas the population dropped from 68,328 in 1890, after some exodus had already occurred, to 50,118 in 1900. The number of farms fell from 14,311 to 8952 in those counties during the same period. In 27 counties of Nebraska west of the 100th meridian there were 15,284 less people in 1900 than a decade before, and 6018 fewer farms. Many of the small towns that were once thought to be future metropolises ceased to exist altogether.[43]

The drought and subsequent failure of hundreds of frontier farmers finally laid to rest for all time the idea that rainfall followed the plow. While there were numerous experiments at rainmaking during the 1890s, these too were futile. Many people now began to take a more realistic view of the Great Plains as an agricultural region and sensibly concluded that farming practices and organization must be adjusted to meet conditions of a semiarid climate. The entire attitude changed. Perhaps this is nowhere better illustrated than in the report of the Kansas State Board of Agriculture for 1895–1896. The president of the board said that more than any of its predecessors, this volume was designed as an agricultural work rather than as an "immigration document." Articles were included on crops, practices of cultivation, and other practical matters. In other words, state agricultural departments, experiment stations, farm journalists, and even newspaper editors turned their attention to developing and publicizing successful farming techniques for the region. By the 1890s experiments with dry farming, including subsoiling, summer fallowing, and other practices to conserve the limited moisture were receiving attention. New crop strains, especially Turkey Red wheat, were also introduced and found to be more suitable for the area. The hard years of the 1890s then brought emphasis upon adjustment, new techniques, and a different type of farm organization.[44]

Farmers harvesting grain with a header in Kansas during the late nineteenth century. (The Kansas State Historical Society, Topeka)

Although most pioneer settlers had some livestock, their main effort had been directed toward cash grain farming. The drought and crop failures of the 1890s caused farmers who remained on the Central Plains to shift more heavily toward livestock as a producer of income. They continued to raise some cash crops, especially wheat, but the main emphasis was upon producing feed for cattle and sheep, and perhaps a few hogs. Contrary to much popular opinion, grain farming expanded on the Central Great Plains despite the discouraging conditions between 1889 and 1897. The retreat of population did not mean a corresponding decline of grain acreage in western Kansas and Nebraska. What happened was that corn, the traditional pioneer crop in that region, gave way to wheat, which was better suited to the soil and climate. Grain sorghums also grew in popularity. The wheat acreage in 24 counties west of the 100th meridian in Kansas increased from 87,057 in 1889 to 427,314 acres in 1896. Meanwhile, corn in those counties declined from 357,591 to 270,828 acres.[45] Cattle numbers advanced markedly. In other words, grain farming did not retreat in the face of drought and hard times, but farmers adjusted and organized their crop farming more closely around a livestock economy. This combination provided a much better chance of success and kept the region from being abandoned to the open range.

The dry years of the late 1880s and 1890s stimulated the whole question of water conservation and irrigation on the Great Plains. Indeed, from Kansas to Dakota irrigation became one of the most lively topics of the day as farmers, agricultural journalists, politicians, and newspaper

The Central Plains Frontier, 1878-1896 - 133

Harvesting corn in Norton County, Kansas, during the 1890s. (The Kansas State Historical Society, Topeka)

editors sought a way to insure good crops on the semiarid plains. There was widespread national interest in water policies and irrigation during the late 1880s, but nowhere did the matter come in for more lively discussion than in the Plains States. Irrigation had been carried on for several years along the Arkansas and Platte rivers east of the Rockies, but by 1889 there were only 1662 Colorado farmers who irrigated some 137,493 acres in the counties along those rivers in the eastern part of the state. In western Kansas and Nebraska some 733 farmers irrigated 32,562 acres.[46]

But attention was not confined to irrigation from the major rivers. It was suggested that draws and creeks be dammed up, that deep artesian wells be drilled, and even that small plots be irrigated from wells using windmills to pump water into earthen storage tanks. In 1891 the editor of the Denver *Republican* wrote that the salvation of agriculture in eastern Colorado lay "in the reservoirs and the underground strata of water."[47] The *Nebraska Farmer* reported in 1894 that "it is plain to be seen that Nebraska is rapidly drifting toward irrigation." A short while later the editor said that Nebraska had 143,100 acres under ditch, which was more than 12 times as much as was reported in 1889.[48]

The *Kansas Farmer* reported that the dry years had set people to thinking about how best to succeed in farming in the western part of the state. It was unAmerican, the editor wrote, to turn the area over exclusively to large stockmen because the farming class deserved its share of the lands. Irrigation, he continued, was the answer as had been proven by the large crops raised around Garden City on lands irrigated from the Arkansas River.[49] The editor of the Goodland *News* wrote in 1895

Constructing the Eureka Canal in Ford County, Kansas, during the 1880s. (The Kansas State Historical Society, Topeka)

that anyone who had talked about windmill irrigation a year before would have been considered a crank. Now, though, only cranks were against it. "Probably never in the history of the world has there been so radical a change in agriculture, or in views regarding it, as the last year has brought forth, not only in Sherman County, but all over the West."[50] Joseph L. Bristow who published *The Irrigation Farmer* between February 1894 and November 1896 was one of the leading promoters of irrigation in Kansas.[51] During the 1890s the state of Kansas dug 20 experimental irrigation wells.

Dakotans who had suffered from the same destructive droughts as their neighbors to the south also were enthusiastic about the prospects of irrigation after 1889. The *Dakota Farmer* reported in 1890 that interest was so intense in irrigation among its readers that a special section would be devoted to the question beginning a month later. Further concern about irrigation was reflected when the South Dakota legislature created the office of State Engineer of Irrigation in 1890. Farmers in Dakota were particularly hopeful that they could tap the large underground reservoir of water that underlay the James River Valley. In May 1891 the *Dakota Farmer* devoted a special edition to irrigation and headlined its main story: "Greatest Artesian Basin in the World." Already scores of deep wells had been drilled in South Dakota and some crops had been irrigated from them.

The Central Plains Frontier, 1878-1896 - 135

A farmer operating a sod buster pulled by a four-horse team on the Great Plains, about 1908.

Many residents of the Great Plains reasoned that the federal government should help to finance irrigation works for drought-stricken farmers. Governor Silas A. Holcomb of Nebraska told the legislature in 1895 that the national government had spent millions of dollars on levees, and it was just as sensible to "direct its efforts toward turning the waters of the western tributaries of the Mississippi River into great reservoirs, and thence into irrigation ditches for the development of sections of the country which produce very little."[52] Professor Garry A. Culver at the State University of South Dakota argued that Dakotans had paid some $20 million to the federal government for lands and that it was "simple justice" for the government to pay back part of this amount "to enable these two states to properly irrigate their lands."[53] As early as 1890 Senator Gideon C. Moody of South Dakota pleaded with Congress to appropriate at least $10 million to put down experimental wells.[54] However, at this time the federal government did not go beyond studying the whole problem of irrigation. The Carey Act, passed in 1894, provided for donations up to 1 million acres of land to certain states if part of the land was irrigated and cultivated, but this measure was of little or no value to the semiarid plains states.

The adjustments and changes in farm organization that began to occur in the 1890s on the Central Plains Frontier continued into the twentieth century. As a result, a more stable and prosperous farming economy developed. The new settlers who moved into the region after 1896 had the experience of earlier pioneers to guide them. Neither the farmers nor the promoters of initial settlement knew the limitations and requirements for successful dry land farming. Not even the state or federal governments understood much about it. Consequently, the farmers who settled on the Great Plains in the 1880s underwent tremendous hardships, and many of them completely failed, but out of their experiences came a more accurate and realistic view of the region's true nature and a recognition of the type of agriculture that could succeed there. The agricultural pioneers, then, made an important contribution, although the cost in suffering and human misery was high.

◁ 8 ▷

Agricultural Settlement in Oregon and Washington

While pioneers rapidly occupied the Western Prairies and large parts of the Great Plains after the Civil War, another farming frontier hundreds of miles farther west beckoned to restless home seekers. The hundreds of settlers who had migrated to the Oregon Country in the 1840s and 1850s had only begun to exploit the region's rich agricultural resources. In some localities, however, agriculture had become well established by the time of the Civil War. John Minto, who had trekked overland to Oregon in 1844 and settled in the Willamette Valley, reported in 1862 that he lived in a "roomy cottage house" and cultivated from 40 to 60 acres of land, including 17 acres of orchard. He also raised cattle, poultry and swine, and bred and sold purebred merino sheep.[1] Strictly pioneer agricultural conditions had also passed around Vancouver and Olympia in Washington Territory. At Walla Walla far to the east, local agriculture was firmly rooted by 1861.

The numerous mining frontiers in the Pacific Northwest stimulated agricultural production in both Oregon and Washington. During the 1850s strikes were made in southern and eastern Oregon, near Fort

Colville in northeast Washington, and on the Fraser River in Canada. After 1860 even more important gold rushes occurred in Idaho and Montana. The miners needed food, and Washington and Oregon farmers were in a favorable position to supply the mining towns. By 1861, for example, farmers in Walla Walla County of southeastern Washington produced substantial quantities of grain, cattle, and other supplies for the mining camps in Idaho and Montana.

Despite this regional stimulus to agricultural production, development of the farmers' frontier in the Pacific Northwest was greatly hindered by the region's isolation and the lack of railroad transportation. Before the 1870s farmers had to rely primarily on rivers and wagon roads to move their crops to market, and neither of these means was satisfactory. In 1866 Governor George L. Woods told the legislature that "a general system of railroads in Oregon is an absolute necessity," and urged the state to give whatever encouragement it "rightfully can to these great enterprises."[2] The editor of the *Morning Oregonian* of Portland wrote in 1865 that a railroad through the Willamette Valley was "what is needed to make Oregon a great state." Without railroads farmers in Oregon and Washington would be seriously handicapped, he declared. The governors of Washington Territory also pleaded for more and better transportation facilities during the 1860s. In his message to the legislative assembly in December 1867, Governor Marshall Moore insisted that completion of the Northern Pacific to Puget Sound was absolutely essential to the region's growth and prosperity. Railroads, he said, were not a mere convenience, "but a vast machinery for building up of empires."[3] In 1865 the entire question of farm marketing was pointed up further when the *Oregonian* declared that thousands of bushels of the finest fruit were lying on the ground and many farmers did not pick or box their apples because it did not pay to ship them.

In addition to practical problems of this nature facing farmers in the Pacific Northwest, the region was not well known enough to draw many new settlers. Washington editors were especially sensitive on this point. The *Pioneer and Democrat* published at the territorial capital of Olympia argued that Washington offered more inducements to settlers than either Oregon or California, but added: "Our Territory is not yet even fairly known."[4]

This observation had a large measure of truth. Except for a few areas, Oregon and Washington made up a rich but largely unsettled frontier. In 1860, the year after Oregon entered the Union and 7 years after Washington became a territory, there were only 64,059 people in the region.[5] Most of this population was west of the Cascades, mainly in the Willamette Valley. A smaller number lived between the Columbia River and Puget Sound. Oregon had 5806 farms, but Washington had a meager 1330. Only a sprinkling of settlement had penetrated east of the Cascades. Walla Walla County in the southeast corner of Washington had 188 farms in 1860, most of which had been settled the year before. However, by the eve of the Civil War, Midwesterners were beginning to give more attention to Oregon and Washington as a farming frontier. One traveler who had recently arrived in Olympia reported in 1859 that he had passed some 5000 emigrant wagons on the road between Salt Lake City and Walla Walla. He estimated that at least one-third of them would settle in Oregon and Washington. Walla Walla, he said, was presently full of emigrants.[6]

When emigrants from the Midwest or the East arrived in the Pacific Northwest, they found a considerably different environment than that to which they were accustomed. Moreover, there were great differences and variations within the region itself. The climate, vegetation, and general appearance of western Oregon and Washington differed greatly from the region east of the Cascade Mountains. West of the mountains the rainfall was much heavier. Most of the area was thickly covered with timber, and the climate was mild. In a large part of western Washington and Oregon settlers had to clear their land of brush and trees before planting crops, much as their forefathers had done on the Atlantic Seaboard 2 centuries earlier. There was some untimbered land along the rivers, but open prairie was mainly confined to the Willamette Valley.

East of the Cascades the climate was entirely different. It was dry, there was little timber, and in late summer the sagebrush and bunch grass lands presented a sterile and forbidding appearance. The rolling hills covered with bunch grass initially provided grazing for a thriving livestock industry, but in time farmers found that the uplands in eastern Washington and northeastern Oregon would raise large crops of wheat even though annual rainfall usually totaled less than 18 inches. Since most of the rainfall east of the Cascades occurred between November and March, farmers had to adjust their farming practices to meet this situation. One Oregon citizen declared as early as 1853 that farm experience in states east of the Rocky Mountains would be of little value in the Pacific Northwest. "Our climate, seasons, and soil differ from those of all of them," he wrote, "and agriculture and horticulture here must be conducted upon different systems. New experiments must be tried, and new modes adopted."[7]

Despite different climatic conditions, farmers from the older settled regions found that they could raise about the same crops that they were accustomed to growing in the Midwest. Most of the main cereals, except corn, did well, especially wheat. Even corn was raised as a garden crop by many settlers. Farmers from the central and eastern sections of the United States soon discovered that fruit growing was amazingly successful almost everywhere on this northwestern frontier. Within a few years after settlement the average farmer in the Willamette Valley, around Puget Sound, or at Walla Walla was growing an abundance of apples, pears, peaches, cherries, and other fruits. One observer near Olympia wrote in 1865 that "five years ago, fruit was a rarity for which our tongues continually watered, with only now and then a taste; now we have a sufficiency ourselves, and much to spare our British neighbors."[8]

In spite of what appeared to be favorable conditions for agricultural settlement and the movement of some pioneers into the region, there was no stampede of farmers into the Pacific Northwest immediately after the Civil War. Compared to the rushing stream of settlers who pushed into western Minnesota, southeastern Dakota, and especially into Nebraska and Kansas, the migration of settlers to Washington and Oregon seemed insignificant. Why should prospective farmers in the older Midwest want to go to the distant Northwest when they could get excellent land on the nearby prairie frontier, which was fairly close to railroads and markets? As late as the 1870s it was still a long, difficult trip from Iowa or Missouri to Oregon or Washington.

Even after completion of the Union Pacific in 1869, the rest of the trip from San Francisco to Portland or the Puget Sound area had to be made by boat. The Oregon and California Railroad Company was chartered in 1870, and it shortly began to build southward from Portland, but the through line to San Francisco was not finished until December 1887. The Northern Pacific, for which people in Washington and Oregon had such high hopes of early completion in the late 1860s, ran into financial difficulties and did not provide through connections from the East to Portland and Tacoma until September 1883. The lack of direct rail transportation between the Midwest and the Pacific Northwest undoubtedly was the major factor that deterred migration to Oregon and Washington after 1865. Additional deterrents to more rapid settlement of the Pacific Northwest were the slowness of government land surveys and occasional Indian disturbances.

Consequently, the agricultural frontier made only meager advances in Oregon and Washington during the 1860s. Writing on "Our Agricultural Resources," the editor of the *Washington Standard* declared that "those portions of our territory adapted to agriculture, are being slowly developed," and, he added, "the best agricultural tracts are not yet taken up." A few weeks later the editor wrote that he had been trying to publicize the territory's agricultural resources but had "failed in awakening the interest their importance merits."[9] The statistics bear out this observation for both Washington and Oregon.

The number of farms in Oregon rose from 5086 in 1860 to 7587 in 1870, a modest increase of only about 30 percent. In contrast, the number

Andrew R. Siegmund hauling wheat to market in Oregon. (Oregon State Library)

of farms in Nebraska advanced 450 percent during the same decade and in Kansas more than 350 percent. Between 1860 and 1870 the number of farms in Washington Territory increased from 1330 to 3127. There was a considerable advance in improved farm acreage and production throughout the settled portions of the Pacific Northwest in the 1860s, but this resulted from expansion by already established farmers rather than from a large influx of new settlers. For example, wheat production in Oregon rose from 826,776 bushels in 1859 to 2,340,746 a decade later. While the number of farms was increasing less than one third, wheat production rose nearly 200 percent.[10]

The livestock economy was more flourishing in eastern Oregon and Washington than was crop farming. Large herds of cattle and sheep ranged the hills and river valleys fattening on the nutritious bunch grass. They were then driven eastward to Montana, Idaho, and other markets. Referring to the Columbia River Valley, the commissioner of the General Land Office wrote in 1868 that the particular vegetation of that area sustained thousands of horses, cattle, and sheep, "and is justly called the glory of the vegetable kingdom in that region."[11] Counties in the

Willamette Valley also had thousands of cattle and sheep. But Umatilla County in northeast Oregon and neighboring Walla Walla County just to the north were the leading livestock counties in Washington and Oregon. The surveyor general of Washington wrote in 1870 that he believed the eastern part of the territory could support a large farming population, but so far grazing had remained the chief aspect of agriculture there.[12]

The slow progress of farm settlement in Oregon and Washington brought insistent demands for official encouragement of immigration, as well as for better transportation facilities. Declaring that the western half of Washington Territory "is about as sparse . . . as it was ten years ago," Governor William Pickering told the legislative assembly in December 1866 that roads must be built across the Cascades so settlers could easily reach the lower Columbia Valley and the Puget Sound area. Impatient because the Oregon government took no official action to promote emigration from the East and abroad, the Board of Statistics, Immigration and Labor Exchange Association, which had been formed in Portland in August 1869, urged Governor L. F. Grover to support an energetic program of immigration encouragement. A representative of the association wrote Grover in 1870 that Oregon especially needed a farming population to establish permanent homes and to develop the state's resources.[13]

It was not until 1872, however, that the Oregon legislature approved the appointment of a Commission of Immigration. But even then no money was appropriated to carry on a promotion program, and the commission had to rely on donations from private businessmen. Nonetheless, arrangements were made to distribute pamphlets, answer letters of inquiry, and to publicize the state in other ways. *Oregon and Her Resources*, which boasted of the state's agricultural prospects, was published in 1872. In 1874 Oregon established a State Board of Immigration, but the members served without salary and did not have funds for a large-scale publicity program. The Oregon State Immigration Society, a private corporation, was chartered in 1877. Operating in Portland on private funds, it distributed a wide variety of promotional material. In Washington the official efforts to draw immigrants were equally ineffective. Governor Edward S. Salomon urged the legislative assembly in 1871 to set up a territorial board of immigration, and Governor Elisha P. Ferry repeated the recommendation 2 years later. Although the legislature took no action in 1873, the next year a group of women organized an immigration association. Viewing the valuable work of this voluntary group, the legislature in 1875 and during subsequent years provided pamphlets for distribution and gave other types of assistance. However, neither Oregon nor Washington went into the business of immigration promotion like the states east of the Rocky Mountains.[14]

The propagandistic publications that were distributed were similar in content and design to those published in other frontier states and territories. These pamphlets boasted of the rich soil, the wide variety of crops, and the ease with which a settler could make a living. One observer wrote in 1869 that there was no part of the world in the temperate zone "where a man can obtain a living so easily, and live so long, as he can in Washington Territory west of the mountains [Cascades]." Promoters also argued that there were no cold winters or hot summers, that water and timber were abundant, at least west of the Cascades, and that farmers did not have to combat drought and grasshoppers. Admitting that hard times prevailed everywhere, the editor of the *Willamette Farmer* declared in 1874 that farmers in Oregon were immeasurably better off than those poor settlers in Kansas, Nebraska, and Dakota who were suffering from drought and having their meager crops devoured by ravenous grasshoppers.[15]

Those who were interested in attracting new immigrants to the Pacific Northwest were disturbed when California seemed to be enticing many settlers supposedly on their way to Oregon and Washington. In 1874 a writer for the *Willamette Farmer* accused California of standing astride the main arteries of transportation and deterring people from migrating to Oregon. He declared that the "parched plains of southern California are talked up as a paradise and the immigrant is directed thither instead of being permitted to work his way to better opportunities to be found to the northward." Then the writer insisted that Oregon must have direct rail communication with the East "completely independent of California."[16]

What conditions confronted farmers who did migrate to the Pacific Northwest in the first decade after the Civil War? Where did they locate, how did they get land, what did they raise, and in general how did farmers fare on this distant frontier? The acquisition of land was the first problem facing new settlers. By 1865 most of the prairie land in the heart of the Williamette Valley was already in private hands, although much of it was not under cultivation. In 1850 Congress had passed the Oregon Donation Act, which granted to qualified persons who had been in Oregon before September 1, 1850, a half-section of land, or a full section of 640 acres to a man and his wife. Persons who settled between December 1, 1850, and December 1, 1853, were to receive 160 acres if single and married couples were to receive 320 acres. Under this law 7317 donation claims were filed for 2,563,577 acres. The terms of the law applying to Oregon were extended to Washington Territory in 1854, although only 985 claims were entered there for a total of 290,215 acres.[17]

The Donation Acts permitted early occupants to acquire either 640 or 320 acres of the most easily worked prairie lands, but this was far more than the average family could use or cultivate in the 1850s and

James Gist's homestead, near Mehama, Oregon. (Oregon State Library)

1860s considering the stage of agricultural technology and the lack of transportation and markets. Consequently, almost constant demands were made during the late 1860s and early 1870s that these large land holders sell part of their holdings in order to increase settlement. The land ought to be subdivided and occupied by actual settlers, said the editor of the *Willamette Farmer*, rather than remain in the hands of large landholders. Thickly settled communities based on small and productive farms, he said, would not only be better for the economy but would sustain schools, churches, and other social institutions.[18]

By 1870, however, a newcomer who desired good improved land in the Willamette Valley found that he had to pay as much as $15 to $30 an acre, and a well developed farm could command as high as $50 an acre. This was far more than the ordinary pioneer could pay. Consequently, he bought land in the foothills and valleys of the tributaries of the Willamette River or in the heavily covered timber lands in the area between Vancouver and Puget Sound. Good unimproved land in these areas sold for $8 to $15 an acre, but rougher lands could be purchased for around $5 an acre, and sometimes less. In 1875 the *Willamette Farmer* wrote that a settler could find fairly satisfactory land at a price

Agricultural Settlement in Oregon and Washington - 145

of from $2 to $10. The Northern Pacific Railroad advertised farm lands in 1872 at $2.50 to $7 an acre and offered credit over a 7-year period.[19]

Like other states and territories, Oregon and Washington had several million acres of land for sale, which they had obtained for internal improvements, schools, and other purposes. A new settler then might buy land from a private party, from the state or territorial government, or the railroads. Finally, of course, he could preempt or homestead part of the public domain. The areas open for homesteading were not considered the most desirable because they were usually not close to transportation and markets. Therefore, relatively few homesteads were filed in either Washington or Oregon in the 1860s and 1870s. Between 1863 and 1880 only 9785 homesteads covering 1,268,899 acres were entered in Oregon and 9504 in Washington.[20] The total homestead entries of 19,289 filed in Washington and Oregon during this period was small compared to the 62,379 in Minnesota and 58,560 in Nebraska.

Once a settler had acquired land, his next task was to build a house and prepare some land for cultivation. Construction of a home was not difficult in western Oregon and Washington where timber was so abundant. It was both easy and cheap to build a log house, but many pioneers used rough boards if there was a sawmill nearby. The boards were placed upright, and the cracks between them were covered with another strip of lumber. The ordinary house was 14 to 16 feet wide and about 20 feet long. Logs were also split for rail fencing to enclose gardens and small fields. The next problem for the pioneer was to clear his land of brush and trees. Farmers generally cut the timber in June, let it dry until September, and then burned it. This was hard work, and many farmers who had left the prairies of Iowa or Missouri found clearing land a distasteful and heartbreaking job. A popular song, which described the difficulty of clearing land, said:[21]

> *I took up a claim in the forest*
> *And set myself down to hard toil*
> *For three years I chopped and I niggered*
> *But never got down to the soil.*

After trying to establish farms in heavily wooded areas, some pioneers became disgusted and moved east of the Cascades or returned to the Midwest.

The main cereal crops of pioneer settlers in the Pacific Northwest were wheat and oats. The Willamette Valley was known for its wheat production even before the Civil War, and wheat had also been grown successfully for many years in the Puget Sound area. Reports of 30 to 60 bushels an acre were common. By 1869 Oregon farmers were producing 2,340,746 bushels of wheat with production centering in Yamhill, Polk,

Lane, Linn, Benton, and Marion counties. Farmers raised nearly as many oats, which were used to feed livestock. Most settlers also grew potatoes and other vegetables as well as fruit, which throve in this region. Farmers east of the Cascades also raised wheat and oats. In 1869 Walla Walla County produced 110,905 bushels of wheat, more than half the total raised in Washington Territory. Fruits and vegetables also did well. While crops were important, most of the early settlers, both west and east of the Cascades, depended heavily on livestock and livestock products for their living.

The economic condition of agricultural pioneers on this isolated frontier can best be understood by looking at a few local communities and at some individual farmers. The manuscript census of agriculture reveals that there were 17 farmers in Fall Creek township of Lane County, Oregon (Eugene) in 1870. Their land holdings varied from 40 to 660 acres, and the improved acreage ranged from a low of 6 to a high of 480 acres. Farms were valued at between $400 and $3000 each. Every settler had milk cows and 15 of the 17 made butter. All the farmers reported horses, and 12 owned sheep. The main crops in the township were wheat, oats, hay, and potatoes. Of the 17 farmers, 12 raised wheat, 14 produced oats, 12 cut hay, and 14 raised potatoes. Five of the settlers had fruit and seven sold a few dollars worth of forest products. The value of farm production varied from a low of $145 to a high of $1024. However, most farmers in the township raised between $200 and $600 worth of livestock, grain, and other products.

One of the farmers in Fall Creek township was John H. Hill, a 36-year old native of Illinois. He had only 6 acres of improved land, 70 acres that were unimproved, and 20 acres of woodland. His farm was valued at $800. In 1869 Hill raised 150 bushels of oats, 15 bushels of potatoes, and made 25 pounds of butter. His livestock consisted of three horses, two milk cows, one "other cattle," and three pigs. The total value of his production was given as $237. Nearby lived James Vickers, who had migrated from Arkansas. He had 320 acres of land with about 60 acres under cultivation. The rest was unimproved agricultural land and woodland. Vickers valued his farm at $1200, or a little less than $4 an acre. He had two horses, two milk cows, and 30 swine. During 1869 the family made about 100 pounds of butter. Vickers raised 200 bushels of wheat, 150 bushels of oats, 14 bushels of potatoes, and 1 ton of hay. He estimated the value of his products for 1869 at $317.[22] The same picture of small, diversified agricultural operations also prevailed north of the Columbia River in Washington.

East of the Cascades in Washington and Oregon, most of the settlement in 1870 was in Walla Walla and Umatilla counties. More than one-fifth of all the farms in Washington were around Walla Walla, and

Umatilla ranked eighth among Oregon's 17 counties in the number of farms. As was true west of the mountains, the amount of land held by farmers in the drier eastern section varied a great deal, and the quarter-section farm was much less common than on the prairie-plains frontier. In Walla Walla County, for example, of the first 80 farmers listed in the census of 1870 only 30 of them had the traditional 160 acres. Farm organization centered around a livestock economy supplemented by the production of cereals, especially wheat and oats, and hay, potatoes, fruits and vegetables.

As was common on other agricultural frontiers, many settlers arrived in the Pacific Northwest with meager capital resources. Although it was often said that a poor farmer who worked hard could acquire financial independence, more caution prevailed on this point in Oregon and Washington than on the prairie-plains frontier. Even the promotional agencies frankly admitted that a farmer needed some money to establish a paying operation. In *Oregon and Her Resources* a prospective settler was told that if he did not have enough money to pay for a farm, he should at least be able to meet the first installment in cash and have enough funds to purchase livestock and other needed property to put the farm on a paying basis. In the 1880s the Oregon State Board of Immigration declared that farmers who intended to immigrate to that state should have at least sufficient capital to make them independent for 1 year. Older farmers were admonished not to go to the Pacific Northwest unless they had some money. One bit of official advice from the Oregon Board of Immigration in 1887 concluded: "families who contemplate settling on government lands will require, after providing for all traveling expenses, from $500 to $800, with which to meet the cost of putting up a house, for livestock, seed, farming implements, provisions and so forth."[23] Many farmers, however, arrived with less than the desired amount of capital. Some of them earned needed money by taking off-farm work in the lumber and fishing industries, but most successful farmers gradually built up their store of capital from the production of their farms.

Although life was hard for the agricultural pioneers in the Pacific Northwest during the 1860s and 1870s, it was probably easier for a poor man of limited capital to get established and to make a living than it was on the prairie-plains frontier in the same period. The main disadvantage was the cost of getting to Oregon or Washington. But once a settler and his family arrived, they could usually make a livelihood. While timber was scarce in some areas east of the mountains, west of the Cascades settlers had the advantage of free building material and fuel. Lumber could also be sold, which meant that farmers had another cash crop. Moreover, crop failures were rare. The region was not entirely devoid of occasional droughts and damage from insects as the local promoters claimed, yet difficulties of this kind were infrequent. Because so many kinds of vegetables, fruits, and berries did well, an enterprising farmer could raise a large part of the necessary family provisions. Unlike the pioneers in parts of Dakota, Nebraska, and Kansas, settlers in the Willamette Valley or the Puget Sound Basin, or even in the Walla Walla Valley, did not have to worry about whether they could grow enough potatoes or other staples to supply the kitchen table. The milder climate also reduced livestock losses, and the average per acre crop production was usually higher in Washington and Oregon than in the states east of the Rockies. Because of these factors, the periodic want and destitution prevalent on the prairie-plains frontier in the late nineteenth century was virtually unknown in the Pacific Northwest.

One of the worst handicaps for pioneer farmers in Washington and Oregon continued to be the lack of adequate transportation and markets. The high cost of moving commodities to market tended to keep the farm price of agricultural products low. For example, in 1872 wheat brought as much as $1.45 to $1.50 a bushel in Portland, but the price paid to farmers at Corvallis about 80 miles south was only 70 cents.[24] As mentioned earlier, fruit in the Willamette Valley was often not even harvested because there was no profitable market at hand, although one authority estimated that in 1865 $100,000 worth of apples were shipped from Portland to San Francisco.[25] The main artery of transportation that connected settlers east of the Cascades with oceangoing vessels was the Columbia River. However, the portages required at the Cascades and at the Dalles farther up the river made this means of transportation slow and costly.[26]

The transportation situation was improved somewhat during the 1870s by the building of local railroads. In 1873 the Northern Pacific was completed from Kalama on the Columbia northward to Tacoma. This especially helped farmers in the Cowlitz Valley. Two years later the Walla Walla and Columbia Railroad connected by rail the 32 miles between Walla Walla and Wallula on the Columbia River. Additional construction also occurred in the Willamette Valley. However helpful these local lines may have been, they did not solve the basic problem. One of the worst aspects of the Panic of 1873 on the Pacific Northwest was the general effect that it had on retarding the building of railroads. This extended the period of isolation for Washington and Oregon.

There was no letup in the demand for a transcontinental railroad, which would provide direct connections between the Northwest coast and the Midwest. The editor of the *North-West Tribune* told of a farmer near Colfax in eastern Washington who had recently taken 500 pounds of cheese to town but could sell only 12 pounds. No market existed, the editor declared, because merchants could not ship the produce out of the territory and, consequently, trade was limited to home demand.

"Nothing but a railroad," he concluded, "will ever be able to carry the surplus produce of this country to where it can find a market."[27]

The main market outlet for farmers in the Pacific Northwest was first at Astoria and later at Portland, about 110 miles inland on the Columbia River, which became the main shipping point by 1870. Wheat was transported on riverboats to Astoria or Portland where it was loaded on oceangoing vessels for shipment to other parts of the United States or abroad. Much of the coastal trade was with San Francisco, and by 1869 Portland was becoming a busy center for the shipment of wheat and flour.

Despite the slow development of transport and market facilities in Oregon and Washington, agriculture made substantial progress in the 1870s. The number of farms in Oregon more than doubled between 1870 and 1880, increasing from 7587 to 16,217. The percentage increase was nearly as large in Washington Territory where the number rose from 3127 to 6529.[28] In the decade of the 1870s wheat production expanded in Oregon from 2,340,746 to 7,480,010 bushels. Except for Umatilla County, and to a lesser extent Union County, which was also in the east, most of this increase was in the Willamette and Umpqua valleys. While Washington produced much less wheat, total production increased from 217,043 in 1869 to 1,921,322 a decade later. Nearly half the wheat production in Washington was in Walla Walla County, but by 1879 Columbia and Whitman counties were beginning to produce several hundred thousand bushels. During the 1870s there was a tremendous expansion of wheat production in the eastern counties of Walla Walla and Umatilla. Output in Umatilla County jumped from only 28,209 to 915,571 bushels between 1869 and 1879, an increase of more than 30 times. Production of 779,907 bushels in Walla Walla County in 1879 represented a rise of 350 percent during the previous decade. Frontier conditions had passed in this region, and the growing number of commercial farmers needed markets. It is no wonder that insistent demands continued for better and cheaper transportation.

The growing number of farms and increased cultivated acreage indicated that the Pacific Northwest agricultural frontier was becoming better known among prospective farmers. More and more settlers were seeking opportunities there. Most of the pioneer farmers who migrated to Oregon and Washington in the period from 1870 to 1890 came from the midwestern states of Missouri, Iowa, Illinois, Indiana, and Ohio. For some it was the second, third, or even fourth move. The manuscript population census, which records the birthplace of family members, presents a revealing picture of restless pioneers who were ever seeking a new El Dorado. For example, a 35-year old farmer in Umatilla County had arrived there after at least two earlier moves. He had been born in Maine and married a girl from Indiana. The first children had been born in Minnesota, a 4-year old child was born in California, and two additional children were born in Oregon. Quite a number of settlers in Washington and Oregon arrived by way of California.[29]

Up to about 1875 most of the newcomers sought farms west of the Cascades. Outside of Umatilla County in Oregon and Walla Walla County in southeastern Washington, the millions of acres of rich valley and rolling prairie land east of the mountains still awaited the agricultural pioneer. By the middle 1870s, however, farmers began to occupy the area northeast of Walla Walla to the Snake River. Several hundred settlers moved into Columbia and Garfield counties, which lay mostly in an area between the Snake River and the Blue Mountains east of Walla Walla.[30] Farther north, some stockmen and farmers were beginning to settle in the Palouse country between the Snake River and Spokane Falls, and at the same time settlers pushed south and southwest from Umatilla County into Union, Grant, and Baker counties. Here occurred the phenomenon of some farmers moving from west to east, from the Willamette Valley and the Puget Sound area to eastern Washington and Oregon.

Outside of stock raisers, farmers had largely avoided the high bench lands, which were covered with bunch grass, as well as the sagebrush lands, in eastern Oregon and Washington, because it was thought they would not produce cereals. By the late 1870s this idea was changing. The Surveyor-General of Washington wrote in 1879 that "the hills and upper table and even the sage-brush lands"[31] would produce fine wheat. Although most of eastern Washington and Oregon received less than 20 inches of rainfall annually, most of it fell in gentle showers during the winter months. At first, most farmers planted spring wheat, but within a few years they learned that winter wheat did better under the prevalent rainfall pattern and general climatic conditions.[32]

The Palouse country became one of the most fabulous wheat-growing areas in the entire United States. An extensive rolling plateau of about 2500 feet elevation, it extends about 60 miles north and south and 50 miles east and west. The soil is extremely fertile, dark loam of volcanic origin. Organized in 1871, Whitman County makes up the heart of the Palouse region, which also extends into northwest Idaho. The normally dry appearance of the area, as well as the hills and steep slopes, convinced the first settlers that the region was fit only for ranching accompanied by small-scale farming in the creek and river bottoms. Gradually, however, farmers found that wheat would grow well on the sidehills and hilltops.

After 1875 settlement began to increase throughout the eastern parts of Washington and Oregon, and by 1880 the trickle had grown into a mighty stream. Emigrants came from the Midwest and Plains States, California, as well as from the Williamette Valley and western Washing-

Agricultural Settlement in Oregon and Washington - 151

ton. While many settlers arrived by rail and water, thousands made the long overland trip by wagon. On July 29, 1876, the *Washington Standard* reported that many emigrants were arriving at Walla Walla from the Plains States, and a few weeks later another dispatch said that 17 immigrant wagons, mostly from Kansas, were on their way north from Walla Walla in search of farms. One observer reported in July 1880 that "a few days ago a train passed through Walla Walla, en route to the Spokane Country, which had made the passage from Bates County, Missouri, in the short time of 90 days, with horse teams."[33] As a result of this migration, pioneer farmers quickly scattered over much of eastern Washington between Walla Walla and Spokane. In the fall of 1881 it was reported that "in every direction from Cheney [Spokane County], for miles and miles, a great amount of breaking has been done this year preparatory for sowing next year. The soil looks black and rich, and the enormous yield this year justifies us in the belief that next year" grain production would surprise everyone.[34]

Again it was land that drew farmers to the Palouse and surrounding areas of eastern Washington and Oregon. Years later when some of the early settlers were asked why they settled in the Palouse region, they gave such replies as, "father had heard and read glowing accounts about the fertile prairies of eastern Washington;" "we found all the good land taken up in the Willamette Valley and we heard there was still plenty of land in the Palouse Country;" or "we were driven out of Kansas by the grasshoppers and were looking for a better farming country."[35] The earliest settlers stayed within about 20 miles of the Idaho border. It was widely held in the late 1870s and early 1880s that the western part of the Palouse region where the rainfall fell to between 12 and 15 inches was not suitable for crop farming. However, as the better lands to the east were occupied the newer settlers had to seek land in the drier area farther west. At first these farmers concentrated on raising livestock, but by the middle 1880s they found that wheat would also do well there because the meager moisture usually fell at the right time.

A huge amount of government land was available in eastern Oregon and Washington, but the railroads and other transportation companies also held large acreages. The Northern Pacific Railroad, for example, owned about one-half the rich farm land in Whitman County. This was sold to settlers for between $2 and $10 an acre, depending upon the location and quality of the land. In some cases credit up to as much as 10 years was extended to farmers who bought railroad land. Although there was no boom in government lands on this frontier comparable to that in Dakota, Kansas, and Nebraska in the same period, thousands of homesteads, timber culture entries, and preemption claims were filed. In the decade following June 30, 1880, there were 22,692 homesteads entered in Washington and 14,774 in Oregon. Of the 22,692 homesteads filed in Washington Territory during the 1880s, final entries were made on 8673, or about 38 percent.[36] The problem of farmers getting land did not seem to be a serious one.

As in most pioneer areas, grain-raising was begun on a small scale in the Palouse region. However, farmers soon brought in the latest machinery and greatly enlarged their acreages. One observer reported that in 1877 10 theshing machines, 95 sulky plows, 100 noble plows, 15 gang plows, 41 reapers, 14 mowers, 21 horse rakes, 14 headers, six harvesters, two self binders, and other machinery were shipped up the Columbia and Snake Rivers to Almota to be used in Whitman and other nearby counties.[37] By the 1880s, gang plows, drills, reapers, headers, and threshers were all in widespread use in eastern Washington and Oregon as wheat growing became very highly mechanized in that region. Midwesterners were amazed when they first saw four- and six-horse teams plowing, or even more teams pulling a header over the steep hillsides of the Palouse. It was a remarkable sight.

The threshed grain was handled differently in this region than it was in the Midwest, where it was hauled in a wagon directly from the threshing machine to an elevator or granary. The wheat growers (locally called ranchers) sacked the grain as it came from the thresher, a system also followed in California. The sacks were then left stacked in the fields without any shelter until it was convenient for the farmer to move them to market or storage. The grain did not suffer damage because rain scarcely ever fell during that time of year. Elevators were not common in the Palouse and surrounding areas until after about 1890.

Throughout the 1880s wheat became the major cash crop of farmers in the great Inland Empire of Washington. Looking north and west from the Blue Mountains in southeastern Washington, one observer declared in 1883 that the whole area looked like one vast wheat field. "We gaze for miles and see nothing but fields of grain, stretching away in one continuous succession of farms until they blend with the distance," he wrote. "Such another view cannot be seen on the continent."[38] By the late 1880s farmers began to take up land in the Big Bend country west of Spokane, a dry region previously thought to be fit only for stockmen. However, by 1889 there were 1327 farmers in Lincoln County where it was found that both oats and wheat did well. In that year more than 300,000 bushels of wheat were raised. Settlers continued to move into that area, and on June 12, 1890, the Spokane Falls *Review* declared that ranch lands were "now fast being converted into wheat fields. . . ."

By 1889 the main wheat-growing counties of eastern Washington contained 8617 farms. This was 47 percent of the total farms in Washington, and they produced 93 percent of the territory's wheat crop. The crop of 1890 was simply tremendous in the Palouse country. One writer said: "Never saw anything like it in my life. It is piled everywhere, thousands upon thousands of tons." The railroads could not handle the deluge of wheat, even though in October eight to 10 trains a day passed through Palouse City. In February 1890 the elevator company at Rosalia reported that it was shipping 70 carloads of wheat daily.[39] Large amounts of wheat were also grown in eastern Oregon, especially in Umatilla and Union counties.

The rapid advance of the transportation frontier in the Pacific Northwest during the 1880s did much to stimulate commercial agricultural production, and played a large part in bringing pioneer farming to an end in many communities. When track was laid between Celilo and Wallula in 1882, Walla Walla County wheat farmers had direct rail service to Portland. In September 1883 the long-delayed Northern Pacific was completed and traffic was opened between Portland and Saint Paul. The main line of the Northern Pacific and some of its branch lines ran through, or close to, some of the finest wheat lands in eastern Washington. A year later the Oregon Short Line joined the Oregon Railway and Navigation Company at Huntington, Oregon, providing railway connections between Oregon and the Union Pacific in Wyoming. In 1887 the Northern Pacific built through the Yakima Valley and over the Cascades to Seattle. Altogether, these and other lines broke down the region's isolation and opened up additional markets for farm products.[40]

Although wheat was the main cereal crop in eastern Washington and Oregon, farmers did not devote their entire efforts to wheat growing. They also raised oats, barley, Irish potatoes, and forage crops. Many of the pioneer settlers also planted fruit trees. As one pioneer put it, people "craved fruit." By the 1880s fruit was a source of considerable income to farmers in eastern Washington. Apples, peaches, pears, and cherries were the leading fruits in Columbia, Walla Walla, Whitman, and Spokane counties. In 1883 the Northern Pacific began plans to transport fruit in refrigerator cars from eastern Washington and Oregon, and one obsever predicted that the farmer who owned a bearing orchard would have a "veritable gold mine."[41] Large-scale, commercial fruit growing, however, did not develop until well into the 1890s. Most farmers continued to rely on a combination of grain farming and livestock production. Fruit-growing for the average small farmer was important mainly because it helped supply his family table with good food.

Although parts of eastern Washington and Oregon could be farmed successfully under conditions of natural rainfall, large areas in that region required irrigation for crop production. If farmers, for example, were to settle on the arid, sagebrush lands in the Yakima and Kittitas valleys where the rainfall was around 8 inches a year, some means of irrigation had to be found. Although these lands appeared barren, they were extremely productive when watered. The earliest settlers east of the Cascades, including Marcus Whitman, successfully irrigated some crops. In 1866–1867 experiments with irrigation began near Yakima, and at about the same time a few farmers started to irrigate small tracts in the Okanogan country farther north. By 1870 there were small spots of irrigated agriculture around Walla Walla, Yakima, and other places in eastern Washington, and in Umatilla County, Oregon. These early attempts at irrigation in eastern Washington and Oregon were a part of the general movement to reclaim arid lands throughout all of the West.

During the 1870s a few settlers moved into the Yakima Valley and diverted water from the Yakima River and other streams to irrigate small patches of hay, wheat, vegetables, and fruit trees. But this area still remained the domain of the cattlemen. In 1880 there were only 226 farms in Yakima County, and these were mostly cattle ranches. The cost of clearing and ditching the land, as well as the expense of diverting water, discouraged most farmers from moving into the region. Moreover, there was not even a good wagon road from Yakima to the Columbia River. In the 1880s, however, a number of large irrigation companies were organized, which built ditches and sold land to farmers with a perpetual water right. The price varied from about $40 to $60 an acre. Among the prominent firms were the Moxee Ditch Company and the Northern Pacific, Yakima and Kittitas Irrigation Company.[42] By 1889 about 15,129 acres were under irrigation in Yakima County and 25,212 in Kittitas.[43] Specialized agriculture developed early in this region because the high cost of land and water made it imperative to concentrate on high income crops. By 1890 fruit, vegetables, and to some extent dairying had all become important. Cereals were of secondary importance. In 1891, for instance, 92 carloads of potatoes were shipped out of the Yakima Valley, and in 1895 fruit exports reached 30 carloads. Irrigation continued to expand in Washington during the 1890s. By 1899 there were 3153 farmers who irrigated 135,470 acres. Of these 101,061 were in Kittitas, Yakima, and Walla Walla counties.

At the same time irrigation was developing rapidly in the arid regions of eastern Oregon. By 1899 about 387,095 acres were being irrigated there, which was more than twice the figure in Washington. However, in Oregon a much larger part of the irrigated acreage was devoted to grass and forage rather than to fruits and other specialized crops. In other words ranchers were irrigating in order to raise a supply of winter feed.

By the 1890s the frontier period of agricultural settlement in Oregon and Washington was drawing to a close. There were still millions of acres of unsettled land both east and west of the Cascades, and the number of farms continued to grow. But pioneering in the true sense was all but

Agricultural Settlement in Oregon and Washington - 155

gone. Improved transportation and marketing facilities had been created, and new farmers who might venture into the forest or onto the plains east of the Cascades were usually not far from a well-developed community.

West of the mountains the farms tended to be small and diversified. The average-sized farm in the region between the Columbia and Puget Sound in 1900 was between 100 and 150 acres, and farmers raised mainly wheat, oats, hay, vegetables, fruits, and livestock. This pattern of production was established early and did not vary much over the years. There were some areas of agricultural specialties. For instance, in the Puyallup Valley near the southern end of Puget Sound farmers began raising hops about 1870 and by 1890 Pierce and King counties were producing 7 million pounds annually. Wheat continued to be the main cereal crop in the Willamette Valley, but, as mentioned earlier, farmers there were generally quite diversified.

East of the Cascades in the area from Walla Walla to Spokane a huge cereal empire had developed where by 1900 highly mechanized, large-scale operations were common. The farms in Walla Walla and Whitman counties averaged 633 and 379 acres, respectively. Many farmers in this region also raised fruit and vegetables and maintained herds of livestock, but the major emphasis was upon wheat. By the turn of the century the importance of irrigated farming in eastern Washington and Oregon was well recognized, and already much had been done to reclaim thousands of the arid but fertile acres. The main problem was to control the water resources so that more land could be brought under cultivation. Throughout all the area east of the Cascades, farmers and ranchers pastured thousands of cattle and sheep on the rough, dry prairies, which were unsuited for crop production.

Although not nearly as many farms were established in Oregon and Washington during the late nineteenth century as there were in the Dakotas, Kansas, and Nebraska, farmers who did settle in the Pacific Northwest built a successful farm economy.[44] They adjusted their crop and farm organizational patterns to fit the climatic and soil conditions, which were new to many of the settlers, and within a remarkably short time they laid the base for a varied and productive agricultural economy.

◁ 9 ▷

The Farmers' Frontier in California, 1850-1900

When the United States took control of California in 1848, few Americans had any idea about, or interest in, the agricultural possibilities of that distant and unfamiliar frontier. During the preceding years, Mexicans and some American settlers from east of the Rockies had engaged in a primitive, easy-going, pastoral type of farming, but other than a few ranchers who had large herds of cattle the production of agricultural commodities was small. There were only 872 farms in the entire state when the first census of agriculture was taken in 1850.

The Gold Rush of 1849 changed all this. The initial effect of the frantic search for gold disrupted business and agriculture as men left their businesses and abandoned growing crops in the mad pursuit of elusive riches in the foothills east of Sacramento. This situation, however, did not last long. The influx of thousands of people into the San Francisco Bay region and the accompanying demand for food products convinced some settlers that there was more profit in raising high-priced grain, vegetables, fruits, and livestock than there was in working a pan or sluice box. One old man advised his sons: "Plant your lands; these be your best gold fields, for all must eat while they live."[1]

The rapidly increasing demand for food by the thousands of gold seekers was met within a remarkable short time by the established producers who enlarged their operations and by settlers who opened up new farms. It was estimated that in 1852 California had 110,748 acres of crops, and 3 years later the State Agricultural Society reported 461,772 acres under cultivation, of which 148,595 were in wheat and 108,924 acres in oats.[2] Governor John Bigler may have exaggerated slightly when he said that by 1854 agricultural production was generally sufficient to supply the home market, but California was rapidly approaching that position. The production of potatoes and onions was equal to demand as early as 1852, and in 1856 some 33,088 bushels of wheat and 114,572 barrels of flour were exported from San Francisco to eastern markets and abroad. A writer for the agricultural census of 1860 declared that "one of the most wonderful features of the grain trade is its growth and development on the Pacific Coast." California, he said, had until recently been almost entirely dependent upon imports of grain, but now frequent dispatches tell of ships "loaded with wheat" sailing from San Francisco for Liverpool or London. "Riches, other than gold, have been found on the soil," he concluded. The State Agricultural Society reported in 1857 that California was as eminent in agriculture as in mining, and 2 years later the editor of the Sacramento *Daily Union* declared that the most notable feature of California's agriculture was its ability to meet the need for home consumption.[3] This condition was achieved because of the rapid expansion of this far western farmers' frontier.

Between 1850 and 1860 the number of farms rose from 872 to 18,716. Most of the new farm making in the 1850s occurred fairly close to the main centers of population. The region within about 100 miles south, southeast, east, northeast, and north of San Francisco, and including the counties of Alameda, Santa Clara, Contra Costa, Sonoma, Mendocino, San Joaquin, Sacramento, Yolo, and Solano contained most of the farms. Outside of this region, Los Angeles County was the only other area that had any substantial agricultural enterprise. In other words, settlement was largely confined to the middle portion of the Central Valley plus small areas west of the coastal ranges.

California's great Central Valley stretches from Redding in the north about 450 miles south to below Bakersfield. It is a vast trough-like plain some 40 to 70 miles wide, bordered on the east by the Sierra and on the west by the coastal ranges. It includes about 11,500,000 acres of land. The northern portion is drained by the Sacramento River and much of the southern part by the San Joaquin. The great majority of California's good farmland lies is this Central Valley, which contains fertile soil but where moisture is deficient in many areas. The average annual rainfall at Sacramento is about 16 inches. At Fresno to the south the annual average precipitation is less than 10 inches, and at Bakersfield only about 6 inches of rain fall each year.

When emigrants arrived in California, they were often shocked and dismayed as they looked westward from the crest of the Sierra across the Sacramento Valley toward San Francisco. If they came in the summer, as most of them did, the vegetation was dry, the ground was cracked, and the temperature was often above 100 degrees. The entire valley looked desolate and inhospitable. Could this be the rich and productive California about which they had read? Some of the early emigrants went on to Oregon or returned to the Midwest before they really understood the region's agricultural possibilities. Many of the goldminers who did not see enough of California to realize the varied forms of farming that might be developed, gained the impression that California was a desert. Failing to find gold, they then left the state. One newcomer who drove south from the San Joaquin River into the center of the great plain reached a point where he lost sight of the surrounding mountains through the haze. Unable to see anything but barren plain, he reportedly exclaimed: "My God! we're out of sight of land."[4]

There were a few perceptive individuals who recognized the valley's true potential. While time may have dimmed his memory I. N. Hoag, who achieved prominence in immigration and agricultural promotion, recalled years later that when he returned from the mines in October 1849, he reached a point where he could view the vast expanse of level plains stretching westward to the opposite coastal range. Suddenly, Hoag said, he realized that the Valley "looks more like the Garden of Eden than the barren country we have all taken it to be."[5] The Central Valley may not have been a Garden of Eden, but it was soon found that the land was suitable for wheat, barley, and other crops if farmers adjusted their operations to fit the climate and soils.

One of the first things that settlers from the Midwest had to realize was that most of what they had learned back home did not apply on this new agricultural frontier. They could not simply transfer the old procedures and ways of doing things and expect to succeed. The rainfall pattern, for example, was entirely different from that in the Midwest and was more like that in eastern Washington and Oregon. There were not really four seasons, but two—a wet and dry season. Most of the moisture fell between November and May. The hot, rainless summers left the soil so baked and hard that a plow could hardly penetrate the ground until after the late fall rains began. Most of the plowing by early settlers was done in November and December after which the grain was planted. By January, when snow blanketed the upper Mississippi Valley, the fields were beginning to turn green in California. At the same time the valley pastures and foothill ranges began to show signs of renewed life. Conditions were so different from the areas where most of the emigrants had learned their agricultural lessons that some of the state's leading farmers and businessmen became convinced that something must be done to collect and distribute accurate information about California's agriculture. Consequently, the California State Agricultural Society was established in 1854.

Although it may have seemed that nature was turned around for the emigrant from the Midwest, he quickly adjusted to new conditions. One of the most notable things about California agriculture was how soon farmers discovered the best use of their land and what crops were most successful under particular climate and soil conditions. In fact, this was true all over the western agricultural frontier during the late nineteenth century. The main exception to this generalization was the slowness with which farmers abandoned corn in western Nebraska and Kansas. But in a surprisingly short period, farmers throughout the West found what products did best and they did this without the help of colleges of agriculture or extension services.

The first farmers in the Sacramento Valley occupied the bottom lands, although some settlers moved into the foothills of the Sierra near the mining camps and to hilly land close to San Francisco Bay where they raised crops and livestock. Even though the area immediately adjacent to the Sacramento River flooded periodically, this land was part of the earliest settled portions of Yolo and Sacramento counties. One observer said that in a wet year the Sacramento Valley looked like a great inland sea, and later levees were built to contain the water. Nonetheless, as early as 1849 and 1850 farmers began growing crops along the river. Vegetables and fruits did best there, except in dry seasons when wheat and barley grew well. By the middle 1850s vegetable and orchard farms had developed for miles on each side of the river. A committee of the California State Agricultural Society reported in June 1857 that one farmer 3 miles from Sacramento kept four wagons running into town daily with vegetables for the local market. He also had fruit trees and vineyards.[6] Farther back from the river on the flat lands of Yolo and Solano counties the land was ideal for wheat and barley, the state's two leading cereal crops.

Some valley farmers also had land in the nearby foothills, but in the initial years of settlement this was generally used only for grazing. These mountain spurs, which extended into the valley, were covered with nutritious bunch grass and some wild oats. But as early as 1860 the editor of the *California Farmer* said that he was gratified to see the hills back of Benicia producing a good crop of grain. People had previously thought these highlands were almost worthless, he continued, but now they were proving very valuable. Grain, orchards, and vineyards were all being planted on the foothills.[7] Although some of the foothills along the Sierra and elsewhere remained unsettled for another 2 decades or more, it is clear that in some localities the value of these lands was recognized during the first few years of the state's agricultural development. This was true mainly, however, only in areas close to San Francisco Bay or the Pacific Ocean.

Pioneer farming and well established agriculture, small operations and tremendous estates, developed side by side in the middle sections of the Central Valley. Probably no agricultural frontier in the United States presented a picture of such sharp contrasts as the region around Sacramento, Stockton, and San Jose during the 1850s and 1860s. For example, Jerome C. Davis lived on Putah Creek about 12 miles west of Sacramento. His farm covered 8000 acres of rich valley land, of which 1000 acres were enclosed by a good fence. Davis pumped water from Putah Creek with a 10-horsepower steam engine to irrigate his orchards and vineyards. In 1856 he had 400 acres of wheat and barley on unirrigated land, which produced more than 30 bushels to the acre. Another large operator 3 miles west of Davis had 1600 acres under fence, and his farm contained a large amount of additional land. A thousand acres of wheat and barley were harvested on this place in 1856, and the machinery included 20 wagons, 50 plows, 25 harrows, two threshing machines, seven reapers and mowers, four hay presses, and other implements. Farther west toward the foothills John Wolfskill had more than 11,000 acres of land, and he had already become widely and favorably known for the great variety and quality of his fruit. A visiting committee of the State Agricultural Society found many other farms around Sacramento, Stockton, San Jose, and in the Napa Valley, which were large, productive, and apparently prosperous. Reporting on its visits, the committee often referred to the large and commodious farm homes and the fine hospitality extended to its members. These farmers seemed to be enjoying a good life as early as the middle 1850s and had passed beyond the frontier stage.[8]

Representatives of the State Agricultural Society confined their visiting and reports to the large and well-to-do farmers. They failed to mention the hundreds of pioneers who were pushing into the Central Valley and trying to establish homes for themselves and their families. To get information on these people it is necessary to go to the manuscript census of agriculture, where an account of their land, livestock holdings, and field productions are recorded. Vacaville township in Solano County was about 30 miles west of Sacramento. Consisting both of flat bottom land and foothills, this township had 389 farmers in 1860. While John Wolfskill and some of his neighbors had already established large agricultural enterprises, there were many small farmers in the area. Josiah Root, for instance, had 120 acres of improved land, which he valued at $1100. He owned one horse, five milk cows, 12 other cattle, five swine, and valued his machinery at $50. In 1859 he raised 50 bushels of wheat, 100 bushels of barley, 100 tons of hay, and made 100 pounds of butter.

Pioneer conditions were more characteristic in Tremont township, which was located entirely in the valley bottom east of Vacaville. In 1860 there were 83 farmers in the township, but many of them had no improved land, which probably means that they settled on their farms the year before. Only seven of these farmers grew any wheat in 1859. In one part of the township several farmers concentrated on market gardens, and about half the settlers had milk cows. Some pioneer farmers reported no land at all, but this did not mean that they were laborers. These settlers were small ranchers who ran their cattle and sheep on the public domain or on unoccupied portions of large estates and were in the process of becoming established farmers. In Putah township of Yolo County the census reveals that one landless farmer had 800 sheep and another 60 head of cattle. The picture was much the same in eastern Alameda County, which was newly settled in 1860. Only 12 out of 68 farmers in Murray township had improved land, and only eight raised wheat in 1859. Forty-one of the 68 settlers had 160 acres of land, which they valued at $200 to $500, and their principal enterprise was raising sheep and cattle.

The first settlers who moved into the Central Valley and along the foothills in the late 1850s were generally stockmen. But in a very short time most of these farmers began growing wheat, barley, and oats. During the 1860s the livestock industry showed a relative decline as thousands of Central Valley farmers concentrated their efforts on wheat raising. Almost from the outset of settlement, farmers also developed fruit production. The editor of the Sacramento *Daily Union* declared in 1859 that one of the most distinguished characteristics of California agriculture was the progress that had been made in raising fruit. Besides apples, pears, peaches, small fruits, berries, vine-growing and wine-making had proven successful. Los Angeles County was particularly noted for its grapes. Within a decade after statehood, the *Daily Union* correctly predicted that orchard fruits "will ever constitute an important feature of our state's agriculture."[9] Commercial fruit growing was an aspect of the farmer's frontier that was different to many new emigrants.

As an increasing number of pioneers sought to establish farm homes on the California frontier they were faced with the problems of land monopoly and the uncertainty of land titles. During the Mexican period several hundred large land grants had been made to residents in California. John A. Sutter was only one of many occupants of California in the 1840s who held thousands of acres under this system. By the treaty of Guadalupe Hidalgo the owners of these lands were to have their titles confirmed by the United States government. However, after American occupation many questions arose about the validity of the claims. In 1851 Congress enacted a law that provided for setting up a board of commissioners to take testimony and to determine the legality of the grants. Decisions of the board could be appealed to the courts. Once title had been established, the land was to be surveyed and any land in rejected claims was to revert to the public domain. Although 563 claims were eventually confirmed, the system of confirmation worked a genuine hardship on the grantees to prove their claims in court in the face of unfriendly public opinion both in California and in Congress. The deep-seated feeling against big estates and land monopoly, which was so strong in American thinking, brought the large landholders under severe criticism regardless of any legal rights. The sentiment against them was especially bitter among squatters.[10]

In his annual message of 1854 Governor John Bigler declared that the unsettled condition of land titles was the greatest obstacle to California's future agricultural expansion. Until the boundaries of the Mexican land grants were definitely determined, he said, settlers would hesitate to locate preemption claims. The State Agricultural Society reported in 1859 that 227 private ranches had been surveyed, which covered 4,067,640 acres or an average of 17,920 acres each. The society complained that the average large estate contained enough land for 112 farms of 160 acres each. Other claims totaling 14,712,358 acres were in various stages of litigation.[11] A decade later land monopoly was still considered a hindrance to the small farmer. The State Agricultural Society declared that, despite excellent natural advantages for agriculture, California did not have as many farmers as it should have. The reason for this was that millions of acres were held in large estates and the land was left uncultivated and unproductive. Moreover, the Central Pacific Railroad held several million acres. In 1869 two citizens of Yolo County wrote that land monopolists had raised a barrier to immigration "more insurmountable than the Sierras—harder to overcome than the deserts which lie between us and the people we covet."[12]

Since most of the best land had fallen into private hands by the 1860s, the new settler found that he had to pay considerably more than the government price of $1.25 an acre, and good land for homesteading was virtually nonexistent. Undeveloped lands held by individuals and the railroads sold for between $2 and $10 an acre. Lands that could be purchased for the lower figure were largely in the foothills or in the southern counties where it was too dry to grow grain under natural rainfall conditions. In fact, the State Agricultural Society reported in 1870 that there were no cheap lands left that were suitable for grain.

The price and kind of land available in Yolo County west of Sacramento was discussed in detail by two residents of Woodland in 1869. They explained that there was no government land in the county on which a poor man could settle and make a living. While many acres were for sale, the price was far beyond what an ordinary immigrant could pay. Yolo County, these men declared, could support four times as many people as presently lived there if they could acquire land. But prices of improved land ranged from $30 to $50 an acre, and some sold for as much as $200. Government land, or that which could be purchased for $2 to $4 an acre, was in the foothills or mountain districts fit only for vines and orchards. These lands did not appeal to the poor immigrant because he could not afford to wait 3 or 4 years for his orchards and vineyards to produce. Furthermore, there was little opportunity for renters. These observers reluctantly concluded that Yolo County "can offer no good reasons why immigrants should seek her borders; and this remark applies to the state at large." Certainly, there was nothing in California, they said, that would cause a settler to pass up government lands in Kansas or Nebraska and move to California—nothing, that is, except climate.[13] The *Pacific Rural Press* also charged that inordinately high land prices were deterring immigration.

The critics of land monopoly may have been too pessimistic about the opportunities yet open for farmers, but they touched on one of the most serious problems for agricultural development in California. Despite all the advertising in the 1860s and 1870s about California being a place for the poor pioneer to be successful at farming, it actually took more capital to begin operations there than most anywhere in the trans-Missouri west. The citizen who looked at the situation honestly admitted that the chance for a new settler to succeed without some financial backing was not very good.

There were relatively few homesteads entered in California compared to the states on the prairie-plains frontier. During the 7 years between 1863 and 1869, inclusive, only 2848 homesteads were filed in California for a total of 414,861 acres. This was fewer homesteads than were entered in Minnesota during 1867 alone, and covered less land than that held by a dozen large proprietors. Beginning in 1871 homesteading in California began to increase, and during the following decade between 1000 and 2000 homesteads were usually filed each year. The high point of homestead filing before 1880 in California occurred in 1876 when 3584 entries were made. This was the highest figure for any state that year.[14]

The 2848 homesteads filed in California before 1870 indicated a scarcity of good government land available for public entry and also reflected a general slowness in establishing new farms during the 1860s. Part of this was because of the distance of California from the Midwest and the lack of direct railway transportation before the Union Pacific and Central Pacific were completed in 1869. This continued uncertainty surrounding land titles and the dry years of 1863 and 1864 also discouraged farmers and retarded settlement. But more important was the fact that tremendous amounts of good land were still available in the two tiers of states and territories west of the Mississippi River. Considering the entire western agricultural frontier, distant California was not in a favorable position to compete for pioneer settlers. The number of farms in California rose only from 18,716 in 1860 to 23,724 in 1870. The great increase in agricultural output, which saw wheat production, for example, advance from 5,928,470 bushels in 1859 to 16,676,702 in 1869, came from the expansion of established agricultural enterprises rather than from new farms.

Californians believed that an average increase of only about 500 farms a year during the 1860s was due to the lack of railroad transportation and the scarcity of immigration. The *California Farmer* declared in March 1865 that the state's greatest need was for more people to occupy the fertile valleys and hillsides. The Board of Agriculture explained a year later that "our resources are so much greater than our ability to develop, that the demand for immigration may be said to be universal." Governor H. H. Haight told the legislature in 1869 that the encouragement of immigration from the eastern states and Europe was recognized by all who were "interested in our material development." California had tremendous resources, he said, but needed "an agricultural population" to develop them.[15]

A wide variety of promotional literature was aimed at enticing farmers to California. Bentham Fabian's, *The Agricultural Lands of California* (1869) declared that "no country in the world offers to the farmers greater inducements than does California. In general, land is rich and cheap." However, Fabian denied his own statement when he later admitted that in the Napa Valley land sold from $25 to $100 an acre, and in Yolo County "every acre of it is settled on and held at a high price." *All About California and the Inducements to Settle There* (1870), published by the California Immigrant Union emphasized the availability of railroad land. As was true in other western states and territories, special immigration agents and railway representatives did everything they could to foster immigration. The California Immigrant Union, formed by a group of San Francisco businessmen in November 1869, spent $24,931 during the next 2 years in promotional activities. It distributed 28,943 pamphlets and leaflets in the United States and 13,680 abroad.[16]

By 1870 the promoters had overdone themselves and people who arrived in California found hard times and limited opportunities. The editor of the *California Farmer* wrote that anyone working to attract more immigrants in California was a candidate for the insane asylum. There were 20,000 to 40,000 men out of work in San Francisco, he said; what the state needed was capitalists with money to invest, not just more people. The *Pacific Rural Press* warned newcomers not to come to California "without some money." After several years of hard times, the editor said that farmers would eventually get favorably located "and none of these will starve or suffer for want to shelter, though they may have to rough it for a season. . . ."[17]

The demand for improved transportation was as insistent as that for more immigration. This plea was met by completion of the Central Pacific and Union Pacific, the building of numerous branch lines, and construction of other major railways. But the early joy at the sight of steaming trains soon turned sour. The State Board of Agriculture reported in 1871 that the railroads had brought in neither the immigrants nor the capital that had been expected. Moreover, the large land holdings of the railroads aroused bitter complaints. Governor Haight insisted that the government had been too liberal in its land grants and argued that the public lands belonged to the public. If some remedy were not provided, he said in 1871, people who had been "defrauded . . . of their rightful patrimony" might revolt in the future.[18]

Following the early period of settlement when demand for food products exceeded supply, marketing became a problem for California farmers. Initially, much of the barley was sold to teamsters who hauled goods to the mining camps, while wheat was disposed of at local mills. Farmers shipped their produce on the rivers and hauled fruit and grain overland from Yolo and Solano counties to Suisun Bay, where they were loaded on boats and taken to San Francisco. By the 1870s railroads were providing much of the transportation to San Francisco from the producing regions and large quantities of agricultural produce were being exported from California. In 1869, 5,530,624 bushels of wheat, 390,519 barrels of flour, 40,126 bushels of potatoes, 91,211 pounds of cheese, 109,488 pounds of butter, and 87,546 pounds of hams and bacon were exported from San Francisco. By 1876 wheat exports totaled 9,693,231 bushels and large amounts of other agricultural products were also shipped abroad and to eastern markets.[19] Most of California's fruit and vegetables continued to be sold locally, although in 1876, 13,746 pounds of dried apples and more than $100,000 worth of other fruit plus 31,699 gallons of wine were exported.

During the decade from 1870 to 1880 the number of farms in California increased from 23,724 to 35,934. However, the average size of farms continued to be large, dropping only from 482 to 462 acres. Criticism of huge estates and demands that large landowners sell part of their holdings at reasonable prices to newcomers had little or no effect on opening up farming opportunities for the poor emigrant in the most productive areas. Consequently, thousands of the new farms had to be located in the foothills and in the southern part of the Central Valley where irrigation was necessary for assured crop production.

By the early 1870s people were just beginning to appreciate the foothills, bordering the Central Valley. While the foothills in Sonoma, Marin, Napa, and Solano counties had long been cultivated, the hilly areas beyond the reach of bay and ocean fogs had been regarded as of little value. But farmers were now proving that the Sierra foothills were highly productive, especially for vineyards and orchards.[20] Since there was practically no cheap land still available in the great valleys where dry-land farming could be carried on successfully, the main prospect for new farmers was in the foothill region.[21] Only there could a settler obtain land for $1.25 to $2.50 per acre. In 1878 one observer estimated that approximately 3 million acres were avaliable for settlement under the federal land laws in the foothills of the Sierra. With better transportation and communication, he believed that happy people would soon dot "the foothills from one end of the state to the other."[22] This region did provide the main outlet for frontier settlement. During the 1870s, for example, the number of farms in Butte County, which had a good share of hilly land, rose from 510 to 999, and more than half the total ranged between 100 and 500 acres in size.[23]

New farms could also be opened up in the southern San Joaquin Valley, but the cost was high because of the need for irrigation. Although dry farming had been partially successful in the northern half of the Central Valley, severe droughts and periodic crop failures had emphasized the need for irrigation, especially in the area south of Stockton. In 1863 and 1864 crops were a total failure throughout parts of the Central Valley, and thousands of cattle perished. Governor Frederick F. Low declared that the drought of 1864 could prove useful if it showed the need of providing a general system of irrigation for "our noble expanse of valley land." In its report for 1864–1865, the State Board of Agriculture called on the federal government to grant public land to the state for the purpose of financing irrigation projects. Disastrous droughts in 1870–1871 and again in 1876–1877 resulted in heavy agricultural losses and continued to emphasize the need for irrigation. The editor of the *Pacific Rural Press* wrote in October 1871 that debt was the only crop raised during the preceding long drought.

By the 1870s irrigation had become a matter of statewide concern. The *Pacific Rural Press* declared late in 1871 that several years of poor crops in the San Joaquin Valley and elsewhere had "drawn attention to the necessity for some general system of irrigation."[24] In a memorial to Congress in 1872 the California legislature asked that alternate sections of land be granted to irrigation companies that were constructing irrigation ditches. The dry plains, legislators said, could not be settled by men of small means until water was made available. Governor Romualdo Pacheco declared in 1875 that irrigation had become of paramount importance to California. "Agriculture, which has been our leading industry," he observed, "has met with a serious check on the very threshold of a vast expansion." Much good land that was capable of being converted into farm homes, he continued, was worthless and would remain so until "redeemed by baptism." In 1881 Governor George C. Perkins explained that the southern part of California could not be farmed successfully without irrigation and that dry farming would "bring defeat to the man of humble means" and monopoly of land by a few big operators would be the outcome if irrigation were not provided.[25]

By the 1870s, then, California agriculture was at the crossroads. Except for the foothills, most of the land that was suitable for dry-land farming had been occupied. There was no room left for the new settler unless he was prepared to buy an improved farm at high prices. While land in the foothills could be acquired quite cheaply, it was not easy to develop a paying farm there. These lands were best suited to vineyards and orchards rather than grain, and the capital costs of establishing an orchard or vineyard were high, and returns came in slowly. In some areas it was estimated that it took $50 an acre to bring an unirrigated vineyard into production.[26] If irrigation were necessary, it would be $15 to $20 more.

The farming frontier in California was definitely tied to the growth of irrigation, and the development of facilities to transport water longer distances from the main rivers and streams. Action by individuals, companies, or government, or a combination of all three, was needed to overcome the handicaps of nature and break the bonds that circumscribed agricultural growth. Despite the glowing accounts published about opportunities for farmers in California, a realistic view showed that there was even less cause for poor settlers to pass up Minnesota, eastern Dakota, Nebraska, or Kansas and move to California in the 1870s than there had been a decade earlier.

Irrigation of dry California lands was nearly as old as settlement. During the Spanish and Mexican periods, streams had been diverted around Los Angeles and elsewhere to water crops of fruit, vegetables, and grain. Expansion of irrigation continued in the early American period. In 1856 William Wolfskill in Los Angeles County had 45,000 grape vines, a large number of orange trees, 1000 bearing apple trees and other fruits.[27] Former Governor John G. Downey wrote in 1860 that Los Angeles and San Bernardino counties had 2 million grape vines and with an "increased supply of water for irrigation" many times that number could be grown.²⁸ As mentioned earlier, farmers around Sacramento were also irrigating fruit and vegetables in the 1850s. By 1867 some 10,000 acres were under irrigation in Los Angeles County and 21,000 acres in Yolo County.²⁹ These two counties had about 44 percent of the total irrigated crop land, most of which was in vines, orchards, and vegetables, with some grain and grass. By 1870 the most extensive vineyards in the state were in the bottom lands of the Los Angeles, San Gabriel, and Santa Ana rivers. Alfalfa had become a major irrigated crop in Yolo County. In Kern County at the south end of the Central Valley the first irrigation ditches were constructed between 1858 and 1860, although very little progress was made there before 1867.³⁰

Recognizing the limitations of dry-land farming, Californians worked hard to expand irrigation facilities after 1870. The Fresno River canal was started in November 1872, and by 1874 a dam, headgates, and canal had been completed. Farther north the Farmers' Irrigation Company of Merced took water from the Merced River. The Kings River and San Joaquin Company diverted water from the San Joaquin River and by 1874 was operating a canal about 40 miles long.³¹ By 1877 the Board of Agriculture estimated that there were 611 irrigation ditches in the state that provided water for 202,955 acres. This was nearly three times the acreage under irrigation in 1867. Merced County ranked first with 37,000 acres, but it was closely followed by Los Angeles County, which reported 36,750 acres under ditch. By 1879 the total acreage being irrigated rose to 292,885. About 188,000 of these acres were on the San Joaquin plains, 82,485 acres in Los Angeles and San Bernardino counties, and 13,400 in the Cache Creek area of the Sacramento Valley and smaller amounts elsewhere.³²

Because of the large capital requirements to build dams, headgates, and canals, most of the irrigation projects undertaken during the 1870s were constructed by water, land, and railroad companies, who then sold land to prospective farmers along with a water right. These firms diverted large amounts of water from the rivers and streams under the doctrine of prior appropriation, which came into direct conflict with the principle of riparian rights that Americans had taken from the English. Under the practice of riparian rights, the use of water was limited to the owners of the land along the stream and all others were prohibited from using the water if that use diminished or altered the flow. If the riparian system were strictly followed, it would prohibit the diversion of water from streams and rivers except by those who held adjoining lands. This would confine irrigation to a small area along the creeks and rivers, leaving the more distant lands without water. Such a system was obviously a deterrent to establishing many new farms distant from the main water channels.

In the California mining camps the doctrine of prior diversion or appropriation had developed. This gave both riparian and nonriparian owners the right to divert water for beneficial use. The first priority went to the person who established the initial appropriation. Consequently, irrigation in California first developed under the common law of riparian rights and the statuatory code of appropriation. When the appropriators began to take large quantities of water from the rivers and streams, a fierce battle ensued between the riparianists and appropriationsts. The courts were filled with suits of water owners, appropriators, and rival companies during the 1870s and early 1880s. This situation continued until the Wright Law was passed by the California legislature in 1887, which provided for the creation of irrigation districts. As C. C. Wright said, this measure was passed "with the object in view that there might be created a special government for the one purpose of developing and administering the irrigation water for the benefit of the people." The greatest obstacle to successful functioning of the irrigation districts was lack of confidence in district bonds, necessary to raise money to build irrigation works. However, the district system was a great advance over the unsettled conditions prior to 1887 because it assured a wider distribution of water, which was absolutely essential for the creation of new farms in the arid sections of California.[33] As Governor George Stoneman told the legislature in 1885, the whole controversy over irrigation policy was not just one between riparian claimants and appropriators of water, or a contest between corporate interests and individual interests. The real conflict was whether irrigation would be held along the river valleys or whether water would be moved out onto the dry, fertile plains.

Despite the conflicts over water rights in California between 1870 and 1886, rapid progress occurred in irrigated agriculture. By 1889 about 13,732 farmers were irrigating 1,004,223 acres of land, mostly in the area between Stockton and Bakersfield. Kern, Tulare, and Fresno counties contained nearly half the total irrigated acreage. By this time 26 percent of California's farms were irrigated, covering 8⅕ percent of the improved farm acreage. Besides irrigating from rivers and streams, Californians drilled hundreds of deep wells to tap the subterranean supply of water. By 1889 about 2000 wells were used to irrigate 38,378 acres in California.[34] At that time California had more irrigated agriculture than any other state, although by 1900 Colorado had pushed into first place.

The increase of irrigated agriculture in the arid sections was also reflected in the expansion of specialized crops for which California was rapidly becoming famous. The value of the state's orchard products rose from $1,384,480 in 1869 to $2,071,314 in 1879. While the value of orchard products was not given in the census of 1890, the production of 1,654,636 bushels of apples, 970,941 bushels of apricots, 154,063 bushels of cherries, 1,691,019 bushels of peaches, 577,444 bushels of pears, and 1,202,573 bushels of plums and prunes in 1889 indicated a tremendous growth in fruit growing during the 1880s. Irrigation also permitted a great expansion of citrus fruit. By 1889 California had 13,196 acres of bearing orange trees, which produced 1,245,047 bushels of oranges valued at $2,271,616. The citrus industry was concentrated in San Bernardino and Los Angeles counties. Market gardens also developed on a commercial basis, and the value of products reached $1,420,565 by 1889. Although not all the vineyards were under irrigation, much of the expanded viticulture industry depended upon an artificial water supply. California had 155,272 acres of bearing vines in 1889 and produced 1,372,195 boxes of raisins and 14,626,000 gallons of wine plus many tons of table grapes. Vineyards, however, were not confined to any particular area, and farmers raised grapes all the way from the foothills of the Sierra Nevada in the north to San Diego in the south.[35] By the middle 1880s large quantities of California fruit were reaching the Midwest, the East, and even foreign markets. In 1887 Omaha received 89 carloads of fruit from California while 59 and 92 carloads were shipped into Kansas City and Saint Louis, respectively. Dried and canned fruit were also exported outside the state. Moreover, many kinds of nuts, including almonds, pecans, and walnuts, were grown commercially and sold all over the country.

One of the most notable characteristics of California agriculture was the fact that such a large percent of the total product was represented by specialized crops, found to be so well suited to the soils and climate. Although cereals continued to be important, 64 percent of the value of all crops by 1899 came from noncereal commodities. Specialized, commercialized farming began very early in the history of California farming, and this trend gained momentum as the nineteenth century progressed. By 1900 the number of specialties was probably greater, and the degree of commercialization higher, than in any other state in the Union.

The effect of irrigation went far beyond increased production. Wherever water could be brought to otherwise fertile but nonproductive soil, the price of land shot up to fantastic heights. In 1889 the editor of the Sacramento *Daily Record-Union* warned prospective settlers from the Midwest that they must be prepared for the shock of being asked $300 to $500 an acre for a bearing vineyard. Actually, this was an underestimate, and some orchard and vineyard land was valued at $1000 to $1500 per acre. Unimproved arid land, which would hardly bring $5 an acre before water was made available, often commanded $100 to $200 after water was supplied. This, of course, greatly increased the amount of capital needed by new settlers, even if they sought to establish intensive farming on only a small plot of 40 acres or less.

One farmer who settled in the San Bernardino Valley in the late 1880s bought 10 acres for $100 an acre. With his wife, three children, and one part-time hired hand he set out walnut trees, planted 3 acres of raisin grapes, 1 acre of assorted fruits, 3 acres of alfalfa, some strawberries and blackberries, 1 acre of wheat, and some corn and vegetables. He had two cows and some chickens. During the first year he sold eggs, butter, potatoes, green corn, and other products for a total of $886. By living frugally, he and his family spent only $365, leaving a profit of about $50 an acre. After his vines began to produce, it was estimated that his income would increase some $2000 anually. According to the editor of the Sacramento *Daily Record-Union*, the experience of this pioneer family on the desert of southern California could be duplicated many times. However, he admitted that many small farmers of this kind had failed.[36]

In much of the farming area between Stockton and San Diego, dryland wheat and barley fields began to be divided into smaller farms for orchards and vineyards during the 1880s. In parts of the state, said the editor of the Sacramento *Daily Record-Union*, this change amounted to an agricultural revolution. The increasing percentage of small, specialized, highly capitalized and productive farms reflected this important trend. About 14 percent of California's farms were between 10 and 50 acres in 1880, while 22 percent and 29 percent were in this category in 1890 and 1900, respectively. In Los Angeles County, for example, the average size of farms declined from 337 to 136 acres during the 2 decades before 1900. The average size of farms in Fresno County, where irrigation expanded rapidly after 1880, was only about half as large in 1900 as it had been 20 years before.

Although there was a tremendous expansion of orchards, vineyards, and garden vegetables by California farmers after 1880, cereals, especially wheat, continued to be highly important and was the state's main agricultural export commodity. From the outset of settlement, wheat had been the major grain crop, and some farmers planted it 10 and 15 years in succession. The mania for wheat was not unlike that experienced in parts of Minnesota, Dakota, and Kansas in the 1870s and 1880s. One editor wrote in 1868 that in the wheat country the main topics of conversation were rain and the Liverpool market. Lands in the northern part of the Central Valley, which could be farmed without irrigation, and areas where it was too costly to get water on the land for fruit growing, dryland wheat, and barley farming made up an important part of the state's agriculture. It should be emphasized again, however, that after 1880 there was little room for new settlers. The best land was occupied, what could be purchased was expensive, and the mechanization of California cereal production demanded capital requirements far beyond

172 - *The Farmers' Frontier in California, 1850-1900*

A scene of a farm and repair shop. San Lorenzo, Alameda County, California, 1878. (Bancroft Library, University of California)

the means of most pioneers seeking new homes. Consequently, wheat production remained in the hands of big operators who were highly mechanized and specialized. About 6 percent of the wheat was irrigated in 1899, but most of it was raised under conditions of natural rainfall. Summer fallowing was adopted in the drier regions where it took all the moisture that could be conserved in 2 years to raise one crop.

Between 1869 and 1889 California's wheat production jumped from 16,676,702 to 40,869,337 bushels. Both acreage and production dropped somewhat by 1899, but California ranked sixth among the nation's leading wheat-growing states. Bonanza operations much like those in the Red River Valley of North Dakota and Minnesota also developed in California. In other words, where proprietors had large acreages and sufficient capital and labor, they could and did establish large-scale, highly commercialized wheat farming. On large wheat ranches the land was plowed with gang plows and sown with a broadcast seeder sometime between September and December. Harvesting was done with 12-foot headers pulled by six horses or mules. The cut grain was elevated into wagons from the header platform, after which it was stacked or taken directly to the steam-powered thresher. The threshed wheat was placed in sacks holding about 2¼ bushels and later hauled to market. Much of the labor required at harvest time was employed on a temporary basis, and Chinese coolies were often used in the grain fields. Almost from the beginning of settlement wheat-growing in California was highly mechanized.[37]

Although there were experiments with a combined harvester-thresher in California as early as 1868, and perhaps earlier,[38] it was not until the late 1870s that these machines proved practical. A combined harvester-thresher was tried near Modesto in 1877, but it was not entirely successful. During 1877–1878, several combines built by Holt and Rice at Stockton were used on nearby farms. These machines cut and threshed the wheat in one operation. They were pulled by 16 to 20 horses or mules at about 2½ to 3 miles an hour, cutting a swath 16 to 18 feet wide. In one operation 35 to 40 acres of grain a day could be cut, threshed, sacked, and made ready for market. Although only a few combines were in use by 1880, their popularity increased among the big producers during the following years.[39]

There were some huge wheat ranches in California by the 1870s and 1880s. Three large farms in the San Joaquin Valley covered 36,000, 23,000, and 17,000 acres, respectively, much of which was in wheat. The largest of these farms raised 1,440,000 bushels of wheat in 1872. With land stretching for 17 miles, when men started to plow in the morning they ate lunch at a midway station and reached the end of the field by nightfall. After eating supper and staying all night, the workers then returned to the other end of the field the next day.[40] While wheat production only averaged about 13 bushels per acre in the 1880s, which was among the lowest of the western states, large-scale, mechanized production made wheat the most profitable crop on hundreds of thousands of acres.

During the early years of American settlement, California farmers plowed and planted too late to get the best crop of wheat. Because they did not begin to plow until after the rains started in November or December, it was often January or February before the wheat was sown. As a result, wheat often did not mature before dry, hot weather set in. By the 1870s farmers were either summer fallowing or plowing earlier with their improved plows. Then they sowed their wheat in the dry soil, or, as it was known, dusted it in. The wheat lay dormant until the first rains came when it began to grow. This method of wheat farming proved much more successful because it took advantage of every bit of rainfall.

Besides raising grain, fruit, vegetables, nuts, and many other products, California farmers carried on an extensive livestock business. Both large ranchers and small farmers had stock and dairy cattle. Dairymen who lived in the Central Valley often took their cows to the foothills and mountain plateaus during the hot summer months and engaged in a sort of nomadic dairy system. There they made butter and kept it fresh in the cold streams and snow banks. When the weather turned cold, these farmers took their herds back to the home place. Some dairymen lived in the foothills, and one writer said in 1878 that "mountain butter has become a standard article over the whole coast."[41]

California agriculture quickly passed through the pioneer stage. In a remarkably short time farmers learned the problems and peculiarities of the state's climate and soils and adjusted their operations to them. By the 1870s and 1880s the main patterns of agricultural production had been established. Because of the limited amount of land that was suitable for dependable dryland farming, farmers turned to irrigation and developed an intensive, highly commercialized type of agriculture. In some places 10 or 15 acres of land were much more valuable and productive than a quarter-section in Kansas or Nebraska. At the same time some areas lent themselves to extensive operations where large amounts of land, labor, and capital were employed to raise thousands of bushels of wheat and barley.

Indeed, the picture of California agriculture at the end of the nineteenth century was one of endless variation and richness. Moreover, a good balance had been achieved. In 1899 about 26 percent of the farmers derived their principal income from grain and hay, 25 percent from fruit, 21 percent from livestock, 12 percent of the operators received a majority of their income from dairy produce, and the remainder from miscellaneous operations. California ranked fourteenth among all states in value of farm products in 1899, but was exceeded only by Iowa, Kansas, Minnesota, Nebraska, and Texas in the states that drew most of their settlers after 1865. It seemed as though California had lived up to the claims of even its most boastful promoters. Yet, it never became a haven for many poor settlers who hoped to get a better stake in the West's agricultural life. Except in a few areas, California farming took capital, knowledge, and business acumen, which most frontiersmen in the late nineteenth century did not possess.

Expansion of California's farming frontier had been sparked by the Forty-Niners. A decade later, the Fifty-Niners in Colorado and other Rocky Mountain states stimulated agricultural beginnings in that region. By the 1870s and 1880s not only farmers in California but those in all of the Rocky Mountain states were sharing the common experience of developing farm and irrigation practices, which would permit successful production in the arid and semiarid West.

◁ **10** ▷

The Rocky Mountain Farming Frontier

When Senator Benjamin Wade once visited Utah, he met an old friend from Ohio. How do you like this country, Wade asked? "Very well," his friend replied. "It would make a nice country if there was a little better society and plenty of water." To this Wade retorted, "I should think so. A little better society and plenty of water would make hell a paradise." While this story is probably apocryphal, it points up the key to agricultural development in the vast Rocky Mountain region all the way from the Bitter Root Valley of western Montana to the Rio Grande Valley in New Mexico. That essential element was water.

The area that ultimately made up the states of Montana, Idaho, Wyoming, Utah, Colorado, New Mexico, Arizona, and Nevada covers 897,010 square miles, or some 590,086,400 acres. The eastern portions of Montana, Colorado, Wyoming, and New Mexico are a part of the Great Plains, but the remainder of this huge region consists of mountain ranges, dry plateaus, sandy deserts, and fertile river valleys. With few exceptions the entire region is arid, and crops do not do well without irrigation. The Mormons, however, found as early as 1847 that where water was applied to the gray, dry, sterile-looking soil, abundant crops could be raised. Their success with irrigated farming along the west edge of the Wasatch Range in Utah encouraged the development of irrigation in scores of small and large river valleys all over the arid West.

Here was a vast frontier largely unknown to pioneer farmers and one, which, because of its aridity, would require all of the initiative, imagination, and energy they could muster before it could be brought into production. Despite some local successes in agriculture, no one in 1860 had any idea how much of the tremendous landscape between El Paso and Missoula was suitable for agriculture, and few cared. There was still plenty of good land in the states and territories east of the 98th meridian. Why would anyone even consider going to the Rocky Mountain territories to farm? The area was inhabited by savage Indians, most of the land was not surveyed, and there were no markets for produce outside of a few army posts. The census of 1860 showed a population of only 174,924 people, mostly in New Mexico (which then included Arizona), Utah, and Colorado. About 10,000 of these people gave their occupation as farmers, but the census takers listed only 8812 farms. Because population and farms in western Montana and Idaho were included in the Washington territorial returns, there was undoubtedly a little larger population and a few more farms than the above figures indicate. A fair estimate seems to be that in 1860 there were about 9000 farms in the area that later comprised the Rocky Mountain States. Practically all were in New Mexico and Utah.

In any event, production was small. New Mexico produced 709,304 bushels of corn and 434,309 bushels of wheat in 1859, while farmers in Utah grew 384,892 bushels of wheat, meager amounts of corn and oats and 141,000 bushels of Irish potatoes. In both territories the farmers ran cattle and sheep.[1] Settlement was mostly confined to a small area east and south of Salt Lake, along the Rio Grande between Santa Fe and El Paso, and near the mountains north and south of Denver. Otherwise, except for small isolated settlements this great expanse of territory was nearly as innocent of agricultural development as it has been centuries before.

The mining rushes into Colorado, Nevada, Idaho, Montana, and elsewhere after 1859 created a sudden interest in the agricultural possibilities of the Rocky Mountain region. By this time California and Oregon were self-sufficient, but they did not yet have large surpluses to export. Moreover, the cost of transporting flour, vegetables, and other provisions from either Oregon or California, to say nothing of Missouri or Iowa, to mining camps in Colorado, Montana, and Idaho was extremely high. Thus the influx of thousands of people into the mining communities stimulated agricultural production in the immediate vicinity of the mines as well as in the peripheral areas such as Walla Walla and the Mormon settlements. As in California, the demand for commodities in these isolated places increased prices to where it was more profitable to raise wheat, potatoes, or meat than it was to pan for gold. One Observer estimated in 1866 that Montanans were spending $1 to $1½ million annually for Utah flour.[2]

During the 1860s several thousand farms and ranches were established within reasonable marketing distances of the mines. In Montana several hundred farmers and ranchers moved into the Gallatin, Jefferson, and Madison River valleys west of Bozeman. "Beautiful ranches have sprung up like magic upon the Sun, Deerborn and Prickly Pear rivers," wrote Inspector General D. B. Sacket in July 1866. He said that the valley "in front of Helena, through which meanders the Prickly Pear, Ten Mile and Silver creeks, dotted with its fine farms, covered with herds of cattle and sheep, presents as beautiful a panorama as the eye ever rested upon. . . ."[3] By 1870 there were 851 farms in Montana, of which 178 were in Gallatin County (Bozeman)—the main center of the territory's agricultural development. In Gallatin County alone 84,494 bushels of wheat, 68,520 bushels of oats, and 37,530 bushels of barley were grown in 1869, which was 47, 45, and 43 percent respectively of the territory's production of these crops. From this area products could be hauled to Virginia City and other mining camps. Montana farmers also raised 91,477 bushels of Irish potatoes and produced 408,080 pounds of butter. They had 12,432 milk cows and 22,545 head of other cattle. Farm production was determined to a large extent by the market demands. Wheat was made into flour, oats was sold to teamsters, and potatoes and butter found ready buyers.

About 200 to 300 miles southwest across the mountains from Helena a sprinkling of farmers gradually moved to supply the needs of prospectors at Orofino, Pierce City, Florence, and other Idaho mining towns. The valleys of the Clearwater, Salmon, Payette, and Boise rivers on the west side of the territory were well situated in relation to the diggings that were drawing thousands of prospectors by 1861. The volcanic soil of the Boise and Payette valleys was almost unbelievably rich when irrigated. These early agricultural settlements were either in, or adjacent to, the great Snake River Valley, which covers much of southern and western Idaho. While a large part of the main Snake River Valley was later brought under cultivation, the first farmers and ranchers settled mainly along the Boise and Payette rivers, where it was quite easy to divert water for irrigation. Moreover, this was fairly close to some of the principal mining districts, such as the one around Idaho City.

The increasing demand for food by the thousands of miners in Idaho during the 1860s far exceeded production by local farmers. By 1870 there were only 414 farms in the entire territory. About 65 percent of the total, or 269 farms, were in Ada County, where the capital of Boise City was located. Seven other counties reported farms, but none of them had more than 35. The main cereal crops were wheat, oats, and barley. Practically all the 75,650 bushels of wheat produced in 1869 were raised in the Boise Valley. Besides cereals, Idaho farmers and ranchers grew 64,534 bushels of potatoes, $16,865 worth of garden vegetables, and produced 111,480 pounds of butter. Meat and milk were provided from 9934 head of milk cows and other cattle.[4] Considering that Idaho had a population of about 15,000 in 1870, it is easy to see why the territory was not yet self-sufficient in food production. Consequently, large quantities of farm products continued to be imported from around Walla Walla, and from Utah.

While the agricultural frontier was establishing a foothold in the mountain and river valleys of Montana and Idaho in the 1860s, the Mormons were rapidly expanding their farming operations in the Great Basin of Utah. By the time of the mining strikes, Mormon farmers had laid a productive base so that agricultural output could be enlarged to meet much of the increased demand. It was in Utah more than anywhere else that farmers first brought the natural factors of agricultural production— land and water—together most effectively in the great arid region of the Rockies. As indicated earlier, most of the first irrigators in the west simply settled along the streams and rivers and diverted water to their land under the right of riparian ownership. As long as there were only a few irrigators and water was plentiful, this system worked satisfactorily. But after all of the land was taken up near the river, agriculture could not expand unless water could be moved some distance away from the stream. It was here that the problem of social control arose. The Mormons were important not only because they were the first Anglo-Americans to develop productive farming in the arid West but also because they worked out a system of public control in the diversion and use of water. In other words, they shaped their institutions to conform to the environment. Community control of water as practiced by the Mormons ran counter to the strong tradition of individualism among Americans, but it was the only feasible system if large amounts of arid land were to be made productive.

Almost immediately after arriving in the Salt Lake Valley in July 1847, the Mormons planted crops and did their first irrigating. Uncontrolled livestock ruined everything but the potatoes, and during the winter of 1847–1848 people suffered terribly. They ate thistles, bark, roots, crows, wolf meat, and anything else that would sustain life. The next year, 1848, hordes of crickets swarmed over the growing crops creating panic and despair. Just when it appeared that all would be lost, sea gulls miraculously appeared and devoured the ravenous insects. A partial crop was harvested a few months later. Meanwhile, the Mormons built log houses and some adobe structures, and worked out their land and water policies.

Land was distributed to settlers mainly on the principle of use. In an area where irrigation was essential for crop production, this meant that only small plots were granted to individual farmers. The average size of farms in Utah in 1850 was 51 acres, but by 1860 this had been reduced to 25 acres. By keeping farms small, the Mormons could spread the available water over a greater number of farms and provide homes for more people. The Mormons forsook the riparian principle and decided at the outset that water would be publicly rather than privately owned. Brigham Young declared that "there shall be no private ownership of the streams that come out of the canyons, . . ." Following 1847 the Mormons constructed dams and ditches on a community basis, and water rights were connected with land utilization. A public official was named to supervise the distribution of water for agricultural, industrial, and personal use. Apportionment of water was controlled by a "watermaster" selected by the Mormon high council.[5] The farmers themselves built and maintained the dams, canals, and ditches on a cooperative basis under the general supervision of a Mormon official. When Utah became a territory, the principle of the community control of water was confirmed, and in 1865 the legislature provided for the creation of irrigation districts. In this way irrigation water remained under the regulation of actual users. Encouraged by their religious beliefs, the Mormons worked together as a cooperative and cohesive group and avoided the problems of land and water monopoly that were so common in some parts of the West.

Mormon land and water policies presented something of a frontier paradox. The system of group control of land and water was contrary to the individualism and independence so often associated with the western frontier. On the other hand, the distribution of water on the basis of actual use cut out land speculation and gave more farmers a stake in society. The Mormon policies definitely contributed to economic democracy.

During the 30 years after original settlement the Mormons played an important and unique role in expanding the western agricultural frontier. These saintly farmers, however, did not leave the Salt Lake City settlement and move to new areas by themselves. The usual individualistic pioneering so characteristic of the American frontier had no place among the Mormons. Rather, the establishment of new communities was a planned and organized group effort. During the 1850s scores of farming villages were created in the Great Basin, where as had been true from the beginning of Mormon settlement, land and water were distributed by community action.

The rush of thousands of people to the California goldfields provided a sharp economic stimulant to the budding Mormon economy. Finding themselves on one of the main routes to California, Great Basin farmers sold grain, flour, vegetables, and livestock to the travelers. A good harvest in 1850 gave the Mormons substantial surpluses for sale. Moreover, they were able to buy supplies at cheap prices from those passing through. For a short time pioneer farmers in Utah found themselves in the unusual position of getting high prices for what they sold and paying cheap prices for what they bought. Good crops continued until 1855 when a devastating drought and hordes of grasshoppers reduced production throughout the territory from one third to two thirds of normal. The church historian wrote in the summer of 1855 that "about two-thirds of the grain in Utah County is destroyed, and a large black bug is devouring the potatoes."[6] The winter of 1855–1856 was unusually severe, and thousands of cattle died. Although they were less destructive, grasshoppers returned in 1856. As a result of these scourges of nature, thousands of people suffered want and privation; however, none starved.

By 1860 most of the 3635 farms in Utah were located in Weber, Davis, Salt Lake, Utah, and San Pete counties. This included the area roughly between Ogden and Ephraim. About 38 percent of the 77,219 improved acres were concentrated in Salt Lake and Utah counties.[7] Production of wheat reached 384,892 bushels in 1859, or an average of around 106 bushels per farm. Wheat sometimes yielded as much as 50 to 60 bushels to the acre. Smaller amounts of corn, oats, barley, peas, and beans were also grown. Utah farmers raised an average of about 40 bushels of Irish potatoes each. A flourishing livestock industry developed as farmers ran cattle and sheep on the hills and in the mountains. The territory had 24,926 head of cattle, excluding oxen, and 37,322 sheep in 1859. Butter and wool were both major farm commodities. Orchard products such as apples, peaches, pears, berries, and other fruits, and garden vegetables were grown for both home use and for sale.

During the 1860s, there was a steady but very modest growth of agriculture in Utah. Although the Union Pacific and Central Pacific did not give the territory through railway connections until near the end of the decade, farmers found markets for flour, vegetables, and dried and canned fruit in the mining camps of Montana, Idaho, and Nevada. Wheat, corn, oats, and barley continued to be the main cereal crops, while potatoes, sorghum, fruits, and vegetables were also raised. A small amount of tropical fruit and a few bales of cotton were grown along the Virgin and Colorado rivers in the southern part of the territory in the late 1860s.[8] There were 1273 new farms established in the territory during the decade, and the improved agricultural acreage rose about 53 percent. The population, however, jumped from about 40,000 to 86,000, an increase of more than 100 percent between 1860 and 1870. The main factor tending to deter more rapid agricultural expansion in the Great Basin was that the extension of irrigation canals and ditches to new lands was a hard, slow process, and there was a limit on the amount of land that could be

The Rocky Mountain Farming Frontier - 181

irrigated from flowing streams. In other words, the physical limitations of land and water under rather primitive irrigation technology restricted more rapid agricultural development. Futhermore, most non-Mormons preferred to settle somewhere else rather than to come under the political and economic control of the Mormons. Also throughout the 1860s, Utah, like all of the Rocky Mountain region, remained isolated. Even after the Union Pacific arrived, high-cost irrigated agriculture could not compete with the low-cost production of prairie farmers to the east.

In the vicinity of Denver another major pocket of irrigated agriculture was developing in the 1860s. Although the Mormon success with irrigated farming gained national attention, Colorado was not far behind its western neighbors. The isolated farmers and ranchers quickly expanded their production after 1859 to meet the demands for food in the Colorado mining camps. Settlers along the Arkansas, Platte, and smaller rivers and streams planted grain and vegetables to supply the local market. A correspondent reported in the fall of 1861 that he had observed many fine farms in the Platte Valley and within 2 more years 50,000 bushels of grain were being produced in the Platte watershed. Another reporter from Canon City on the Arkansas wrote in October 1862 that "all kinds of grain or vegetables grown in Illinois will grow here. . . ." He said that wheat made 30 to 40 bushels to the acre, corn made 30 to 40 bushels, and potatoes made up to 400 bushels. A little earlier Governor John Evans declared that "crops now standing on the farms in the valleys of the various branches of the South Platte and Fontaine-qui-Bouille afford most encouraging prospect."[9] Thus from the beginning of permanent settlement in Colorado, farmers began diverting water from the rivers and streams that flowed eastward out of the snow-capped Rockies to irrigate crops along the semiarid base of the mountains.

Yet during the 1860s agricultural expansion was slow in Colorado. By 1870 there were only 1728 farms and ranches in the entire territory. Lack of transportation, limited markets, insufficient knowledge about the region in the Midwest that might provide settlers, grasshopper infestations in 1864 and 1867, and inexperience in the practices of irrigation all tended to retard more rapid growth. But even as early as 1870 the value of the territory's agricultural production reached an estimated $3,500,000, which nearly equaled the $4 million value of bullion.[10]

By 1870 some of the handicaps to more rapid agricultural settlement were being removed. In June 1870 the Denver Pacific Railroad connected with the Union Pacific at Cheyenne, giving Colorado citizens direct rail communication with the rest of the country. A few months later, in September 1870, the Kansas Pacific was completed between Kansas City and Denver, and in 1871 the Denver and Rio Grande opened service between Denver and Colorado Springs. The meeting of the transportation and farming frontiers in Colorado around 1870 had a mutually expansive effect.

Besides providing transportation, the railroads immediately began to promote settlement as a means of selling their lands and increasing passenger and freight traffic. In 1869 the Denver Pacific contracted with the National Land Company, which undertook the task of encouraging settlement and selling railroad lands. The National Land Company entered into similar agreements with other railways, and an intensive promotional effort was carried on during 1870 and 1871. Although the promoters exaggerated the simplicity and profits of irrigation farming, their work removed much of the ignorance about agricultural possibilities in Colorado and stimulated a considerable increase in settlement. Many of the newcomers settled in farm colonies.

One of the first group colonization efforts in Colorado was made by the German Colonization Company, which located land in the Wet Mountain Valley south of Canon City in March 1870. Initially this was to be a cooperative venture in settling poor urban Germans on the frontier, but the scheme failed within a few months. Many people left before fall, and only a few remained to create successful farms. The Chicago-Colorado Colony was founded in a good agricultural area watered by Boulder and St. Vrain creeks in Boulder County in 1871. The most important colony, however, was the Union Colony, which founded Greeley and opened up the surrounding area in Weld County. Organized by Nathan Meeker, agricultural editor of the New York *Tribune* and named after the paper's famous editor, the first settlers arrived in the valley of the Cache la Poudre in April and May 1870. The colony committee had purchased a large block of land from the Denver Pacific plus other holdings and then filed on vacant government land. The colony was an incorporated company run by an executive committee. Settlers were required to have good character and to pay an initiation and membership fee of $155. For this payment, the colonist received land, the services of the colony officers, and any benefits of the group's cooperative efforts. Colonists who were granted or bought land were also supposed to get a supply of water for irrigation. There was no thought here of individuals getting control of the water supply. Irrigation was to be a community affair. Early in the colony's history the company hired teams and scrapers and constructed two ditches, one to furnish water for Greeley and the other to irrigate outlying land. Another company project was that of building a fence to enclose colony property.[11]

The Colorado colonies had some idealistic features—the manufacture and sale of liquor were forbidden in the Greeley colony—, but community settlement was mainly a practical means of conquering an isolated and arid frontier. There were several advantages in group migration. Land could be purchased at less cost in large lots by associations than by individual farmers, railroad transportation was often cheaper, people were safer, and emigrants enjoyed the social advantages that accompanied compact settlement. Most important, however, was the fact that the work of building dams and ditches for irrigation could be done much more effectively by joint effort. Individual farmers did not have either the financial ability or the technical know-how to build expensive and complex irrigation systems necessary to reclaim much arid land. One settler might make a small ditch with a plow and irrigate a few acres adjacent to a river or creek, but it took many teams and scrapers as well as engineering skill to construct a canal large enough to provide water for several score or even hundreds of farmers. Companies such as the one that organized the Greeley Colony were able to provide the necessary irrigation facilities for substantial agricultural expansion.

Not all emigrants who went to Colorado became farmers, since the communities offered employment for other kinds of labor. However, hundreds of hopeful pioneers from New York, Pennsylvania, the old Northwest, Missouri, and Iowa migrated to the Colorado frontier in the 1870s to try their hand at irrigated farming. This was a different type of agriculture than most of them were used to and not all emigrants succeeded, or even stayed in Colorado. Those who remained played an important part in reducing the ever-narrowing farmer's frontier.

Publicity about and promotion of the Colorado colonies did much to stimulate the interest of prospective farm settlers in Colorado. During the 1870s irrigated farming expanded rapidly along the eastern base of the mountains all the way from Trinidad in the south to Fort Collins in the north. In 1871 the Greeley *Tribune* said that "people are now busy putting in grain under this Canal (No. 2), and the whole region is said to be rapidly crystallizing into a farming scene." This scene was either being, or was soon to be, repeated all along the eastern edge of the Rockies. Other large irrigation canals were constructed, and the acreage under cultivation advanced rapidly. There were also scattered settlements in the parks and valleys west of the front mountain ranges. In the spring of 1878 a group of Mormons from Georgia, Alabama, and Tenessee settled in Conejos County, and by 1880 there were more than 100 farmers and ranchers in the San Luis Valley along the headwaters of the Rio Grande.[12]

Between 1870 and 1880 the number of farms in Colorado rose from 1738 to 4506. The main cereal crops were wheat, oats, and corn, and by 1879 Colorado produced more wheat than any other Rocky Mountain state or territory. Irish potatoes were also a big crop, especially after the founding of the Union Colony. As early as 1871 the Greeley *Tribune* carried potato marketing news. Potatoes were sold locally, in the mining camps, and at military posts in the region, and were also shipped east.

In 1877 2000 carloads of potatoes were shipped out of Greeley. Products from market gardens were also grown in several Colorado counties. However, fruit growing did not become a significant farming enterprise until after 1880. Like other new settlements, farmers grew what did best in the soil and climate and also aimed their production at the available markets.[13]

One of the main problems of agricultural development throughout all of the arid West was the control and distribution of water. In most places the first occupants settled on the bottom lands along the streams and constructed small ditches to meet their individual requirements for irrigation. During the early period of settlement there was plenty of irrigation water for all farmers and ranchers who lived along the streams, and they could divert it cheaply and without hurting their neighbors. Farmers simply threw up a dam made of logs or brush and forced the water into the ditches, which they made to their fields with a plow or scraper. This was a simple technique that supplied water for small-scale, individual irrigation.

However, when groups like the Union Colony began tapping the rivers and creeks with large irrigation ditches to take water to the distant table lands, the important question of water rights and priorities arose. Conflicts occurred between small farmers and big appropriators as well as between large land and irrigation companies. For instance, a sharp controversy developed between the Greeley and Fort Collins communities in 1874 when the Poudre could not supply enough water for both settlements. Since Fort Collins was closer to the source of the river, irrigators there appropriated most of the water, leaving little or none for their Greeley neighbors some 25 miles downstream. As mentioned earlier, similar controversies developed in California.

The difficulties in Colorado led to the inclusion of a provision in the state constitution that gave prior appropriators the better right to use of water in the streams. A few years later the legislature provided for the regulation of this new property right. The laws of 1879 and 1881, which became the basis of the Colorado System, divided the state into 10 water districts consisting in most cases of a complete watershed. In each district a water commissioner was to be appointed to divide the stream flow on the basis of prior rights. The district courts, acting as administrative boards, were to adjudicate conflicting priorities.

The law of 1881 strengthened the system of regulating water rights by providing for a state hydraulic engineer to measure the streams.[14] The passage of these laws went a long way to provide the social control needed to obtain the most beneficial use of water for irrigation purposes. Pioneer western irrigators were strong individualists, but a majority of them soon saw that without group control of water resources confusion and conflict would hamstring the development of irrigated agriculture. California experienced just such a conflict in the 1870s and 1880s before passage of the Wright Act in 1887. Indeed, economic growth in the western states was dependent upon the wisest use of water resources, and this could not be left to individual choice. Consequently, most of the western states eventually adopted the Colorado system of the public control of irrigation water. Colorado residents and other westerners who had to rely on irrigation did not adapt existing institutions to new conditions, but they created entirely new institutions to meet their peculiar needs.

Irrigated agriculture also developed farther south in New Mexico and Arizona. The Indians had first irrigated crops in that area hundreds of years earlier, and the Spanish-Americans continued a primitive, self-sufficient type of agriculture after they settled in the region. They raised a little grain, some vegetables and fruit, as well as cattle and sheep. Agricultural progress, however, was slow because of a limited market and primitive methods. Between 1850 and 1860 population of New Mexico Territory (Arizona became a separate territory in 1864), increased from 61,547 to 83,009 and the number of farms from 3750 to 5086. The production of corn nearly doubled, and wheat raising showed a marked increase. During the 1860s, however, farming and ranching in New Mexico and Arizona actually lost ground. Although corn production was up, the number of cattle and sheep decreased between 1859 and 1869, wheat output declined, and the total number of farms dropped. Farming was of minor significance in these two territories in 1870.[15]

After about 1868 the territorial governors, surveyor-generals, and local boosters repeatedly declared that fine agricultural opportunities awaited farmers in the Pecos, Rio Grande, Salt, Gila, Colorado, or other river valleys, but these desert reaches had little appeal to settlers who could get good land in Minnesota, Dakota, and central Nebraska, and Kansas. Occasional Indian trouble, especially the Apache raids in the 1860s, gave the area bad publicity and deterred settlement. Moreover, the small amount of land available for dry land farming, the problem of working out suitable water and irrigation policies, and especially the lack of railroad transportation, all combined to keep settlers out of this new southwestern frontier. For example, transcontinental railway transportation was not provided until completion of the Southern Pacific in 1882. The Santa Fe did not reach Albuquerque from Colorado until the spring of 1880, after which it built southward to Deming. The isolation of this area may have been typified by the story about the celebrants who sent telegrams to many dignitaries, including the Pope in Rome, after the Southern Pacific arrived in Tucson in 1880. The Pope's alleged reply was: "Am glad railroad has reached Tucson, but where in hell is Tucson?"[16]

By 1880 there were 25,043 farms and ranches scattered throughout the eight Rocky Mountain territories and states, of which about 38 percent were in Utah. Farm production had not yet become significant in this vast region, and agriculture was still largely confined to meeting the needs of mining camps and other local markets. For example, Colusa County, California, grew more wheat and more than half as much barley in 1879 than all the farms in the Rocky Mountain area combined. This extensive area showed up somewhat better as a producer of livestock. The Census of 1880 reported 1,334,867 head of cattle, excluding oxen, and 3,630,442 sheep, but this was less sheep than were raised in California and only about half as many cattle as were found in Iowa.[17]

Expansion of the farmer's frontier in the Rocky Mountain region was encouraged to some extent by government land policies. Despite the inapplicability of the Homestead Act to the arid Rocky Mountain region, it played a larger part in the early agricultural settlement of the area than has been generally recognized. As long as population was sparse and there was room for new farmers along the creeks and rivers, homesteading was feasible. Of course, 160 acres of land was of little value if it were distant from water. Up to June 30, 1880, about 16,933 homestead entries were made, the largest numbers being in Colorado and Utah. Wherever possible, settlers located on or near a creek or river in order to have water for livestock and irrigation. Of the total homestead filings, 4904, or about 29 percent, were completed through final entry. During the next 5 years an additional 7893 final entries were made. Most of these would have been homesteads on which settlers made their original filings before June 30, 1880. A few could have been veterans who filed after 1880 and who were permitted to deduct the period of their armed service from the 5-year residence requirement. Others were probably filed by miners who had no intention of farming. But it seems safe to assume that about two-thirds of those who filed a homestead entry before June 30, 1880, eventually gained ownership of the land through the regular residence requirement. A fair estimate would be that between 40 and 50 percent of the 25,043 farms in the Rocky Mountain territories and states by 1880 were established as homesteads. Only 2855 entries were made under the Desert Land Act in the 4 years up to 1880. This law was used mainly by ranchers and land speculators who were trying to gain control of key areas for irrigation and pasture rather than by people who actually wanted to farm.[18]

By the 1880s it was apparent that agricultural expansion in the arid region would be severely limited unless larger and more efficient irrigation systems made better use of the water. In other words, most of the land that could be irrigated easily and with simple techniques had been taken up. Water was becoming scarce at critical times during the growing season, valleys were becoming crowded, and conditions for newcomers were discouraging. An observer in Utah wrote in 1885 that "I find the settlements crowded up to their utmost capacity, land and water all appropriated, and our young people as they marry off have no place to settle near home. . . ."[19] A little later a farmer near Greeley said that "we lose our potato crop nearly every year because of the shortage of water at the proper time."[20] Commenting on the Boise City Board of Trade's attempt to lure emigrants to the Boise Valley, the editor of the Idaho *Daily Statesman* wrote on June 14, 1888: "The real truth is, there is no place for emigrant farmers to come here and settle on government land." There was plenty of land, he continued, but "it is land that must be irrigated, and there are no ditches to bring the water to it."

One problem was how to store a water supply and to build larger ditches and canals to carry water to the hundreds of thousands of acres of dry but fertile lands away from the streams and river bottoms. Not many new farms could be established unless water could be taken to the bench lands. Although there was still much to be learned about irrigation engineering, the main question was how to finance the expensive reservoirs and canals, which would be necessary to provide enough water throughout the entire growing season. Large-scale irrigation systems cost far more than individual farmers could afford. In his report on the arid lands in 1878, J. W. Powell emphasized that the larger streams could not be tapped for irrigation except by the use of "cooperative labor or aggregated capital."[21] But who would provide the necessary capital? Among the alternatives were associations of farmers, private corporations, the states, the federal government, or some combination of them all.

Despite the supposed independence of westerners, they never hesitated to seek government help when government wealth and power seemed necessary to the economic development of their section. Frontier individualism was simply overpowered by self-interest. By the 1870s leaders throughout the Rocky Mountain region were pleading for federal aid to develop irrigation. Governor John L. Routt of Colorado declared in 1876 that reservoirs were absolutely essential to store irrigation water, but that neither the state nor private enterprise could bear the expense. He recommended that public land be granted to the states to aid these projects. John C. Fremont, Governor of Arizona Territory, argued that somehow the federal government must help "to increase the water supply." The resulting advantages, Fremont explained, would be "so great as to make it incumbent on the government in the ordinary care of its property to give the required aid, which, if effectively supplied, would involve an expenditure too large and comprehensive for individual enterprise." Without a supply of irrigation water, he concluded, "this country cannot be used for what it is worth."[22]

The editor of the Idaho *Daily Statesman* of Boise wrote on November 14, 1889, that following proper surveys, the "entire Northwest will not only ask, but demand liberal and generous government aid for building reservoirs and opening ditches for irrigating these immense areas of arid government land. It is a pretty state of affairs indeed, if a government which can legally appropriate scores of millions annually for the improvement of harbors and rivers, may not set aside from the surplus a few million for making its own land saleable, and fit for American homes." He declared that the West meant to get this assistance through political power. "We are determined to prove that what has been good for the Eastern gander these many years, will be equally good for the Western goose." Arguments favoring federal assistance in building irrigation works were couched in terms of national interest, but they were motivated primarily by local self-interest. It was a recognized fact that local and regional economic development would be seriously checked unless more efficient use could be made of water. It was argued that if irrigation were expanded, more farms could be created, the government could sell more land, and the nation as a whole would benefit.

The multitude of questions surrounding water use and irrigation were of overwhelming concern throughout the arid west by the 1880s. Powell's *Report on the Lands of the Arid Region of the United States* in 1878 greatly contributed to this general interest. In August 1886 the United States Senate asked for a report on irrigation, prepared by Richard R. Hinton under the direction of the Commissioner of Agriculture. Hinton's study was largely descriptive and he did not say much about the crucial matters of irrigation policy. He did conclude, however, that agriculture could be greatly expanded in the mountain region if the supply of water were "properly conserved, protected, and distributed, under the wise and conservative direction of the national and state governments. . . ."[23]

An increasing number of westerners and government officials who knew the actual situation in the irrigated areas were moving to the position that the entire problem could best be handled by the national government. Arizona's congressional delegate Marcus A. Smith argued that private enterprise could never provide the necessary water for irrigation unless monopolies were formed. "The government for its own protection and for the well-being of the people must assume this duty," he said. Smith declared that "the available agricultural lands are nearly exhausted. The over-crowded laborer seeking a western home finds a useless desert staring him in the face. . . . Will you not give him a chance? . . . Sirs, make homes for your people," he pleaded, "Save your lands from monopoly. Redeem the arid lands. . . ."[24] Fear was especially strong that the best reservoir sites would fall into the hands of private corporations, thereby creating a monopoly of water resources. Representative George G. Symes of Colorado said that people throughout the arid regions wanted to save "the natural sites for reservoirs from the grasp of private corporations" and reserve them for future homesteaders.[25] The view that government should play such a positive role, however, was by no means unanimous. Idaho's Governor, Edward A. Stevenson, wrote in 1887 that he had long believed that desert lands must be reclaimed by private enterprise, and he favored giving 320 acres of desert land to each settler who would combine with his neighbors to build canals and ditches.

On March 20, 1888, Congress authorized an investigation of the water resources of the arid region and in a subsequent appropriation bill reserved from sale or entry all lands that might be needed for reservoir sites or canals, or were susceptible to irrigation by such works. The effect of the latter measure when finally enforced was to prohibit entry on public lands between the 100th meridian and the Pacific Ocean until the law was changed. While westerners wanted a survey of water resources, they strongly objected to closing the public domain until the study of reservoir sites, watersheds, and related problems had been completed. Major Powell, who directed the survey, came under vicious attack by those who accused him of slowing down the "resistless tide of humanity" into the West. "We want crops, . . . and we cannot wait until this geological picture and topographical picture is perfected," said one westerner. Regional interests soon prevailed, and in August 1890 Congress revoked the provision that had closed lands susceptible to irrigation and all entries that had been made in good faith after 1888 were declared valid.[26]

Meanwhile, the Senate decided to conduct its own investigation of irrigation problems in the arid region. During the fall of 1889 a committee traveled extensively throughout the West taking testimony from engineers, businessmen, farmers, and political leaders. The general tenor of the remarks was that government had the responsibility of at least completing a proper hydrographic survey and drilling experimental deep wells. Many witnesses, though, believed that the federal government should go further and actually construct the needed irrigation systems.[27] The extensive debate and investigations indicated that Congress was groping for a workable reclamation policy but that conflicts of interest within the West, differences between easterners and westerners, and lack of reliable hydrographic data made it difficult to develop satisfactory policies.

Some reservoir sites were reserved after 1888, and in 1894 the Carey Act offered up to 1 million acres to any state in the arid region that would see that the lands were irrigated and occupied by settlers. While it was not clear whether the states or private enterprise would actually construct the irrigation works, this law recognized that expansion of irrigation depended upon government encouragement if not outright participation in building irrigation facilities. But it was not until passage of the Newlands Act in 1902 that the federal government began to provide a direct subsidy to construct irrigation works. This law provided that funds derived from the sale of public lands in the arid states were to be used for surveying, constructing, and maintaining irrigation works under the direction of the Secretary of the Interior. But the development of irrigation in the twentieth century was part of a different frontier—the frontier of expanding government functions and powers identified with an urban, industralized America.

What was actually happening to irrigated farming in the Rocky Mountain states and territories while public officials were arguing over water, the region's life blood? Because of a careful survey of irrigation by the Census Bureau in 1889, fairly accurate information on irrigated agriculture became available for the first time. Between 1880 and 1890 the number of farms in the eight Rocky Mountain states and territories nearly doubled, increasing from 25,043 to 49,398. Of this number 34,656, or 70 percent, were operated by irrigators who by 1889 had brought water to 2,332,440 acres of land. Within another decade, the number of irrigators had risen to 69,059, and the land under irrigation reached 5,293,619 acres. The percentage of irrigated farms fell slightly because of settlement in eastern Colorado and New Mexico.

The expansion of irrigated agriculture before 1900 was made possible by the construction of larger irrigation facilities by groups of farmers and private corporations. But the expense of building irrigation facilities generally exceeded the estimates, and many water companies and cooperative ventures ran into financial difficulty in the late 1880s and 1890s. As mentioned in connection with California, one of the problems that irrigation districts faced was failure to interest investors in district irrigation bonds. In any event, by 1890 around $15,639,000 had been invested in irrigation systems throughout the Rocky Mountain region. This averaged about $6.60 for each acre being irrigated. By 1899 the initial per acre cost of irrigation systems was nearly $8. In other words, the expense rose as larger facilities and more land was brought under cultivation. Moreover, water rights increased rapidly in value.

After the early settlers had occupied most of the areas that could be irrigated cheaply, the capital requirements on irrigated farms was high. Thus, it is not surprising that the number of farms remained relatively small in this region. Actually, there was little to attract a poor man. A new settler had to buy a farm with a water right, which might cost $10 an acre or more. This greatly increased the cost of farm-making. If a pioneer moved into an area where water was not yet available, he was unable to raise anything and might starve before ever really becoming established.

Under these conditions, it is not surprising that within a year after the opening of Oklahoma Territory, there were more farmers on that rolling prairie than in any of the Rocky Mountain states or territories, except Colorado and Utah. In addition to the capital costs many farmers did not think they would like irrigated farming. Much of the advertising directed at prospective settlers tried to convince them that farming by irrigation represented a good rural life.

Most of the irrigated acreage in the 1880s and 1890s was devoted to cereals and forage. Alfalfa became a leading hay crop in most of the irrigated valleys and provided feed for the growing livestock industry. Practically all the irrigation was for forage in Wyoming and Nevada, where ranching was the main agricultural activity. However, in 1889, except in those two areas, cereal crops occupied from 21 to 63 percent of the irrigated land in the Rocky Mountain region. There were a few spots of important dry-land farming, notably in Nez Perce and Latah counties in northwest Idaho, which were part of the famous Palouse wheat country.[28]

Because of the growing expense of irrigation, the general trend was toward the production of specialized commodities such as vegetables and fruits, which had a higher value. Between 1889 and 1899, for example, Colorado moved from twenty-first to sixteenth among all the states in potato production. Many kinds of garden vegetables were grown, and the value of market garden products and small fruits increased nearly 500 percent in the last decade of the nineteenth century. Orchard products also grew in importance. In three Colorado counties peach production rose from 26,678 bushels in 1889 to 160,097 in 1899. Peaches, pears, plums, apples, and other fruits were also grown by many farmers in Idaho and Utah.

Despite some rather remarkable percentage increases in crop production, farming in the states and territories of the Rocky Mountains was quite insignificant when considered from a national viewpoint. Crops for the entire region were valued at only $55,991,522 in 1899 compared to more than twice that figure for Kansas alone. Even the vaunted and much written about livestock and ranching industry was hardly of major significance in the total agricultural picture, except in the case of sheep raising and wool production. In 1900 Iowa alone had 90 percent as many cattle as the eight Rocky Mountain states and territories combined.[29]

In summary then, the Rocky Mountain region provided only limited opportunity for agricultural pioneers in the late nineteenth century. The number of farms established was small, only 101,327 by 1900, and except in a few localities commercial production was not highly significant. The natural geography of the region was basic to the lack of agricultural development. But continued isolation from centers of population, the

192 - The Rocky Mountain Farming Frontier

problems and cost of irrigation, and the inability to compete with low-cost production of midwestern farmers all joined to make this vast area the least important part of the farmer's frontier after the Civil War.

In many parts of the Rocky Mountain region frontier conditions were relatively brief. This was especially true in Utah and along the eastern base of the Rocky Mountains in Colorado where large groups of pioneers settled within a short time. Yet, new frontiers were being continually opened between 1860 and 1900 as farmers pushed up river valleys or onto the dry bench lands, where by irrigation they successfully combined the region's land and water resources. More than in any other part of the West, the frontier concepts of independence and individualism seemed at variance with actual conditions in the Rocky Mountain region. The need to irrigate that vast arid domain called for group effort or government action, or both. However, Rocky Mountain farmers successfully adjusted to new agricultural conditions, and adjustment was a highly important frontier trait.

◁ **11** ▷

Pioneering in West Texas, Indian Territory, and Oklahoma, 1860-1900

While farmers spread over a series of prairie, plains, valley, and mountain frontiers between Kansas City and San Francisco after 1860, another frontier called to hopeful agricultural pioneers. This was the Southwest of Texas and Oklahoma. Farm settlement there, however, lagged behind some other western regions, not because of lack of interest but mainly because of Indian barriers. Migration into northwest Texas was nearly stopped by the fierce Comanches until after 1875, and Oklahoma was reserved for the Five Civilized Tribes and certain plains Indians until after 1889. So while farmers were pushing into other parts of the prairie-plains frontier, Oklahoma was legally denied to white settlers. Moreover, by the 1880s farmers were reaching the dry areas of west Texas where scarcity of rainfall slowed the westward movement.

By 1860 the western edge of settlement in north Texas was just west of Gainesville near the 98th meridian. From there the frontier extended southwestward to about 75 miles west of Fort Worth and then southward to the Rio Grande. Within the thinly settled area along this line, and farther west to the 100th meridian, there were millions of acres still awaiting stockmen and farmers when the last Confederate troops surrendered in 1865. Indeed, the extensive area northwest, west, and southwest of Fort Worth appeared ideal to agricultural pioneers. The region enjoyed a relatively mild climate, it contained substantial areas of productive soil, land was fairly cheap, and until a farmer got west of Childress or Abilene, he could count on an average annual rainfall of more than 20 inches.

Viewing this region in 1858, one promoter wrote that the most suitable areas in which to settle were "the upper waters of the Brazos, Colorado, Guadalupe or Red River, where the country is rolling, the water pure, the lands rich, the atmosphere salubrious and invigorating, the hills affording a fine range for cattle, horses, sheep and hogs. . . ."[1] Evidently many farmers agreed with this evaluation of West Texas because hundreds of them settled in the newly organized counties west and southwest of Fort Worth during the 1850s. By 1860, for example, pioneers were thinly scattered over Wise, Parker, Palo Pinto, Erath, and Comanche counties, and a few farmers had gone even farther west. In 1860 there were 396 farms and ranches in Parker and 163 in Palo Pinto County, the first two counties west of Fort Worth.[2] It was obvious that by the time of the Civil War farmers were ignoring the old axiom that farming could not succeed west of the Brazos.

Although Fort Belknap was established on the Upper Brazos in 1851, the early settlers in this region, as well as those farther south, were harrassed by hostile Indians. Throughout the 1850s the loss of life and property among pioneer settlers was extremely heavy. According to one authority, the Indians killed and plundered "up to within the sound of the church bells in San Antonio," and even farmers near Fort Belknap itself were attacked. In 1859, for instance, the Indians stole livestock, burned buildings, and killed men, women, and children all the way from San Saba to the Red River. People "forted up" for their own protection, but they were hardly a match for their attackers. But even the dangers of frontier life did not stop the emigrant tide. In 1860 when the Indian threat to farmers and ranchers in Palo Pinto County was very great, several loads of settlers from Missouri arrived searching for new homes. Despite the Indian peril, westward migration continued.[3] Individuals, single families, and groups of families all made their way to northwest Texas. They came mainly from East Texas and the southern states, but many also emigrated to Texas from the Midwest.

During the 1860s, however, settlement retreated all along this Texas frontier. Neither the few Confederate troops nor local militia was able to protect the farmers and ranchers in West Texas against the destructive Indian depredations. There was no other major part of the agricultural frontier in the trans-Mississippi West that was blocked so long and so effectively by hostile Indians, mostly Kiowa and Comanche. Hundreds of settlers left their homes and withdrew eastward to the safety of more thickly settled communities. The frontier retreated as much as 100 miles and during part of the 1860s, life and property were not safe very far west of Fort Worth. Consequently, most of the western counties lost population between 1860 and 1870, and farming was virtually abandoned. General Randolph Marcy wrote in 1871 after traveling from Fort Griffin to Fort Richardson near Jacksboro that he saw fewer people along the way than when he had made the same trip 17 years before.[4]

In 1860 Wise County had 3160 people, but only 1450 remained in 1870, and the number of farms had dropped from 149 to 82. There was not a single farm reported in Palo Pinto County in 1870, although 163 had been listed in the census a decade before. Farther south in Comanche and Erath counties population remained about even, and the agricultural frontier was stationary during the 1860s. But even the worst Indian attacks could not completely depopulate the Texas frontier as some cattlemen and a few farmers stayed on or left temporarily and then returned.[5] In any event, relentless military pressure forced the Indians to surrender, and by the end of 1875 this block to agricultural settlement had finally been removed.

Although it had taken a decade or more to defeat the Indians and open the country for settlement, the West Texas frontier now attracted thousands of land hungry pioneers. During the 1870s a vast ranching empire was created in the area between Wichita Falls and San Angelo, and cattle raising became the principal agricultural enterprise. But this did not deter the dirt farmers. They moved into the Cross Timbers and rapidly settled Montague, Jack, and Palo Pinto counties, and then advanced westward onto the rolling prairies to settle in Young, Stephen, Throckmorton, and Shackelford counties. Young County reported only 17 farms in 1870, but it contained 463 within another decade. Farther south in Comanche, Brown, and Coleman counties the number of farms also grew rapidly, and in Gillespie County, the second west of Austin, there were 671 farms in 1880 compared to only 369 10 years earlier. Some restless pioneers had gone as far as Abilene while others were working their way up the south side of the Red River west of Wichita Falls.[6]

As was true on other agricultural frontiers, most settlers arrived in wagons containing their personal belongings, a plow, an ax, and a few other tools and implements, and were pulled by a team of mules or oxen. These pioneers usually had one or more milk cows and often a few head of other cattle. In the Cross Timbers or along the rivers and creeks they built log houses, but farther west in the plains the first settlers generally lived temporarily in dugouts or half-dugouts. In some areas, such as around Fredericksburg west of Austin, which was settled by German immigrants, the settlers used local limestone to build houses. Still farther west adobe was the most common building material. There were very few sod houses on the West Texas frontier like those that were so common in Kansas and Nebraska. This was partly due to the consistency of the turf, which did not make good sod, and the fact that the first settlers lived along the creeks and rivers where they found timber for building purposes. The large ranchers, of course, hauled lumber to build their homes.

Even before building a home, the frontier farmer had to acquire land. Unlike other parts of the West where the federal government administered the public lands and settlers could get a farm under the national land laws, Texas retained and disposed of its own public lands. From the beginning of Texas history, the state adopted liberal land policies to attract and hold population. The Constitution of 1836 gave land to heads of families and to single persons then living in Texas, and subsequent laws made grants to those who immigrated to the state, remained at least 3 years, and performed the duties of citizenship. The laws of 1838 and 1841 actually applied the homestead principle in limited areas.

In 1845 the legislature passed a preemption measure, which offered 320 acres of land to the head of a family and 160 acres to a single person who had settled, or who would settle upon, the public domain. The price was 50 cents an acre. In 1854 a homestead law was enacted that granted 160 acres from the unclaimed public domain to indviduals who would live on the land for 3 years and cultivate it. Beginning in 1858 the state sold land in lots of no less than 160 acres and no more than 1280 at $1 per acre. In addition to these and other laws, which provided for acquiring land directly from the state, Texas gave millions of acres to railroads between 1854 and 1882, and this land was offered for sale.[7] Thus, there were several ways by which a settler could get land. In West Texas during the 1870s and 1880s the price usually ranged from a low of 50 cents to as much as $8 or $10 an acre. In 1867 around Weatherford in Parker County land was quoted at between $1 and $10 an acre, while in Comanche County it sold for 50 cents to $5.[8] The legislature later modified its land policy as settlers moved into the extreme western part of the state. Under a law of 1895 a farmer or cattleman could acquire 640 acres of agricultural land at $2 an acre and three additional sections of grazing land at $1, making a total of 2560 acres. Long-term credit extending over 40 years at only 3 percent interest was also provided in this legislation.

Corn was the main crop of early West Texas farmers, but they also grew small quantities of wheat, oats, barley, and rye. Most settlers planted corn because it was easy to grow and harvest by hand labor or with primitive implements. Moreover, many West Texans had emigrated from sections of the South, where corn products were important in the family diet. For example, in 1870 farmers in Comanche County raised 39,292 bushels of corn compared to only 3368 bushels of wheat. In Parker County farther north production of corn was more than five times greater than that of wheat. Throughout the 1870s, and even into the 1880s, corn continued to be the principal grain crop in the northwestern frontier counties.[9]

Production of wheat gradually increased on this frontier, although it did not develop to the extent hoped for by some of the crop's early advocates. One writer claimed in 1867 that there was no finer wheat land in the nation than the red, rolling prairies of the Upper Brazos. He told of one farmer on the Clear Fork of the Brazos who had raised 42 bushels of wheat to the acre.[10] However, by 1879 wheat production in the area remained small. In Young County the total acreage averaged only about 4.2 acres per farm,[11] but by 1889 wheat had become the major crop in the counties along the Red River northwest of Wichita Falls. From the beginning West Texas farmers grew winter wheat. Besides being best suited to the climate and rainfall pattern, winter wheat provided winter pasture for livestock. In addition to cereals West Texas farmers raised Irish potatoes, sweet potatoes, vegetables, and sorghum.

Perhaps the most important agricultural development in the 1870s and 1880s was the westward expansion of cotton culture. Production of cotton in Comanche County grew from only 28 bales in 1869 to 2098 bales in 1879. Farther north in Young County no cotton was grown in 1869 but 554 bales were produced a decade later. Some cotton was also being raised west of Wichita Falls along the Red River as early as the late 1870s. As farmers pushed farther west into Hardeman, Haskell, Jones, Taylor, and Runnels counties, cotton culture spread with them. One of the main problems facing cotton farmers on the Texas frontier was the distance from cotton gins and markets. When one farmer raised a small amount of cotton in Fisher County west of the 100th meridian in 1881, he had to haul it 100 miles to a gin at Coleman.[12] By the late 1880s cotton was being grown by many farmers around Abilene, and some was raised even farther west.[13]

Like other frontier farmers, settlers in West Texas in the 1870s and 1880s maintained a combined crop-livestock enterprise. However, livestock played a larger part in the agricultural operations of farmers in this area than on the Kansas and Nebraska frontiers. In 1879 farms in some of the western pioneer counties had an average of only 10 to 25 acres of cereals plus a few acres of other crops, but it was common for farmers and ranchers to have anywhere from 25 to 65 head of milk cows and other cattle. This meant that while the dirt farmer might own eight to 12 head of cattle, of which three or four were milk cows, his neighbor was a small rancher who ran 100 head or more. Butter was an important product and it was sold for cash and traded for groceries at the local store.

One of the problems that faced Texas pioneers was that of protecting their crops against marauding livestock. Unlike many western states and territories that passed herd laws, Texas clung to the open range principle, favoring the rancher over the dirt farmer. Consequently, farmers had to bear the labor and expense of fencing their fields from roving livestock. After the introduction of barbed wire in the 1870s, ranchers began to fence the open range, partly to control their stock and partly to discourage the encroachment of so-called nesters. Sometimes farmers and small ranchers found themselves completely surrounded by miles and miles of barbed wire. By the early 1880s fence-cutting wars broke out all over West Texas as those who favored "free grass" and others who found their access to water cut off took matters into their own hands and cut the fences. The situation became so serious that early in 1884 a special session of the legislature made fence-cutting a felony and required the building of gates every 3 miles. In general this legislation reached a compromise that both sides accepted.[14]

By the late 1870 and early 1880s large ranchers had been established throughout most of West Texas, including the high plains west of the Cap Rock. The Cattle Kingdom stretched all the way from No Man's Land in the north to the Edwards Plateau in the South. But if ranchers believed that this area was suited only for grazing and that they could escape the intrusion of dirt farmers, they were badly mistaken. As early as 1878 Paris Cox, an Indiana Quaker, bought about 50,000 acres in Crosby County just east of where Lubbock was later established. Grain and vegetables were planted in 1879, and by 1882 10 families lived in the Cox community. These farmers raised feed for the surrounding ranchers.[15]

By growing small amounts of grain and sorghum for winter feed, the large ranchers themselves encouraged the advance of the agricultural frontier into West Texas. In 1887 grain and vegetables were being grown on the XIT Ranch, and the next year a report said that Colonel Charles Goodnight had raised 100 acres of good wheat in Donley County southeast of Amarillo. Indeed, part of an earlier prophecy by an owner of the XIT was beginning to come true. Looking at the Panhandle, he wrote: "What a clean stretch of land! Why I could start a plowpoint into the soil at the south line and turn a furrow two hundred miles long without a break—and I'll live to see the day when the plow will push the cattle off this range and grain crops will be fed to dairy cows."[16] While cows were never pushed out of the Panhandle, grain crops did eventually occupy a large part of the land. The large cattlemen knew that eventually they must "give way for a multitude of smaller cattlemen and actual settlers," said the Tascosa *Pioneer* on March 30, 1887.

The isolation of the Texas Panhandle was broken in 1888 when the Fort Worth and Denver City railroad cut across the area from the southeast and met the Denver, Texas and Fort Worth at Texline in the extreme northwest corner of the state. Settlers now had direct rail communication to the northern Panhandle plains, and a number of towns began to grow, including Amarillo, which was established in July 1887. The Tascosa *Pioneer* advised on January 28, 1888: "Come to the Panhandle for cheap lands; come for rich and productive soil; come for health; come for seasonable summers and balmy winters; come and raise cereals, fruits, vegetables, sorghum, grains, grasses and forage. . . ." And people came. On June 9, 1888, the Tascosa *Pioneer* wrote that "wagons with white tops, rope-bottomed chairs, tow-heads, brindle cows, yellow dogs and a pervading air of restlessness have poured through this week in the direction suggested by Horace Greeley."

Farmers were also encouraged to occupy the plains farther south, where it was said that they could make a good living raising feed to support a modest livestock operation. The Crosby County *News* appealed to farmers in East Texas by saying: "emancipate yourself. Throw off the yoke of slavery fixed upon you by King Cotton. Sell out that old farm, buy you [sic] some cows and mares, or both and a bunch of sheep, then come to Crosby County and start you a ranch or stock farm."[17] Farther south along the line of the Texas and Pacific, which reached Midland in 1881, a few settlers sought farms in Nolan, Mitchell, Howard, and Midland counties. The Texas and Pacific had large amounts of land for sale, and it appealed to prospective immigrants by boasting of the region's agricultural capabilities. Local promoters also praised the area in a most exaggerated fashion. Despite the fact that rainfall at Midland averaged only about 16 inches a year, one publicity tract published in 1884 was entitled, "Garden of the Southwest, Midland County on the Staked Plains of West Texas, the Most Desirable Locality on the Continent for Homeseekers."[18] Perhaps unaware of its false nature, a writer in the *Prairie Farmer* of Chicago declared that a new and promising agricultural region was opening up on the high plains around Midland and that wheat would make 20 to 35 bushels per acre and oats as much as 100 bushels.[19]

But most of this discussion amounted to nothing more than talk. Large-scale cattle raising continued to dominate the southern plains in the 1880s and 1890s. In 1890 there were only 29 farms in Midland County. Most of these had been established after 1888, and no grain production was reported for the county in 1889. However, during the 1890s several hundred farms and small ranches were established in the counties between Abilene and Midland. For most of these settlers farming was subsidiary to the main business of raising livestock.[20]

As settlers pressed westward along the Texas frontier they ran into the problem of periodic droughts, as did the pioneers in western Kansas, Nebraska, and eastern Colorado. In 1886 a terrible drought struck most of the region west of Fort Worth. The crops and grass burned up, springs and creeks went dry, and thousands suffered want and privation. Many people were forced to leave the region at least temporarily. A sign chalked on a deserted cabin door in Blanco County told the story: "250 miles to the nearest post office; 100 miles to wood; 20 miles to water; 6 inches to hell. God bless our home! Gone to live with wife's folks." One observer saw 45 wagons going east through Jacksboro in a single day in October 1886. While many people left the country, and some counties lost population, others were able to hang on. More than 28,000 individuals received nearly $100,000 in state aid, and people were also assisted by private contributions of money, food, and clothing. But even this severe drought could not keep people out of the region, and some westward migration continued in the face of most discouraging circumstances. As one authority has written, "at all times there were two streams of covered wagons; one going west and the other going east."[21] Despite intense hardships, during this period most of the wagon tongues were pointed west all along the southern Great Plains frontier.

By 1900 there were 5904 farmers, small stockmen, and large ranchers in the 60 counties west of the 100th meridian in Texas between the northern Panhandle and San Angelo. In much of this area the large ranches were being broken up and hundreds of the detested nesters, or dirt farmers, had moved in. But, as mentioned earlier, crop farming was supplementary to the main business of raising and marketing livestock, and most of the crops were consumed on the farms and ranches rather than sold in distant markets. Texas land laws permitted the acquisition of large acreages and, consequently, a ranching economy continued to predominate throughout most of West Texas. The average-sized farm or ranch in Potter County (Amarillo) in 1900 was 8662 acres, and in Lubbock County 9710 acres. In only a few counties west of the 100th meridian was the average size below 2000 acres in 1900. Thus in West Texas the land units were more in line with the needs for making a living on the Great Plains, in contrast to western Kansas and Nebraska, where thousands of farmers were trying to earn a livelihood on 160 or 320 acres. Because of the large land holdings and slowness of settlement in western Texas, settlers there were probably the most isolated and lonesome of those on any agricultural frontier in the late nineteenth century. Quarter-section farming had its drawbacks, but it at least produced a better social life. Unlike western Kansas and Nebraska, where a new farmer might be 5 or 10 miles from a neighbor for 1 or 2 years (but usually not more than that), this condition persisted in West Texas well into the twentieth century.

While farmers edged westward in Kansas and Texas, after 1870 Indian Territory remained an island of rich farm and pasture lands denied to covetous white settlers. Yet, an important part of the last agricultural frontier was being developed here. In the 1820s and 1830s the federal government moved the Five Civilized Tribes—Cherokee, Choctaw, Chickasaw, Seminole, and Creek—to the region west of Arkansas and between the 37th parallel and the Red River, or what became the eastern part of the present state of Oklahoma. Indian territory was mostly rolling, partly wooded, and interlaced with numerous rich creek and river bottoms, including those of the Arkansas, Canadian, and Red rivers. While people had little reliable information about the region at the time of the removals, it was generally thought that white men would never want to live in the area.

Despite the harsh disruption of their society and economy east of the Mississippi, the Five Civilized Tribes soon developed a moderately prosperous agricultural economy. By the time of the Civil War most full bloods had small tracts under cultivation, lived in rude log houses, and raised enough grain, vegetables, and meat for the family table with perhaps a little surplus for sale. Some of the mixed bloods took up land in the rich river bottoms, cultivated large tracts, and marketed substantial quantities of grain, cotton, and livestock. Land was owned on a tribal or communal basis, but there was nothing under tribal law to keep an energetic Indian farmer from expanding his operations into a large-scale enterprise. Labor was provided by hiring whites under a permit system while others owned Negro slaves. For example, in the Chickasaw Nation Colonel Pittman Colbert cultivated between 300 and 400 acres of cotton and raised enough corn to supply his family and 150 slaves. The Choctaw Robert M. Jones farmed four plantations and shipped 700 bales of cotton in 1851. Farmers of this type lived in large frame mansions and enjoyed a life comparable to the planters of the Old South. The main outlet for agricultural products was down the Red and Arkansas rivers to the Mississippi and then to New Orleans, although some produce was sold to federal military establishments in the region. Indian livestock farmers raised thousands of cattle, but there was little market for them until demand was created by California immigrants in the 1850s.

The Civil War brought temporary disaster to the Five Civilized Tribes, many of whom had sympathized with the Confederacy. At the close of hostilities they found their farms ruined, buildings burned, and livestock stolen. They were also faced with the problem of fitting the freedmen into their agricultural economy. Perhaps worst of all was the loss of a large part of their western lands on which the federal government settled thousands of Indians from other tribes in the years between 1865 and 1880. Despite these difficulties, agriculture was restored in a remarkably short time. It was estimated that 6,420,195 bushels of corn were raised in the Five Nations in 1872. Wheat, oats, potatoes, sorghum, cotton, and other crops were also widely grown, and the Indians had thousands of head of livestock. By 1883 the Five Tribes had about 400,000 acres under cultivation.[22]

Full bloods continued a small, pioneer, self-sufficient type of farming much as they had developed before the Civil War, and as late as 1893 one observer wrote that "it is a rare thing to find a full-blood in the Indian Territory who is living comfortably on as much as a quarter section of land under cultivation." On the other hand, the mixed bloods and inter-married whites expanded their acreages into huge estates, often of several thousand acres, and carried on extensive commercial operations. They improved their farming practices, bred better livestock, and, in general, established a fairly sound agricultural economy. Indian farmers suffered from low prices, periodic droughts, lack of markets, and other problems, but in this respect they were not different from other western settlers in that period.

Most of the labor on commercial farms was performed by whites under a permit system developed by the various tribes. The white settler paid a fee that varied at different times and in different Indian Nations from as low as 25 cents to $25 a year. Once a white had a permit, he could farm Indian land on a share basis. Other whites entered the Indian Nations illegally, while some gained tribal membership through marriage. By 1880 about 6000 whites lived illegally upon Indian lands and around 15,000 were there under the permit system. The mixed bloods were glad to have noncitizen whites do most of their farming, but they strongly objected to white domination and the loss of any of their land, which became an increasing threat. The trickle of white settlement that began in the 1860s developed into an uncontrollable torrent by the 1880s. By turning over the labor to whites, the Five Civilized Tribes expanded the agricultural frontier in their Nations but at the same time this system played a big part in giving the whites eventual supremacy.

Immediately after the Civil War land-hungry farmers, speculators, businessmen, and other whites began to look longingly at Indian lands owned by the Five Tribes. The white man's view had not changed since the days of Andrew Jackson. Even though the Indians were utilizing some of their land for grazing and farming, outsiders looked at the vast untilled acreages and insisted that the Indians had much more land than they needed. Throughout the 1870s and 1880s bills were introduced in Congress to create a territory of Oklahoma with the idea that all the land not actually occupied by Indians would be thrown open to white settlement. However, the Indians were temporarily successful in resisting this move.

But law or no law, whites were determined to acquire a large part of the Indian lands. A delegation of Cherokee, Creek, and Choctaw declared in a memorial to Congress in 1870 that "an almost countless swarm of squatters" was hovering about the borders of their lands "awaiting the hour when they can enter upon them."[23] This was no exaggeration. In fact, the squatters would not wait on the slow process of legislation, and in the early 1870s they pushed illegally into Cherokee Territory south of the Kansas border. An agent for the Osages reported in 1872 that hundreds of settlers had moved into the best lands between Coffeyville and the Arkansas River, and that they were virtually defying the government to move them out.[24] Federal troops soon ejected these squatters, but throughout the 1870s pressure by intruders increased. An Indian Colonization Society was formed at Chetopa, Kansas, and despite the stationing of troops along the Kansas border and in Indian Territory white farmers continued to invade Indian lands. On April 26, 1879, President Rutherford B. Hayes forbade any trespassing "by emigrants on the Indian Territory," but the government had a difficult time enforcing this policy. In May 1879 federal troops found a group of settlers on the right bank of the Chickaskia River on Cherokee lands who "were commencing to break ground" for crops.[25]

By the late 1870s an intense and organized campaign had developed to open Indian lands to whites. Interest was especially high after Elias C. Boudinot, a mixed-blood Cherokee and Washington D.C. lawyer, wrote an article proclaiming that there were 14 million acres of government land available for settlement in Indian Territory. These lands, he said, remained after the cessions and assignments to various tribes. Boudinot's article was published on February 15, 1879, in the Chicago *Times* and during the next few months it was reprinted in scores of other newspapers and distributed as a leaflet. Hearing of this new El Dorado, landless pioneers headed toward Indian Territory. By the spring of 1879 hundreds of prospective homesteaders gathered at Baxter Springs, Independence, and other southern Kansas towns. Some of them pushed across the border onto Indian lands. By May 5 one observer said that "over 50,000 acres are already taken by squatters [on the Quapaw Reservation in the northeast part of Indian Territory] and hundreds are pouring in in wagons, on horseback and in every conceivable manner."[26] But federal troops soon cleared the area of most of these so-called "boomers."

Their most conspicuous leader was David L. Payne, a native of Indiana who had moved around the West for many years before settling near Wichita, Kansas, in 1871. While general efforts were made to open all of Indian Territory, Payne and his followers concentrated on occupying the so-called unassigned lands in the central part of the region. This area consisted of nearly 2 million acres and was bordered on the north by

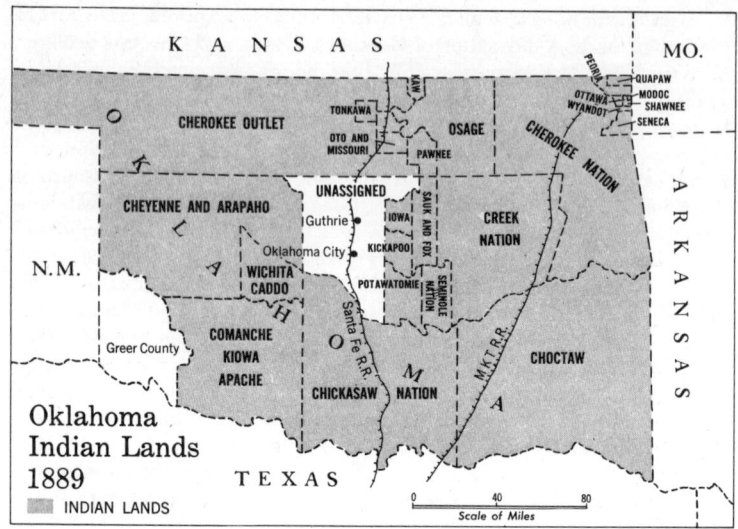

Oklahoma Indian Lands 1889

the Cherokee Outlet, on the west by the Cheyenne and Arapaho reservation, on the south by the South Canadian River, and on the east by lands owned by Potawatomi, Kickapoo, Iowa, and other tribes. This region contained fertile, rolling prairie land covered in places by blackjack oak and other timber, and was well watered by the South Canadian, North Canadian, and Cimarron rivers.[27]

In December 1879 Payne formed what he called the Oklahoma Colony, which was to be made up of individuals and families who wanted to settle in the unassigned part of Indian Territory. He announced on January 1, 1880, that a colony of 5000 to 10,000 people would be organized "and move upon these lands in one body on or about the 15th of March."[28] Payne described the Oklahoma lands in most glowing terms. "There is no finer body of country in the United States," he wrote. "It is well watered, well timbered, . . . For all agricultural purposes, stock, grain, cotton, tobacco and fruit raising, it cannot be excelled by any other section of the country between the Atlantic and Pacific." He said that the climate was "nearly like that of California" and argued that it was the only part of the public domain "now open and within reach of the people this side of the Rocky Mountains that is worth occupying."

On April 26, 1880, Payne and about 150 followers slipped across the Kansas line west of Arkansas City and headed south toward the unassigned lands of Oklahoma. Eluding federal troops, they arrived at the present site of Oklahoma City 6 days later. On May 3 Payne wrote that the public lands in Indian Territory were "not only open to settlement, but settled." He declared: "we are here to stay."[29] The boomers were soon busy building cabins, staking their claims, and preparing for permanent settlement. However, federal troops quickly arrived and escorted the land-hungry settlers back to Kansas. Before his death in 1884 Payne led other raids into Indian Territory. While he did not establish any permanent settlement, he did much to advertise the country, and his enthusiastic reports whetted the appetites of prospective settlers for these lands. Defeat of settlement seemed to make the "forbidden land" even more desirable and Payne's descriptions of Oklahoma got increasingly idyllic. In one pamphlet he wrote that "no other territory . . . in the world, presents features and advantages at all commensurate with the beautiful land of Oklahoma, the garden spot, the Eden of modern times—richest of all of them both in dollars from the soil and health for the people."[30]

The work of Payne and other boomers, however, was not in vain. As vanguards of the agricultural frontier, they finally achieved what they wanted when on March 2, 1889, Congress, after providing for the final Indian claims, authorized transferring the unassigned lands to the public domain. On March 23 President Harrison announced that this part of Indian Territory, generally known as Oklahoma, would be open for settlement on April 22, and that the existing United States land laws would be in force. This meant that the area could be homesteaded.

Since there were many more homeseekers than land available for farms, government officials adopted a new technique to equalize opportunity among prospective settlers. This was the land run. In preparation for the rush of settlement, people were permitted to travel through Indian lands to the borders of the Oklahoma District where they camped to await the official opening under the eyes of federal troops. Precisely at 12 noon on April 22, 1889, soldiers fired their pistols signaling the opening, and the mad scramble for land followed. Newsman and promoter Fred L. Wenner described the scene: "Along the line as far as the eye could reach, with a shout and a yell the swift riders shot out, then followed the light buggies or wagons and last the lumbering prairie schooners and freighters' wagons, with here and there even a man on a bicycle and many too on foot,—above all a great cloud of dust hovering like smoke over a battlefield. It was a wild scramble, a rough and tumble contest filled with excitement and real peril."[31]

Before nightfall hundreds of settlers had staked out farms and prepared to file claims on their land, while tent cities like Guthrie and Oklahoma City rose from the prairies around previously settled railroad stations. Nothing like this had ever happened before on the American frontier. Within a few hours an uninhabited land had been almost fully claimed and much of it was occupied. One settler wrote on the evening of the run: "Never dreamed we'd have such close neighbors. People are around staking claims and settin' up tents. The whole prairie is covered with things [tents] and some people were even plowin' this afternoon."[32]

Some settlers had sneaked into the Oklahoma District and staked out choice land before the official opening. A few of these so-called sooners had invaded the region so early that they had gardens and fields growing when the first legal landseekers arrived. One story told of a man who made the run on a fine race horse, but when he got to his desired site he found a settler plowing the land with a team of oxen. The man on the race horse charged that the farmer was a sooner and that he had broken the law and forfeited his claim by entering the territory before the legal time. However, the farmer stoutly insisted that he had not entered the Oklahoma District before 12 noon. The rider then offered to buy the team of oxen. When asked why he wanted them, he replied that he was in the racing business and wanted to put those oxen in the race![33]

By June 30, 1889, 9 weeks after the opening, 5764 homesteads had been filed on 903,962 acres of land in the Oklahoma District. Within another year an additional 7033 homesteads had been entered for 1,081,883 acres. Not all of these filings resulted in established farms because some individuals filed on land and then failed either to construct buildings or to plant crops. These people did not want to farm, but hoped to sell a relinquishment or simply hold their claim for speculative gain. The census bureau found that by June 1, 1890, there were 7678 farms in the six counties that made up the heart of Oklahoma Territory, plus 232 more in Beaver County comprising the Oklahoma Panhandle, which was a noncontiguous part of the territory.[34]

Although a few farmers plowed some ground and planted crops in 1889, settlement came too late for much agricultural activity. One farmer recalled that "I used the axe to chop holes in the sod to plant the first corn crop. I put in eight acres the first year."[35] While some settlers grew a little corn, vegetables, and even a few bales of cotton, most of them spent their time building a house, digging a well, and breaking ground for the following season. The majority of settlers lived in dugouts, half dugouts, sod houses, or in crude log cabins. By the crop season of 1890 hundreds of farmers were planting corn, wheat, and oats, as well as vegetables and fruit trees. As had been true on earlier agricultural frontiers, most of these pioneer farmers were poor and initially they endured many hardships. Most settlers did not get a crop planted in 1889, and little was raised in 1890 because of a severe drought. This meant that farmers had to exist 2 successive years without crops or income from their land. Crops failed again in 1894 as a result of the

George M. De Groff, an attorney-at-law, in front of his law and real estate office at Guthrie, Oklahoma Territory, shortly after the Run of '89. (Division of Manuscripts, Library, University of Oklahoma)

widespread drought, which afflicted much of the Western Prairie and Great Plains region. However, production was good from 1891 to 1893.

Even before the opening of Oklahoma, the Dawes Act of 1887 provided that after Indians were given individual farms, surplus reservation lands could be made available to white settlers. Wherever Indian reservations contained good farm land, intense pressure soon developed to force the Indians to take allotments, return the remainder of the land to the public domain, and open it to white farmers. It should be kept in mind, however, that this law did not apply to the Five Civilized Tribes.

The land run of 1889 was only the beginning wedge of white settlement into former Oklahoma Indian Lands. During the 1890s the agricultural frontier burst into one former Indian reserve after another. In 1891 there was a rush of settlers into Sac and Fox, Iowa, Shawnee and Potawatomi lands east of Oklahoma Territory. The following year

208 - *West Texas, Indian Territory, and Oklahoma, 1860-1900*

The U.S. Land Office in Guthrie, Oklahoma Territory, May 27, 1889. (Division of Manuscripts, Library, University of Oklahoma)

about 25,000 settlers staged a mad run to claim surplus Cheyenne and Arapaho lands to the West. The biggest land run of all was in the Cherokee Outlet, which was opened September 16, 1893. On that day some 100,000 pioneers in search of land raced to obtain one of the 40,000 claims. Each of these areas was added to Oklahoma Territory, which was organized in May 1890, and in 1896 another region, Greer County, was attached to Oklahoma by a decision of the United States Supreme Court. In 1901 the remainder of southwestern Oklahoma was opened, following allotment of lands to the Kiowa, Comanche, Wichita, Caddo, and Apache Indians. However, the government abandoned the customary run as a means of acquiring land and adopted a lottery system. About 170,000 persons registered in hopes of drawing one of the 6500 claims.[36] In 1906 an area known as Big Pasture in the southwest was sold at public auction to qualified homesteaders.

Meanwhile, farmers had been moving into No Man's Land, a rectangular region west of the 100th meridian and bounded by Texas, New Mexico, and Kansas. Later known as the Oklahoma Panhandle, settlement in the eastern part of this region occurred after 1885 as an extension of the rush into southwestern Kansas. Since there was no government in the area, settlers could not get title to land. However, they established farms under squatter's rights. By 1887 it was estimated that there were 6000 farmers and townsite boomers in what came to be Beaver County. Drought, hard times, and failure to obtain legal land titles caused many people to soon abandon No Man's Land. In 1889 hundreds of these settlers made the run into the Oklahoma District. Beaver County was organized in 1890, and squatter rights were recognized after surveys were completed. In June 1890, however, there were, as mentioned earlier, only 232 farms in the county.[37]

Settlement in the original Oklahoma District was unusual in that practically all the land was available for homesteading. Unlike the situation throughout most of the West, huge acreages had not been given to corporations nor did the government hold large amounts for cash sale. Probably nowhere in the West was the ideal of using the public lands to provide homes for actual settlers more completely fulfilled than in Oklahoma Territory. To be sure there was sale of relinquishments and commutations, but these did not discourage settlement, stimulate land monopoly, or deter farm-making.

In the areas attached to the original Oklahoma Territory farmers could homestead in the sense that they could locate and file on a particular quarter section, but the laws required a cash payment varying from $1.50 in the Cheyenne-Arapaho country to as much as $2.50 an acre in the eastern portion of the Cherokee Outlet. Government officials held that some cash must be derived from the lands to compensate for the expense of liquidating Indian claims, but settlers insisted that they should be treated just like those on other parts of the public domain. Dick T. Morgan, president of the Free Homes League, declared that Oklahoma settlers were being discriminated against. "It may have the words—the voice of the homestead law," he said, "but it has the hairy hands of the old pre-emption law, requiring the lands to be purchased."[38] Following several years of effort led by congressional delegate Dennis Flynn, Congress passed the Free Homes Bill in May 1900. This law provided that unoccupied public domain in Oklahoma Territory could be entered free under the Homestead Act and that any unpaid amounts already owed by settlers on government lands would be cancelled.[39]

Like other frontiers, Oklahoma was pictured as an agricultural paradise by land companies, newspaper editors and other promoters. One writer declared that the soil was unexcelled in fertility, that nearly all crops, including cotton, flourished, that "all kinds of fruits grow as luxuriantly as in southern California." The hot summer days, he said, were cooled by a "delightful breeze from the gulf."[40] The editor of the Watonga Republican boasted that Blaine County was "the greatest wheat country in the world," and that farmers could raise "corn bigger than sawlogs and watermelons bigger than whales." The Arapaho *Arrow* ad-

210 - *West Texas, Indian Territory, and Oklahoma, 1860-1900*

A homesteader and his family on their claim in Oklahoma Territory shortly after the Run of '89. (Division of Manuscripts, Library, University of Oklahoma)

vised: "Go to plowing, sow every acre of wheat you possibly can this fall and next year it will be said of you, 'Verily, he is 'in it.' "[41] A broadside published about 1900 announced that southwestern Oklahoma had experienced only one crop failure in 12 years and that the healthful climate attracted invalids who "come here and regain their health." There was hardly any business for doctors in Oklahoma. Much of the Advertising connected with settlement in Oklahoma adopted a kind of frantic touch. It was said that the opportunity to acquire a free home was fast disappearing in America. "The Time Is Short! Oklahoma. The Last Chance," was the title of one broadside. Another filing agent wrote, "accept your last chance or forever hold your peace."[42]

Most of Oklahoma Territory was settled in the brief period between 1889 and 1901. This did not mean that all of the farm land was taken, but most of the best agricultural areas were occupied. By 1900 there were 62,495 farms in what only about a decade before had been sparsely settled Indian reservations. No other part of the agricultural frontier had been possessed so quickly by farmers and stockmen. Meanwhile, Congress forced the Five Civilized Tribes and other Indians who lived in Indian Territory between Oklahoma and Arkansas to take individual land allotments. Although the alloting of lands took several years after the

The Time is Short!

●●●●●●●●●●●●●●●●

OKLAHOMA

●●●●●●●●●●●●●●●●

THE LAST CHANCE!

●●●●●●●●●●●●●●●●

The Kiowa, Comanche, Apache and Wichita Reservations will soon be opened to settlement. These lands consist of about 3,303,610 acres; bounded on the north by Oklahoma, on the west and south by Texas, and on the east by the Chickasaw Nation. The famous Wichita Mountains, said to contain gold, silver, lead, copper and coal, are located near the center of this country. The topography of this country is level and undulating; it has sufficient timber for all farm purposes and is the best watered country I ever saw; its streams and tributaries abound in fish, with plenty of deer, turkey, chicken and quail left for sportsmen. The soil of this country is black loam, sandy loam, mulatto and red, all of which are very productive. A greater diversity of crops is raised here than in any country on earth. Cotton, corn, wheat, oats, barley, rye, Kaffir corn, sorghum, broom corn, millet, alfalfa, castor beans, etc., are successfully raised. All vegetables simply grow in abundance. The rainfall in Oklahoma is from 35 to 45 inches, and in this new country from 43 to 55 inches, insuring a crop every year. Oklahoma has had but one substantial crop failure in twelve years. The Great Rock Island Railroad runs along the entire eastern border of this country, giving an outlet to the north, east, west, and the gulf on the south. This company also has a line running from Chickasha west, through the northern part of this country, into Texas, and a line running from Anadarko south, to Fort Sill. When this country opens, it becomes a part of Oklahoma. The exemption laws of Oklahoma are as liberal as those of any state or territory. Any kind of farm work can be done here every month in the year. Stock run on pasture the year round, without shelter or feed, and do well. This is a healthful climate; many invalids come here and regain their health.

All the Reservations in this Territory have been opened by "Race or Run." This manner of opening, for various reasons, has grown in disfavor, and the prevalent opinion now is that this opening will be made by the President without date, so the exact time is not known. Under the law, it has to be before August 6, 1901. Under the law, the rights of soldiers, sailors and marines have not been abridged. They can file their declaratory through an agent. This can be done for less money than it would take to pay railroad fare here, to say nothing of delay, hotel bills and other expenses. Besides, those away from here would not know when to come. And, again, this country will be opened when you are in the midst of your crops. After your selection is made by an agent, you have six months in which to get to your claim and transmute. You will find unscrupulous parties flooding the mails with unwarranted statements, who have no interest in you, other than to get your money. Of such, I caution you to BEWARE. I have practiced law for over 30 years, and have practiced before the courts and United States Land Offices of this Territory, and before the departments at Washington. I have never done any crookedness to be censured for. I have been in this country since the opening. I am a Past Post-Commander of Kingfisher Post No. 2. I have filed hundreds of Declaratories for my comrades, and given general satisfaction. I am familiar with the land to be opened to settlement, and can make you as good selection as any one, for less money than those who have no interest in your welfare. The comrade who fails to get 160 acres of this fine land, for a home in his old days, misses the best opportunity of his life. Give this Circular to some Comrade.

For Terms and Pareiculars write me. Always inclose postage for reply. I have a few sectional maps of Oklahoma and the country to be opened to settlement. Will send you one for 20c in stamps.

Correspondence Solicited. Send for blank Declatory Statement.

Yours in F. C. and L.

M. M. Duncan,
Kingfisher, Oklahoma.

A typical piece of literature, widely circulated over the country before the opening of the Kiowa, Comanche Lands in Oklahoma Territory, 1901. (Division of Manuscripts, Library, University of Oklahoma)

212 - West Texas, Indian Territory, and Oklahoma, 1860-1900

Using a one-mule walking plow to break land for cotton in Indian Territory, about 1905. (Division of Manuscripts, Library, University of Oklahoma)

passage of the Curtis Act in 1898, the census of 1900 listed 45,505 farms in Indian Territory.[43]

Corn and wheat were the principal grain crops in Oklahoma Territory. While corn was raised by almost every farmer for both food and livestock feed, wheat was the main money crop. Governor William C. Renfrow reported in 1893 that wheat averaged about 20 bushels per acre throughout the territory. On some farms production was as high as 40 bushels.[44] However, like farmers throughout much of the Western Prairies and Great Plains, Oklahoma settlers suffered from poor crops in 1894 and 1895. From 100 acres of land in Woods County, a farmer grew a total of only 76 bushels in 1894, and 367 bushels in 1895. But the next year he raised 3800 bushels on the same land. The first good wheat crop after 1893 in all parts of the territory did not come until 1897.[45] After the two crop failures in 1894 and 1895 the Kingfisher *Free Press* said on October 31, 1895, that wheat raising was "a fake and a fraud" and advised greater diversification.

Oklahoma farmers did not have to wait long, if at all, for railroads to connect them with markets in Wichita or Kansas City. The Santa Fe built through the Oklahoma District in 1887, 2 years before the opening. Other lines extended into the wheat country of northwestern Oklahoma, and within a few years large quantities of wheat were being moved out of Kingfisher, Enid, and other towns. During the season of 1897, some 826 carloads of wheat, or 578,000 bushels, were shipped from Kingfisher.[46]

Farmers in Oklahoma Territory also produced oats, kaffir corn, milo maize, and other feed crops. Cotton grew in importance, too, and by 1899 producers raised 72,012 bales. The Kingfisher *Free Press* said that every Oklahoma farmer ought to have a field of cotton. The editor argued that it was a sure crop and enjoyed a cash market. "Farmers who raise cotton" continued the editor in a rather unrealistic vein, "never need to mortgage their livestock and farm implements to live on."[47] But Kingfisher and Blaine County were too far north for much successful cotton production. While there was some undue emphasis upon wheat in parts of Oklahoma Territory, farmers were quite well diversified in both crops and livestock almost from the beginning of settlement.

Oklahoma undoubtedly represented the best part of the agricultural frontier still remaining around 1890. At the time the territory was opened, most of the public land yet available for settlement was in the semiarid Great Plains or in the Mountain and Pacific coast states, where irrigation was necessary. It is not surprising that there was such a rush for farms in Oklahoma and Indian Territory where the land was not only fertile but where rainfall was generally adequate to produce crops. The central part of Oklahoma received an average of more than 30 inches of precipitation annually, and even as far west as Woodward and Elk City, which are west of the 99th meridian, yearly rainfall exceeded 20 inches. To be sure, those who advertised Oklahoma lands greatly exaggerated the region's prospects, but considering the areas open to settlement at the time, Oklahoma was by far the most desirable.

People migrated to Oklahoma from the Midwest, East, South, and from abroad. The northern part was settled mainly by Kansans, Missourians, and people from states north of the Ohio River. The southern part of the territory drew population from Arkansas, Texas, and other states from the Middle and Lower South. Both climate and the source of immigration determined farm production patterns. The north central and northwestern part of Oklahoma was an extension of the rich wheat lands of central Kansas and was settled by people experienced in wheat growing. In the central section of the territory wheat was also a major crop, but there cotton soon became an important product. Farther south cotton became the main cash crop. Throughout the entire territory livestock made up a big part of most farm enterprises. While Oklahoma farmers were soon confronted with common problems of markets, low prices, unfavorable weather, and erosion and soil depletion, early prospects for the hopeful settler who wanted to acquire that coveted piece of land seemed better in Oklahoma than anywhere in the United States.

◁ **12** ▷

The End of the Farmers' Frontier

Within a generation after the Civil War the most desirable parts of that great expanse of territory between Missouri and California had been largely occupied. The magnetic power of free or cheap land had done its work, and in a remarkably short time the agricultural frontier was gone. To be sure, there were still millions of acres on the Great Plains and in the Rocky Mountain region, which could be obtained under government land laws or at cheap prices from private owners. In fact, more land was disposed of under the Homestead Act between 1898 and 1917 than between 1868 and 1897. But these were mostly marginal lands except when irrigated or used for livestock ranges. Unless one could irrigate or ranch on a large scale, good opportunities for new settlers on the public domain were gone.

The great majority of entries filed on government land after about 1898 were made by petty speculators who had no intention of farming. The Commissioner of the General Land Office reported in 1904, for example, that 2756 homesteads were commuted at the Minot, North Dakota, land office between April 1, 1903, and March 31, 1904, while only 293 final entries were made on the basis of residence requirements. In other words, about 90 percent of the proofs on homesteads at that office were perfected under the commutation clause, and most of the land fell into the hands of land and cattle companies. The original entryman got $500 or $600 for his trouble of filing and going through the motions of settlement, and then returned to his former home. This was not only true on the Great Plains but in some of the timber and mining belts as well.[1] So while millions of acres were homesteaded after 1900, farmers established only a relatively few additional farms or ranches. By the 1890s the United States had entered a new phase of its history, when, for the first time since colonial days, a man could not push a little farther west and take up land on which he and his family could make a living. At least this opportunity existed in only a few places and for a very limited number of settlers.

One of the most notable things about the history of the American West in the late nineteenth century was the speed with which farmers occupied the unsettled regions suitable for agriculture. Pulled by the prospect of free or cheap land, encouraged by the railroads, enticed by private and official promotional agencies, and driven by the perennial hope of better things over the horizon, hundreds of thousands of restless pioneers soon conquered the agricultural frontier. The West experienced a number of frontiers, but it was the farmers who furnished most of the population, exploited the most valuable resource, and were mainly responsible for bringing the frontier in the United States to a close after nearly 3 centuries. Although thousands of Germans, Scandinavians, and other immigrant groups took up land in the American West after the Civil War, the great majority of those who spread out over the last frontier were native Americans from the Midwest and East. Except in Texas and Oklahoma, not many southerners were in the vanguard of westward settlement.

What kind of life did western pioneers lead during the late nineteenth century? Space does not permit a full answer to this question, but some brief observations are in order. Conditions, of course, varied in time and place, but settlers on the outer fringe of settlement had many common experiences. One of the main characteristics of frontier farming was the drudgery and hard work. It was not easy to carve a farm from the raw prairie, the desert, or the forest of the Pacific Northwest. Whether a farmer was breaking sod on the prairie-plains, clearing land in western Oregon or Washington, or plowing an irrigation ditch in Colorado, it was back-breaking toil. Moreover, much farm work was dull and monotonous. Diaries of frontier farmers carry entries day after day that report, "plowed today," "breaking prairie," "hoeing corn," or "cradled wheat." Even into the 1880s, when farm machinery became somewhat cheaper and more efficient, thousands of pioneers did much of their planting, cultivating, and harvesting by hand.

The daily existence of housewives was a round of caring for children, washing, baking, cleaning, sewing, doing outside chores, and even working in the fields during busy times. One frontier woman in northwestern Kansas recorded in her diary early in 1873: "done my housework then made fried cakes, squash pies, baked wheat bread and corn bread, cut out a night dress and partly made it." But often at the end of a long, hard day, she wrote, "am very tired"; and no doubt she was. Most nineteenth-century Americans, however, believed that hard work never hurt anyone, and on this score frontiersmen were not prone to self-pity. They only complained after their toil failed to produce a decent living.

All people are faced with human tragedy from time to time, and frontier farmers suffered their full share. Ill health, accidents, loss of crops and livestock, and even death itself, struck many farm homes. Often far from relatives and loved ones who might comfort them, these disasters weighed heavily upon families trying to make a start in a new country. Charles Thresher who settled 7 miles from Topeka told about the death of his young son in 1873. Evidently sick with diphtheria, no medicine seemed to help the boy. At "½ past 5 this A. M. [October 12] he died after much suffering," Thresher wrote. "Made his pants aunty sent him and burried him [sic] about sun down. All well with him." The next day Thresher went to Topeka and bought a coffin for $10. Elam Bartholomew, a Rooks County, Kansas, pioneer described the death of his baby in 1887: "it became evident that the hour of dissolution was near at hand and as the death dews began to gather on his pallid little brow, I took him from the arms of Mrs. O. P. Coy who had been holding him, and sitting down in the rocking chair held him tenderly until about half past three oclock when the dreaded summons came from the dark angel and with a light struggle his spirit, sinless from his birth, and made white in the blood of the Lamb, took its flight and went to mingle with the angelic hosts beyond the river, in the boundless ocean of God's love." Even though several neighbors came by to offer condolences, grief and emptiness overwhelmed Bartholomew.

Sadness was sometimes compounded with loneliness on the frontier. However, the loneliness on western farms has often been misunderstood. It is true that sometimes pioneer families were quite isolated and did not see neighbors very often. But this was the exception rather than the rule. Most settlers in the West were not lonesome because they were beyond easy traveling distance to neighbors, but because they desperately missed families, loved ones, and friends in the communities from which they had migrated. Most pioneers had strong emotional ties with their former homes. One poor and pregnant woman in western Kansas wrote in 1894 that "if I was in Iowa I would be all right." John A. Sanborn, a settler in southwestern Nebraska in the 1880s, wrote that it was a "red letter day" when his father and mother had come to visit from Illinois. It was an especially joyful occasion because upon departing, the parents gave Sanborn and his wife each $20.

Shortage of cash was one of the most common experiences of settlers on the frontier. For long periods of time many families existed without more than a token amount of money. Mrs. Mattie Oblinger wrote from Kansas in 1876 that "we have been very busy and most of the time without stamps and money." While most pioneer households handled only a small amount of cash during the early years of settlement, some money was essential to buy such things as coffee, sugar, kerosene, farm machine repairs, and other items. Besides selling products from their farm, settlers in hard times gathered and sold buffalo bones, they sought off-farm work on railroads, in nearby towns, or in distant harvest fields. They also borrowed and accepted gifts from relatives. It cannot be determined how much capital relatives provided for frontier farmers in the late nineteenth century, but diaries and correspondence reveal that it was a large sum. John Sanborn, for example, received a draft for $100 from his father in September, 1887, which he said "will help me out of debt." A settler who moved to near Hastings, Nebraska, in the spring of 1875 received $47.50 from his father and a little later $29.40 from his uncle. Thousands of western farmers like Sanborn and Gregory got financial help from midwestern and eastern relatives.

The constant worry over having enough money was intensified by the uncertainties of crops and prices. Many pioneers tightened their belts through the spring and summer with the expectation that things would improve with the sale of crops or livestock in the fall. But often they saw their grain destroyed by drought or hail, and livestock succumb to disease. At other times good crops sold at extremely low prices, resulting in a very small income. These conditions brought hopelessness and despair to many frontier farmers. During the early years of settlement most farm families did not handle over $300, and more often as little as $100. Even after a decade on a western farm, families commonly spent only $500 or $600 annually for both living and operating expenses.

Scarcity of money meant that many settlers had to go into debt. Diaries of farmers show almost constant need for credit, and the phrase, "did not pay for it," occurs again and again. Pioneer farmers were under constant pressure to find money to pay on store bills, machine notes, and other debts. Interest on short-term loans secured by personal property often ran 2 or 3 percent a month in many western communities during the 1870s and 1880s.

While frontier farm life after the Civil War had its pains and problems, it also had its pleasures and rewards. The stereotype presented by writers such as Hamlin Garland, which shows little but ugliness and poverty, is by no means fully accurate. Western farmers engaged in a wide variety of social activities and enjoyed many good times. In most communities there was a great deal of social visiting. To visit a neighbor usually meant staying for dinner or supper. Elam Bartholomew, who kept better records than most pioneer settlers, preserved a list of the number of people who called at his home in 1880, only 6 years after he migrated to northwestern Kansas. He also recorded the number of meals that his wife served to visitors. Altogether, 1081 persons of all ages visited the Bartholomew home, and Mrs. Bartholomew provided meals for 783 people over 3 years of age. Bartholomew's wife may have been weary, but she was surely not lonesome.

Besides frequent visits with neighbors, farmers organized and attended singing socials, literary and debate societies, spelling bees, Fourth of July celebrations, and Christmas parties. Indeed, many western farmers had a rather busy social life throughout the year, except during planting and harvest seasons. Bartholomew frequently referred to the good times that he and his family enjoyed at the various community affairs. On December 24, 1885, he wrote: "In the evening took wife and the children over to the schoolhouse where we participated in the Christmas tree festivities and enjoyed ourselves very much. We all received a number of pleasing presents. A very large crowd was present and everything went off nicely." Debates held at literary society meetings were a favorite type of entertainment. At the schoolhouse near Bartholomew's place on February 19, 1887, they debated the question: "Resolved that man will do more for the love of money than he will for the love of woman." The women were no doubt flattered when the negative won. Edward Hawkes, a Nebraska farmer, said that his literary society debated whether "there is more enjoyment in poverty than in riches." The judges apparently saw no joy in being poor—perhaps they knew about it from firsthand experience—and decided in favor of the negative side. Much of the social activity centered around the local school. Even church services were held in the schoolhouse during the early years of western settlement. Frontier areas were liberally supplied with different faiths and denominations. After only 6 years of settlement in Phillips County, Kansas, the Presbyterians, Congregationalists, Baptists, Methodists, and Catholics all had organized congregations. However, there were no separate church buildings and religous services were generally held in the schoolhouses. The same thing was true in many other frontier areas.

Pioneer settlers created most of their own entertainment and social life, and family affairs seemed to be especially happy and satisfying

220 - The End of the Farmers' Frontier

occasions. Bartholomew told how he fixed up a Christmas tree in 1881 which, he said, impressed the younger children a great deal. "Popcorn and plenty of apples made the evening pass pleasantly to all of us," he wrote, "and will be a green spot in our memories in years to come." John Sanborn in Nebraska recorded on December 24, 1887, that the family had set up a nice Christmas tree. A package from his parents in Illinois had arrived with presents for all, and three other couples with their children joined in the Christmas Eve festivities. The party was "very successful," he wrote.

The idea that frontier farmers were isolated and went for weeks without seeing a friend or neighbor is mostly imaginary. The speed of settlement was so great in most communities that strictly pioneer conditions did not last very long. Writing to "Dear friends in Indiana," on March 24, 1878, Uriah Oblinger said that, although he had lived in Fillmore County, Nebraska, only 3 years, most of the land had already been taken up and "three new frame houses are going up in the neighborhood at this time." Only 5 or 6 years after the first migration to large sections of eastern Washington, one editor wrote that "the pioneering days, the privations, and the anxious waiting for a better day are over. . . ." After the first 2 or 3 years of settlement, there was relatively little genuine isolation in most newly occupied areas.

Moreover, farmers moved about much more than generally assumed. Just because they had to travel in buggies or wagons pulled by horses did not mean that they were immobile. Mrs. Oblinger explained to relatives that it "does not take long to drive 20 or 25 miles here. . . ." Bartholomew commonly drove about 8 miles to Stockton, Kansas, two or three times a week and 18 miles to Kirwin on other occasions. Even cold winter weather did not force farmers to remain inside. The coming and going of people on the frontier as recorded in their diaries and letters indicate almost constant movement in both summer and winter. The diary of Hiram H. Young who lived 8 miles from Concordia, Kansas, shows between October 2 and 22, 1887, that he or members of his family went to town five times either for business or pleasure. This was an average of once every 4 days. In December 1876 Edward Hawkes traveled to town, had company, or attended some social event 13 out of the 31 days. Sanborn's travels and visits in January 1888 reveal the same picture. On January 23 he went to town and his wife visited neighbors; the next day he went again to Franklin, Nebraska, for coal, and his wife visited friends. They both called on neighbors on the 26th and 27th. On January 28 they drove to town, and Sunday the 29th to church. Then on Monday, January 30, they again went to Franklin to shop. Seven out of 8 days Sanborn and his wife were away from home. Actually, there was about as much travel on the frontier in the winter as in the summer when men were busy in the fields. Below zero weather was no deterrent to wagon travel. Settlers put hay or straw a foot or more deep in the wagon bed, wrapped up in heavy clothes and blankets and thought nothing of driving 8 or 10 miles to town, church, or just to visit on a cold winter night.[2]

Pioneering on the last agricultural frontier was characterized by a mixture of high hopes and bitter disappointment; successes, and failures. Beginning with little more than determination and a piece of land, thousands of western settlers established successful farms on which they were able to make a satisfactory living for themselves and their families. Time and place of settlement, hard work, careful management, temporary sacrifices in their standard of living, and a degree of luck all played a part in these successes. On the other hand, many western farmers were unable to meet the natural and man-made handicaps in the West and failed miserably. These settlers did not conquer the frontier, they were conquered by it. The western agricultural frontier was a powerful winnower and sifter.

Farmers on the prairie-plains frontier suffered especially from a wide variety of natural hazards, which greatly increased the risk of farming and contributed to many failures. Drought, frost, insects, wind, and other uncontrollable elements often destroyed feed and grain crops, as well as contributed to livestock losses. As emphasized earlier, the ultimate success of thousands of pioneer farmers depended upon whether crop conditions were favorable during the first 2 or 3 years of settlement while they were getting established and building up their meager supply of capital. Because of the vagaries of weather and the general climatic conditions in the semiarid and arid sections of the Western United States, it is not surprising that many settlers who were ignorant of natural conditions failed to establish a profitable farm. The amazing thing is that so many succeeded as well as they did.

The farmers' frontier encouraged individualism and self-sufficiency because settlers had to rely mainly on their own resources. But western pioneers in the late nineteenth century were practical enough to know that the solution to some of their problems required group effort. Facing droughts, grasshopper plagues, and other natural hazards, which were outside of their control, settlers turned easily and almost naturally to government for assistance. Moreover, farmers soon realized that cooperative action was necessary to expand irrigation facilities in the arid West and that the distribution of water could not be left to individual choice. In other words, western farmers had no basic objections to meeting their problems through group action, even when that cooperation was provided by government, if there was no other practical solution.

If frontier farmers sometimes compromised their independence, they maintained a basic optimism in the face of difficult circumstances. Particularly on the prairie-plains frontier in the 1870s and 1890s, natural hardships severely tested the courage and endurance of settlers. However, these hard-pressed pioneers kept looking for better things. Surely conditions would be better next year. A correspondent from Osborne County, Kansas, wrote on March 31, 1882, that "we are still hopeful, and while our wheat crop may be cut short by continued drouth, we are looking for a good season for summer crops." Writing after the crop failure in parts of western Kansas in 1879, another observer said that the residents of the region "still have a living faith in this part of the state, and so long as they can be kept from starvation, and there is any chance or hope for the future, they will not leave." Some did give up, but many settlers remained optimistic about the future even after several years of light crops or total failures. The farmer who dried out or lost his crop some other way would be found in his fields the next spring so long as he could get seed to plant.

Success in western farming was closely associated with adjustment to the geography and climate, which were unlike those found in the East and Middle West, where most of the new settlers came from. The successful frontiersman was one who could and did adapt to new conditions. Nowhere was this better demonstrated than on the agricultural frontier after the Civil War. Whether it was on the semiarid Great Plains, the arid Rocky Mountain states and territories, the Central Valley of California, or eastern Washington and Oregon, farmers quickly adjusted their farming patterns to the different natural conditions. Indeed, this was one of the most striking features of the western agricultural frontier.

Until the true nature of the Great Plains was understood by practical farmers, for example, settlement in that region went through a period of transition and adjustment, which by the 1890s had eliminated most of those who could not adapt their operations to the geography of the area. Thus the farmer who persisted in raising corn in western Kansas soon lost money, while the settler who made the proper adjustments usually succeeded. This involved raising the right grain crops, mainly wheat and kaffir corn, and relying heavily upon livestock. It also meant adopting new farming practices such as summer fallowing and selecting crop strains that would produce best under minimum moisture conditions. Moreover, adjustment meant a recognition of the region's scanty and uncertain rainfall as a permanent condition, and the necessity to provide feed and cash reserves to get one over periods of drought and crop failure.

Walter Prescott Webb in his book, *The Great Plains,* emphasized the problems surrounding a scarcity of wood and water west of the 98th meridian. However, the lack of readily available wood and water was a symptom of a basic problem and not the problem itself. It was not particularly difficult to use cow chips or twisted hay for fuel instead of wood, to put up a windmill rather than using the old hand pump, or to substitute barbed wire for the rail fence. Other than increasing the capital requirements for a new farmer, these factors were not a real deterrent to successful settlement. The basic problem was one of working out and adapting proper farm organization patterns to fit natural conditions on the Great Plains. In the Rocky Mountain region the most meaningful experience for the agricultural pioneers was that of bringing land and water together for production, and solving the problem of the ownership and distribution of water for irrigation. Again, the important question was one of adaptation.

Besides being responsible for settling most of the trans-Mississippi West, the basic importance of the last agricultural frontier was that it accounted for a large part of the tremendous physical expansion that characterized American agriculture in the years from 1860 to 1900. The total number of farms in the United States rose from 2,044,077 to 5,739,657, and improved farm acreage increased from 163,110,720 to 414,793,191 in this period. About 1,141,276 of the new farms and about 130,730,000 acres of improved land were added to the agricultural domain in the 19 western states and territories that were largely or entirely settled after 1860.[3] By 1900 the newly settled western part of the United States raised nearly 50 percent of the cattle, 56 percent of the sheep, about one fourth of the hogs, and 32 percent of the nation's cereal crop. Fifty-eight percent of the wheat was produced in the western states and territories. These figures indicate how important this region had become in the country's total farm output, especially when it is remembered that only about 17 percent of the population lived in that part of the United States.[4] The West, in other words, had become a producer of large agricultural surpluses, especially of grain and meat, and contributed greatly to the over-all farm problem, which became so serious after 1920.

As the farmers' frontier drew to a close, many citizens began to ask what effect the end of new and continued farm settlement would have on American life. What changes would this bring about in the country's economic growth; would it noticeably break the steady pulse of American development or change the American character? The answer to these and other questions was already being given, although it was not so evident to contemporaries who bemoaned the passing of the frontier.

Indeed, the pattern for the nation's future was set long before the last homesteads were filed. This pattern was one where business and industry would consume major energies and set the pace of American life. By 1890 the nation's industries were already producing more wealth than its farms. Farming would continue to be of major, but of secondary importance, and the main influences on American life and character would be urban, not rural. Yet, as the nation assumed first place among the greatest industrial countries in the world, a highly productive agriculture was one of the principal pillars upon which expanding industrialism rested. The nation's industrial development was not deterred or slowed by a struggle to produce enough food for the growing nonfarm sectors of the economy. Instead, American farmers not only produced enough food and raw materials for several of the nation's most important industries, but they turned out huge surpluses that were sold abroad. These farm products earned millions of dollars in foreign exchange and greatly helped to provide the needed capital for development of other aspects of the economy. Here is the true significance of the farmers' frontier and the expansion of agriculture in the late nineteenth century.

NOTES

Chapter 1: The Unknown Land

[1] U.S. Census, *Eighth Census* (1860), "Population."

[2] U.S. Census, *Eighth Census* (1860), "Agriculture," p. 222.

[3] Walter Prescott Webb, *The Great Plains* (Boston, 1931).

[4] "An Account of an Expedition from Pittsburgh to the Rocky Mountains. . . . Commanded by Major Stephen H. Long," Reuben Gold Thwaites, *Early Western Travels* (32 vols., Cleveland, 1905), vol. 14, p. 20.

[5] Thomas J. Farnham, "Travels in the Great Western Prairies," Thwaites, *Early Western Travels*, vol. 28, p. 109.

[6] Data on average rainfall and temperature may be found conveniently in *The Columbia Lippincott Gazetteer of the World*, Leon E. Seltzer, ed. (New York, 1952); see also J. Russell Smith and M. Ogden Phillips, *North America: Its People and the Resources, Development, and Prospects of the Continent as the Home of Man* (New York, 1942); *Climate and Man: Yearbook of Agriculture, 1941* (Washington, 1941); and *Land, Yearbook of Agriculture, 1958* (Washington, 1958).

[7] This figure includes Texas, 42,891; Kansas, 10,400; Minnesota, 18,181; California, 18,716; Oregon, 5806; and the territories of Dakota, 123; Nebraska, 2789; Nevada, 91; New Mexico, 5086; Utah, 3635; and Washington, 1330. U.S. Census, *Eighth Census* (1860), "Agriculture," p. 222.

[8] *Report of Brevet Colonel W. F. Raynolds, . . . On The Exploration of the Yellowstone and Missouri Rivers, in 1859–'60*. Sen. Ex. Doc. No. 77, 40th Cong., 2d Sess. (erroneously cited as the 1st Sess.), 1867 (Ser. No. 1317), pp. 15, 16, 115, and 153. This account includes Raynolds' report and diary as well as the reports of others in the Raynolds' party.

[9] Hazen to Major H. G. Litchfield, October 16, 1866, H. Ex. Doc. No. 45, 45th Cong., 2d Sess., 1867 (Ser. No. 1289), p. 2.

[10] General John Pope, Report on the Department of the Missouri, February 25, 1866. H. Ex. Doc. No. 76, 39th Cong., 1st Sess., 1866 (Ser. No. 1263), p. 2.

[11] Sherman to General J. A. Rawlins, August 24 and 31, and September 12, 1866. H. Ex. Doc. No. 23, 39th Cong., 2d Sess., 1866–1867 (Ser. No. 1288), pp. 7, 9, and 13.

[12] *Report of the Commissioner of the General Land Office*, 1868 (Washington, 1868), pp. 111–114. See also Richard A. Bartlett, *Great Surveys of the American West* (Norman, Oklahoma, 1962).

[13] *Report of the Commissioner of the General Land Office*, 1868, p. 138.

[14] F. V. Hayden, *Sixth Annual Report of the United States Geological Survey of the Territories . . . 1872*, H. Misc. Doc. No. 112, 42nd Cong., 3d Sess., 1873 (Ser. No. 1573), p. 277.

[15] William B. Hazen, "The Great Middle Region of the United States, and Its Limited Space of Arable Land," *North American Review*, vol. 246 (January 1875), p. 22.

[16] *Report of the Commissioner of Patents*, 1857, Agriculture (Washington, 1858), pp. 294–296.

[17] Albert D. Richardson, *Beyond the Mississippi* (Hartford, Connecticut, 1867), p. 77.

[18] Wood Diary, 1863. Minnesota State Historical Society.

[19] William J. Palmer, *Report of Surveys across the Continent in 1867–1868* . . . (Philadelphia 1869), pp. 117 and 133–134.

[20] Samuel Bowles, *Across the Continent: A Summer's Journey to the Rocky Mountains, the Mormons, and the Pacific States* (New York 1866), p. 18.

[21] Ovando J. Hollister, *The Mines of Colorado* (Springfield, Massachusetts, 1867), p. 423.

[22] The *Central Union Agriculturalist and Missouri Valley Farmer*, vol. 2 (December 1870), p. 370.

[23] U.S. Census, *Eighth Census* (1860), "Population," p. 549.

[24] LeRoy R. Hafen, "Utah Food Supplies Sold to the Pioneer Settlers of Colorado," *Utah Historical Quarterly*, vol. 4 (January 1931), pp. 62–63.

[25] James H. Baker and LeRoy R. Hafen, *History of Colorado* (3 vols., Denver, 1927), vol. 2, p. 586.

[26] Alvin T. Steinel, *History of Agriculture in Colorado* (Fort Collins, Colorado, 1926), pp. 49–50.

[27] Baker and Hafen, *History of Colorado*, vol. 2, p. 587.

[28] See the comments of Col. Samuel B. Holabird, "Report on Inspection Trip of the Department of Dakota, 1869," Sen. Ex. Doc. No. 8, 41st Cong., 3d Sess., 1870 (Ser. No. 1440), pp. 1–8; and K. Ross Toole, *Montana, An Uncommon Land* (Norman, Oklahoma, 1959), p. 80.

[29] William S. Greever, *The Bonanza West, The Story of the Western Mining Rushes, 1848–1900* (Norman, Oklahoma, 1963) p. 235.

[30] U.S. Census, *Eighth Census* (1860), "Agriculture," p. 183.

[31] Rawlins to O. E. Babcock, July 23, 1866, in H. Ex. Doc. No. 20, 39th Cong., 2d Sess., 1866–1867 (Ser. No. 1288), p. 11.

[32] *Council Journal of the Eighth Session of the Legislative Assembly of the Territory of Dakota* (Yankton, 1869), p. 203.

[33] Hjelm-Hansen Papers, 1869. Minnesota State Historical Society, Saint Paul. His letter was originally published in *Nordisk Folkebladet*.

[34] *Kansas Farmer*, vol. 4 (July 1867), p. 112.

[35] Ralph C. Morris, "The Notion of a Great American Desert East of the Rockies," *Mississippi Valley Historical Review*, vol. 13 (September 1926), pp. 190–200.

Chapter 2: Land and Immigration Policies in Minnesota, Dakota, Nebraska and Kansas

[1] Jane M. Grout, Diary of a Journey from Wisconsin to Southern Minnesota in 1873. Minnesota State Historical Society; Uriah W. Oblinger to Wife, November 5, 1872. Oblinger Papers. Nebraska State Historical Society; "Letters from a Pioneer Settler in Johnson County, 1864–1868," *Nebraska History Magazine*, vol. 13 (April–June 1932), pp. 130–131.

[2] Harold E. Briggs, "The Settlement and Economic Development of the Territory of Dakota," Doctoral Dissertation, University of Iowa, 1929, vol. 1, pp. 114–149.

[3] "Letters from a Pioneer in Johnson County," pp. 130–131.

[4] Thomas Donaldson, *The Public Domain*. H. Misc. Doc. No. 45, 47th Cong., 2d Sess., 1884 (Ser. No. 2158), p. 349.

[5] Addison E. Sheldon, *Land Systems and Land Policies in Nebraska*, Publications of the Nebraska State Historical Society, vol. 22 (Lincoln, 1936), p. 79.

[6] Twelve U.S. *Statutes at Large*, p. 392 (1862).

[7] Paul W. Gates, *Fifty Million Acres* (Ithaca, New York, 1954), p. 196. The

policy of selling government land suitable for farming by public auction was virtually abandoned after the Civil War, and public lands were reserved for purported settlers under the federal land laws.

⁸ Homer E. Socolofsky, "How We Took the Land," in *Kansas: The First Century*, John D. Bright, ed., (New York, 1956), pp. 291–292.

⁹ Gates, *Fifty Million Acres*, p. 252; Sheldon, *Land Systems and Land Policies in Nebraska*, p. 87; Richard C. Overton, *Burlington West, A Colonization History of the Burlington Railroad* (Cambridge, Massachusetts, 1941), p. 332; and Socolofsky, "How We Took The Land," p. 305. See also Evan E. Evans, "An analytical Study of Land Transfer to Private Ownership in Johnson County, Nebraska," Master's Thesis, University of Nebraska, 1950; Roy M. Robbins, *Our Landed Heritage, The Public Domain, 1776–1936* (Princeton, New Jersey, 1942), chapters 15 and 16.

¹⁰ Land Department, Union Pacific Railroad, *Guide to the Union Pacific R.R. Lands. 12,000,000 Acres, Best Farming Lands in America* (Omaha, 1870). This booklet includes a map showing sections owned by the railroad in the Platte Valley.

¹¹ Gates, *Fifty Million Acres*, p. 234.

¹² See Merrill E. Jarchow, *The Earth Brought Forth, A History of Minnesota Agriculture to 1885* (Saint Paul, 1949), p. 68, on this point as it applied to Minnesota.

¹³ Jarchow, *The Earth Brought Forth*, p. 57. When land was granted for educational purposes under the Morrill Act of 1862, there was not enough public land in some states to cover their allotment. The states were therefore given scrip, which could be exchanged for land in other states and territories. In some cases the scrip was sold to individuals or companies who then entered large blocks of land in the western states and territories.

¹⁴ Sheldon, *Land Systems and Land Policies in Nebraska*, p. 87.

¹⁵ *Kansas Farmer*, vol. 4 (September 1, 1867), p. 144.

¹⁶ *Congressional Globe*, 41st Cong., 2nd Sess., March 12, 1870, p. 2095.

¹⁷ Donald Danker, "The Beginnings of Rural Life in Nebraska," *Nebraska Farmer* (March 21, 1959), p. 74. See Thomas Le Duc's comments on the petty land speculator in "Public Policy, Private Investment, and Land Use in American Agriculture 1825–1875," *Agricultural History*, vol. 37 (January 1963), pp. 3–9.

¹⁸ *Kansas Farmer* vol. 17 (August 20, 1879), p. 272.

¹⁹ Donaldson, *The Public Domain*, pp. 360–361; and Robbins, *Our Landed Heritage*, pp. 218–219. The figures on original entries and final patents under the Timber Culture Act indicate that many of those who filed on land under this law never obtained title to it.

²⁰ The Homestead National Monument is located on the Freeman farm. However, there were many other homesteads filed the same day.

²¹ Donaldson, *The Public Domain*, pp. 350–351; and Socolofsky, "How We Took The Land," p. 297.

²² Donaldson, *The Public Domain*, pp. 353 and 355.

²³ Paul Gates did a great deal to stimulate criticism of the Homestead Act in his article "The Homestead Act in an Incongruous Land System," *American Historical Review*, vol. 16 (July 1936), but he has modified his earlier position in "The Homestead Act: Free Land Policy in Operation, 1862–1935," in *Land Use Policy and Problems in the United States*, Howard W. Ottoson, ed. (Lincoln, 1963), p. 37. See also the discussion in Benjamin H. Hibbard, *A History of the Public Land Policies* (New York, 1924), p. 409; and Fred A. Shannon, *The Farmer's Last Frontier, Agriculture, 1860–1897* (New York, 1945), p. 55.

²⁴ Shannon, *The Farmer's Last Frontier*, p. 55.

²⁵ These results were calculated from Donaldson, *Public Domain*, p. 353 ff.;

Census of Agriculture, 1950, General Report, vol. 2, pp. 51–52, and *Annual Reports of the Commissioner of the General Land Office*, 1881–1885.

[26] Shannon, *The Farmer's Last Frontier*, pp. 58–59.

[27] *Report of the Public Lands Commission*, 1904. Sen. Doc. No. 189, 58th Cong., 3d Sess., 1905 (Ser. No. 4766), pp. 66–67.

[28] Quoted in Peter J. Ristuben "Minnesota and the Competition for Immigrants," Doctoral Dissertation, University of Oklahoma, Norman, 1964, p. 148.

[29] *Central Union Agriculturalist and Missouri Valley Farm*, vol. 4 (June 1872), pp. 164 and 167.

[30] Herbert S. Schell, "Official Immigration Activities of Dakota Territory," *North Dakota Historical Quarterly*, vol. 7 (October 1932), p. 5.

[31] *General Laws of Minnesota*, 1867, p. 53.

[32] Schell, "Official Immigration Activities of Dakota Territory," p. 19.

[33] Ristuben, "Minnesota and the Competition for Immigrants," pp. 58–59.

[34] C. F. Walther and I. N. Taylor, *The Resources and Advantages of the State of Nebraska* (N.P., 1871), p. 6; and *Republican Valley Lands In Nebraska* (Nebraska City, 1872).

[35] Ristuben, "Minnesota and the Competition for Immigrants," p. 109; see also Carlton C. Qualey, *Norwegian Settlement in the United States* (Northfield, Minnesota, 1938), pp. 106–108; and Theodore C. Blegen, ed., *Land of Their Choice, The Immigrants Write Home* (Minneapolis, 1955).

[36] Saint Paul *Pioneer and Democrat*, February 5, 1858.

[37] Ristuben, "Minnesota and the Competition for Immigrants," pp. 184–185.

[38] Marcus L. Hansen, "Official Encouragement of Immigration to Iowa," *Iowa Journal of History and Politics*, vol. 19 (April 1921), p. 173.

[39] Charles L. Green, *The Administration of the Public Domain in South Dakota*, South Dakota Historical Collections, vol. 20 (1940), pp. 97–98.

[40] Paul W. Gates, *The Illinois Central and Its Colonization Work* (Cambridge, 1934).

[41] James B. Hedges, "The Colonization Work of the Northern Pacific Railroad," *Mississippi Valley Historical Review*, vol. 13 (December 1926), p. 330.

[42] L. L. Waters, *Steel Trials to Santa Fe* (Lawrence, Kansas, 1950), p. 241.

[43] Harold F. Peterson, "Early Minnesota Railroads and the Quest for Settlers," *Minnesota History*, vol. 13 (March 1932), pp. 28–29.

[44] Waters, *Steel Trials*, p. 240.

[45] *Kansas in 1875, Strong and Impartial Testimony of the Wonderful Productiveness of the Cottonwood and Arkansas Valleys* (Topeka, 1875), pp. 1–24. The editor of the *Kansas Farmer*, who also was a guest on this trip, reported that the well improved fields and heavy crops were a "continued surprise" to the excursionists. *Kansas Farmer*, vol. 13 (June 30, 1875), p. 204.

[46] *Guide to Union Pacific R.R. Lands, . . .* p. 16; Waters, *Steel Trails*, p. 223; and Overton, *Burlington West*, p. 450.

[47] Overton, *Burlington West*, p. 338.

[48] *Guide to the Union Pacific R.R. Lands, . . .* p. 12.

[49] Harold F. Peterson, "Some Colonization Projects of the Northern Pacific Railroad," *Minnesota History* vol. 10 (June 1929), p. 130.

[50] Saint Paul *Daily Press*, January 7, 1872.

[51] Saint Paul *Daily Press*, January 7, 1872.

[52] Saint Paul *Daily Press*, January 6, 1872.

[53] *Farmers Union*, vol. 7 (May 31, 1873), p. 174.

[54] Jackson (Minnesota) *Republic*, April 24, 1875, and January 22, 1876.

55 *Daily State Journal* (Lincoln, Nebraska), January 3, 1875.

56 *Kansas, Her Resources and Developments* (Cincinnati, 1871).

57 Elam Bartholomew Diary, entry for November 5, 1885. Kansas State Historical Society (Topeka).

Chapter 3: The Upper Midwest and Central Prairie Frontier, 1865–1875

1 For the Indian uprising in Minnesota see William Watts Folwell, *A History of Minnesota* (4 vols., Saint Paul, 1924), vol. 2, chaps. 5, 9, and 10. The Sioux uprising in 1862 was set off by the slow distribution of food and annuities to the Indians by the federal government. However, the basic causes went much deeper. Before troops restored order, some 612 citizens were reported killed in Minnesota and 32 in Dakota Territory. Going west from Winona, Minnesota, in August, Captain Cornelius F. Buck said that he and his troops met "great numbers of settlers from the frontier fleeing to the more thickly settled regions for protection, . . ." *Executive Documents of the State of Minnesota*, 1862 (Saint Paul, 1863), p. 501. On Dakota, consult Harold E. Briggs, "The Settlement and Economic Development of the Territory of Dakota," vol. 1, p. 56.

2 Briggs, "The Settlement and Economic Development of the Territory of Dakota," p. 58.

3 "Treasurer's Report," December 1, 1867, in *Laws of Minnesota*, 1868, p. 198.

4 Thomas Donaldson, *The Public Domain*, pp. 351–352.

5 *Kansas Farmer*, vol. 3 (October 1866), p. 149.

6 Earle D. Ross, *Iowa Agriculture* (Iowa City, 1951); p. 66.

7 *First Annual Message of Governor A. J. Faulk . . . Territory of Dakota*, December, 1866, p. 5.

8 Harold E. Briggs, "The Settlement and Development of the Territory of Dakota, 1860–1870," *North Dakota Historical Quarterly*, vol. 7 (1931–1932), pp. 114–149.

9 *Kansas Farmer*, vol. 9 (May 1, 1872), p. 138.

10 *Fourth Annual Report of the State Board of Agriculture*, Kansas, 1875, (Topeka, 1875), p. 388.

11 Donaldson, *The Public Domain*, pp. 352–353; and *Compendium of the Tenth Census*, 1880, p. 650.

12 Richard C. Overton, *Burlington West*, p. 383.

13 Peter J. Ristuben, "Minnesota and the Competition for Immigrants," p. 154–155.

14 *Saint Paul Pioneer*, April 22, 1867.

15 Ristuben, "Minnesota and the Competition for Immigrants," p. 165.

16 *Fourth Annual Report of the State Board of Agriculture*, Kansas, 1875, p. 67.

17 Beadle to Joseph S. Wilson, August 1, 1870. Records of the General Land Office, Dakota Territory, National Archives, R. G. 49.

18 Jane Grout, Diary, Minnesota State Historical Society.

19 George A. Batchelder, *A Sketch of the History and Resources of Dakota Territory* (Yankton, 1870), p. 248. Reprinted in *South Dakota Historical Collections*, vol. 14 (Pierre, 1928), pp. 181–251.

20 John Ise, ed., *Sod-House Days* (New York, 1937), pp. 12, 52, and 117.

21 Hilda Smith, "The Advance and Recession of the Agricultural Frontier in Kansas, 1865–1900," Masters Thesis, University of Minnesota, 1931, pp. 19–23. See also [Donald F. Danker] "Out of Old Nebraska." News Clipping, Nebraska State Historical Society, 1964.

[22] *Annual Message of Governor Marshall to the Legislature of Minnesota*, January 10, 1868 (Saint Paul, 1868), p. 19.

[23] *Message of Governor Thomas A. Osborn to the Legislature*, September 15, 1874 (Topeka, 1874), pp. 1–5.

[24] Applications for Relief, 1881. Kansas State Historical Society. Filed by county.

[25] Everett Dick, *The Sod-House Frontier* (New York, 1937), pp. 112 and 114.

[26] Kansas State Census, Agriculture, 1895. Norton County. See data on the depth of wells in Beaver Township, Rollins County, Kansas, in the census records. The author was raised on a South Dakota farm near the 99th meridian, where a 16-foot well could not be pumped dry. However, the depth of water varied greatly even in the same locality.

[27] *Fourth Annual Report of the State Board of Agriculture*, Kansas, 1875, p. 402. In Saline County, Kansas, in 1875 there were 94,932 rods of fence, of which 76,217 rods were hedge.

[28] Charles Thresher Diary, 1880. Kansas State Historical Society (Topeka).

[29] Manuscript Census of Agriculture, 1870. Pope County, Minnesota. Minnesota State Historical Society.

[30] Bartholomew Diary, entry for June 27, 1877, vol. 2.

[31] *Kansas Farmer*, vol. 5 (January 1868), p. 4. The Secretary of the Board of Immigration said a man on a homestead could get along at the beginning if he had $300.

[32] Accounts of Fred A. Fleischman, Lake Preston, Dakota Territory. Photostatic copies in the files of the North Dakota Institute for Regional Studies, Fargo.

[33] Mattie Oblinger to Parents, April 12, 1878. Nebraska State Historical Society; and Water, *Steel Trails*, p. 232.

[34] Thresher Diary, for appropriate years. Kansas State Historical Society.

[35] *Executive Documents for the State of Minnesota*, 1873 (Saint Paul, 1874), p. 450; and Manuscript Census of Agriculture, 1870. Minnesota State Historical Society (Pope County, Minnesota).

[36] Kansas State Census, Agriculture, 1875. Russell County. Manuscript copy, Kansas State Historical Society.

[37] Mattie Oblinger to Parents, August 8, 1876. Oblinger Papers, Nebraska State Historical Society.

[38] Thresher Diary for years 1873 and 1876. Kansas State Historical Society.

[39] *Statistics of Minnesota*, 1872, p. 6.

[40] *Farmers Union*, vol. 6 (August 29, 1872), p. 1.

[41] *Statistics of Minnesota*, 1877, pp. 8–10.

[42] Merrill E. Jarchow, *The Earth Brought Forth* (Saint Paul, 1949), pp. 167 and 175.

[43] *Farmers Union*, vol. 8 (August 15, 1874), p. 253.

[44] *Farmers Union*, vol. 6 (October 24, 1872), n.p.

[45] James C. Malin, *Wheat in the Golden Belt of Kansas* (Lawrence, 1944), p. 4.

[46] U.S. Census, *Ninth Census* (1870), "Agriculture," pp. 83, 155, and 199.

[47] Kansas State Census, Agriculture, 1875. Norton County.

[48] *Kansas Farmer*, vol. 4 (September 1, 1867), p. 141.

[49] *Fourth Annual Report of the State Board of Agriculture*, Kansas, 1875, pp. 80–82.

[50] *Compendium of the Tenth Census*, 1880, p. 770.

[51] Malin, *Wheat in the Golden Belt of Kansas*. See chapter 12 for a discussion of the introduction of new varieties.

[52] U.S. Census, *Ninth Census* (1870), "Agriculture," pp. 113, 155, 181, and 199; and *Compendium of the Tenth Census*, 1880, pp. 842, 862, 876, and 884.

Chapter 4: Destitution on the Frontier in the 1870s

¹ William Shadwell to J. F. Wallace, December 2, 1871, Governor's File No. 259, Minnesota State Archives. Hereafter cited as MSA.

² Flower to Horace Austin, October 22, 23, 24, and 25, 1871, Governor's File No. 259.

³ Johnson to Austin, October 30, 1871. Governor's File No. 259 contains receipts, letters, and statements about relief conditions.

⁴ Minnesota State Treasurer's Statement of Receipts and Disbursements, Relief Fund, Governor's File No. 259. An undated interim report showed that the Governor's office had received 649 applications for relief from 37 counties, and that $12,115 had been distributed. Assuming all 649 applicants received something, this would be an average of about $18.82 each.

⁵ *General Laws of the State of Minnesota*, 1872 (Saint Paul, 1872), p. 165; and Saint Paul *Daily Press*, February 1, 1872.

⁶ George M. Rohne to Stephen Miller, January 21, 1873; and E. P. Evans to Governor Austin, February 14, 1873, Governor's File No. 311. MSA.

⁷ *General Laws of the State of Minnesota*, 1873 (Saint Paul, 1873), p. 254.

⁸ *Fourth Annual Message of Governor H. Austin to the Legislature of Minnesota*, January 9, 1874 (Saint Paul, 1874), pp. 26–28.

⁹ Report of H. H. Sibley to the Saint Paul Chamber of Commerce, June 27, 1874. Sibley Papers, AS564, Box 15, Minnesota State Historical Society.

¹⁰ John E. Briggs, "The Grasshopper Plagues in Iowa," *Iowa Journal of History and Politics* vol. 13 (July 1915), pp. 349–391.

¹¹ *Journal of the Senate, State of Minnesota*, 1874 (Saint Paul, 1874), pp. 81–82; and *Fourth Annual Message of Governor H. Austin . . .*, p. 27.

¹² Briggs, "The Grasshopper Plagues in Iowa," p. 379.

¹³ *General Laws of the State of Minnesota*, 1874, pp. 252–254; see also the receipts in Governor's File No. 320, 1874. MSA.

¹⁴ Briggs, "The Grasshopper Plagues in Iowa," p. 381.

¹⁵ Eighteen U.S., *Statutes at Large*, 1875, p. 81.

¹⁶ Jennie Flint to C. K. Davis, February 6, 1874. Governor's File No. 320. MSA.

¹⁷ Junction City *Union*, August 1, 1874.

¹⁸ *Central Union Agriculturalist & Missouri Valley Farmer*, vol. 6 (October 1874), p. 294.

¹⁹ Wichita City *Eagle*, August 13, 1874.

²⁰ *Kansas Farmer*, vol. 12 (August 12, 1874), p. 1.

²¹ *Message of Governor Robert W. Furnas . . . to the Legislative Assembly*, 1875 (Lincoln, 1875), pp. 33–34.

²² Pearl Louise Erickson, "Destitution and Relief in Nebraska, 1874–1875," Master's Thesis, University of Nebraska, 1937, p. 13.

²³ Herbert S. Schell, *History of South Dakota*, p. 120.

²⁴ Stephen Miller to Governor C. K. Davis, July 4, 1874; and Rev. A. Kenter to Rev. J. Lieker, July 4, 1874. Governor's File No. 321. MSA.

232 - Notes

[25] Johannes Janson to C. K. Davis, July 20, 1874. Governor's File No. 321. MSA.

[26] D. Y. Jones to C. K. Davis, October 17, 1874; and letter from Mrs. Jones. Governor's File No. 321. MSA.

[27] Pearl L. Erickson, "Destitution and Relief in Nebraska, 1874–1875," p. 11.

[28] E. Cox to Davis, July 13, 1874; Samuel Carroll to Davis, July 19, 1874; and minutes of a meeting of citizens at Windom, Minnesota, May 26, 1874. Governor's File No. 321. MSA.

[29] *Daily State Journal* (Lincoln), December 1, 1874; and *Grand Island Times*, December 23, 1874.

[30] *Ellsworth Reporter*, January 21, 1875.

[31] *Kansas Farmer*, vol. 12 (December 1874), p. 412.

[32] *Journal of the Senate, State of Minnesota*, 1875, pp. 97–98; and Sibley to C. K. Davis, January 2, 1875, also in the *Journal of the Senate*, pp. 100–106.

[33] Schell, *History of South Dakota*, p. 120.

[34] Erickson, "Destitution and Relief in Nebraska, 1874–1875," p. 52.

[35] *Fourth Annual Report of the State Board of Agriculture*, Kansas, 1875, pp. 41–43.

[36] *Message of Governor Thomas A. Osborn to the Legislature*, September 15, 1874, pp. 1–5.

[37] *Laws of the State of Kansas, Passed at the Special Session of the Legislature in September, 1874* (Topeka, 1874), pp. 255–262.

[38] *Wichita City Eagle*, October 1, 1874.

[39] *Special Message of Governor Thomas A. Osborn to the Legislature of Kansas*, January 26, 1875 (Topeka, 1875), pp. 7–8.

[40] *Wyandotte Gazette*, March 12, 1875.

[41] *Kansas Session Laws*, 1875 (Topeka, 1875), pp. 8–9.

[42] *Message of Robert W. Furnas . . . to the Legislative Assembly*, January 1875, pp. 61–62.

[43] *Nebraska Session Laws*, 1875, pp. 173–175.

[44] *Bismarck Tribune*, September 23, 1874.

[45] *Message of Governor John L. Pennington*, December 7, 1874, p. 6. E. W. Camp, "North Dakota Pamphlets." North Dakota Historical Society.

[46] Schell, *History of South Dakota*, p. 120.

[47] Sibley to Davis, January 2, 1875. In *Journal of the Senate, State of Minnesota*, 1875, pp. 100–106; see the receipts in Governor's Grasshopper Relief File No. 361. MSA.

[48] *General Laws of Minnesota*, 1875, pp. 48, 182, 183, and 184.

[49] *House Journal, Proceedings of the Legislative Assembly of the State of Kansas*, 1875, p. 340.

[50] *Congressional Record*, 43rd Cong., 2d Sess., February 1, 1875, p. 887.

[51] Ord to Adjutant General, October 24, 1874. Records of Adjutant General, National Archives, Record Group 94.

[52] William W. Belknap to President U. S. Grant, November 11, 1874; and O. E. Babcock to Secretary of War, November 12, 1874. Records of Adjutant General, National Archives, R. G. 92.

[53] "Relief of Grasshopper Sufferers," H. Ex. Doc. No. 28, 44th Cong., 1st Sess., 1875 (Ser. No. 1687), p. 2.

[54] Official Journal of Lt. Theodore E. True Relating to Duty of Relief Distribution to Grasshopper Sufferers . . . in Dawson County, Nebraska. Nebraska State Historical.

[55] Dudley to Major George D. Ruggles, November 18, 1874. N. A. R. G. 94.

[56] Eighteen U.S., *Statutes at Large*, 1875, pp. 314–315.

[57] *Omaha Daily Republican*, February 25 and March 14, 1875.

58 "Relief to Grasshopper Sufferers," pp. 6–20. Only seven people received rations in Colorado and 1923 received rations in four counties of Iowa.

59 *Congressional Record*, 43rd Cong., 2d Sess., January 5, 1875, p. 252.

60 *Report of the Commissioner of Agriculture*, 1875 (Washington, 1876), p. 15.

61 D. Patten to Sibley, February 5, 1874. Governor's File No. 321. MSA.

62 Briggs, "The Grasshopper Plague in Iowa," p. 381.

63 The Red Cloud *Chief*, quoted in the Omaha *Daily Bee*, January 12, 1875.

64 Omaha *Daily Republican*, February 5, 1875.

65 William Bird to Governor Davis, June 13, 1874. Governor's File No. 321. MSA.

66 Quoted in *Kansas Farmer*, vol. 12 (August 19, 1874), p. 1.

67 *Fourth Annual Report of the State Board of Agriculture*, Kansas, 1875, p. 265.

68 Alex R. Banks to Governor Thomas A. Osborn, January 4, 1875. Governor's Relief File. KSHS.

69 Donaldson, *The Public Domain*, pp. 353–354.

70 *The Rocky Mountain Locust, or Grasshopper*, Report of Proceedings of a conference of the Governors of Several Western States and Territories . . . Held at Omaha on the 25th and 26th Day of October, 1876, . . . (Saint Louis, 1876).

71 William W. Folwell, A *History of Minnesota*, vol. 3, pp. 96–110; see also Walter N. Trenerry, "The Minnesota Legislator and the Grasshopper," *Minnesota History*, vol. 36 (June 1958), pp. 54–61.

72 James C. Olson, *History of Nebraska* (Lincoln, 1955), p. 184; Jarchow *The Earth Brought Forth*, p. 290; and Malin, *Winter Wheat*, pp. 40–41.

73 Quoted in *Nebraska Farmer*, vol. 1 (May 1877), p. 15.

74 *Kansas Farmer*, vol. 15 (March 21, 1877), p. 1.

Chapter 5: Bonanza Farming in the Red River Valley of the North

1 Chicago *Advance*, August 24, 1871.

2 Saint Paul *Daily Press*, February 22, 1871; and March 10, 1872.

3 The best account of bonanza farming is Hiram M. Drache, *The Day of the Bonanza, A History of Bonanza Farming in the Red River Valley of the North* (Fargo, 1964); see also George N. Lamphere, "History of Wheat Raising in the Red River Valley," *Minnesota Historical Society Collections*, vol. 10 (1905), pp. 2–33; Stanley N. Murray, "Railroads and Agricultural Development of the Red River Valley of the North, 1870–1890," *Agricultural History*, vol. 31 (October 1957), pp. 57–66. See also Murray, "A History of Agriculture in the Valley of the Red River of the North, 1812–1920," Doctoral Dissertation, University of Wisconsin, 1963; and the diary for 1873 and 1874 of R. W. Probstfield who lived 2 miles north of Moorhead. Minnesota State Historical Society.

4 See the reminiscences of Colonel James B. Power published in the Fargo *Forum and Daily Republican*, February 13, 14, and 15, 1912.

5 James B. Power, "History of the Northern Pacific Land Department Transactions from the Commencement of Sales, June 1872 to November 30, 1880." Power Letterpress Book, 1880–1882. North Dakota Institute for Regional Studies, Fargo. Hereafter cited as NDIRS. Drache, *The Day of the Bonanza*, pp. 46–52.

6 Dalrymple to Grandin brothers, March 12, 1876. Bayless Transfer Railroad Company files, Wisconsin State Historical Society. Hereafter cited as BTRC.

7 Oliver Dalrymple to William F. Dalrymple, January 15, 1876, BTRC. William did advance his brother money for expanded wheat operations, but the financial results were disappointing.

8 Dalrymple to Grandin brothers, March 12, 1876, BTRC. One land map of 1876

shows that Dalrymple held 18 sections of land, which probably included the Cass and Cheney properties that Dalrymple managed. These lands were often referred to as the Cass-Cheney-Dalrymple farms.

⁹ Power to George Stark, September 11, 1876. Power Letterpress Book.

¹⁰ Journal of the Amenia and Sharon Land Company, 1876–1892. NDIRS.

¹¹ Manuscript biography of John L. Grandin. Libby Manuscripts, North Dakota State Historical Society, Bismarck.

¹² Hard Wheat Interviews. Richland County. NDIRS.

¹³ *Richland County Gazette*, April 17, 1880; and December 21, 1881.

¹⁴ *Letters from Golden Latitudes*. Booklet published by the Great Northern Railroad. See Drache, *The Day of the Bonanza* for a list of big farms, pp. 80–82.

¹⁵ Dalrymple to William F. Dalrymple, January 15, 1876. BTRC.

¹⁶ James B. Power to Editors of *Country Gentleman*, May 10, 1878. Power Letterpress Book.

¹⁷ U.S. Census, *Tenth Census* (1880), "Agriculture," pp. 181–182.

¹⁸ "Dakota Wheat Fields," *Harper's New Monthly Magazine*, vol. 60 (March 1880), p. 534.

¹⁹ *Nebraska Farmer*, vol. 2 (September 1879), pp. 214–215; New York *Tribune*, April 3, 1879.

²⁰ New York *Tribune*, September 23, 1879.

²¹ P. Donan, *The Land of Golden Grain* (Chicago, 1883), pp. 36 and 43; and *Prairie Farmer*, vol. 51 (March 13, 1880), p. 81.

²² Power, "History of the Northern Pacific Land Department."

²³ Power to Frederick Billings, March 21, 1879. Power Letterpress Book.

²⁴ *Report of the Commissioner of the General Land Office*, 1879, pp. 603–605 and 1880, pp. 615–625; Drache, *The Day of the Bonanza*, p. 27.

²⁵ Fargo *Weekly Forum*, December 9, 1890.

²⁶ Dickinson *Press*, May 2, 1884, and October 24, 1885.

²⁷ *Dakota Farmer*, vol. 10 (November 1, 1890), p. 1.

²⁸ Journal of the Amenia and Sharon Land Company, 1876–1892, for the years 1881, 1882, 1885, and 1888. NDIRS.

²⁹ Breaking the sod was usually done in the summer. The turf would then rot, and in the fall or the following year the land was plowed. This was commonly called backsetting. After harrowing, the land was ready to seed. The breaking, backsetting, and harrowing cost about $4 to $4.50 an acre. By 1885 and 1886 some farmers were using a disc to tear up the broken sod rather than backsetting.

³⁰ Statement by Governor Arthur C. Mellette in Official Council House Letterpress Book, 1889, pp. 345–346. North Dakota State Historical Society.

³¹ U.S. Census, *Tenth Census* (1880), "Agriculture," pp. 181–182 and 194; and *Eleventh Census* (1890), "Agriculture," pp. 371–372 and 379–380. Stutsman County has been included even though it is in the third tier of counties west of the Red River because some large operations were established there on Northern Pacific Lands.

³² "The Bonanza Farms of the West," *Atlantic Monthly*, vol. 45 (January 1880), pp. 33–44.

³³ *North Dakota Farmer*, 1 (January 1886), p. 7.

³⁴ A. R. Dalrymple to William F. Dalrymple, April 20, May 29, and September 9, 1889. BTRC.

³⁵ James Chaffee to W. W. Chaffee, July 6, 1889. Amenia and Sharon Land Company files; and H. S. Chaffee to E. W. Chaffee, July 16, 1889. Chaffee Papers, NDIRS.

36 E. K. Butler to Oliver Dalrymple, December 15, 1885, and February 23, 1888. McCormick Papers, Letterpress Books, 1885 and 1888. Wisconsin Historical Society.

37 B. S. Russell, Statement of Receipts and Expenditures in Dakota accounts of Williams, Deacon and Company and himself. . . . Jay Cooke Papers, Minnesota State Historical Society.

38 Journal of the Amenia and Sharon Land Company, 1876–1892. Entry for 1883. NDIRS.

39 A. R. Dalrymple to William F. Dalrymple, October 15, 1882. BTRC.

40 Power Letterpress Book. Accounts for 1877.

41 A. R. Dalrymple to William F. Dalrymple, April 10, 1889. BTRC.

42 *Report of the Secretary of Agriculture, 1892* (Washington, 1893), pp. 434–435.

43 Power Letterpress Book, Accounts for 1877; Journal of the Amenia and Sharon Land Company, entries for 1886.

44 See William Allen White, "The Business of a Wheat Farm," *Scribner's Magazine*, vol. 22 (November 1897), pp. 531–548, for some of the economic problems faced by bonanza operators. White believed that high land prices "tempted many a bonanza farmer to reduce his acreage."

45 Oliver Dalrymple to L. K. Church, January 3, 1889. Letters to the Governor, Box 147. North Dakota State Historical Society.

46 *The Cultivator and Country Gentleman*, vol. 54 (September 12, 1889), p. 688; and vol. 65 (October 9, 1890), p. 798. For the unfortunate experiences of an English investor in the wheat business, see Morton Rothstein, "A British Investment in Bonanza Farming, 1879–1910," *Agricultural History*, vol. 23 (April 1959), pp. 72–78.

47 Drache, *The Day of the Bonanza*, p. 211.

48 "Bonanza Farms of the West," *Atlantic Monthly*, vol. 45 (January 1880), pp. 33–44.

49 *The Cultivator and Country Gentleman*, vol. 55 (June 12, 1890), p. 464.

Chapter 6: The Great Dakota Boom, 1878–1887

1 New York *Tribune*, April 28, 1877, p. 5.

2 Power to *Pioneer Press*, May 8, 1877. Power Letterpress Book. NDIRS.

3 Wichita *Weekly Beacon*, June 3, 1877.

4 Quoted in *Prairie Farmer*, vol. 56 (July 5, 1884), p. 418.

5 *Prairie Farmer*, vol. 51 (December 4, 1880), p. 385.

6 Samuel Aughey and C. D. Wilber, *Agriculture Beyond the 100th Meridian* (Lincoln, 1880), p. 5. See also Wilber's more extensive study, *The Great Valleys and Prairies of Nebraska and the Northwest* (Omaha, 1881).

7 Quoted in Fred Floyd, "A History of the Dust Bowl," Doctoral Dissertation, University of Oklahoma, 1950, p. 8.

8 *Prairie Farmer*, vol. 51 (July 24, 1880), p. 233; and *Kansas Farmer*, vol. 21 (April 18, 1883), p. 1.

9 45th Cong., 2nd Sess., H. Ex. Doc. No. 73 (Washington, 1878); see also Wallace Stegner, *Beyond the Hundredth Meridian, John Wesley Powell and the Second Opening of the West* (Boston, 1953), pp. 212–231.

10 *Prairie Farmer*, vol. 51 (July 6, 1884), p. 450.

11 Commissioner of Immigration, *Resources of Dakota* (Sioux Falls, 1887), p. 11.

12 *Plain Facts About Dakota, Its Fertile Lands, Its Wonderful Crops, and Its Inexhaustible Resources* (Milwaukee, 1882–1883), pp. 1–20.

[13] *Report of the Commissioner of the General Land Office*, 1879, p. 390.

[14] Charles L. Green, *Administration of the Public Domain in South Dakota*, p. 135; and *Report of the Commissioner of the General Land Office*, 1883, fold out table following p. 303, and also p. 124; and 1884, fold out table following p. 236.

[15] *Report of the Governor of Dakota, 1883* (Washington, 1883).

[16] Quoted in Marc M. Cleworth, "Twenty Years of Brown County Agricultural History, 1880–1899," *South Dakota Historical Collections*, vol. 17 (1934), p. 25.

[17] N. J. Dunham, *A History of Jerauld County* (Wessington Springs, South Dakota, 1910), p. 32.

[18] *Prairie Farmer*, vol. 16 (February 2, 1884), p. 66.

[19] Harold E. Briggs, "The Settlement and Economic Development of the Territory of Dakota," Doctoral Dissertation, University of Iowa, 1929, vol. 1, pp. 178–179 and 194.

[20] L. W. Lansing, "Hand County in the 1880s," *South Dakota Historical Collections*, vol. 22 (1947), p. 363.

[21] *Report of the Public Lands Commission, 1904*, pp. 177–178.

[22] Herbert S. Schell, *History of South Dakota*, p. 173.

[23] For a detailed account of this, see the *Report of the Public Lands Commission, 1904*, pp. 65–126 and 180–183.

[24] Cleworth, "Twenty Years of Brown County Agricultural History," pp. 27–33.

[25] *Prairie Farmer*, vol. 57 (October 17, 1885), p. 679.

[26] Cleworth, "Twenty Years of Brown County Agricultural History," pp. 38 and 40.

[27] Calculated from the U.S. Census, *Tenth Census* (1880), "Agriculture," pp. 36–38 and 1890, pp. 179–180.

[28] Territorial Manuscript Census of Agriculture, 1885. Edmunds and Hand counties, Dakota. South Dakota State Historical Society, Pierre.

[29] *Dakota Farmer*, vol. 7 (December 1887), p. 2; and vol. 8 (March 1888), p. 8.

[30] *Dakota Farmer*, vol. 3 (July 1884), p. 7; vol. 4 (June 1885), p. 8; and vol. 5 (May 1886), pp. 13–14.

[31] *Prairie Farmer*, vol. 57 (October 17, 1885), p. 677.

[32] Schell, *History of South Dakota*, p. 169; and U.S. Census, *Eleventh Census* (1890), "Population," pp. 655 and 606.

[33] *Report of the Governor of Dakota* (Washington, 1886), p. 3.

[34] See *Dakota Farmer*, vol. 6 (April 1887), p. 6; vol. 8 (March 1888), p. 8; (May 1888), p. 10; and vol. 14 (February 15, 1894), p. 5.

[35] *Dakota Farmer*, vol. 6 (March 1887), p. 8.

[36] *Dakota Farmer*, vol. 14 (April 1, 1894), p. 8.

[37] *Dakota Farmer*, vol. 4 (November 1885), p. 5; and vol. 5 (May 1886), p. 5.

[38] *Farm, Stock and Home*, vol. 3 (January 15, 1887), p. 65. This refers to number one hard wheat.

[39] *Dakota Farmer*, vol. 5 (August 1886), p. 14.

[40] U.S. Census, *Eleventh Census* (1890), "Agriculture," p. 383.

[41] *Prairie Farmer*, vol. 42 (March 15, 1890), pp. 161 and 168.

[42] *Yankton Press and Dakotan*, November 1, 1889; and Mellette to J. H. Branton, December 29, 1889. Governor's Letterpress Book, North Dakota State Historical Society (Bismarck).

[43] Undated Manuscript Statement, and Helgesen to Miller, March 12, 1890, File 152, Commissioner of Agriculture and Labor, NDSHS, Bismarck.

[44] Mellette to K. B. Kimmel, February 4, 1890. Governor's Letterpress Book, NDSHS.

45 "Official Statement of South Dakota Relief Committee, June 23, 1890. South Dakota Historical Society, Pierre. Box 2–7.

46 *Yankton Press and Dakotan*, November 1 and 14, 1889; and January 24 and February 5, 1890. See also the Dickinson *Press*, November 9 and 30, 1889, and January 11, 1890.

47 E. Back to Mellette, July 16, 1890. Mellette Papers. South Dakota State Historical Society.

48 *Conklin's Dakotian*, vol. 3 (July 11, 1889), p. 287.

49 See also the *Prairie Farmer*, vol. 61 (June 29, 1889), p. 416; (August 17, 1889), p. 528; and *Yankton Press and Dakotan*, February 11, 1890.

50 *Yearbook of the Department of Agriculture*, 1897, (Washington, 1898), p. 719.

51 Schell, *History of South Dakota*, p. 338.

52 U.S. Census, *Twelfth Census* (1900), "Population," vol. 1, pp. 296–304 and 356–365.

53 Calculated from the U.S. Census, *Eleventh Census* (1890), "Agriculture," pp. 226 and 383; and *Twelfth Census* (1900), Pt. 1, pp. 62 and 110. One of the most penetrating and valid studies of the westward move of grain farming is Charles M. Studness, "Development of the Great Plains Grain Farming Frontier to 1953," Doctoral Dissertation, Columbia University, 1963. See pages 73–91.

Chapter 7: The Central Plains Frontier, 1878–1896

1 *Kansas Farmer*, vol. 16 (September 18, 1878), p. 329.

2 Dodge City *Times*, November 3, 1877.

3 Manuscript Census of Agriculture, Ford County, Kansas, 1880. KSHS.

4 *Annual Report of the Commissioner of the General Land Office*, 1879, p. 610; 1880, pp. 620–621; U.S. Census, *Tenth Census*, (1880), "Agriculture," p. 72.

5 Samuel Aughey and C. D. Wilber, *Agriculture Beyond the 100th Meridian* (Lincoln, 1880). A pamphlet.

6 Figures from *Second Biennial Report of the State Board of Agriculture*, Kansas, 1879–1880, pp. 520–531; *Annual Report of the Commissioner of the General Land Office*, 1879 and 1880; and U.S. Census, *Tenth Census* (1880), "Agriculture," pp. 52 and 70.

7 U.S. Census, *Tenth Census* (1880), "Agriculture," pp. 188–189 and 197–98.

8 *Kansas Session Laws*, 1881, pp. 249–251.

9 Applications for relief. Kansas State Historical Society.

10 Bartholomew Diary, Entry for May 4, 1880. Kansas State Historical Society.

11 Quoted in *Kansas Farmer*, vol. 20 (December 6, 1882), p. 385.

12 Quoted in Dodge City *Times*, March 13, 1884.

13 Quoted in Dodge City *Times*, October 9, 1884.

14 *Prairie Farmer*, vol. 57 (September 26, 1885), p. 622.

15 Quoted in Dodge City *Times*, April 2 and April 23, 1885.

16 *Kansas Farmer*, vol. 23 and (July 23–August 19, 1885), p. 4 of both issues.

17 Hallie Farmer, "The Economic Background of Frontier Populism," *Mississippi Valley Historical Review*, vol. 10 (March 1924), p. 411. For a detailed study of farm credit see Allan G. Bogue, *Money at Interest* (Ithaca, N. Y., 1955).

18 Floyd M. Farmer, "Land Boom of Southwest Nebraska, 1880–1890," Master's Thesis, University of Nebraska, Lincoln, 1936, pp. 40 and 45.

19 *Kansas Farmer*, vol. 23 (August 19, 1885), p. 4; statistics on land filings were

taken from the *Annual Report of the Commissioner of the General Land Office* for the years 1884 to 1887.

[20] State Manuscript Census of Agriculture, Norton County, Kansas 1885. Kansas State Historical Society.

[21] See James C. Malin, "The Kinsley Boom in the Late Eighties," *Kansas Historical Quarterly*, vol. 4 (February 1935), pp. 23–49; and (May 1935), pp. 164–187; Hilda Smith, "The Advance and Recession of the Agricultural Frontier in Kansas, 1865–1900"; Gerld K. Aistrup, "An Investigation of the Relationship Between Climatic Conditions and Population Changes in Western Kansas, 1885–1900," Master's Thesis, Fort Hays State College, 1956; and Charles M. Studness, "Development of the Great Plains Grain Farming Economy Frontier to 1953," pp. 53–60.

[22] *Colorado Farmer*, vol. 28 (October 8, 1886), p. 4.

[23] Robert G. Dunbar, "Agricultural Adjustments in Eastern Colorado in the Eighteen-Nineties," *Agricultural History*, vol. 18 (January 1944), pp. 43–44.

[24] *Field and Farm*, vol. 5 (February 4, 1888), p. 4; and vol. 6 (September 15, 1888), p. 4.

[25] Alvin T. Steinel, *History of Agriculture in Colorado*, p. 253.

[26] Steinel, *History of Agriculture in Colorado*, p. 252.

[27] S. A. Swendson to Governor Lyman Humphrey, November 30, 1889; Alfred Leigh to Humphrey, December 9, 1889; and J. S. Oliver to Humphrey, January 21, 1890. Governor's Relief files, Kansas State Historical Society. The letters and circulars from Kansas citizens to the Governor cited in this chapter hereafter are in the relief file.

[28] Printed circular, October 19, 1889.

[29] Committee of citizens to Governor Lyman Humphrey, February 18, 1890.

[30] S. G. Campbell to Humphrey, September 5, 1890.

[31] Omaha *Daily Bee*, January 16, 1891.

[32] *Third Annual Message of Governor John M. Thayer*. February 5, 1891, pp. 42–45; and Luther P. Ludden, *Report of the Nebraska Relief Commission* (Lincoln, 1892).

[33] G. W. Finlay to Governor Humphrey, January 22, 1891.

[34] Denver *Times*, January 10 and 28, 1891.

[35] *Laws Passed at the Eighth Session of the General Assembly of the State of Colorado*, 1891, pp. 37–39.

[36] Mrs. Susan Orcutt to Governor L. D. Lewelling, June 29, 1894; and W. R. Christy to Brother Broad, December 28, 1894.

[37] William N. Cline to Governor Silas A. Holcomb, February 1, 1895; and Mrs. C. C. Fullerton to Governor Holcomb, February 25, 1895. Holcomb Papers, Nebraska State Historical Society.

[38] Denver *Republican*, February 21 and March 12, 1895. Up to February 21 the *Republican* had collected $2,486.18 in cash.

[39] Luther P. Ludden, *Report of the Nebraska State Relief Commission* (Lincoln, 1895), p. 61.

[40] *Laws . . . Passed by the Legislative Assembly of the State of Nebraska*, 1895, pp. 207–210.

[41] "Report of Commissioners Appointed by Governor Morrill . . . to Solicit and Distribute Aid and Relief to Western Kansas," May 1895. Governor's file. *Kansas Session Laws*, 1895, pp. 394–396.

[42] Quoted in Dunbar, "Agricultural Adjustments in Eastern Colorado," p. 49.

[43] Data taken from U.S. Census, *Eleventh Census* (1890) and *Twelfth Census* (1900), "Population."

44 James C. Malin, "The Adaptation of the Agricultural System to Sub-Humid Environment," *Agricultural History*, vol. 10 (July 1936), pp. 118–141.

45 U.S. Census, *Eleventh Census* (1890), "Agriculture," pp. 366–367, and *Tenth Biennial Report of the Kansas State Board of Agriculture*, 1895 and 1896 (Topeka, 1896), pp. 770–780.

46 U.S. Census, *Eleventh Census* (1890), "Agriculture." Irrigation, pp. 100–101, 266, and 273.

47 Denver *Republican*, February 7, 1891.

48 *Nebraska Farmer*, vol. 18 (August 9, 1894), p. 312; and (September 13, 1894), p. 585.

49 *Kansas Farmer*, vol. 20 (September 13, 1892), p. 293.

50 *Goodland News*, January 17, 1895.

51 A. Bower Sageser, "Editor Bristow and the Great Plains Irrigation Revival of the 1890s," *Journal of the West*, vol. 3 (January 1964), pp. 75–89.

52 *Inaugural Address of Silas A. Holcomb* (Lincoln, Nebraska, 1895), pp. 51–52.

53 State University of South Dakota, *University Bulletin*, No. 1 (Vermillion, 1800), pp. 1–7.

54 *Congressional Record*, 51st Cong., 1st Sess., August 18, 1890, pp. 8742–8743.

Chapter 8: Agricultural Settlement in Oregon and Washington

1 John Minto, "Ten Years of My Middle Life in Oregon." Manuscript Chapter, Minto Papers. Oregon State Historical Society, Portland.

2 *Message of the Governor of Oregon*, September 1866 (Salem, 1866), p. 12.

3 Charles M. Gates, ed., *Messages of the Governors of the Territory of Washington to the Legislative Assembly, 1854–1889*, University of Washington Publications in the Social Sciences, vol. 12 (August 1940), pp. 140–142.

4 *Pioneer and Democrat*, October 16, 1857.

5 *Compendium of the Tenth Census*, 1880 (Washington, 1883), pp. 48 and 58.

6 *Pioneer and Democrat*, September 30, 1859.

7 Quoted in Charles H. Carey, *History of Oregon* (Portland, 1922), p. 803.

8 Olympia *Washington Standard*, October 7, 1865.

9 Olympia *Washington Standard*, July 1 and August 12, 1865.

10 Pertinent tables in U.S. Census, *Eighth Census* (1860), and *Ninth Census* (1870), "Agriculture."

11 *Report of the Commissioner of the General Land Office*, 1868, p. 84.

12 E. P. Ferry to Commissioner of the General Land Office, August 10, 1870. Records of the General Land Office, National Archives, R. G. 49. Ferry later became Governor of Washington Territory.

13 "Communication from the Labor Exchange of Portland, August 23, 1870," in Appendix to the *Inaugural Address of Governor L. F. Grover*, September 14, 1870 (Salem, 1870). One of the promotional pamphlets designed to publicize Oregon's resources was A. J. Dufur, *Statistics of the State of Oregon; Containing a Description of Its Agricultural Development, and Natural and Industrial Resources*. . . . (Salem, 1869).

14 Arthur J. Brown, "Means of Promoting Immigration to the Northwest and Washington to 1910", Masters Thesis, University of Washington, 1942, pp. 30–31.

15 *Wilkeson's Notes on Puget Sound. Being Extracts from Notes by Samuel Wilkeson of a Reconnaissance of the Proposed Route of the Northern Pacific Railroad*

Made in the Summer of 1869 (n.p. 187?), p. 31. *Willamette Farmer*, vol. 6 (November 6, 1874), p. 4.

[16] *Williamette Farmer*, vol. 6 (July 4, 1874), p. 4; and vol. 7 (May 7, 1875), p. 4.

[17] Donaldson, *The Public Domain*, p. 296. See also Jerry A. O'Callaghan, "The Disposition of the Public Domain in Oregon." Doctoral dissertation, Stanford University, 1951.

[18] *Willamette Farmer*, vol. 6 (August 14, 1874), p. 4.

[19] *Willamette Farmer*, vol. 7 (April 30, 1875), p. 4; and *Settler's Guide to Oregon and Washington Territory and to the Lands of the Northern Pacific Railroad on the Pacific Slope* (New York, [1872?]), p. 28.

[20] Donaldson, *The Public Domain*, pp. 351–355.

[21] Quoted in Kenneth O. Bjork, *West of the Great Divide, Norwegian Migration to the Pacific Coast 1847–1893* (Northfield, Minnesota, 1958), p. 546.

[22] Manuscript Census of Agriculture, Lane County, Oregon, 1870. Oregon State Library, Salem.

[23] Oregon State Board of Immigration, *Oregon As It Is* (Portland, 1887); Hugh Small, *Oregon and Her Resources* (San Francisco, 1872); Oregon State Board of Immigration, *Oregon As It Is, Solid Facts and Actual Results* (Portland, n.d.); and *The Pacific Northwest* (New York, 1883).

[24] David S. Halbakken, "A History of Wheat-Growing in Oregon During the Nineteenth Century," Masters Thesis, University of Oregon, 1948, p. 55.

[25] H. O. Lang, *History of the Willamette Valley* (Portland, 1885), pp. 566–567.

[26] Frank B. Gill, "Oregon's First Railway," *Quarterly of the Oregon Historical Society*, vol. 25 (September 1924), pp. 171–235.

[27] *North-West Tribune* (Colfax), August 11, 1880.

[28] *Compendium of the Tenth Census*, 1880, p. 650.

[29] Manuscript Census of Population, Umatilla County, 1870. Oregon State Library.

[30] *The West Shore*, I (December 1875), p. 3.

[31] "Report of the Surveyor-General of Washington," October 9, 1879. H. Ex. Doc. No. 1, 42nd Cong., 2d Sess., 1879–1880 (Ser. No. 1911), p. 471. See also *Washington Standard*, July 1, 1876.

[32] *North-West Tribune* (Colfax), September 22, 1880.

[33] Olympia *Washington Standard*, July 30, 1880.

[34] *North-West Tribune* (Cheney) October 28, 1881.

[35] Fred R. Yoder, "Pioneer Social Adaptation in the Palouse County of Eastern Washington, 1870–1890," *Research Studies of the State College of Washington*, vol. 6 (December 1938), p. 137.

[36] Earl Zimmerman, "A History of the Development of Agriculture in Whitman County, Washington," Bachelor's Thesis, Washington State College, 1916, p. 9; and *Annual Report of the Commissioner of the General Land Office*, for the years 1881 to 1891 inclusive; and *Report of the Public Lands Commission*, 1904, Sen. Doc. No. 189, 58th Cong., 3d Sess., 1905 (Ser. No. 4766), pp. 177–178.

[37] W. H. Leaver, *An Illustrated History of Whitman County* (n.p. 1901), p. 105.

[38] *The West Shore*, vol. 9 (May 1883), p. 102.

[39] Spokane Falls *Review*, February 18, October 8, and December 7, 1890.

[40] Dorothy O. Johansen and Charles M. Gates, *Empire of the Columbia* (New York, 1957), pp. 372–381.

[41] *The West Shore*, vol. 9 (June 1883), p. 139.

[42] See Emmett K. Vandevere, "History of Irrigation in Washington, 1948." Doc-

toral dissertation, University of Washington, 1948. Joyce B. Kuhler, "A History of Agriculture in the Yakima Valley, Washington, 1880–1900." Masters Thesis, University of Washington, 1940.

43 For statistics on irrigation see, U.S. Census, *Twelfth Census* (1900), "Agriculture," pt. 2.

44 In 1900 there were 35,837 farms in Oregon and 33,202 in Washington. They averaged 281 and 256 acres, respectively.

Chapter 9: The Farmers' Frontier in California, 1850–1900

1 Hubert Howe Bancroft, *History of California* (7 vols., San Francisco, 1888), vol. 6, pp. 65–66.

2 *Transactions of the California State Agricultural Society, 1859* (Sacramento, 1860), pp. 342–348.

3 U.S. Census, *Eighth Census* (1860), "Agriculture," pp. 158–159; and Sacramento *Daily Union*, January 26, 1859.

4 Quoted in *Transactions of the California State Agricultural Society, 1874* (Sacramento, 1874), p. 419.

5 Sacramento *Daily Record-Union*, January 2, 1882.

6 *Official Report of the California State Agricultural Society's Fourth Annual Fair, 1857* (Sacramento, 1858), p. 15. On the problem of flooding, see Kenneth Thompson, "Historic Flooding in the Sacramento Valley," *Pacific Historical Review*, vol. 29 (November 1960), pp. 349–360, and Robert L. Kelley, *Gold vs. Grain: The Hydraulic Mining Controversy in California's Sacramento Valley* (Glendale, Calif., 1959).

7 *California Farmer*, vol. 13 (April 5, 1860), p. 60.

8 *Official Report of the California State Agricultural Society's Third Annual Fair, 1856* (Sacramento, 1856); and *1857* (San Francisco, 1858).

9 Sacramento *Daily Union*, January 26, 1859.

10 John W. Caughey, *California* (New York, 1953), chap. 20; Bancroft, *History of California*, vol. 7, p. 542. Bancroft gives 591 as the figure of confirmed claims. Paul W. Gates, "California's Embattled Settlers," *California Historical Society Quarterly*, vol. 41 (June 1962), pp. 99–125.

11 *Transactions of the California State Agricultural Society, 1859*, pp. 361–363.

12 C. P. Sprague and H. W. Atwell, *The Western Shore Gazetteer and Commercial Directory, For the State of California, . . . Yolo County* (San Francisco, 1870), p. 202.

13 The *Western Shore Gazeteer*, pp. 200–203.

14 Thomas Donaldson, *The Public Domain*, pp. 351–355.

15 *California Farmer*, vol. 23 (March 31, 1865), p. 81; *Biennial Report of the State Board of Agriculture . . . 1866 and 1867* (n.p., n.d.), and *Biennial Message of Governor H. H. Haight to the Legislature of the State of California, 1869–1870* (n.p., n.d.), p. 55.

16 "Memorial and Report of the California Immigrant Union," in appendix to the *Journals of the Senate and Assembly*, vol. 3 (Sacramento, 1872), p. 6.

17 *California Farmer*, vol. 33 (February 24, 1870), p. 44; and *Pacific Rural Press*, vol. 1 (January 14, 1871), p. 24, and *Pacific Rural Press*, vol. 9 (April 24, 875), p. 272.

18 *Biennial Message of Governor H. H. Haight to the Legislature . . . 1871–1872*, p. 62.

19 *Commerce and Navigation of the United States, 1869* (Washington, 1870), pp. 178–205; and *1876* (Washington, 1877), pp. 308–350.

20 *Pacific Rural Press*, vol. 1 (July 1, 1871), p. 404.

21 Sacramento *Daily Record-Union*, April 14, 1875.

22 *Transactions of the California State Agricultural Society, 1878* (Sacramento, 1879).

23 U.S. Census, *Ninth Census* (1870), "Agriculture," p. 346; and *Tenth Census* (1880), "Agriculture," p. 34.

24 *Pacific Rural Press*, vol. 2 (December 16, 1871), p. 376.

25 *Biennial Message of Governor R. Pacheco to the Legislature . . . 1875–1876* (n.p., n.d.), pp. 11–12; and *Annual Message of Governor George C. Perkins to the Legislature . . . 1881* (Sacramento, 1881), p. 17.

26 *Transactions of the California State Agricultural Society . . . 1874* (Sacramento, 1875), in appendix to the *Journals of the Senate and Assembly*, 1875–1876, 1, pp. 390–413.

27 *Official Report of the California State Agricultural Society's Third Annual Fair, 1856* (San Francisco, 1856), p. 14.

28 U.S. Census, *Eighth Census* (1860), "Agriculture," p. 163.

29 *Transactions of the California State Agricultural Society . . . 1868 and 1869* (Sacramento, 1870), pp. 152–153.

30 *Annual Report of the State Engineer to the Governor of the State of California. . . .* October 1880 (n.p.), pp. 32–34.

31 *Transactions of the California State Agricultural Society, 1874*, pp. 419–446.

32 *Annual Report of the State Engineer. . . .* October 1880, p. 60.

33 Department of Agriculture, *Irrigation. The Final Report of the Artesian and Underflow Investigation and of the Irrigation Inquiry*, 1892, pp. 95–96 (Ser. No. 2899); and *Irrigation and the Reclamation of Arid Lands*. Senate Rept. 928, 51st Cong., 1st Sess., 1890 (Ser. No. 2707), pp. 248–259.

34 U.S. Census, *Twelfth Census* (1900), "Agriculture," pt. 2, pp. 826–828; and *Eleventh Census* (1890), "Agriculture by Irrigation," p. viii.

35 Data compiled from the Ninth, Tenth, Eleventh, and Twelfth Censuses of Agriculture, 1870, 1880, 1890, and 1900.

36 Sacramento *Daily Record-Union*, November 2, 1889.

37 *California Farmer*, vol. 13 (June 22, 1860), p. 140.

38 Sacramento *Daily Union*, November 21, 1868.

39 *Pacific Rural Press*, vol. 16 (July 20, 1878), p. 40; "Report on the Cereal Production of the United States," *Tenth Census* (1880), "Agriculture," pp. 76–79; and Sacramento *Daily Record-Union*, September 19, 1883.

40 *Pacific Rural Press*, vol. 4 (September 7, 1872), p. 153. This story also appeared in several Midwestern farm papers.

41 Sacramento *Daily Record-Union*, January 26, 1859, and January 1, 1878.

Chapter 10: The Rocky Mountain Farming Frontier

1 U.S. Census, *Eighth Census* (1860), "Agriculture," pp. 178–181 and 222.

2 D. B. Sacket to Adjutant General, July 9, 1866, in H. Ex. Doc. No. 23, 39th Cong., 2d Sess., 1866–1867 (Ser. No. 1288), p. 52–53.

3 H. Ex. Doc. No. 23, 39th Cong., 2d Sess., 1866–1867 (Ser. No. 1288).

4 U.S. Census, *Ninth Census* (1870), "Agriculture," pp. 197, 129, and 349.

5 Leonard J. Arrington, *Great Basin Kingdom, An Economic History of the Latter-Day Saints, 1830–1900* (Cambridge, Massachusetts 1958), pp. 52–53. See also

George D. Clyde, "History of Irrigation in Utah," *Utah Historical Quarterly*, Vol. 27 (January 1959), pp. 28–32.

6 Arrington, *Great Basin Kingdom*, p. 150.

7 U.S. Census, *Eighth Census* (1860), "Agriculture," pp. 180 and 222.

8 U.S. Census, *Ninth Census* (1870), "Agriculture," p. 262. The census reported 22 bales of cotton.

9 Alvin T. Steinel, *History of Colorado Agriculture*, pp. 49–50. Probably the first irrigation in Colorado by an American was done by John Hatcher in Las Animas County south of Trinidad in 1847. See A. W. McHendrie, "The Hatcher Ditch . . . The Oldest Colorado Irrigation Ditch Now in Use," *Colorado Magazine*, 5 (June 1928), pp. 81–91.

10 *Report of the Commissioner of the General Land Office*, 1870, p. 424. The census gave the value of farm production in 1869, including additions to stock, as $2,335,106. U.S. Census, *Ninth Census* (1870), "Agriculture," p. 108.

11 James F. Willard ed., *The Union Colony at Greeley Colorado, 1869–1871* (Denver, 1918), pp. 12–13 and Willard and Colin B. Goodykoontz, eds., *Experiments in Colorado Colonization, 1869–1872* (Boulder, 1926).

12 Nicholas G. Morgan, "Mormon Colonization in the San Luis Valley," *Colorado Magazine*, vol. 27 (October 1950), pp. 269–293.

13 *Report of the Special Committee of the United States Senate on the Irrigation and Reclamation of Arid Lands*, vol. 3, 52nd Cong., 1st Sess., 1890 (Ser. No. 2708), p. 394; and U.S. Census, *Tenth Census* (1880), "Agriculture," pertinent tables.

14 Robert G. Dunbar, "The Origins of the Colorado System of Water Control," *Colorado Magazine*, vol. 17 (October 1950), p. 262; Dunbar, "Water Conflicts and Controls in Colorado," *Agricultural History*, vol. 22 (July 1948), pp. 180–186; and Dunbar, "The Significance of the Colorado Agricultural Frontier," *Agricultural History*, vol. 34 (July 1960), pp. 119–125.

15 U.S. Census, *Eighth Census*, (1860), "Agriculture," pp. 184–185 and 222; and *Ninth Census* (1870), "Agriculture," pp. 209 and 358.

16 William S. Greever, "Railway Development in the Southwest," *New Mexico Historical Review*, vol. 32 (April 1957), p. 157.

17 U.S. Census, *Tenth Census* (1880), "Agriculture," pp. 141 and 177.

18 Thomas Donaldson, *The Public Domain*, pp. 351–355 and 363–364. For an explanation of how the Mormons used the Homestead Law in Utah see Lawrence B. Lee, "The Homestead Act: Vision and Reality," *Utah Historical Quarterly* (Summer 1962), pp. 215–234.

19 Quoted in Arrington, *Great Basin Kingdom*, p. 354.

20 *Report of the Special Committe of the United States Senate on the Irrigation and Reclamation of Arid Lands*, 51st Cong., 1st Sess., Sen. Rept. 928 (4 vols., Washington, 1890), Serials 2707 and 2708, vol. 3, pt. 2, p. 393.

21 J. W. Powell, *Report on the Lands of the Arid Region of the United States*, H. Ex. Doc. No. 73, 45th Cong., 2d Sess. (Washington, 1878), p. 11.

22 *Message of John L. Routt, Governor of Colorado*, November 3, 1876 (Denver, 1876), p. 13; and John C. Fremont, "Report of the Governor of Arizona, November 20, 1879," H. Ex. Doc. No. 1, 46th Cong., 2d Sess., 1879–1880 (Ser. No. 1911), p. 386.

23 Richard R. Hinton, *Irrigation in the United States*. Sen. Misc. Doc. No. 15, 49th Cong., 2d Sess., (Ser. No. 2450), p. 7.

24 *Congressional Record*, 50th Cong., 1st Sess., September 10, 1888, p. 8478.

25 *Congressional Record*, 50th Cong., 1st Sess., September 10, 1888, p. 8469.

[26] *First Annual Report of the Reclamation Service.* H. Doc. No. 79, 57th Cong., 2d Sess. (Washington, 1903), pp. 18–19. See also Everett W. Sterling, "The Powell Irrigation Survey, 1888–1893," *Mississippi Valley Historical Review*, vol. 27 (December 1940), pp. 421–434.

[27] *Report of the Special Committee of the United States Senate on the Irrigation and Reclamation of Arid Lands*, passim.

[28] U.S. Census, *Twelfth Census* (1900), "Agriculture," vol. 2, p. 159.

[29] U.S. Census, *Twelfth Census* (1900), vol. 2, p. 62 and 1, p. 322.

Chapter 11: Pioneering in West Texas, Indian Territory, and Oklahoma, 1860–1900

[1] J. De Cordova, *Texas: Her Resources and Her Public Men* (Philadelphia, 1858), p. 23.

[2] U.S. Census, *Eighth Census* (1860), "Agriculture," pp. 216–217; and (1870), pp. 362–363.

[3] Rupert N. Richardson, *The Frontier of Northwest Texas, 1846 to 1876* (Glendale, California, 1963), pp. 114, 122, and 205.

[4] Richardson, *The Frontier of Northwest Texas, 1846 to 1876*, p. 253. See also Richardson, *The Comanche Barrier to South Plains Settlement* (Glendale, California, 1933).

[5] Richardson, *The Frontier of Northwest Texas*, p. 254.

[6] U.S. Census, *Ninth Census* (1870), "Agriculture," p. 363; and (1880), pp. 89–92.

[7] Rueben McKitrick, *The Public Land System of Texas, 1823–1910* (Madison, Wisconsin, 1918); Aldon S. Lang, *Financial History of the Public Lands in Texas*, (Waco, Texas, 1932); and Richardson, *Texas, The Lone Star State* (New York, 1943), pp. 385–391.

[8] *The Texas Almanac for 1867*, (Galveston, 1867), pp. 95 and 147.

[9] U.S. Census, *Ninth Census* (1870), "Agriculture," pp. 252–259.

[10] *The Texas Almanac for 1867*, p. 221.

[11] U.S. Census, *Tenth Census* (1880), "Agriculture," pp. 92 and 208.

[12] Richardson, *Texas, The Lone Star State*, p. 395.

[13] U.S. Census, *Ninth Census* (1870), "Agriculture," pp. 252–260; (1880), pp. 242–244; and (1890), p. 397.

[14] R. D. Holt, "The Introduction of Barbed Wire Into Texas and the Fence Cutting War," *West Texas Historical Year Book*, vol. 6 (June 1930), pp. 65–79; and Wayne Gard, "The Fence Cutters," *The Southwestern Historical Quarterly*, vol. 51 (July 1947), pp. 1–15. A Texas law of 1840 required that "every gardener, farmer or planter shall make a sufficient fence about his cleared land in cultivation." This was a disadvantage to the crop farmer. In 1873 the legislature amended the original law so that farmers did not have to fence against the incursions of sheep, goats, and hogs. However, a three-fifths vote of the people in a county was necessary to implement this provision, and some counties were specifically exempt.

[15] Roger A. Burgess, "Pioneer Quaker Farmers of the South Plains," *Panhandle-Plains Historical Review*, vol. 1 (1928), pp. 116–123.

[16] J. Evetts Haley, *The XIT Ranch of Texas* (Norman, Oklahoma, 1953), p. 204. See also L. F. Sheffy, "The Experimental Stage of Settlement in the Panhandle of Texas," *The Panhandle-Plains Historical Review*, vol. 3 (1930), pp. 78–103.

[17] Quoted in Sheffy, "The Experimental Stage of Settlement," pp. 94–95.

[18] For settlement in this area see Robert L. Martin, "The City Moves West:

Economic and Industrial Growth of the Southern Llano Estacado," Doctoral Dissertation, University of Oklahoma, 1959, p. 40.

[19] *Prairie Farmer*, vol. 57 (August 22, 1885), p. 533.

[20] Martin, "The City Moves West," p. 37; and U.S. Census, *Eleventh Census* (1890), "Agriculture," p. 386; and 1900, pt. 2, p. 186.

[21] W. C. Holden, "West Texas Drouths," *The Southwestern Historical Quarterly*, vol. 32 (October 1928), p. 107; J. W. Williams, "A Statistical Study of the Drouth of 1886," *West Texas Historical Association Year Book*, vol. 21 (October 1945), p. 105.

[22] The discussion of agricultural development among the Five Civilized Tribes is based mainly on Laura E. Baum [Graebner], "Agriculture Among the Five Civilized Tribes, 1865–1906," Masters Thesis, University of Oklahoma, 1940; see also Gilbert C. Fite, "Development of the Cotton Industry by the Five Civilized Tribes in Indian Territory," *Journal of Southern History*, vol. 15 (August 1949), pp. 342–353. For a general history, see Grant Foreman, *The Five Civilized Tribes* (Norman, Oklahoma, 1934).

[23] Sen. Mis. Doc. No. 143, 41st Cong., 2d Sess., 1870 (Ser. No. 1408), p. 3.

[24] Sen. Ex. Doc. No. 51, 42nd Cong., 2d Sess., 1872 (Ser. No. 1479), pp. 1–2.

[25] Sen. Ex. Doc. No. 6, 46th Cong., 2d Sess., 1879 (Ser. No. 1882), p. 4.

[26] Carl Coke Rister, *Land Hunger, David L. Payne and the Oklahoma Boomers* (Norman, Oklahoma, 1942), p. 44.

[27] See Rister, *Land Hunger, David L. Payne and the Oklahoma Boomers*, for Payne's career.

[28] Leaflet in Boomer Literature File, University of Oklahoma Archives.

[29] Rister, *Land Hunger*, pp. 58–59.

[30] "To Our Oklahoma Colonists," a leaflet in Boomer Literature File.

[31] Fred L. Wenner, "The Great Day Arrives." Manuscript in the Wenner Collection, University of Oklahoma Archives.

[32] Quoted in the *Sunday Oklahoman*, April 19, 1964.

[33] Owen L. Bland Interview, July 28, 1937. Indian-Pioneer Papers, vol. 8, pp. 446–447. Phillips Collection, University of Oklahoma Library.

[34] *Report of the Commissioner of the General Land Office*, 1889, p. 255; and 1890, p. 321; U.S. Census, *Eleventh Census* (1890), "Agriculture," p. 224.

[35] Louis N. Baker Interview, March 21, 1938. Indian-Pioneer Papers, vol. 4, p. 238.

[36] Edward Everett Dale and Morris L. Wardell, *History of Oklahoma* (New York, 1948), pp. 248–266. See also A. M. Gibson, "The Homesteaders Last Frontier," *American Scene*, vol. 4 (1962), p. 26 ff.

[37] Oscar A. Kinchen, "The Squatters in No Man's Land," *Chronicles of Oklahoma*, vol. 26 (Winter 1948–1949), pp. 385–398; see also Gaston Litton, *History of Oklahoma* (3 vols., New York, 1957), vol. 1, pp. 413 ff.

[38] Address of Dick T. Morgan, February 16, 1900. Boomer Literature File.

[39] Twenty-one U.S. *Statutes at Large*, p. 179 (1900).

[40] Fred L. Wenner, *The Homeseeker's Guide* (Guthrie, Oklahoma, n.d.), p. 20.

[41] Watonga *Republican*, August 9, 1893; and Arapaho *Arrow*, July 8, 1892.

[42] Boomer Literature File.

[43] U.S. Census, *Twelfth Census* (1900), "Agriculture," pt. 1, pp. 78 and 114.

[44] *Report of the Governor of Oklahoma*, 1893 (Guthrie, 1893), p. 11.

[45] Jesse Harder, "Wheat Production in Northwestern Oklahoma, 1893–1932," Masters Thesis, University of Oklahoma, 1952, pp. 12–13.

[46] Kingfisher *Free Press*, November 18, 1897.

[47] Kingfisher, *Free Press*, April 29, 1897.

Chapter 12: The End of the Farmers' Frontier

[1] *Report of the Public Lands Commission*, 1904 (Washington, 1905), pp. 72–74.

[2] There is a great lack of studies on rural social and cultural life in the West during the late nineteenth century. The best book on this subject is Everett Dick, *The Sod-House Frontier, 1854–1890*. However, most of my discussion has been based on diaries and correspondence of actual farm settlers. These include the diaries of Elam Bartholomew, Charles A. Thresher, Anne Jones Davies, Mrs. W. W. Dimond, and Hiram M. Young, who settled in Kansas; and those of John Sanborn, Edward Hawkes, George A. Gregory, and John Loder, of Nebraska. Also the Oblinger Letters in the Nebraska State Historical Society contain valuable information. The diary of Mrs. E. B. Boley, who settled near Mandan, North Dakota, describes the life of a pioneer woman. This is located at the North Dakota Historical Society. Hard times on the farm are most adequately revealed in letters written by western farmers to the governors of Minnesota, Kansas, and Nebraska in the 1870s, and Kansas, Nebraska, and the Dakota's in the 1890s. These are located in the state historical societies.

[3] These figures do not include Iowa.

[4] Calculated from the U.S. Census, *Twelfth Census* (1900), "Agriculture" and "Population."

AN ESSAY ON BIBLIOGRAPHY

There is an abundant literature dealing with the settlement of the American West in the late nineteenth century, but a relatively small amount of it deals with the farming frontier. Outside of the pertinent chapters in Fred A. Shannon's, *The Farmer's Last Frontier, Agriculture, 1860–1897* (New York, 1945), and Everett Dick's, *The Sod-House Frontier, 1854–1890* (New York, 1937), there is little of merit. Authors of the older state and regional histories gave only meager attention to the development of farming, and much of what they did write was useless for any real understanding of the settlement, development, and importance of western agriculture. Writers of more recent state histories have done better. Moreover, there is some good material in the two excellent surveys of the West, *Westward Expansion: A History of the American Frontier* (2nd ed., New York, 1960), by Ray A. Billington; and LeRoy R. Hafen and Carl Coke Rister, *Western America: The Exploration, Settlement, and Development of the Region beyond the Mississippi* (New York, 1941).

Histories of agriculture exist for only five of the western states and all but one of these are limited in time and scope. They include Earle D. Ross, *Iowa Agriculture: An Historical Study* (Iowa City, 1951); "A History of the Evolution of Agriculture in Nebraska, 1870–1930," Doctoral Dissertation, University of Nebraska, 1940, by Verne S. Sweedlun; Alvin T. Steinel, *History of Agriculture in Colorado* (Fort Collins, Colorado, 1926); and Samuel L. Evans, "Texas Agriculture, 1880–1930," Doctoral Dissertation, University of Texas, 1960; the best study that concentrates on the pioneer period is *The Earth Brought Forth: A History of Minnesota Agriculture to 1885* (Saint Paul, 1949) by Merrill E. Jarchow. A chapter by Frank Adams, "The Historical Background of California Agriculture" in *California Agriculture* (Berkeley and Los Angeles, 1946), edited by Claude B. Hutchinson is useful but very general. The journal *Agricultural History* contains many articles dealing with special phases of western agricultural development. Also pertinent volumes in *The Works of Hubert Bancroft* (39 vols., San Francisco, 1883–1890), include numerous references to western agriculture in the late nineteenth century. But with few exceptions, readers interested in western farming must search out the reports and observations that are buried in state and federal documents, in historical society publications, newspapers, farm journals, and similar sources. The references found in Everett E. Edwards, *A Bibliography of the History of Agriculture in the United States* (Washington D.C., 1930) are helpful, but emphasize the paucity of writing on western agriculture covering the years between the Civil War and 1900.

In order to get some picture of agriculture and its possibilities throughout the Great West in the 1850s and 1860s as people began pushing into this unknown land, it is necessary to examine the scattered references of contemporaries. A helpful source on early western agricultural prospects is the *Report* of the Commissioner of the General Land Office (Washington D.C.), which was published annually. Remarks by the surveyors-general in the different states and territories on soil, rainfall, crops, production, and land problems are especially good. Observations of army officers stationed in the West, as well as those of government scientists are also useful. Especially valuable are the reports of the *Geological and Geographical Survey of the Territories* published between 1867 and 1879. Most of these documents are in the government document serial set. The best source of statistical information on farms and production in the western states and territories are the censuses of agriculture for 1860, 1870, 1880, 1890, and 1900. The published census, however, has its limitations as the statistics are not broken down below the county level. For data on individual farmers or township totals, one must search through the unpublished manuscript censuses of agriculture. These are not available in any central place, but are located in different historical societies and state libraries of the western states. For instance, the manuscript census of agriculture for California for the years, 1850, 1860, 1870, and 1880 are located at the State Library in Sacramento. In Kansas these records are at the Kansas State Historical Society in Topeka. *The Report of the Commissioner of Agriculture* (Washington D.C.), for the years from 1862 to 1888, contains statistics and a few articles of value for a study of the agricultural frontier.

Some of the best information on western farming can be found in the reports of the various state and territorial agencies that dealt with agriculture. In Kansas, for instance, there was a State Board of Agriculture, which began publishing a report in 1872, and in California the State Agricultural Society began publishing reports as early as 1854. Some states and territories included agricultural statistics in their published executive and legislative documents. In Minnesota the *Report of the Commissioner of Statistics* (Saint Paul) included a section on the state's agriculture. Readers should be warned that both state and federal production statistics are subject to large error because of incomplete returns and the rough estimates of census takers, which are little more than educated guesses.

Another category of materials that have been largely unexploited include the unpublished diaries, letters, account books, and memoirs of pioneer farm settlers in the late nineteenth century. The state historical societies of Minnesota, Kansas, and Nebraska have some of the best farm diaries, and large collections of letters written by farmers are located in the Governors' files of the Minnesota State Archives, and the Kansas and Nebraska state historical societies. Special collections such as the John Minto Papers in the Oregon State Historical Society, Portland, are also valuable sources. The publications of the various western state historical societies all contain published memoirs of early settlers, but most of these are of indifferent value.

Land and Immigration Policies
in Minnesota, Dakota, Nebraska, and Kansas

Land policies and the disposal of the public domain had much to do with the farm patterns established throughout the western United States during the late nineteenth century. For background reading, the articles by Paul W.

Gates, "Research in the History of American Land Tenure," *Agricultural History*, vol. 28 (July 1954), and Thomas Le Duc, "The Disposal of the Public Domain on the Trans-Mississippi Plains: Some Opportunities for Investigation," *Agricultural History*, vol. 24 (October 1950) should be consulted. General accounts on land history include Benjamin H. Hibbard, *A History of the Public Land Policies* (New York, 1924), and Roy M. Robbins, *Our Landed Heritage, The Public Domain, 1776–1936* (Princeton, N. J., 1942). Studies that deal with land policy and disposition in individual states are Paul W. Gates, *Fifty Million Acres: Conflicts over Kansas Land Policy, 1854–1890* (Ithaca, N. Y., 1954); Roscoe L. Lokken, *Iowa Public Land Disposal* (Iowa City, 1942); Charles Lowell Green, *The Administration of the Public Domain in South Dakota*, South Dakota Historical Collections, vol. 22 (1940); Addison E. Sheldon, *Land Systems and Land Policies in Nebraska*, Nebraska Historical Collections, vol. 22 (1936); Jerry A. O'Callaghan, "The Disposition of the Public Domain in Oregon," Doctoral Dissertation, Stanford University, 1951; Reuben McKitrick, *The Public Land System of Texas, 1823–1910* (Madison, Wisconsin, 1918); W. W. Robinson, *Land in California* (Berkeley and Los Angeles, 1948); and Victor Westphall, *The Public Domain in New Mexico, 1854–1891* (Albuquerque, 1965).

Every serious student of public land policy must depend heavily upon the *Report of the Commissioner of the General Land Office* (Washington D.C.) published annually, as well as Thomas Donaldson's monumental study on *The Public Domain*. H. Mis. Doc. 45, 47th Cong., 2d Sess., 1884 (Ser. No. 2158). Perhaps the best study on the actual operation of the Homestead Act is "Kansas and the Homestead Act, 1862–1905," Doctoral Dissertation, University of Chicago, 1957, by Lawrence B. Lee. Lee's articles, "The Homestead Act: Vision and Reality," in the *Utah Historical Quarterly* (January 1960 and Summer 1962), show, among other things, that the Mormons proved up on a high percentage of their homesteads and utilized the Homestead Act to maintain compact settlements. Varying ideas on the value of the Homestead Act as a farm-maker, both expressed by Paul W. Gates, can be seen in the articles cited in footnotes 23 and 26 of chapter 2. Thomas Le Duc has dealt with the role of the farmer as a pretty land speculator in "Public Policy, Private Investment, and Land Use in American Agriculture, 1825–1875," *Agricultural History*, vol. 37 (January 1963). Other phases of land policy and its administration can be studied in John T. Canoe, "The Desert Land Act in Operation, 1877–1891," *Agricultural History*, vol. 11 (April 1937); George L. Anderson, "The Administration of Federal Land Laws in Western Kansas 1880–1890: A Factor in Adjustment to a New Environment," *Kansas Historical Quarterly* (November 1952) and Harold H. Dunham, *Government Handout: A Study in the Administration of the Public Lands, 1875–1891* (Ann Arbor, Michigan, 1941).

Many of the works on land policy in the years between 1860 and 1900 also contain material on immigration promotion and the attempts to attract more farmers to the West. Among the best works on promotion of western immigration by the railroads is Richard C. Overton, *Burlington West* (Cambridge, Massachusetts, 1941), which includes a list of advertising booklets published by some of the western railroads. The articles by James B. Hedges on "The Colonization Work of the Northern Pacific Railroad," in the *Mississippi*

Valley Historical Review, vol. 13 (December 1926), and "Promotion of Immigration to the Pacific Northwest by the Railroads" in the same journal, vol. 15 (September 1928) are excellent; Edna M. Parker, "The Southern Pacific Railroad and Settlement in Southern California," *Pacific Historical Review*, vol. 6 (June 1937), and other articles cited in the footnotes of chapter 2 provide specific information on the extent and techniques of promotion. Stanley N. Murray, "Railroads and the Agricultural Development of the Red River Valley of the North, 1870–1890," *Agricultural History*, vol. 31 (October 1957), provides a wider view of the relation between the railroads and agricultural expansion in that area. Morris N. Spencer has shown how the Union Pacific sought to advance settlement in "The Union Pacific Railroad Company's Utilization of Its Land Grant with Emphasis on Its Colonization Program," Doctoral Dissertation, University of Nebraska, 1950. "The Burlington and Missouri River Railroad Brings the Mennonites to Nebraska, 1873–1878," *Nebraska History* (March 1964) by John D. Unruh Jr., gives an account of how the railroads encouraged group settlement. However, the most revealing information is still to be found in the scores of pamphlets and publications printed by the railroads. The state historical societies of the western states and the railroad archives both contain collections of these pamphlets.

The best and most complete study of immigration promotion by a single state or territory is Peter J. Ristuben, "Minnesota and the Competition for Immigrants," Doctoral Dissertation, University of Oklahoma, 1964. Other important works include Herbert S. Schell, "Official Immigration Activities of Dakota Territory," *North Dakota Historical Quarterly*, vol. 7 (October 1932); Theodore C. Blegen, "The Competition of the Northwestern States for Immigrants," *Wisconsin Magazine of History*, vol. 3 (September 1919), the same author's "Minnesota's Campaign for Immigrants: Illustrative Documents," in *Yearbook of the Swedish Historical Society of America*, vol. 11 (1926), and William H. Russell, "Promoters and Promotion Literature of Dakota Territory," *South Dakota Historical Collections*, vol. 26 (1952). Two volumes of collected promotional and descriptive pamphlets dealing with immigration into Kansas and the West between 1854 and 1926 are located in the Kansas State Historical Society at Topeka. Some of the most active efforts to attract farmers were made by the state and territorial boards and commissions of agriculture. For example, the annual and biennial reports of the Kansas State Board of Agriculture had many characteristics of promotional literature. Another aspect of immigration promotion and settlement has been discussed by James P. Shannon, *Catholic Colonization on the Western Frontier* (New Haven, Connecticut, 1957).

The Upper Midwest and Central Prairie Frontier, 1865–1875

There are only a few general studies that contribute much to the history of the expanding agricultural frontier in Minnesota, Dakota, Nebraska, and Kansas in the first decade after the Civil War. These include Fred A. Shannon, *The Farmers Last Frontier* (New York, 1945); Merrill E. Jarchow, *The Earth*

Brought Forth: A History of Minnesota Agriculture to 1885 (Saint Paul, 1949); chapter 4 in *Early Economic Conditions and the Development of Agriculture in Minnesota* (Minneapolis, 1915), by Edward Van Dyke Robinson; parts of Verne S. Sweedlun, "A History of the Evolution of Agriculture in Nebraska, 1870–1930," Doctoral Dissertation, University of Nebraska, 1940; *pertinent* chapters in John D. Bright, ed., *Kansas: The First Century* (2 vols., New York, 1956); and James C. Malin, *Winter Wheat in the Golden Belt of Kansas* (Lawrence, Kansas, 1944). The two best accounts of Dakota settlement in this period are Harold E. Briggs, "The Settlement and Development of the Territory of Dakota, 1860–70," *North Dakota Historical Quarterly*, vol. 7 (January and June 1933), and the relevant material in Herbert S. Schell, *History of South Dakota* (Lincoln, Nebraska, 1961).

Although scores of reminiscences written by early settlers have appeared in the publications of the state historical societies, very few contain anything of substantial value for studying pioneer agriculture. Among the better contemporary accounts are "Knute Steenerson's Recollections: The Story of a Pioneer," *Minnesota History Bulletin*, vol. 4 (August–November 1921); E. D. Haney, "The Experiences of a Homesteader in Kansas," *Kansas Historical Collections*, vol. 17 (1926–1928); Paul H. Giddens, "Eastern Kansas in 1869–1870," *Kansas Historical Quarterly*, vol. 9 (November 1940), which is a collection of contemporary newspaper accounts, and Frank W. Dean, "Pioneering in Nebraska, 1872–1879—A Reminiscence," *Nebraska History*, vol. 36 (June 1955). There have been many good studies of foreign migration to the western frontier. Carlton C. Qualey, "Pioneer Norwegian Settlement in Minnesota," *Minnesota History*, vol. 12 (September 1931), deals with one important group, while Thomas P. Christensen has considered "Danish Settlement in Minnesota," *Minnesota History*, vol. 7 (December 1927). Other studies include Sarka B. Hrbkova, "Bohemians in Nebraska," and Joseph Alexis, "Swedes in Nebraska," both in the *Publications of the Nebraska State Historical Society*, vol. 19 (1919). An unpublished thesis of special value is Hilda Smith, "The Advance and Recession of the Agricultural Frontier in Kansas, 1865–1900," Masters Thesis, University of Minnesota, 1931. Other valuable Masters Theses, all done at the University of Nebraska, include Mary Ann Jakl, "The Immigration and Population of Nebraska to 1870," 1936; Evan E. Evans, "An Analytical Study of Land Transfer to Private Ownership in Johnson County, Nebraska," 1950; and Edwin A. Schaad, "An Agricultural History of Lancaster County, 1856 to 1900," 1939.

One of the best sources of information on agricultural settlement and farm life are the published and unpublished diaries of farmers. Two of the finest published diaries are, "The Diaries of a Nebraska Farmer, 1876–1877," edited by Clarence S. Paine in *Agricultural History*, vol. 22 (January 1948), and Powell Moore, ed., "A Hoosier in Kansas, The Diary of Hiram H. Young, 1886–1895," vol. 14 (May, August, and November 1946) and vol. 15 (February and May 1947). Although it covers an earlier period, Rodney C. Loehr's *Minnesota Farmers' Diaries: William R. Brown, 1845–46, Mitchell Y. Jackson, 1852–63* (Saint Paul, 1939), are also very helpful for insights into farm life and early settlement. Undoubtedly the best unpublished diary of a western farmer in the late nineteenth century is that of Elam Bartholomew, who lived in Rooks County, Kansas. Bartholomew's multivolume diary and that of Charles A. Thresher, who lived near Topeka, are located in the Kansas State Historical Society, Topeka. The Nebraska State Historical Society has the John A. Sanborn, John Loder, and other important farm diaries, which cover parts of the late nineteenth century. The Minnesota State Historical Society has, among others, farm diaries by John E. Cummins, who lived near Eden Prairie, the John S. Harris family papers and diaries, and the diary of R. W. Probstfield, who resided near Moorhead. A pioneer farm woman's life is revealed in the diary of Mrs. E. B. Boley, who settled northwest of Mandan, North Dakota, in 1878. Her diary is in the North Dakota State Historical Society, Bismarck.

The agricultural journals published in the western states contain abundant materials on settlement and expansion of farming during the late nineteenth century. Among the most important and useful are the *Kansas Farmer* (Topeka), which began publication in 1863; the *Farmers' Union* (Minneapolis) is especially good for the years 1867 to 1877; the *Minnesota Farmer and Stockman* (Minneapolis) covers the years from 1877 to 1887; the *Nebraska Farmer* (Lincoln) for 1877 and later years; and the *Dakota Farmer* (Huron and Aberdeen), which was started in 1881.

State government publications also contain a great deal of pertinent material on agricultural conditions during the first decade after the Civil War. The messages of the Governors to the legislature and the reports of the territorial Governor of Dakota to the Secretary of Interior, often describe the current farm situation. States and territories making up the upper midwest prairie frontier also made half-hearted attempts to gather agricultural statistics. In Minnesota, for instance, the governor's messages, local agricultural statistics, and other materials are included in *Executive Documents of the State of Minnesota* (Saint Paul). The *Annual Report of the State Board of Agriculture* in Kansas and later the *Biennial Report of the State Board of Agriculture* carries data on farms, land, crop production, and other materials by county. The most convenient source of statistics on agriculture in Nebraska is *Nebraska Agricultural Statistics, Historical Record, 1866–1954* (n.p., n.d.). The U.S. Census, *Ninth Census* (1870), "Agriculture," is indispensable, but the best source of information on particular farm operations is the federal manuscript census of agriculture. For Kansas, Nebraska, and Minnesota in 1870 these can be located in the state historical societies of these states. The most complete state census of agriculture is that of Kansas and should be consulted in the Kansas State Historical Society for the years 1865 and 1875.

Destitution on the Frontier in the 1870s

The hardships suffered by frontier farmers in the 1870s can be most clearly understood by reading the letters written by farmers themselves. Hundreds of letters and reports describing hard times caused by drought, grasshoppers, and other natural hazards in the 1870s are available in the files of state officials in Minnesota, Nebraska, and Kansas. The Governors' files in the Minnesota State Archives in Saint Paul and those located in the Nebraska and Kansas State Historical Societies are the best sources of information on frontier destitution and relief. The Henry H. Sibley Papers at the Minnesota State Historical Society also contain a great deal of material on relief problems in Minnesota.

Conditions in Nebraska and the actions taken to relieve want and suffering have been considered by Robert N. Manley, "In the Wake of the Grasshoppers: Public Relief in Nebraska, 1874–1875," *Nebraska History*, vol. 44 (December 1963); Pearl Louise Erickson, "Destitution and Relief in Nebraska, 1874–1875," Masters Thesis, University of Nebraska, 1937; Othman A. Abbott, "Plagues of Grasshoppers and Other Experiences," *Nebraska Historical Magazine*, vol. 11 (July–September 1928), and *Message of Governor Robert W. Furnas, Governor of Nebraska* (Lincoln, 1875). For the situation in Kansas, see "Rocky Mountain Locust Invasion," in the *Fourth Annual Report of the State Board of Agriculture* (Topeka, 1875); Hilda Smith, "The Advance and Recession of the Agricultural Frontier, 1865–1900," Masters Thesis, University of Minnesota, 1931, and the *Kansas Farmer*, vol. 12 and 13 (1874 and 1875). An extensive account of grasshopper raids in Minnesota can be found in William Watts Folwell, *A History of Minnesota* (4 vols., Saint Paul, 1921–1930), vol. 3. The response of the Minnesota legislature to the needs of settlers is traced in Walter N. Trenerry, "The Minnesota Legislator and the Grasshopper, 1873–77," *Minnesota History* (June 1958), and the plight of farmers on the Minnesota frontier is described in "Some Farmers' Accounts of Hardship on the Frontier," *Minnesota History*, vol. 37 (March 1961), edited by Gilbert C. Fite.

The role of the U.S. Army in providing relief to grasshopper sufferers on the frontier is reported in the *Letter from Secretary of War, Accompanying Copies of Reports and Recommendations of Generals Pope and Ord Relative to the Ravages of Grasshoppers*, Sen. Ex. Doc. No. 5, 43rd Cong., 2d Sess., 1874 (Ser. No. 1629) and *Relief of Grasshopper Sufferers*, H. Ex. Doc. No. 28, 44th Cong., 1st Sess., 1875 (Ser. No. 1687). John T. Schlebecker's article on "Grasshoppers in American Agricultural History," *Agricultural History*, vol. 27 (July 1953), and *The Rocky Mountain Locust, or Grasshopper, Report of Proceedings of a Conference of the Governors in Several Western States and Territories . . . October, 1876, . . .* (Saint Louis, 1876) should also be consulted. For another kind of hardship see James C. Malin, "Dust Storms Part Two, 1861–1880," *Kansas Historical Quarterly*, vol. 14 (August 1946).

Bonanza Farming in the Red River Valley of the North

Bonanza farming in the Red River Valley of the North has attracted wide interest among both popular writers and scholars. The most important book on the subject is Hiram M. Drache's, *The Day of the Bonanza, A History of Bonanza Farming in the Red River Valley of the North* (Fargo, 1964). There are two unpublished doctoral dissertations, which add a great deal to the history of agricultural settlement and expansion in the Red River Valley.

Arthur H. Moehlman, "The Red River of the North: An Analysis of the Advance of the Frontier of Settlement in the Area, 1850–1900," University of Michigan, 1934, and "A History of Agriculture in the Valley of the Red River of the North, 1812 to 1920," by Stanley N. Murray, University of Wisconsin, 1963. The article by Harold E. Briggs, "Early Bonanza Farming in the Red River Valley of the North," *Agricultural History*, vol. 6 (January 1932), is also good. One of the best special studies is by Morton Rothstein, "A British Investment in Bonanza Farming, 1879–1910," *Agricultural History*, vol. 33 (April 1959).

Older but still useful studies are Warren Upham, "The Settlement and Development of the Red River Valley," *Collections of the Minnesota Historical Society*, vol. 8 (1898), John L. Coulter, "Industrial History of the Valley of the Red River of the North," *Collections of the State Historical Society of North Dakota*, vol. 3 (1910), and George N. Lamphere, "History of Wheat Raising in the Red River Valley," *Collections of the Minnesota Historical Society*, vol. 10, pt. 1 (1905). There is no good biography of Oliver Dalrymple, perhaps the best-known bonanza farmer, but John S. Dalrymple's, *No. 1 Hard: Oliver Dalrymple, The Story of a Bonanza Farmer* (Minneapolis, 1960) provides some worthwhile information.

Many articles were written by contemporaries and appeared in the farm and popular journals. A sampling of these include C. C. Coffin, "Dakota Wheat Fields," *Harper's Monthly Magazine*, vol. 60 (March 1880); P. Bigelow, "The Bonanza Farms of the West," *Atlantic Monthly*, vol. 45 (January 1880); A. M. Anson, "Harvesting Wheat in Dakota," and D. J., "Dakota As a Farming Country," both in the *Cultivator and Country Gentleman*, vol. 47 (January 19, 1882, and October 26, 1882). The use of steam power on the bonanza farms has been discussed by Reynold M. Wik, *Steam Power on the American Farm* (Philadelphia, 1953).

The federal censuses of agriculture and of population for the years 1870, 1880, and 1890 provide invaluable data for a study of farming in the Red River Valley. Finally, the records in the North Dakota Institute for Regional Studies at Fargo are absolutely basic in any investigation of bonanza farming. Files there include the letterbooks of James B. Power, who was land agent for the Northern Pacific Railroad, and records of the Amenia and Sharon Land Company, of the Grandins, Oliver Dalrymple, and other bonanza operators.

The Great Dakota Boom, 1878–1887

The best surveys of agricultural settlement in Dakota outside of the Red River Valley are chapters 12 and 13 in Herbert S. Schell, *History of South Dakota* (Lincoln, Nebraska, 1961), Harold E. Briggs, "The Great Dakota Boom, 1879 to 1886," *North Dakota Historical Quarterly*, vol. 4 (January 1930), and the relevant parts of Briggs, *Frontiers of the Northwest, A History of the Upper Missouri Valley* (New York, 1940). The older *History of Dakota Territory* (2 vols., Chicago, 1915), vol. 1, by George W. Kingsbury, contains a considerable amount of material on pioneer farm settlement and immigration into Dakota. The most complete study of immigration promotion into Dakota is Herbert S. Schell, "Official Immigration Activities of Dakota Territory," *North Dakota Historical Quarterly*, vol. 7 (October 1932). The early migration of Norwegians into Dakota has been examined by Peter J. Ristuben, "History of the Early Norwegian Settlements in Southeastern South Dakota," Masters Thesis, University of South Dakota, 1957.

There are numerous histories of counties in Dakota as well as in those of other western states, but most of them add very little to the history of the agricultural frontier. The main exception to this is Marc M. Cleworth's, "Twenty Years of Brown County Agricultural History, 1880–1899," *South Dakota Historical Collections*, vol. 17 (1934). Cleworth catches the expansionist spirit, which was prevalent on this frontier, and shows clearly the history of settlement and agricultural development in that community. A great deal of information on the farmer's frontier in Dakota can be obtained from government publications. The *Report of the Governor of Dakota* prepared annually for the Secretary of the Interior was published separately and in some years was included in the government serial set. A section was usually included on the progress of farming. Important publications that include statistical data on agriculture, population, and other matters are *Resources of Dakota* (Sioux Falls, 1887), an official publication prepared by the Commissioner of Immigration, and Frank H. Hagerty, *The State of South Dakota, The Statistical, Historical and Political Abstract* (Aberdeen, 1889).

The growing interest in, and development of, irrigation that arose following dry years in the late 1880s and early 1890s have been discussed by James Realf Jr., "Irrigation Problem in the Northwest," *Arena*, vol. 4 (June 1891), Samuel H. Lea, *Irrigation in Dakota* (Washington, 1909), and Lowell E. Whiteside, "A History of Irrigation in South Dakota," Masters Thesis, University of South Dakota, 1955.

The Central Plains Frontier, 1878–1896

Many of the same works cited in the footnotes and bibliography for chapter 3 also include materials valuable for a study of western agriculture in the 1880s as farmers pushed onto the Great Plains. Besides Walter Prescott Webb's, *The Great Plains* (New York, 1931), the writings of James C. Malin are especially important in providing an understanding of the elements necessary for successful farming on the semiarid plains. See especially Malin's article on "The Adaptation of the Agricultural System to Sub-Humid Environment," *Agricultural History*, vol. 10 (July 1936), and "The Kinsley Boom in the Late Eighties," *Kansas Historical Quarterly*, vol. 4 (February and May 1935), which shows how the boom psychology in western Kansas was even greater in the nonfarm sector of the economy than it was in agriculture. In "The Turnover of Farm Population in Kansas," *Kansas Historical Quarterly*, vol. 4 (November 1935), Malin explains how farm population changed in different rainfall belts within the state. Finally, Malin provides stimulating insights into the problems of western farming in parts of his *Winter Wheat in the Golden Belt of Kansas*

(Lawrence, Kansas, 1944) and *The Grassland of North America: Prolegomena to Its History* (Lawrence, Kansas, 1947). Leola Howard Blanchard's *Conquest of Southwest Kansas* (Wichita, 1931) contains some material on agriculture in that region. Two of the most interesting and revealing books on pioneer farm life in north central Kansas are Howard Reude, *Sod-House Days: Letters from a Kansas Homesteader, 1877–78* (New York, 1937), edited by John Ise, and Ise's, *Sod and Stubble, The Story of a Kansas Homestead* (New York, 1936). The latter deals with the experiences of Ise's parents and is full of human interest. Jeff. Jenkins, *The Northern Tier, or Life Among the Homestead Settlers* (Topeka, Kansas, 1880) contains three chapters that deal with land and agricultural settlement in north-central Kansas. One of the most revealing studies of settlement in one portion of the Great Plains is Gerld K. Aistrup, "An Investigation of the Relationship Between Climatic Conditions and Population Changes in Western Kansas, 1885–1900," Masters Thesis, Fort Hays Kansas State College, 1956. Unfortunately, there are very few detailed studies of western agricultural communities, but A. D. Edwards, *Influence of Drought and Depression on a Rural Community: A Case Study in Haskell County, Kansas,* Social Research Report No. 7, United States Department of Agriculture (Washington, January 1939) analyzes the agricultural development of one county.

For the westward movement of farming in Nebraska see chapter 16 in James C. Olson, *History of Nebraska* (Lincoln, 1955), and Verne S. Sweedlun, "A History of the Evolution of Agriculture in Nebraska, 1870–1930," Doctoral Dissertation, University of Nebraska, 1940. Promotional in nature, but still containing a good deal of worthwhile information on farm settlement, land prices and other matters is *Johnson's History of Nebraska* (Omaha, 1880), by Harrison Johnson. The boom spirit and rapid occupation of southwestern Nebraska is considered by Lloyd M. Farmer, "Land Boom of Southwest Nebraska, 1880–1890," Masters Thesis, University of Nebraska, 1936. No student of western farming can afford to miss Arthur F. Bentley's, *The Condition of the Western Farmer as Illustrated by the Economic History of a Nebraska Township*, Johns Hopkins University Studies in Historical and Political Science, vol. 11 (Baltimore, 1893), which considers Harrison township in Hall County located between the 98th and 99th meridians. The most revealing study of the westward move of grain farming onto the Great Plains is Charles M. Studness, "Development of the Great Plains Farming Frontier to 1953," Doctoral Dissertation, Columbia University, New York, 1963.

Agricultural settlement and the problems of farming on the plains of eastern Colorado in the late 1880s and 1890s have been discussed by Alvin T. Steinel, *History of Agriculture in Colorado* (Fort Collins, Colorado, 1926), and Robert G. Dunbar, "Agricultural Adjustments in Eastern Colorado in the Eighteen-Nineties," *Agricultural History*, vol. 18 (January 1944). On irrigation development along the Arkansas River see Joseph O. Van Hook, "Settlement and Economic Development of the Arkansas Valley from Pueblo to the Colorado-Kansas Line, 1860–1900," Doctoral Dissertation, University of Colorado, 1933.

Problems surrounding the settlement and success of farmers who settled on the Great Plains can also be traced in the *Kansas Farmer* (Topeka), the

Nebraska Farmer (Lincoln), and the *Colorado Farmer* (Denver). Statistical material is most conveniently found in the United States Census of Agriculture for 1880, 1890, and 1900, but the *Biennial Report of the State Board of Agriculture*, Kansas, (Topeka) and the *Annual Report, Nebraska State Board of Agriculture* (Lincoln) for 1883 and subsequent years also provide a great deal of useful information. Both the Kansas and Nebraska state historical societies have scrapbooks and clipping collections, which deal with agriculture in those states.

Agricultural Settlement in Oregon and Washington

There is no general history of agricultural development in the Pacific Northwest, but some pertinent material can be found in such general works as *Empire of the Columbia, A History of the Pacific Northwest* (New York, 1957), by Dorothy O. Johansen and Charles M. Gates; Charlotte Shackleford, *Building a State, Washington 1889–1939* (Tacoma, 1940); Charles H. Carey, *History of Oregon* (Portland, 1922), and H. O. Lang, ed., *History of the Willamette Valley* (Portland, 1885). Many references to agriculture, land policies, and farm problems during the late nineteenth century are included in the messages of the governors. The most convenient places to find these are in the *Messages of the Governors of Oregon, 1866–1917*, bound in a single volume and located in the Oregon State Library, Salem, and Charles M. Gates, ed., *Messages of the Governors of the Territory of Washington to the Legislative Assembly, 1854–1889* (Seattle, 1940).

The migration and promotion of immigration to the Pacific Northwest can be followed in Dan E. Clark, "The Movement to the Far West During the Decade of the Sixties," *Washington Historical Quarterly*, vol. 17 (April 1926); Arthur J. Brown, "The Promotion of Emigration to Washington, 1854–1909," *Pacific Northwest Quarterly*, vol. 36 (January 1945); James B. Hedges, "Promotion of Immigration to the Pacific Northwest by the Railroads," *Mississippi Valley Historical Review*, vol. 15 (September 1928), and Kenneth O. Bjork, *West of the Great Divide: Norwegian Migration to the Pacific Coast, 1847–1893* (Northfield, Minnesota, 1958).

The matter of acquiring land has been most fully discussed by Jerry A. O'Callaghan in "The Disposition of the Public Domain in Oregon," Doctoral Dissertation, Stanford University, 1951. Wheat raising and its importance in the agricultural development of Oregon has been fully considered by David S. Halbakken, "A History of Wheat-Growing in Oregon During the Nineteenth Century," Masters Thesis, University of Oregon, 1948.

There are several studies that cover some phase of settlement and the expansion of agriculture east of the Cascades. These include R. E. Zimmerman, "A History of the Development of Agriculture in Whitman County, Washington," Bachelors Thesis, Washington State College, Pullman, 1916; Robert C. Nesbit and Charles M. Gates, "Agriculture in Eastern Washington, 1890–1910," *Pacific Northwest Quarterly*, vol. 37 (October 1946); "Early Farming in Umatilla County," by C. A. Barrett in the *Quarterly of the Oregon Historical Society*, vol. 16 (December 1915), and Joyce B. Kuhler, "A History of Agriculture in the Yakima Valley, Washington, 1880 to 1900," Masters Thesis, University of Washington, 1940. Parts of Fred R. Yoder's, "Pioneer Social Adaptation in the Palouse Country," *Research Studies of the State College of Washington*, vol. 6 (1938) provide some highly useful information on why farmers settled in that region. One of the finest studies of migration into a part of eastern Washington is Carl F. Reuss's, "The Pioneers of Lincoln County, Washington, A Study in Migration," *Pacific Historical Quarterly*, vol. 30 (January 1939). On the development of irrigation consult Emmett K. Vandevere, "History of Irrigation in Washington," Doctoral Dissertation, University of Washington, 1948. Some worthwhile information on farming and early settlement in Washington can be found in the collection of reminiscences entitled *Told by the Pioneers* (3 vols., n.p., 1937), edited by F. I. Trotter and others, and generally referred to as the Washington Pioneer Project.

Despite a sizeable amount of writing on various phases of pioneer farming in Oregon and Washington, the serious student must rely mainly on the newspapers, farm journals, and the published and unpublished censuses of agriculture. The unpublished census of agriculture for Washington Territory is available for 1860, 1870, and 1880 in the Washington State Library, Olympia; for Oregon these records are at the Oregon State Library in Salem, but only for the years 1850, 1870, and 1880. The 1860 returns are missing. The *Willamette Farmer*, which began publication in 1869 at Salem, is extremely informative on all phases of agricultural development.

The Farmers' Frontier in California, 1850–1900

A number of general histories of California, or those dealing with particular sections of the state, contain important materials on the settlement and development of agriculture in the American period. John W. Caughey's, *California* (Englewood Cliffs, N. J., 1953) deals with land problems, ranching and crop farming. Robert G. Cleland has discussed some of the difficulties connected with establishing a workable agriculture during the pioneer years in his book, *The Cattle on a Thousand Hills; Southern California, 1850–1870* (San Marino, Calif., 1941). There are several chapters in volume 1 of Joseph A. McGowan's, *History of the Sacramento Valley* (3 vols., New York and West Palm Beach, 1961), which explain the development of farming in that area. In the *History of California*, (vols. 23 and 24 of Bancroft's *Works*, San Francisco, 1888 and 1890), there is a great deal of undigested information on various aspects of California farming, land policies, and emigration promotion. Osgood Hardy has shown the general trends in the state's agriculture in, "Agricultural Changes in California, 1860–1900," *Proceedings of the Pacific Coast Branch of the American Historical Association* (1929).

On land policies and problems readers should see W. W. Robinson, *Land in California* (Berkeley and Los Angeles, 1948), which is comprehensive but lacks critical interpretation; R. L. Allen, "The Spanish Land Grant System As an Influence in the Agricultural Development of California," *Agricultural History*, vol. 9 (July 1935), and two articles by Paul W. Gates, "California's Agricultural College Lands," *Pacific Historical Review*, vol. 30 (May 1961) and

"California's Embattled Settlers," *California Historical Society Quarterly*, vol. 41 (June 1962), which deals with the controversy between settlers and large land holders in the 1850s.

One of the best sources on the early development of farming in California is the official reports of the California State Agricultural Society and later those of the State Board of Agriculture. The title varies, but the first report appeared in 1854. The study by E. W. Hilgard and others under the direction of the United States Commissioner of Agriculture entitled, *Report on the Climate and Agricultural Features and Agricultural Practices and Needs of the Arid Regions of the Pacific Slope* (Washington, 1882) also contains much valuable information on the development of farming in California up to that time. Two articles that picture the extent and methods of wheat growing are Horace Davis, "Wheat in California," *Overland Monthly*, vol. 1 (November 1868), and Alfred Bannister, "California and Her Wheat Culture," *Overland Monthly*, Second Series, vol. 12 (July 1888). H. D. Dunn wrote a contemporary description of California agriculture as he saw it in the 1860s in "California— Her Agricultural Resources," *Report of the Commissioner of Agriculture, 1866* (Washington, 1867).

Publications, largely promotional in nature but still containing worthwhile information on early farm settlement and the prospects for farming in California, include Titus Fey Cronise, *The Agricultural and Other Resources of California* (San Francisco, 1870); John S. Hittell, *The Resources of California, Comprising Agriculture, Mining, Geography, Climate, Commerce* (San Francisco, 1863) and later editions; Bentham Fabian, *The Agricultural Lands of California: A Guide to the Immigrant As to The Productions, Climate and Soil* . . . (San Francisco, 1869), and J. S. Silver, "Farming Facts for California Immigrants," *Overland Monthly*, I (August 1868). Silver's article emphasizes that California agriculture is different from that east of the Rockies and it advises prospective settlers on the requirements for successful farming. The role of colony migration in the settlement of California has been discussed by Virginia E. Thickens, "Pioneer Agricultural Colonies of Fresno County," *California Historical Society Quarterly*, vol. 25 (March and June 1946).

Irrigation and water policy can be studied in the *Report of the State Engineer to the Legislature of the State of California—Session of 1880* (Sacramento, 1880), *and Report of the Special Committee of the United States Senate on the Irrigation of Arid Lands*, vol. 2, The Great Basin and California. Sen. Rept. 928, 51st Cong., 1st Sess., 1890 (Ser. No. 2707). The *California Farmer*, which began publication at San Francisco in 1854, and the *Pacific Rural Press*, started in 1871, are essential to any study of California's agricultural history in the pioneer period. The federal manuscript census of agriculture for California is located at the California State Library in Sacramento and covers the census years 1850, 1860, 1870, and 1880.

The Rocky Mountain Farming Frontier

Alvin T. Steinel's, *History of Agriculture in Colorado* (Fort Collins, Colorado, 1926) is the only systematic treatment of agricultural development in any of the Rocky Mountain states and territories. However, there is a great deal of valuable material on farming in Utah during the late nineteenth century in Leonard J. Arrington's, *Great Basin Kingdom; An Economic History of the Latter-Day Saints, 1830–1900* (Cambridge, Mass., 1958). Bancroft's *Works*, including the *History of Washington, Idaho and Montana, 1845–1889*, vol. 31 (San Francisco, 1890), and volumes 26, 17, and 25 cover other territories and states in the Rocky Mountain region. Material in the Bancroft volumes is valuable and often hard to locate elsewhere, but there is no organized presentation of farm settlement or agricultural development.

The best sources on agriculture are the federal censuses of agriculture, the annual *Report of the Commissioner of the General Land Office* (Washington, D.C.), and the discussions and statistics found in the yearly reports of the territorial governors to the Secretary of Interior, especially for the 1870s and 1880s. Some of these reports are in the government document serial set, but they were also generally published as separates.

Among the more worthy special studies dealing with certain phases of settlement, land disposition, and general agricultural development are Victor Westphall, "The Public Domain in New Mexico, 1854–1891," Doctoral Dissertation, University of New Mexico, 1956; Lawrence B. Lee, "The Homestead Act: Vision or Reality," *Utah Historical Quarterly*, Vol. 30 (Summer 1962), which provides an evaluation of the Homestead Act; Joseph Earle Spencer, "The Development of Agricultural Villages in Southern Utah," *Agricultural History*, vol. 14 (October 1940); Mrs. James D. Agnew, "Idaho Pioneer of 1864," *Washington Historical Quarterly*, vol. 14 (January 1924), which is a fairly good memoir of early settlement near Boise, and Leslie L. Sudweeks, "Early Agricultural Settlements in Southern Idaho," *Pacific Northwest Quarterly*, vol. 28 (April 1937).

On the important questions of water policy and irrigation, readers will find good background material in John T. Canoe, "The Beginnings of Irrigation in the United States," *Mississippi Valley Historical Review*, vol. 25 (June 1938). One of the most significant studies is that of Robert G. Dunbar, "The Origins of the Colorado System of Water-Right Control," *Colorado Magazine*, vol. 27 (October 1950). Other basic works include Joseph O. Van Hook, "Development of Irrigation in the Arkansas Valley," *Colorado Magazine*, vol. 10 (January 1933); Paul L. Murphy, "Irrigation in the Boise Valley, 1863–1903: A Study in Pre-Federal Irrigation," Masters Thesis, University of California, Berkeley, 1948, and relevant parts of Arrington's, *Great Basin Kingdom*. Two of the best accounts written by contemporaries are Nelson A. Miles, "Our Unwatered Empire," *North American Review*, vol. 150 (March 1890) and Walter Gillette Bates, "Water-Storage in the West," *Scribner's Magazine*, vol. 7 (January 1890).

The best sources on irrigation, however, are still the *Report of the Special Committee of the United States Senate on the Irrigation of Arid Lands*, vol. 3, Sen. Rept. 928, 51st Cong., 1st Sess., 1890 (Ser. No. 2708), and the U.S. Census, *Eleventh Census* (1890), "Agriculture," and entitled "Irrigation in the Western Part of the United States;" see also the same source (1900), pt. 2, "Irrigation."

Pioneering in West Texas, Indian Territory, and Oklahoma, 1860–1900

The history of farm settlement in the Southwest during the late nineteenth century and the subsequent development of agriculture has been almost totally neglected. Carl Coke Rister gave farming only slight attention in his, *The Southwestern Frontier, 1865–1881* (Cleveland, 1928), and *Southern Plainsmen* (Norman, Oklahoma, 1938). There is some useful material on the westward movement of agriculture in Samuel L. Evans, "Texas Agriculture, 1880–1930," Doctoral Dissertation, University of Texas, 1960, but references to frontier farming are limited. The best account of westward migration in Texas during the first decade after the Civil War is *The Frontier of Northwest Texas, 1846 to 1876* (Glendale, California, 1963) by Rupert N. Richardson. An excellent brief survey of the westward march of agriculture in Texas is W. C. Holden, "The Development of Agriculture in West Texas," in *Readings in Texas History* (Dallas, 1929) edited by Eugene C. Barker. On Texas land policy readers should consult Reuben McKitrick, *The Public Land System of Texas, 1823–1910* (Madison, Wisconsin, 1918), and Aldon S. Lang, *Financial History of the Public Lands in Texas*, (Waco, Texas, 1932).

Progress of the farming frontier in Indian Territory can be traced in the fine study by Laura Edna Baum [Graebner], "Agriculture Among the Five Civilized Tribes, 1865–1906," Masters Thesis, University of Oklahoma, 1940. Two important articles dealing with Indian agricultural development are, "The Public Land Policy of the Five Civilized Tribes," and "Pioneer Indian Agriculture in Oklahoma," *Chronicles of Oklahoma*, vol. 23 (Summer and Autumn 1945), by Norman A. Graebner. The latter article deals with the period before 1860.

The pressure by white settlers to open the unassigned lands in Indian Territory, the area known as Oklahoma, has been most fully discussed by Carl Coke Rister, *Land Hunger: David L. Payne and the Oklahoma Boomers* (Norman, Oklahoma, 1942). Good chapters on the boomer movement and the initial settlement in Oklahoma can be found in volume 1 of Gaston Litton, *History of Oklahoma* (4 vols., New York, 1957). An excellent source on early farming activities in Indian Territory and Oklahoma, but one that should be used with caution, are the interviews made with early settlers in 1937 and collected in the "Indian-Pioneer Papers," 116 volumes, located in the Phillips Collection, University of Oklahoma Library. A file of Boomer Literature and other materials that deal with Oklahoma land openings are available in the Manuscripts Division, University of Oklahoma Library. For Oklahoma Territory the reports of the governors to the Secretary of Interior in the 1890s (Washington, D.C.) tell a great deal about agricultural development during the first decade of settlement. *The Report of the Commissioner of the General Land Office* (Washington, D.C.) gives the number of homesteads filed and other important data. Little has been done on the history of crops, but Jesse Harder's "Wheat Production in Northwestern Oklahoma, 1893–1932," Masters Thesis, University of Oklahoma, 1952, and Gilbert C. Fite, "Development of the Cotton Industry by the Five Civilized Tribes in Indian Territory," *Journal of Southern History*, vol. 15 (August 1949) show early development of wheat and cotton. As is true for other parts of the West in the late nineteenth century, serious students must rely heavily on the censuses of agriculture and the local newspapers.

INDEX

A

Agricultural adjustment, on Central Plains, 131–133
Agricultural frontier, slow development of, in Oregon and Washington, 140; rapid expansion of, 35–38
Agriculture, importance of Western, 223–224; potential in West unknown, 6–7; in West in 1860s, 13–14
Amenia and Sharon Land Company, 80, 85, 90, 92
Arid region, need for irrigation in, 187–190
Arkansas River Valley, and agriculture, 10
Armstrong, Moses K., 27, 34, 35
Aughey, Samuel, 96
Austin, Horace, 49, 57

B

Bartholomew, Elam, 44
Beadle, W. H. H., 37
Bigler, John, as Governor of California, 162

Bonanza farms, acquiring land for, 76–77; capital for, 88; decline of, 90–93; economic problems on, 87–90; mechanization and production on, 81–85; profits on, 90; in Red River Valley, 76–86; size of, 80–81
Boudinot, Elias C., 203
Bowles, Samuel, 10
Burlington railroad, 28, 31, 38
Butter, as important farm product, 47, 146, 197–198

C

California, agricultural conditions in, 158–159; agricultural products of, 165; demand for railroads in, 164–165; farming in, 157; farming in foothills of, 159, 166–167; irrigated farming in, 167, 169; land monopoly in, 161–163; large farms in, 160, 171; orchard products in, 169; pioneer farmers in, 160–161

265

266 - Index

California State Agricultural Society, 157, 159

Capital, acquisition of, by borrowing, 119, by pioneers, 46; on bonanza farms, 88; for irrigated farming, 187, in California, 168; need for, in Oregon, 147, by pioneers, 42, 43–45

Carey Act, 135, 189

Central Plains, decline of boom in, 126; rapid settlement of, 118–123; slow agricultural expansion in, 114–116

Central Valley (California), 157

Chaffee, E. W., 80

Cherokee Outlet, land run in, 208

Coastal States, geography of, 5–6

Colorado, farming in, 11, 181; settlement in eastern, 123–124; value of farm production in 1870, 181

Colorado System, of irrigation, 184–185

Combined harvester-thresher, use of in California, 173

Commutation, under Homestead Act, 17, 101

Concordia, Kansas, rush of homesteaders to, 36

Corn, in Dakota, 104; in eastern Colorado, 125; as first crop of Kansas and Nebraska pioneers, 50–51, 117

Cotton, in Indian Territory, 201; in Oklahoma, 206; in Utah, 180; westward advance of, in Texas, 197

Cox, Paris, 198

Credit, 119

Crops, in Arizona and New Mexico, 185; in California, 170; in Dakota, 104–106, yield of, 1894, 110; in Oklahoma, 206, 212–213; in Oregon and Washington, 153; of pioneer farmers, 40, 50–51; in Rocky Mountain region, 191; in Texas, 196–197; in Utah, 180; in Washington, 147

D

Dakota, crops in 104–106; destitution in, 108–109; as a farming area, 100; frontier in, 1860s, 35–36; immigration to, 35–36, 83, 99–101; increase of farms in, 94; population increase in, 94; rapidity of settlement in, 106; rush of settlement to, 100–101; wheat in, 103–105

Dakota Territory, and emigrants, 24–25

Dalrymple, Oliver, begins farming in Red River Valley, 79; in financial difficulty, 87; improves farm practices, 92; manages wheat farms, 80–81; wheat production by, 84–85

Davis, C. K., 59, 60, 63

Davis, Jerome C., 160

Dawes Act, 207

Desert Land Act, entries under, 186; terms of, 23

Destitution, on Central Plains, 127–129; among Dakota settlers, 108–109; on Minnesota frontier, 56–58; among pioneer settlers, 58–63

Donation Acts, 143
Drought, in California, 166, 170; in eastern Colorado, 126; in Kansas, 61, 115; in Oklahoma, 206–207; in Texas, 200
Dudley, N. A. M., 63, 69–70

F

Farm colonies, in Colorado, 182–183
Farm prices, 74
Farmers, property of pioneer, 40; success or failure of pioneer, 40–41; in West Texas in 1900, 200
See also Pioneer farmers
Farmers' frontier, expansion of, 1860–1900, 223; importance of, 223–224; quick end of, 216
Farming, development of, in West in 1860, 10–11; first development of, in Colorado, 11; near mining camps, 11–12; westward expansion of, to 1880, 53–54
Farms, in California in 1850s, 157, 165; in Colorado, 1870s, 183; diversification on, 53; in eastern Washington, 155; establishment by homesteading of, 22–23; on Kansas frontier, 50–51; increase of, in upper Midwest in 1860s, 35; large, in Red River Valley, 77–78; number of, in West in 1860, 2; operations of, in western Kansas and Nebraska, 123–124; in Oregon and Washington, 138–139, 140–141, 149; in Rocky Mountain region in 1860, 176, in 1880, 186, in 1900, 191; size of, in Dakota, 111; in Utah, 180; in West Texas, 200
Farnham, Thomas J., 3
Fence cutting, in Texas, 198
Fencing, 43–44
Five Civilized Tribes, agriculture of, 201–202
Fleischman, Fred A., 44–45
Foreigners, in Dakota, 106
Foster, James S., 25
Free Homes League, 209
Freeman, Daniel, 20
Fremont, John C., 187
Frontier, in Dakota in 1860s, 35–36; farmers', in 1860, 2; natural hazards on, 55–57; in northwest Iowa, 35; passing of, in Oregon and Washington, 154–155; recession of, in Texas, 194–195; swift advance of, 99–100
Frontier relief, demand for federal aid, 68–69; provision by army of, 69–71; role of state governments in, 57–59, 66–68
See also Relief
Frontiers, blending of, 12
Fruit, in Pacific Northwest, 146, 148, 153
Furnas, Robert W., 62

G

Gilpin, William, 9
Government, role of, in frontier relief, 57–59, 66–68, 69–71
Grandin Brothers, 81

Grapes, in California, 161, 167
Grasshoppers, conference on, 73; description of, 61; destruction of crops by, 58, 60–63
Great American Desert, 117
Great Dakota Boom, decline of, 106–107; end of, in 1887, 108; reasons for, 97–98
Great Plains, changing ideas on, 9–10; changing image of, 14; descriptions of, 3, 7–8, 10; farming adjustments on, 132, 223; geography of, 3–4; land units on, in Texas, 200
Great West, geography of, 3–6
Greeley Colony, 182–183
Greeley, Horace, 37

H

Hayden, F. V., 8
Hazen, W. B., 7, 9
Hinton, Richard R., 188
Hoag, I. N., 158
Homestead, first filed, 20
Homestead Act, abuses under, 24; criticisms of, 21; evaluation of, 21–24; terms of, 16–17
Homesteading, in Nebraska, 37
Homesteads, in California, 163; in Colorado, 124; commutation, 17, 101; in Dakota in 1880s, 99; decline in filing for, in Kansas and Nebraska, 115–116; entries decline, 72–73; entries in Oregon and Washington in 1880s, 151–152; filed after 1897, 215–216; final entries in Dakota, 101; increase of, in late 1860s and early 1870s, 20–21; in Kansas in 1884–1887, 120; and Major Powell, 97; in Oklahoma Territory, 206, 209; in Oregon and Washington, 145; in Red River Valley, 83–84; in Rocky Mountain region, 186; sale of relinquishment on, 40–41, 101
Hops, in Washington, 155
Houses, dugout, 40, 43; in Pacific Northwest, 145; sod, 40, 43, 118; on Texas frontier, 195–196

I

Idaho, early farming in, 177–178; need for irrigation in, 188
Immigration, campaigns to attract, 24–25; encouragement of, in Oregon and Washington, 142–143; promotion of, in California, 164
Indian Territory, white invaders of, 202–203
Indians, and frontier movement in Texas, 194–195
Irrigation, in California, 166–171; in Colorado, 183; Colorado System of, 184–185; companies, in eastern Washington, 154; deep wells for, 169, 189; demand for, in Dakota, 134; demand federal aid for, 135, 188–190; in eastern Washington, 154; expansion of, 133; and Hinton report, 188; and investigation by Senate Committee, 189–190; among Mormons, 179–180; need for, on Great Plains, 132–133; in Rocky Mountain region, 190;

and water policies in California, 169; in the Yakima Valley, 154

J

Johnson, A. S., 29

K

Kansas, boom of 1880s in, 117–119; destitution in, 1881, 42; frontier relief in, 65–67; homesteading in, 36; pioneer farm operations in, 50–53, 121–122; rush to western, 119–120; seeks emigrants, 26; slow agricultural expansion in, 113–116

Kansas Central Relief Committee, 65

L

Land, abundance of, 13–14; acquisition by purchase, 17; attraction of, 15–16; availability of, 19–20; discontinuance of grants to railroads, 19; lottery system for, 208; monopoly in, 18–19; monopoly in California, 161–163; no lack of, for farmers, 111; policies in Oklahoma, 206; policies in Texas, 196; prices, 18, 31, in California, 162–163, 166, 170–171, in Oregon, 144, in Texas, 196; and railroads, 17–18, 31; scarcity of, for poor farmer in California, 162; selection of, by pioneers, 39–40; 76–77; speculation in, 18–20; in Willamette Valley, 143

Land run, 206–207

Livestock, in California, 173–174; east of the Cascades, 141; raised by Mormons, 180; on Texas frontier, 197

Long, Major Stephen H., 3

M

Machinery, on California farms, 160, 173; in Dakota, 105; in Palouse Country, 152; on pioneer farms, 44

Marshall, William R., 35, 41

Mattson, Hans, 29

Mechanization, on bonanza farms, 81, 85; of California farming, 172–173

Meeker, Nathan, 182

Mellette, Arthur, 109

Milk cows, 53

Mining, and farming, 137–138

Minnesota, destitution in, 57; early wheat production in, 48–50; and emigrants, 25; frontier relief in, 57–59, 63, 65; relief provided settlers in, 57

Minnesota Immigration Board, 27

Minto, John, 137

Montana, early farming in, 12, 177

Moody, Gideon C., 135

Morgan, Dick T., 209

Mormons, agricultural development by, 178–180; in Colorado, 183; hardships among, 178; water policies of, 179

Moxee Ditch Company, 154

N

National Land Company, 182
Nebraska, agricultural expansion in, 114; frontier relief in, 67; homesteads in, 37; rush to western, 119–120
Nebraska Immigration Association, 26
Nebraska Relief and Aid Society, 67
Newlands Act, 190
New Mexico, slow growth of agriculture in, 185; small farm production in, 176
Northern Pacific Railroad, completion to West Coast of, 153; and immigration, 27; land policies of, 76–77; reaches Moorhead, 38; slow completion of, 140

O

Oklahoma, as a farming frontier, 213–214; glowing reports of, 204; land rush in, 205
Oklahoma Colony, formation of, 204
Oklahoma Territory, opening of, 205
Orchard products, in California, 169
Ord, E. O. C., 69
Oregon, agricultural progress in, 149
Osborn, Thomas A., 65–66

P

Pacific Northwest, agricultural isolation of, 138–139; climate of, 139
Palouse, crops in, 150–151
Payne, David L., 203–205
Pike, Zebulon Montgomery, 3
Pillsbury, John S., 73
Pioneer farmers, as land speculators, 19; life of, 216–220; operations of, 46–47
See also Farmers
Pioneer farming, decline of, in California, 174
Pioneering, in Nebraska and western Kansas, 121–122; in Oregon and Washington, 146
Platte River Valley, farming prospects in, 11
Pope, General John, 7, 70
Population, loss of, in Dakota, 110–111; in Nebraska and western Kansas, 123; in Oregon and Washington, 138
Potatoes, in Colorado, 183–184
Powell, John Wesley, 187; favors large homesteads, 97, 187; reports on arid lands, 24; warns against crop farming in the West, 95–96
Power, James B., 76, 80, 83, 84; refutes John W. Powell, 95–96
Prairie fires, in Minnesota, 56
Preemption law, terms of, 17

R

Railroads, in Colorado, 181–182; demand for, in California, 164; in eastern Colorado, 124; expansion of, on Central Plains, 118; and immigration, 27–29, 31; need for, in Oregon and Washington, 138; in

Pacific Northwest, 148; sell land, 31; and settlement in Dakota in 1880s, 97–98; western support for, 32–33; westward push of, 38

Rainfall, abundance on Central Plains, 96, 119; in eastern Colorado, 124; on Great Plains in 1880s, 98; increase of, 129; in West, 4–5

Ramsey, Alexander, 25

Raynolds, W. F., 6–7

Red River Valley, description of, 75–76

Relief, for Kansas farmers, 115–116; role of Minnesota in, 57–59; for settlers on Central Plains, 127–131; voluntary contributions for, 57–59, 65
See also Frontier relief

Reservoir sites, preservation of, 188

Rocky Mountains, description of, 175–176; farms in, 176; geography of, 3

Routt, John L., 187

S

Sacramento Valley, 159

Santa Fe Railroad, expansion of, in New Mexico, 185; and immigration in Kansas, 29–30; reaches Emporia, 38; suggestions on capital needs of settlers, 42–43

Scandinavian Immigration Society, 26

Settlement, discouraging factors in, 34–35; in eastern Colorado, 123–125; edge of, in 1860, 2; in Kansas and western Nebraska, 119; in Texas Panhandle, 198–199; westward push of, in late 1860s, 37

Sherman, General W. T., 7

Sibley, H. H., 59, 65, 68, 71

Sioux Indian uprising (1862), 34

Sioux Reservation, partial opening of, 110

Sooners, in Oklahoma, 206

Speculation, in Kansas and Nebraska, 123

State relief, in Colorado, 129; demands for, to help destitute on frontier, 64–68; for grasshopper sufferers, 57–60; in Nebraska, 128–129

T

Texas, frontier settlement in northwest, 194–196; land policies in, 196

Timber Culture Act, terms of, 20

U

Union Colony, founded, 182–184

Union Pacific Railroad, 31, 38; and land in Nebraska, 17

United States Army, relief efforts of, 69–70

United States Geological Survey, reports of, 8

Utah, early agriculture in, 178–180

W

Wade, Benjamin, 175

Walla Walla, early agriculture near, 138, 140

Washington, agricultural progress in, 149
Water policies, of Mormons, 179
Water problem, in arid West, 6; in Rocky Mountain region, 187–188
Wells, depth of, 43
Wheat, in California in 1850s, 147, in 1860s, 164; in eastern Washington, 152–153; in Kansas, 51–52; large-scale production of, in California, 173; as main crop in Dakota, 103–104, in Oregon, 141, in Willamette Valley, 145–146; in Palouse Country, 151–153; as pioneer crop in Dakota and Minnesota, 48–49; prices of, 88, 89, 148; production in Red River Valley, 84–86; Turkey Red, 52; in Walla Walla County, 146
Wolfskill, John, 160
Wolfskill, William, 167
Wright, C. C., as California legislator, 169
Wright irrigation law, 169, 185

X

XIT Ranch, in Texas, 198

Y

Yakima Valley, 154

HISTORY

HISTORIES OF THE AMERICAN FRONTIER

Edited by
RAY ALLEN BILLINGTON

AMERICA'S FRONTIER HERITAGE
—*RAY ALLEN BILLINGTON*

THE NORTHERN COLONIAL FRONTIER, 1607-1763
—*DOUGLAS E. LEACH*

THE REVOLUTIONARY FRONTIER, 1763-1783
—*JACK M. SOSIN*

MINING FRONTIERS OF THE FAR WEST, 1848-1880
—*RODMAN WILSON PAUL*

THE TRANSPORTATION FRONTIER:
TRANS-MISSISSIPPI WEST, 1865-1890
—*OSCAR O. WINTHER*

THE FARMERS' FRONTIER, 1865-1900
—*GILBERT C. FITE*

2798700